ENGLISH
FOR EVERYONE

LIBRO DE ESTUDIO
BUSINESS ENGLISH

AUDIO GRATUITO
web y app
www.dkefe.com

Autora

Victoria Boobyer es escritora, ponente y formadora de profesores freelance con experiencia en la enseñanza del inglés y la gestión de profesores. Su interés principal se centra en el uso de libros de lectura fácil y un uso pedagógico constante de la tecnología en la formación.

Consultor del curso

Tim Bowen ha enseñado inglés y ha formado profesores en más de 30 países en todo el mundo. Es coautor de libros sobre la enseñanza de la pronunciación y sobre la metodología de la enseñanza de idiomas, y autor de numerosos libros para profesores de inglés. Actualmente se dedica a la escritura de materiales, la edición y la traducción. Es miembro del Chartered Institute of Linguists.

Consultora lingüística

La profesora **Susan Barduhn** cuenta con una gran experiencia en la enseñanza del inglés y la formación de profesores. Como autora ha participado en numerosas publicaciones. Además de dirigir cursos de inglés en cuatro continentes, ha sido presidenta de la Asociación Internacional de Profesores de Inglés como Lengua Extranjera y asesora del British Council y del Departamento de Estado de Estados Unidos. Actualmente es profesora de la School for International Training en Vermont, Estados Unidos.

ENGLISH
FOR EVERYONE

LIBRO DE ESTUDIO NIVEL 1

BUSINESS ENGLISH

Edición Estados Unidos Jenny Siklos, Allison Singer
Edición del proyecto Lili Bryant, Laura Sandford
Edición de arte Chrissy Barnard, Paul Drislane, Michelle Staples
Edición Ben Ffrancon Davies
Asistencia editorial Sarah Edwards, Helen Leech
Ilustración Edwood Burn, Michael Parkin, Gus Scott
Dirección editorial Daniel Mills
Dirección de la edición de arte Anna Hall
Dirección de la grabación de audio Christine Stroyan
Diseño de cubierta Ira Sharma
Edición de cubierta Claire Gell
Dirección editorial de cubierta Saloni Singh
Dirección de desarrollo del diseño de cubierta Sophia MTT
Producción, preproducción Andy Hilliard
Producción Mary Slater
Dirección editorial Andrew Macintyre
Dirección de arte Karen Self
Dirección general editorial Jonathan Metcalf

DK India
Dirección de la edición de arte sénior Arunesh Talapatra
Edición de arte sénior Chhaya Sajwan
Edición de arte Meenal Goel, Roshni Kapur
Asistencia de edición de arte Rohit Dev Bhardwaj
Ilustración Manish Bhatt, Arun Pottirayil,
Sachin Tanwar, Mohd Zishan
Coordinación editorial Priyanka Sharma
Dirección de preproducción Balwant Singh
Diseño sénior DTP Harish Aggarwal, Vishal Bhatia
Diseño DTP Jaypal Chauhan

Primera edición americana, 2018
Publicado en Estados Unidos por DK Publishing
345 Hudson Street, Nueva York, Nueva York 10014
DK es una División de Penguin Random House LLC

Copyright © 2017 Dorling Kindersley Limited
© Traducción al español: 2017 Dorling Kindersley Limited

Producción editorial de la versión en español: Tinta Simpàtica
Traducción: Ruben Giró i Anglada

Publicado en Gran Bretaña por Dorling Kindersley Limited.
Un registro de catálogo para este libro está
disponible en la Biblioteca del Congreso.

ISBN: 978-1-4654-7394-3
Impreso y encuadernado en China

Los libros de DK están disponibles con descuentos especiales cuando se
compran en cantidades para su venta promocional, su uso como regalo
corporativo, recaudación de fondos o uso educativo. Para más detalles,
contacte con: DK Publishing Special Markets, 345 Hudson Street, New
York, New York 10014 – SpecialSales@dk.com

Todas las imágenes: © Dorling Kindersley Limited
Para más información ver: www.dkimages.com

www.dkespañol.com

Nivel ❶ Contenidos

Nivel **2** Contenidos ver página 194

Cómo funciona el curso

English for Everyone está pensado para todas aquellas personas que quieren aprender inglés por su cuenta. La edición de inglés de negocios contiene las expresiones y construcciones inglesas imprescindibles para las situaciones de negocios más habituales. A diferencia de otros cursos, todo ello se practica y aprende de una manera enormemente visual. El curso se divide en dos niveles, ambdos incluidos en este libro. La mejor manera de progresar es seguir el libro por orden utilizando el audio de la web y la app del curso, y hacer las tareas del libro de ejercicios al acabar cada unidad para consolidar con la práctica lo aprendido.

LIBRO DE EJERCICIOS

LIBRO DE ESTUDIO

Número de unidad El libro está dividido en unidades. El número de unidad te ayuda a seguir tu progreso.

Qué vas a aprender La unidad comienza con un resumen de lo que aprenderás en ella.

Módulos Cada unidad se compone de distintos módulos que debes seguir por orden. Puedes tomarte un descanso tras completar cualquiera de ellos.

Aprendizaje del idioma Las secciones con fondo de color te presentan nuevo vocabulario y gramática. Estúdialas con atención antes de hacer los ejercicios.

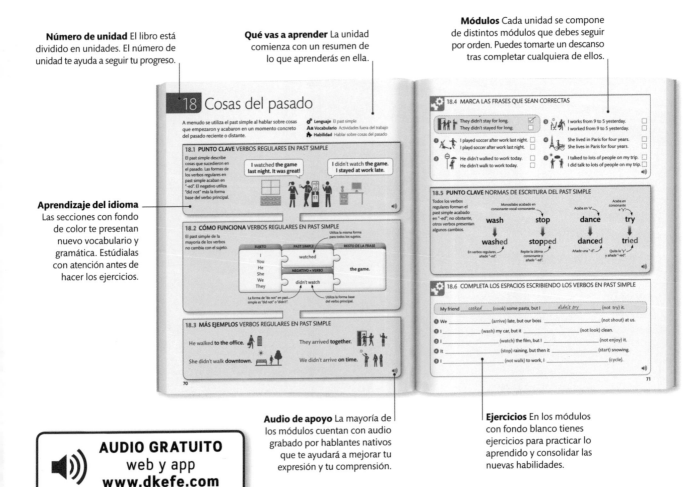

Audio de apoyo La mayoría de los módulos cuentan con audio grabado por hablantes nativos que te ayudará a mejorar tu expresión y tu comprensión.

Ejercicios En los módulos con fondo blanco tienes ejercicios para practicar lo aprendido y consolidar las nuevas habilidades.

AUDIO GRATUITO
web y app
www.dkefe.com

Módulos de idioma

El vocabulario aparece contextualizado en situaciones de negocios habituales. Cada módulo de aprendizaje muestra el inglés adecuado para una situación determinada, además de puntos generales del inglés para que mejores la fluidez general.

Número de módulo Cada módulo tiene su propio número para que puedas seguir tu progreso y te sea fácil localizar el audio correspondiente.

Titular del módulo El tema que se va a tratar aparece aquí junto con una breve introducción.

Frases de ejemplo Cada nuevo aspecto lingüístico se presenta en contextos típicos de empresa. Los destacados en color y las notas explicativas facilitan la comprensión de las nuevas estructuras.

Guía gráfica Ilustraciones sencillas y claras ayudan a entender el sentido de las nuevas estructuras y a saber en qué situaciones profesionales debes utilizarlas.

Audio de apoyo Este símbolo indica que las frases de ejemplo del módulo están disponibles en grabaciones de audio.

Guía de formación Estas guías visuales desmenuzan la gramática inglesa en sus componentes básicos para mostrar gráficamente cómo funcionan incluso las estructuras más complejas.

Vocabulario A lo largo del libro tienes módulos de vocabulario que recogen las palabras y las expresiones más útiles del inglés para los negocios, e incluyen pistas visuales que te ayudarán a recordarlas.

Espacio para escribir Es útil que escribas la traducción de los términos, pues tendrás así tus propias páginas de referencia.

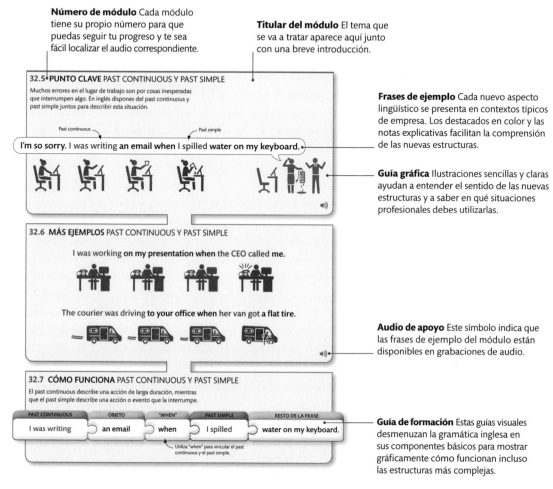

32.5 **PUNTO CLAVE** PAST CONTINUOUS Y PAST SIMPLE

Muchos errores en el lugar de trabajo son por cosas inesperadas que interrumpen algo. En inglés dispones del past continuous y past simple juntos para describir esta situación.

Past continuous — Past simple

I'm so sorry. I was writing **an email when** I spilled **water on my keyboard.**

32.6 **MÁS EJEMPLOS** PAST CONTINUOUS Y PAST SIMPLE

I was working **on my presentation when the CEO called me.**

The courier was driving **to your office when** her van got **a flat tire.**

32.7 **CÓMO FUNCIONA** PAST CONTINUOUS Y PAST SIMPLE

El past continuous describe una acción de larga duración, mientras que el past simple describe una acción o evento que la interrumpe.

PAST CONTINUOUS	OBJETO	"WHEN"	PAST SIMPLE	RESTO DE LA FRASE
I was writing	an email	when	I spilled	water on my keyboard.

Utiliza "when" para vincular el past continuous y el past simple.

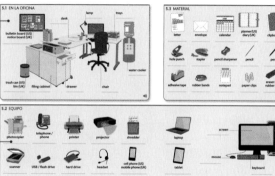

9

Módulos de ejercicios

Cada ejercicio está cuidadosamente graduado para que profundices y contrastes lo que has aprendido en la unidad. Si haces los ejercicios a medida que avanzas, recordarás mejor los conceptos, y tu inglés será más fluido. Cada ejercicio indica con un símbolo qué habilidad vas a practicar con él.

 GRAMÁTICA
Aplica las nuevas reglas en distintos contextos.

LECTURA
Analiza ejemplos del idioma en textos reales en inglés.

ESCUCHA
Comprueba tu comprensión del inglés hablado.

VOCABULARIO
Consolida tu comprensión del vocabulario clave.

ESCRITURA
Practica produciendo textos escritos en inglés.

CONVERSACIÓN
Compara tu dicción con los audios de muestra.

Número de módulo
Cada módulo tiene su propio número, para que te sea fácil localizar las respuestas y el audio correspondiente.

Instrucciones En cada ejercicio tienes unas breves instrucciones que te dicen qué debes hacer.

41.6 COMPLETA LOS ESPACIOS CON LAS PALABRAS DEL RECUADRO

Do you have _____enough_____ bread?

1. I've eaten _____ many chocolates.
2. How _____ glasses do we need?
3. There's too _____ sauce on this.
4. How _____ should we tip here?

much   much   many
    too   ~~enough~~

Respuesta de ejemplo La primera respuesta ya está escrita, para que entiendas mejor el ejercicio.

Espacio para escribir
Es útil que escribas las respuestas en el libro, pues te servirán para repasar lo aprendido.

Ejercicios de conversación
Este símbolo indica que debes decir las respuestas en voz alta y compararlas a continuación con su audio correspondiente.

Ayuda gráfica
Las ilustraciones te ayudan a entender los ejercicios.

Ejercicios de escucha Este símbolo te avisa de que debes escuchar el audio para poder responder a las preguntas.

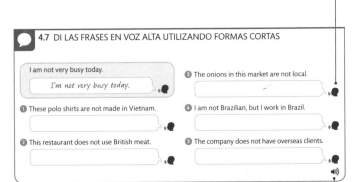

4.7 DI LAS FRASES EN VOZ ALTA UTILIZANDO FORMAS CORTAS

I am not very busy today.
    I'm not very busy today.

1. These polo shirts are not made in Vietnam.
2. This restaurant does not use British meat.
3. The onions in this market are not local.
4. I am not Brazilian, but I work in Brazil.
5. The company does not have overseas clients.

Audio de apoyo Este símbolo indica que las respuestas a los ejercicios están disponibles en grabaciones de audio. Escúchalas tras completar el ejercicio.

20.6 ESCUCHA EL AUDIO Y NUMERA LAS IMÁGENES EN SU ORDEN

Audio

English for Everyone incorpora abundantes materiales en audio. Te recomendamos que los utilices al máximo, pues te ayudarán a mejorar tu comprensión del inglés hablado y a lograr una pronunciación y un acento más naturales. Escucha cada audio tantas veces como quieras. Páralo y vuelve atrás en los pasajes que te resulten difíciles, hasta que estés seguro de que has entendido bien lo que se dice.

EJERCICIOS DE ESCUCHA
Este símbolo indica que debes escuchar el audio para poder responder a las preguntas.

AUDIO DE APOYO
Este símbolo indica que dispones de audios adicionales que puedes escuchar tras completar el módulo.

AUDIO GRATUITO
web y app
www.dkefe.com

Mide tu progreso

El curso está pensado para que te sea fácil comprobar tu progreso, e incorpora para ello resúmenes de lo aprendido y módulos de repaso. Se incluyen las respuestas de todos los ejercicios, con lo que podrás ver si has entendido correctamente cada apartado.

Checklist Cada unidad termina con un recuadro en el que podrás marcar las habilidades que hayas aprendido.

07 ✓ CHECKLIST

⚙ Respuestas cortas ☐	**Aa** Información de contacto ☐	🗣 Intercambiar datos de contacto ☐

Módulos de repaso Al final de cada grupo de unidades tienes un módulo de repaso en el que se resumen con más detalle los aspectos aprendidos.

Casillas de verificación
Marca las casillas de los puntos con los que te sientas seguro. Vuelve a repasar los que te hayan resultado más difíciles.

✪ REPASA LO QUE HAS APRENDIDO EN LAS UNIDADES 01-07

NUEVO LENGUAJE	FRASE DE EJEMPLO	☑	UNIDAD
PRESENTAR Y PRESENTARSE ANTE OTRAS PERSONAS	Good morning. My name's **Alisha Sharma**. This is **my colleague, Edward**.	☐	1.1, 1.5
PRESENT SIMPLE PARA DESCRIBIR ACTIVIDADES DIARIAS EN EL TRABAJO	We have a team meeting every Tuesday. The CEO works weekends if we're busy.	☐	2.1
PAÍSES Y NACIONALIDADES	These new mopeds are from Italy. I'm Brazilian, but I work in the US.	☐	4.1, 4.2, 4.3
FRASES NEGATIVAS	I'm not French. I'm Canadian. The printer doesn't work!	☐	4.6
FORMULAR PREGUNTAS	Do you have an appointment? Where is the staff room?	☐	6.1, 6.4, 6.8
INTERCAMBIAR DATOS DE CONTACTO, RESPUESTAS CORTAS	Is this your email address? Yes, it is. Do you have a business card? No, I don't.	☐	7.1, 7.2, 7.7

29

29.2 ◀))
1 It's a special one for fire safety.
2 There's a nice café across the street.
3 We're meeting clients later this afternoon.
4 I have saved all the documents.

29.3 ◀))
1 Is your stapler broken? You **can** use mine.
2 She **doesn't have to** come to the training session. She did it last year.
3 You **have to** turn off the light if you're the last person to leave the office.
4 He **has to** test the fire alarm every Wednesday morning.
5 We **don't have to** wear a jacket and tie in the summer months.

29.4 ◀))
1 Not given 2 False 3 True
4 True 5 False

29.8 ◀))
1 Could you **tell** Jan to call me back?
2 Could you **check** this report?
3 Would you mind **ordering** more pens?
4 Could you **mop** the floor, please?
5 Could you **come** to today's meeting?
6 Would you mind **calling** back later?
7 Would you mind **turning** the light off?
8 Could you **wash** these cups, please?
9 Could you **pass** around the reports?
10 Would you mind **booking** me a taxi?
11 Could you **show** our clients around?

29.9
1 False 2 False 3 True 4 True

29.10 ◀))
1. Could you book a meeting room?
2. Could you send Sam Davies an email?
3. Could you call our supplier?
4. Would you mind booking a meeting room?
5. Would you mind sending Sam Davies an email?
6. Would you mind calling our supplier?

Respuestas Tienes las respuestas de todos los ejercicios al final del libro.

Número de ejercicio Para que las localices más fácilmente, las respuestas indican el número del ejercicio.

Audio Este símbolo indica que puedes escuchar el audio de las respuestas.

01 Conocer a nuevos colegas

Puedes utilizar inglés formal o informal para presentarte o dar la bienvenida a nuevos colegas y compañeros de trabajo, según la situación y la persona de que se trate.

⚙ **Lenguaje** Abecedario y deletrear
Aa Vocabulario Presentaciones y saludos
🧩 **Habilidad** Presentarte a los colegas

1.1 PUNTO CLAVE PRESENTARTE

En inglés dispones de diversas expresiones educadas para presentarte o dar la bienvenida a los compañeros de trabajo.

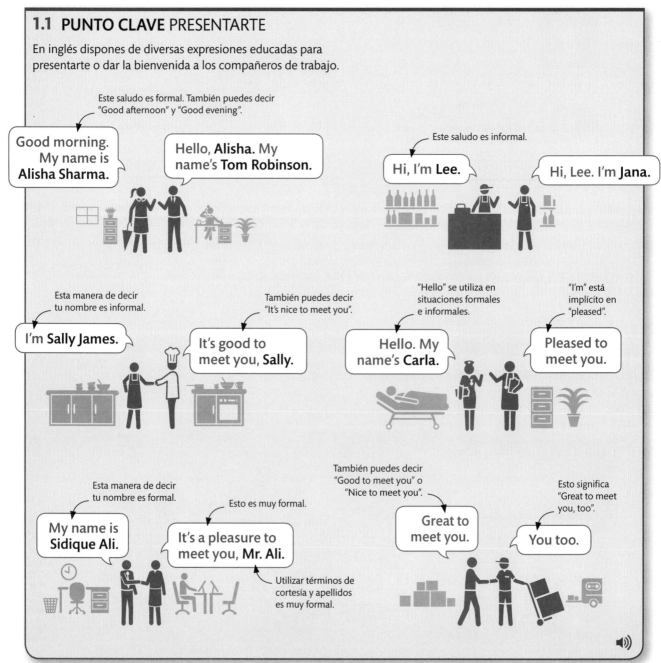

Este saludo es formal. También puedes decir "Good afternoon" y "Good evening".

Good morning. My name is **Alisha Sharma.**

Hello, **Alisha.** My name's **Tom Robinson.**

Este saludo es informal.

Hi, I'm **Lee.**

Hi, Lee. I'm **Jana.**

Esta manera de decir tu nombre es informal.

I'm **Sally James.**

También puedes decir "It's nice to meet you".

It's good to meet you, **Sally.**

"Hello" se utiliza en situaciones formales e informales.

Hello. My name's **Carla.**

"I'm" está implícito en "pleased".

Pleased to meet you.

Esta manera de decir tu nombre es formal.

My name is **Sidique Ali.**

Esto es muy formal.

It's a pleasure to meet you, **Mr. Ali.**

Utilizar términos de cortesía y apellidos es muy formal.

También puedes decir "Good to meet you" o "Nice to meet you".

Great to meet you.

Esto significa "Great to meet you, too".

You too.

12

1.2 COMPLETA LOS ESPACIOS CON LAS PALABRAS DEL RECUADRO

It's good to _____*meet*_____ you.

1. Hello. My _____ Sebastian.

2. Good _____ . My name is Joe Carr.

3. Hi, Marie. _____ Clive.

4. It's great to meet you, _____ , Sven.

5. It's a _____ to meet you.

afternoon	pleasure	~~meet~~
I'm	name's	too

🔊

1.3 PRONUNCIACIÓN EL ABECEDARIO

Escucha cómo se pronuncian las letras del abecedario en inglés cuando se dicen solas.

Aa Bb Cc Dd Ee
Ff Gg Hh Ii Jj Kk
Ll Mm Nn Oo Pp
Qq Rr Ss Tt Uu
Vv Ww Xx Yy Zz

🔊

1.4 ESCUCHA EL AUDIO Y MARCA LOS NOMBRES QUE OIGAS

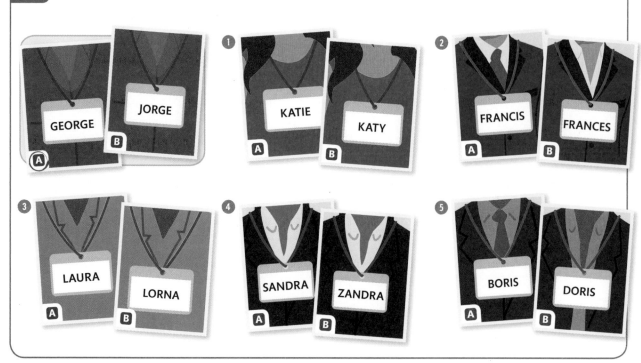

- GEORGE (A) / JORGE (B)
- 1. KATIE (A) / KATY (B)
- 2. FRANCIS (A) / FRANCES (B)
- 3. LAURA (A) / LORNA (B)
- 4. SANDRA (A) / ZANDRA (B)
- 5. BORIS (A) / DORIS (B)

1.5 PUNTO CLAVE PRESENTAR A OTRAS PERSONAS

También puedes utilizar expresiones educadas formales
e informales para presentar a compañeros de trabajo.

Esta presentación es formal.

> May I introduce **Maria Diaz**? Maria is our sales manager for Europe.

> It's good to meet you, **Maria**.

> It's a pleasure to meet you too.

Esta presentación es informal.

> **Amit**, meet **Edward**. **Edward, Amit and I work together**.

> Great to meet you, **Edward**.

Esta presentación es formal.

> I'd like you to meet **Zoe Carr**.

> It's nice to meet you, **Ms. Carr**.

Utiliza "this is" para presentar a otras personas en situaciones menos formales.

> This is **my new assistant, Levi**.

> Hi, **Levi**. Good to meet you.

1.6 VUELVE A ESCRIBIR LAS FRASES CORRIGIENDO LOS ERRORES

Hello, Sam. Nice meet you.
Hello, Sam. Nice to meet you.

❶ To meet you, it's a pleasure, too.

_____

❷ Hi, I'm name's Adedeyo.

_____

❸ Greet to meet you.

_____

❹ This my new colleague, Martin.

_____

❺ Marisa, meeting Roula, my partner.

_____

❻ It's good to meet to you, Katherine.

_____

❼ I may introduce Claudia Gomez, our new CEO?

_____

1.7 ESCUCHA EL AUDIO Y RESPONDE A LAS PREGUNTAS

Jill tiene trabajo nuevo y asiste a una reunión con sus nuevos colegas, Mr. Singh y Daniel.

What is Jill's role at the company?

Design assistant	☐
Finance manager	☑
Intern	☐

❶ What is Jill's last name?

Greene	☐
Cheam	☐
Green	☐

❷ How long has Mr. Singh been working with Spandone and Co.?

14 years	☐
15 years	☐
16 years	☐

❸ What is Mr. Singh's role at Spandone and Co.?

Lawyer	☐
CEO	☐
Accountant	☐

❹ Which two people are meeting for the first time?

Jill and Daniel	☐
Jill and Mr. Singh	☐
Daniel and Mr. Singh	☐

1.8 COMPLETA LOS ESPACIOS CON LAS PALABRAS DEL RECUADRO Y DI LAS FRASES EN VOZ ALTA

May I _introduce_ Marta Lopez?
Marta and I _work_ together.

❶ Hello, Mr. Lucas. It's a _____ to meet _____ .

❷ Ashley, _____ André. André and I work on the _____ project.

❸ _____ , Sophie. My _____ Rachel Davies. Great to meet you.

❹ _____ is my colleague, Hayley. We went to college_____ .

❺ It's _____ to meet you, Cori. _____ name's Angel.

❻ Hello, James. _____ really nice ____ meet you. My name's Alex.

good	together	It's	My	to
~~introduce~~	name's	pleasure	Hello	
meet	same	you	This	~~work~~

🔊

---

01 ✓ CHECKLIST

⚙ Abecedario y deletrear ☐   **Aa** Presentaciones y saludos ☐   🧩 Presentarte a los colegas ☐

02 Actividades diarias en el trabajo

Utiliza el present simple para hablar de cosas que haces de manera habitual, como las tareas diarias o las rutinas del trabajo.

⚙ **Lenguaje** Present simple
Aa Vocabulario Actividades en el trabajo
🧩 **Habilidad** Hablar de rutinas del trabajo

2.1 PUNTO CLAVE EL PRESENT SIMPLE

Utiliza el present simple para hablar de cosas que pasan de manera habitual como parte de una rutina.

Every morning, we prepare the food and Justin sets the tables.
🔊

2.2 CÓMO FUNCIONA EL PRESENT SIMPLE

En los verbos regulares, utiliza la forma base del verbo para formar el present simple con "I", "you", "we" y "they". Con "he", "she" e "it", añade "s" a la forma base.

SUJETO	VERBO	RESTO DE LA FRASE
I / You / We / They	prepare	the food every morning.
He / She	prepares	

2.3 MÁS EJEMPLOS EL PRESENT SIMPLE

"Be" con "I" es "I am" y se contrae como "I'm".

I'm a lifeguard at the local pool.

La forma de present simple de "be" con "he", "she" e "it".

Mia is an excellent tour guide.

They have a meeting every morning.

We usually stop for tea and coffee at 11.

La forma de present simple de "be" con "we", "you" y "they".

Stephanie works from home on Mondays.

We are always busy in the evening.

🔊

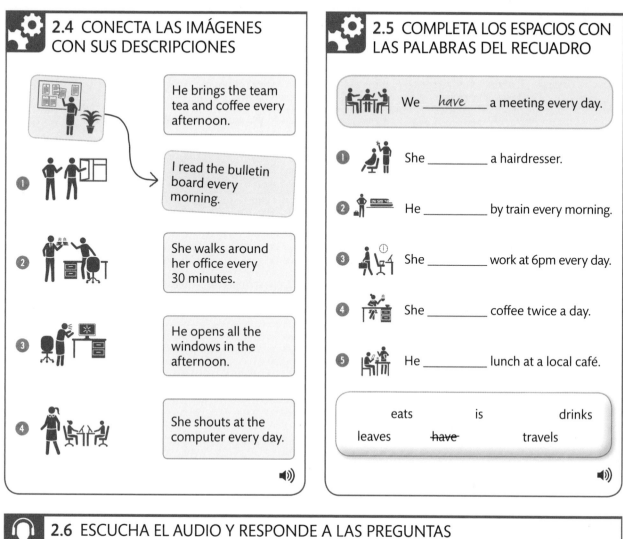

2.4 CONECTA LAS IMÁGENES CON SUS DESCRIPCIONES

He brings the team tea and coffee every afternoon.

I read the bulletin board every morning.

She walks around her office every 30 minutes.

He opens all the windows in the afternoon.

She shouts at the computer every day.

2.5 COMPLETA LOS ESPACIOS CON LAS PALABRAS DEL RECUADRO

We __have__ a meeting every day.

1 She _____ a hairdresser.

2 He _____ by train every morning.

3 She _____ work at 6pm every day.

4 She _____ coffee twice a day.

5 He _____ lunch at a local café.

eats	is	drinks
leaves	~~have~~	travels

2.6 ESCUCHA EL AUDIO Y RESPONDE A LAS PREGUNTAS

Zoe ha empezado a trabajar en un café. Su jefe le explica las tareas diarias en el trabajo.

The café opens at 10am.
True ☑ False ☐ Not given ☐

1 All the staff arrive at 8am.
True ☐ False ☐ Not given ☐

2 Zoe checks the tables before the café opens.
True ☐ False ☐ Not given ☐

3 Everyone has a break at 11:30pm.
True ☐ False ☐ Not given ☐

4 Employees eat lunch in the kitchen.
True ☐ False ☐ Not given ☐

5 The café closes at 6pm.
True ☐ False ☐ Not given ☐

2.7 ⚠ ERRORES COMUNES EL PRESENT SIMPLE CON "HE", "SHE" E "IT"

Es fácil olvidarse de añadir la "s" a la forma base del verbo en el present simple al utilizar pronombres de la tercera persona del singular: "he", "she" e "it".

Añade una "s" a la forma base del verbo.

The CEO works on Sundays. ✓

The CEO work on Sundays. ✕

Aquí está el error.

2.8 TACHA LA PALABRA INCORRECTA DE CADA FRASE

She ~~make~~ / makes tea and coffee before the team meeting every Friday.

1. The head of marketing speak / **speaks** for about an hour at every team meeting.

2. Arianna and Gabriel **read** / reads their emails first thing every morning.

3. The photocopier stop / **stops** working if we don't load the paper carefully.

4. The owners of the hotel **visit** / visits it at the end of every month.

5. The cleaner start / **starts** work at 6am every day. The office is always clean in the mornings.

🔊

2.9 USA EL DIAGRAMA PARA CREAR OCHO FRASES CORRECTAS Y DILAS EN VOZ ALTA

I work from Monday to Friday.

| I / You / She / My manager | work / works / have / has | from Monday to Friday. / a meeting every morning. |

🔊

OUR TEAM

Meet the manager

Our Head of Customer Services describes a typical working day

Sumiko Akimoto, our Head of Customer Services, describes a typical day at work. "Every morning, even in the winter, I ride my bicycle to work. I arrive at work early and then walk through the departments to talk to the staff. It is important for me to know what is happening in the company so that I can share any useful information with clients. Next, I read my emails and use them to help me write a list of things to do during the day. I rarely do everything on the list, but it's useful to help me plan my day.

During my morning coffee break, I talk to my team members about my list and sometimes delegate tasks to them. At lunchtime, many of my colleagues go to a local Italian restaurant to eat, but I stay in the office and eat a packed lunch. I like to deal with all my emails by 5 o'clock. Sometimes I can leave work at 5:30, but I usually leave at 6 o'clock. To help me relax after work, I turn off my phone as soon as I get home."

Sumiko cycles to work every day.	True ☑	False ☐
❶ She reads her emails first thing every morning.	True ☐	False ☐
❷ She writes a list of things to do that day.	True ☐	False ☐
❸ She meets her colleagues to talk about the day's work.	True ☐	False ☐
❹ Sumiko goes to a local restaurant for lunch every day.	True ☐	False ☐
❺ She tries to deal with all her emails by 5 o'clock.	True ☐	False ☐
❻ Sumiko always leaves work at 6 o'clock.	True ☐	False ☐
❼ She turns her phone off when she gets home.	True ☐	False ☐

02 ✔ CHECKLIST

⚙ Present simple ☐   **Aa** Actividades en el trabajo ☐   🧩 Hablar de rutinas del trabajo ☐

3.1 PAÍSES

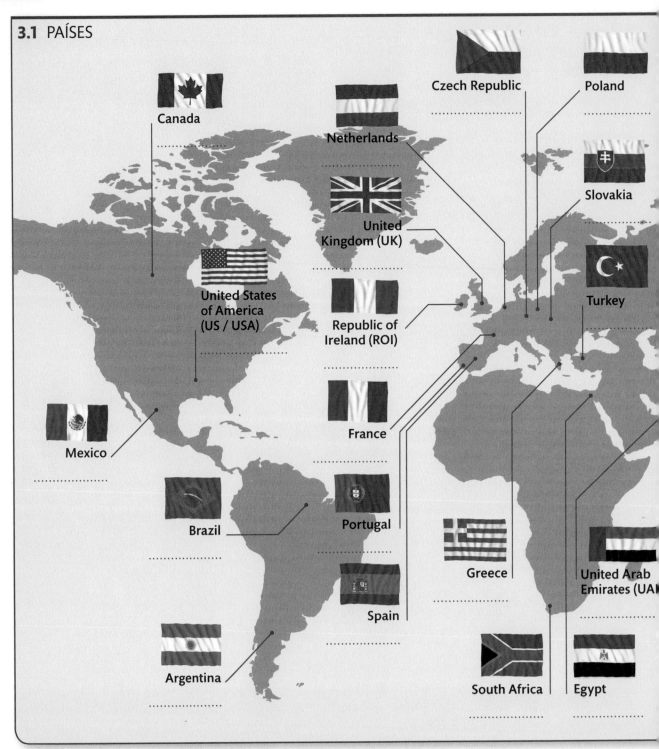

Canada

Netherlands

Czech Republic

Poland

United Kingdom (UK)

Slovakia

United States of America (US / USA)

Republic of Ireland (ROI)

Turkey

Mexico

France

Brazil

Portugal

Greece

United Arab Emirates (UA

Spain

Argentina

South Africa

Egypt

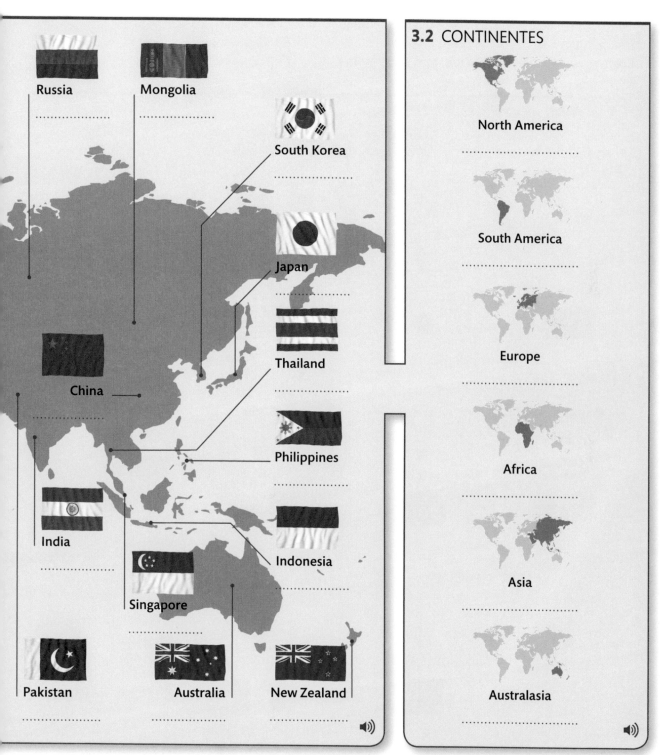

Russia

Mongolia

South Korea

Japan

Thailand

China

Philippines

India

Indonesia

Singapore

Pakistan

Australia

New Zealand

North America

South America

Europe

Africa

Asia

Australasia

04 Empresas en todo el mundo

En inglés se utiliza "from" o adjetivos de nacionalidad para hablar del origen de los productos o las personas. "From" también sirve para hablar de tu empresa o departamento.

Lenguaje Expresiones negativas
Aa Vocabulario Países y nacionalidades
Habilidad Decir de dónde son las cosas

4.1 VOCABULARIO ADJETIVOS DE NACIONALIDAD

Los adjetivos de nacionalidad se basan en los nombres de los países. La mayoría terminan en "-ese", "-an", "-ish", "-ean" o "-ian", pero también los hay irregulares.

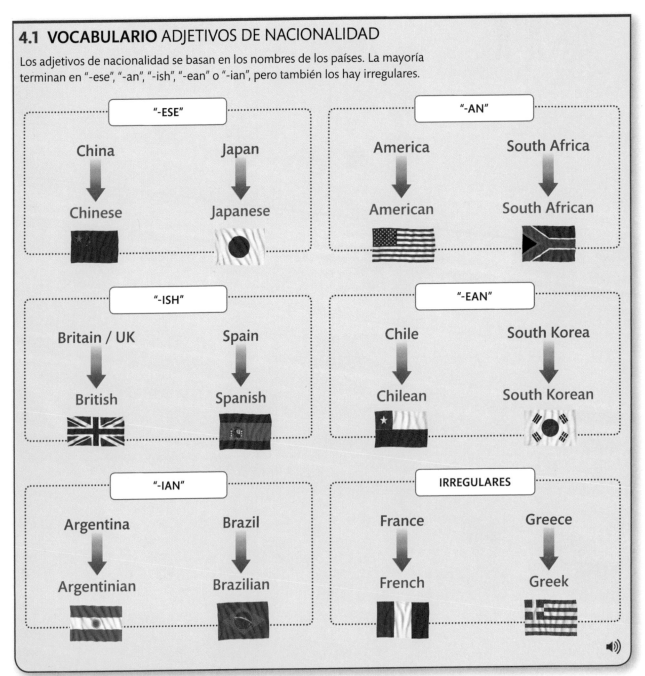

"-ESE"
China → Chinese
Japan → Japanese

"-AN"
America → American
South Africa → South African

"-ISH"
Britain / UK → British
Spain → Spanish

"-EAN"
Chile → Chilean
South Korea → South Korean

"-IAN"
Argentina → Argentinian
Brazil → Brazilian

IRREGULARES
France → French
Greece → Greek

4.2 PUNTO CLAVE PAÍSES Y NACIONALIDADES

Para decir dónde se ha fabricado un producto o de qué país viene alguien, utiliza "from" y el nombre del país, o un adjetivo de nacionalidad.

"FROM" + PAÍS

These new mopeds are from Italy.

ADJETIVO DE NACIONALIDAD

These new mopeds are Italian.

4.3 MÁS EJEMPLOS PAÍSES Y NACIONALIDADES

These smartphones are from Japan.

The new CEO is from Switzerland.

These Indian dresses are excellent value.

I'm Russian, but I regularly visit the US.

4.4 TACHA LA PALABRA INCORRECTA DE CADA FRASE

These monitors are from China / ~~Chinese~~.

1. I'm on the Europe / European sales team.
2. Our Chile / Chilean office is in Santiago.
3. We sell leather shoes from Spain / Spanish.
4. My job is to watch the Asia / Asian markets.
5. Book a trip to Mexico / Mexican with us.

4.5 ESCUCHA EL AUDIO Y CONECTA LOS PRODUCTOS CON SU LUGAR DE ORIGEN

France   Canada   Asia   Italy   Africa   India

4.6 PUNTO CLAVE CONTRACCIONES NEGATIVAS

Al añadir "not", convertimos en negativa una expresión positiva.
"Not" se utiliza a menudo en su forma contraída.

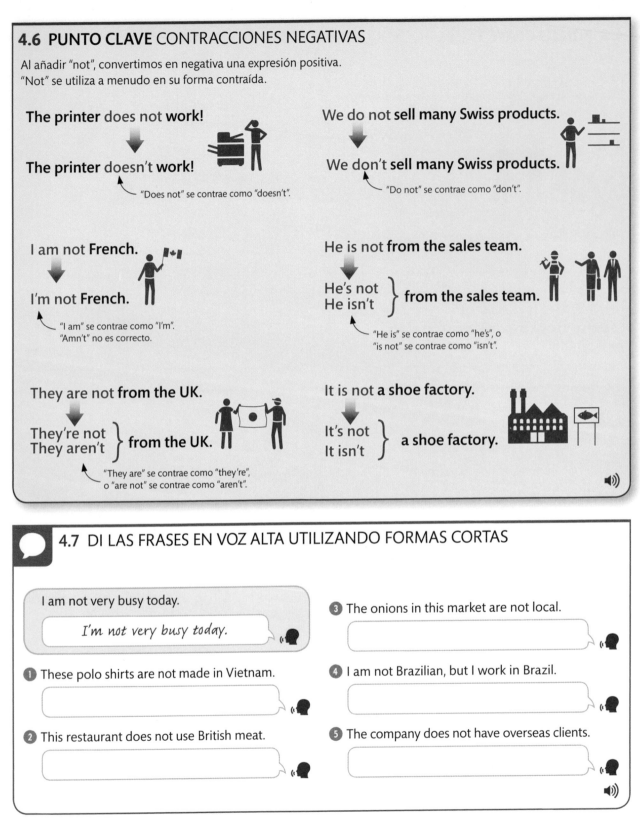

The printer does not **work!**

⬇

The printer doesn't **work!**

"Does not" se contrae como "doesn't".

We do not sell many Swiss products.

⬇

We don't sell many Swiss products.

"Do not" se contrae como "don't".

I am not **French.**

⬇

I'm not **French.**

"I am" se contrae como "I'm".
"Amn't" no es correcto.

He is not **from the sales team.**

⬇

He's not
He isn't } **from the sales team.**

"He is" se contrae como "he's", o
"is not" se contrae como "isn't".

They are not **from the UK.**

⬇

They're not
They aren't } **from the UK.**

"They are" se contrae como "they're",
o "are not" se contrae como "aren't".

It is not **a shoe factory.**

⬇

It's not
It isn't } **a shoe factory.**

4.7 DI LAS FRASES EN VOZ ALTA UTILIZANDO FORMAS CORTAS

I am not very busy today.

I'm not very busy today.

❶ These polo shirts are not made in Vietnam.

❷ This restaurant does not use British meat.

❸ The onions in this market are not local.

❹ I am not Brazilian, but I work in Brazil.

❺ The company does not have overseas clients.

24

4.8 PUNTO CLAVE EXPLICAR DÓNDE TRABAJAS

"From" también sirve para hablar de una empresa o departamento.

> **I'm George. I'm** from the marketing department **in New York.**

> **And this is Barbara. She's** from QuickStyle Printers.

> **I'm Nisha. I'm** from finance.

A veces la gente omite "the" y "department" cuando dicen de qué departamento son.

4.9 LEE EL PERFIL DE LA EMPRESA Y RESPONDE A LAS PREGUNTAS

Guitar City is a new company.
True ☐ False ☑

1 Giorgio Michalis is from Greece.
True ☐ False ☐

2 Giorgio has one Guitar City guitar.
True ☐ False ☐

3 Pete Donnelly works in production.
True ☐ False ☐

4 The guitars are made of wood from rainforests.
True ☐ False ☐

5 Each guitar has a beautiful wood pattern.
True ☐ False ☐

6 Some of the artists are Polish.
True ☐ False ☐

Guitar City

HOME | PRODUCTS | ABOUT | CONTACT

About us

Established in 1965, Guitar City makes guitars for some of the most famous musicians in the world. The award-winning Greek guitarist Giorgio Michalis always uses our guitars and believes that they are the best that he has ever played. "The sound of all my Guitar City guitars is amazing," he says.

Our guitars are mostly made from recycled aluminum and are much lighter than the usual, wooden ones. Pete Donnelly from our production department also says that these guitars are better for the environment. "We do not use any wooden materials from rainforests and we make all the main guitar body parts from recycled materials."

Guitar City guitars also look really great. They do not have the natural beauty of wood, but each guitar is hand painted by a top artist from our creative design team. With artists from Kenya, Poland, Mexico, and Laos, we have designs to suit everyone.

---

04 ✔ CHECKLIST

⚙ Expresiones negativas ☐   **Aa** Países y nacionalidades ☐   🧩 Decir de dónde son las cosas ☐

5.1 EN LA OFICINA

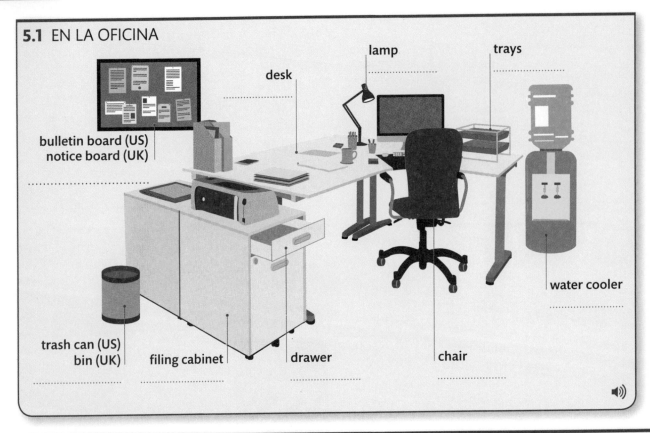

lamp

trays

desk

bulletin board (US)
notice board (UK)

water cooler

trash can (US)
bin (UK)

filing cabinet

drawer

chair

5.2 EQUIPO

photocopier

telephone /
phone

printer

projector

shredder

scanner

USB / flash drive

hard drive

headset

cell phone (US)
mobile phone (UK)

5.3 MATERIAL

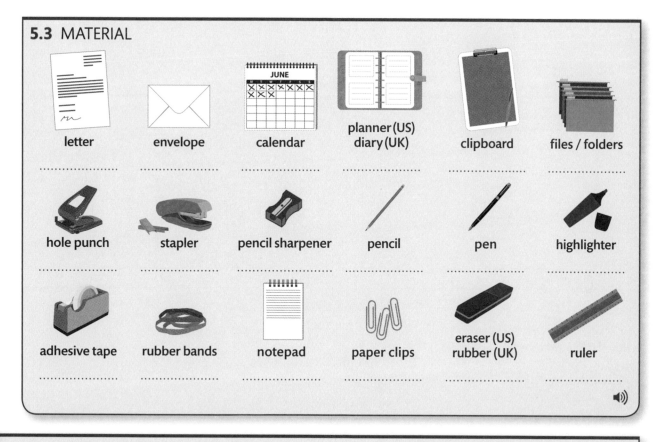

letter · **envelope** · **calendar** · **planner (US) diary (UK)** · **clipboard** · **files / folders**

hole punch · **stapler** · **pencil sharpener** · **pencil** · **pen** · **highlighter**

adhesive tape · **rubber bands** · **notepad** · **paper clips** · **eraser (US) rubber (UK)** · **ruler**

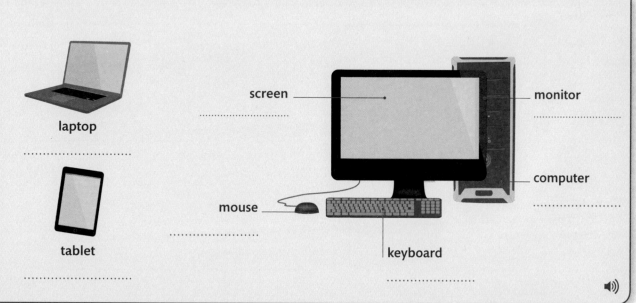

laptop

tablet

screen

monitor

mouse

computer

keyboard

06 Preguntar cosas en el trabajo

Es importante utilizar el orden adecuado de las palabras y los pronombres interrogativos en las preguntas en inglés, especialmente si son preguntas abiertas.

⚙ **Lenguaje** Formular preguntas
Aa Vocabulario Material de oficina
🧩 **Habilidad** Preguntar a los colegas

6.1 PUNTO CLAVE PREGUNTAS SIMPLES CON "TO BE"

Is this **where I can pay?**

No. Our machines are broken.

Are the meeting rooms **all busy?**

Yes. I'm afraid so.

6.2 CÓMO FUNCIONA PREGUNTAS SIMPLES CON "TO BE"

En frases afirmativas, el sujeto aparece antes del verbo. En frases interrogativas, se invierten el sujeto y el verbo.

This is **where I can pay.**

Is this **where I can pay?**

Verbo — Sujeto

6.3 VUELVE A ESCRIBIR LAS PREGUNTAS PONIENDO LAS PALABRAS EN SU ORDEN CORRECTO

| this | Is | desk? | my |

Is this my desk?

❶ | open? | windows | the | Are |

❷ | phone | working? | Is | your |

❸ | your | files? | these | Are |

❹ | that | Is | drawer | locked? |

❺ | desk | his | clean? | Is |

28

6.4 PUNTO CLAVE PREGUNTAS SIMPLES CON "DO"

Para formular preguntas en frases sin el verbo "to be", empieza la pregunta con "do" o "does".

Do you **have an** appointment?

No. Could I make one for today, please?

Does he **work with you**?

Yes, he works in my office.

6.5 CÓMO FUNCIONA PREGUNTAS SIMPLES CON "DO"

"DO / DOES"	SUJETO	VERBO	RESTO DE LA FRASE
Do	I / you / we / they		
Does	he / she	have	an appointment?

"Does" corresponde a la tercera persona de "do".

Utiliza la forma base del verbo.

6.6 COMPLETA LOS ESPACIOS CON "DO" O "DOES"

_____Do_____ they come in early?

1. _____ he have a key for this drawer?

2. _____ your laptop have a DVD drive?

3. _____ Jim and Tom have new screens?

4. _____ you keep pens in your desk drawer?

5. _____ Sarah write the minutes?

6. _____ all employees have wall calendars?

6.7 ESCUCHA EL AUDIO Y NUMERA LAS PREGUNTAS EN EL ORDEN QUE APARECEN

Karen ha empezado a trabajar y hace algunas preguntas sobre la empresa a su colega Kim.

A Are the refreshments in the kitchen free? ☐

B Do you have parties for everyone? ☐

C Are there weekly team meetings? ☐ 1

D Is there a code for the Wi-Fi? ☐

E Does the CEO visit the office regularly? ☐

29

6.8 PUNTO CLAVE FORMULAR PREGUNTAS ABIERTAS

Utiliza pronombres interrogativos como "when", "where", "how" o "why"
para formular preguntas que no puedan contestarse con "sí" o "no".

Where is the staff room?

Go down to the second floor.

When does Mia start work?

She usually starts at nine.

6.9 MÁS EJEMPLOS PREGUNTAS ABIERTAS

El "do / does" auxiliar va antes del sujeto.

How does the scanner work?

What would you like to drink?

Invierte el sujeto y el verbo para formular preguntas abiertas con "to be".

Where is the cafeteria?

Why is he late?

El verbo principal va al final en las preguntas sin "to be".

Who is giving the presentation?

When does the meeting start?

6.10 TACHA LA PALABRA INCORRECTA DE CADA PREGUNTA

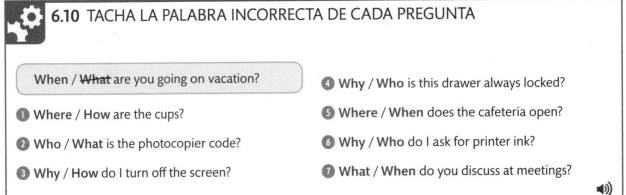

When / ~~What~~ are you going on vacation?

① Where / How are the cups?

② Who / What is the photocopier code?

③ Why / How do I turn off the screen?

④ Why / Who is this drawer always locked?

⑤ Where / When does the cafeteria open?

⑥ Why / Who do I ask for printer ink?

⑦ What / When do you discuss at meetings?

6.11 CONECTA LAS PREGUNTAS CON LAS RESPUESTAS CORRECTAS

Where is the stationery cabinet? ———→ It's across from the meeting room.

1 Who do I ask about taking a day off?

2 When is the restaurant usually busy?

3 Why is the stationery cabinet locked?

4 How does this coffee machine work?

5 What time does the meeting start?

You need to talk to Anne in HR.

So that Marie can control the stock.

At 2 o'clock. We usually start on time.

It's always full on weekend evenings.

Turn it on and then select your drink.

6.12 MARCA LAS PREGUNTAS QUE SEAN CORRECTAS

Who is in your team? ☑
What is in your team? ☐

1 What I can do to help you? ☐
What can I do to help you? ☐

2 Do you know where the key is? ☐
Does you know where the key is? ☐

3 When does the store open? ☐
When do the store open? ☐

4 Who do I connect the keyboard? ☐
How do I connect the keyboard? ☐

5 Why is her desk always a mess? ☐
Why does her desk always a mess? ☐

6.13 COMPLETA LOS ESPACIOS CON LAS PALABRAS DEL RECUADRO Y DI LAS PREGUNTAS EN VOZ ALTA

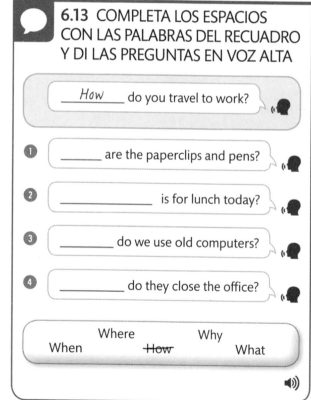

___How___ do you travel to work?

1 _____ are the paperclips and pens?

2 _____ is for lunch today?

3 _____ do we use old computers?

4 _____ do they close the office?

When   Where   Why   ~~How~~   What

---

07 Datos de contacto

Existen diversas expresiones para obtener y ofrecer información cuando se hacen nuevos contactos profesionales.

⚙ **Lenguaje** Respuestas cortas
Aa Vocabulario Información de contacto
🧩 **Habilidad** Intercambiar datos de contacto

7.1 PUNTO CLAVE INTERCAMBIAR DATOS DE CONTACTO

Es útil saber cómo preguntarle la información de contacto a un cliente o a un compañero de trabajo. Se pueden adaptar determinadas expresiones a muchas situaciones diferentes.

These products look great! Do you have a website?

En inglés británico también se utiliza "Have you got...?".

Yes! Here's my card with all the details.

How can I reach you for more information?

"Give me a ring" también se utiliza, especialmente en inglés británico.

Just give me a call.

Call me. Here's my number.

Drop me a line.

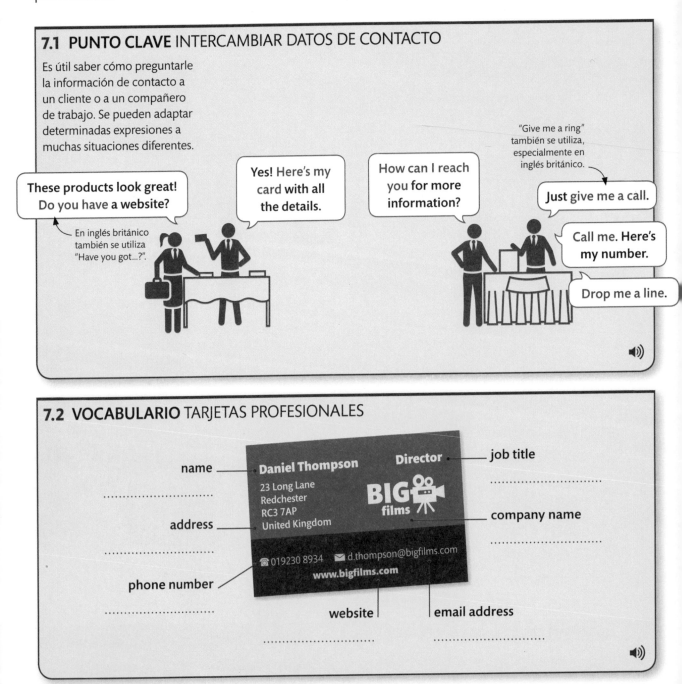

7.2 VOCABULARIO TARJETAS PROFESIONALES

name
address
phone number
job title
company name
website
email address

Daniel Thompson — **Director**
23 Long Lane
Redchester
RC3 7AP
United Kingdom
BIG films
☎ 019230 8934 ✉ d.thompson@bigfilms.com
www.bigfilms.com

7.3 PRONUNCIACIÓN DIRECCIONES DE CORREO ELECTRÓNICO

En inglés los símbolos "@" y "." de las direcciones de correo electrónico se pronuncian de una manera concreta.

(at) (hyphen) (underscore) (dot)

sue@super-cleaning_team.com

"Com" se pronuncia como se escribe; pero dominios como **.co.jp** y **.co.uk** se deletrean. Este último se pronuncia "dot co dot yu key".

7.4 ESCUCHA EL AUDIO Y NUMERA LAS DIRECCIONES DE CORREO EN EL ORDEN QUE APARECEN

Seis personas dan sus datos de contacto a alguien que acaban de conocer.

A c.j.jones@global-exec.com ☐

B joe@worldmail.co.jp ☐

C c.jones@global-exec.com ☐

D jay.jones@globalmail.com ☐ 1

E globalmail@jonesbrothers.com ☐

F c.j.jones@global-exec.co.fr ☐

7.5 TACHA LA PALABRA INCORRECTA DE CADA FRASE

> Just ~~make~~ / give me a call when you're ready.

1. Do you do / have a website I can look up?
2. Your job title / name isn't listed here.
3. Just fall / drop me a line for more details.
4. How can I reach / touch you to follow up?
5. Is this your phone number / address?
6. Here's my contact / business card.
7. Say / Call me to arrange a meeting.
8. Drop me a line / word to follow up next week.

7.6 MIRA LAS TARJETAS PROFESIONALES Y RESPONDE A LAS PREGUNTAS

> McKay & Sons is a travel agent. True ☐ False ☑

1. McKay and Sons has a website. True ☐ False ☐
2. Steven McKay is a Web Designer. True ☐ False ☐
3. Nancy Li has a website. True ☐ False ☐
4. City Zoo is on Madison Avenue. True ☐ False ☐
5. Nancy works in Human Resources. True ☐ False ☐
6. Nancy has an email address. True ☐ False ☐

McKay & Sons
Architects
www.mckayandsons.com
Steven McKay
Managing Director
📞 1200 400 589
✉ s.mckay@mckayandsons.net

City Zoo
2045 Mason Avenue, Madison, WI 54229
Nancy Li
Assistant Zoologist
(608) 233-4487
nancyli@cityzoo.org

7.7 PUNTO CLAVE RESPUESTAS CORTAS

A menudo escucharás respuestas cortas, como por ejemplo "Yes, I am", en entornos de trabajo en los que se hable inglés. Es más educado utilizar una respuesta corta que contestar solo "Yes" o "No".

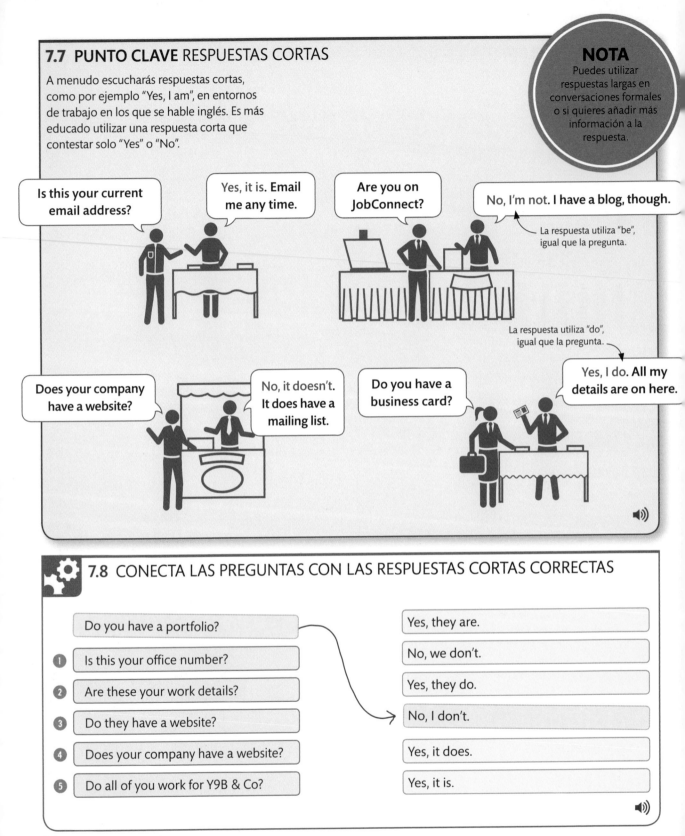

Is this your current email address?

Yes, it is. **Email me any time.**

Are you on JobConnect?

No, I'm not. **I have a blog, though.**

La respuesta utiliza "be", igual que la pregunta.

La respuesta utiliza "do", igual que la pregunta.

Does your company have a website?

No, it doesn't. **It does have a mailing list.**

Do you have a business card?

Yes, I do. **All my details are on here.**

7.8 CONECTA LAS PREGUNTAS CON LAS RESPUESTAS CORTAS CORRECTAS

Do you have a portfolio?

1 Is this your office number?

2 Are these your work details?

3 Do they have a website?

4 Does your company have a website?

5 Do all of you work for Y9B & Co?

Yes, they are.

No, we don't.

Yes, they do.

No, I don't.

Yes, it does.

Yes, it is.

7.9 COMPLETA LOS ESPACIOS Y RESPONDE EN VOZ ALTA

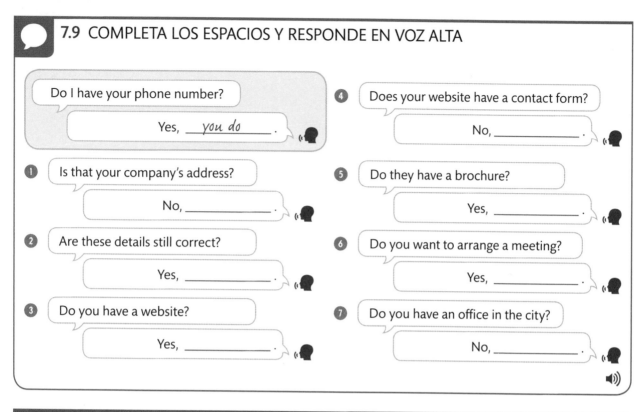

Do I have your phone number?

Yes, _you do_ .

1 Is that your company's address?

No, _____ .

2 Are these details still correct?

Yes, _____ .

3 Do you have a website?

Yes, _____ .

4 Does your website have a contact form?

No, _____ .

5 Do they have a brochure?

Yes, _____ .

6 Do you want to arrange a meeting?

Yes, _____ .

7 Do you have an office in the city?

No, _____ .

---

07 ✔ CHECKLIST

⚙ Respuestas cortas ☐   **Aa** Información de contacto ☐   🧩 Intercambiar datos de contacto ☐

♻ REPASA LO QUE HAS APRENDIDO EN LAS UNIDADES 01–07

NUEVO LENGUAJE	FRASE DE EJEMPLO	☑	UNIDAD
PRESENTAR Y PRESENTARSE ANTE OTRAS PERSONAS	**Good morning.** My name's **Alisha Sharma.** This is **my colleague, Edward.**	☐	1.1, 1.5
PRESENT SIMPLE PARA DESCRIBIR ACTIVIDADES DIARIAS EN EL TRABAJO	**We have a team meeting every Tuesday. The CEO works weekends if we're busy.**	☐	2.1
PAÍSES Y NACIONALIDADES	**These new mopeds are** from Italy. **I'm Brazilian, but I work in the US.**	☐	4.1, 4.2, 4.3
FRASES NEGATIVAS	I'm not **French.** I'm **Canadian.** **The printer** doesn't **work!**	☐	4.6
FORMULAR PREGUNTAS	Do you have **an appointment?** Where is **the staff room?**	☐	6.1, 6.4, 6.8
INTERCAMBIAR DATOS DE CONTACTO, RESPUESTAS CORTAS	**Is this your email address?** Yes, it is. **Do you have a business card?** No, I don't.	☐	7.1, 7.2, 7.7

Capacidades y experiencia

En inglés se utiliza el verbo "have" para hablar de las capacidades, la experiencia y los atributos profesionales. También se usa "have got" en inglés británico informal.

⚙ **Lenguaje** "Have", "have got", artículos
Aa Vocabulario Trabajos y capacidades
🧩 **Habilidad** Redactar un perfil profesional

8.1 PUNTO CLAVE "HAVE"

Utiliza "have" con sustantivos para hablar de las cualidades o experiencia de alguien.

"Have" es un verbo irregular. Su tercera persona es "has".

I have good computer skills.

My assistant has an excellent phone manner.

8.2 MÁS EJEMPLOS "HAVE" Y "HAVE GOT"

He has excellent negotiation skills.

"Have got" se utiliza en inglés británico informal oral.

Have you got any catering experience?

They don't have good people skills.

Para las expresiones negativas, se utiliza "do not" o "don't", su forma contraída, antes de "have".

She's got a positive attitude.

Esta forma corta de "has got" es informal.

8.3 CÓMO FUNCIONA FRASES AFIRMATIVAS CON "HAVE"

SUJETO	"HAVE" / "HAS"	RESTO DE LA FRASE
I / You / We / They	have	good computer skills.
He / She	has	

Con "he", "she" e "it", utiliza "has".

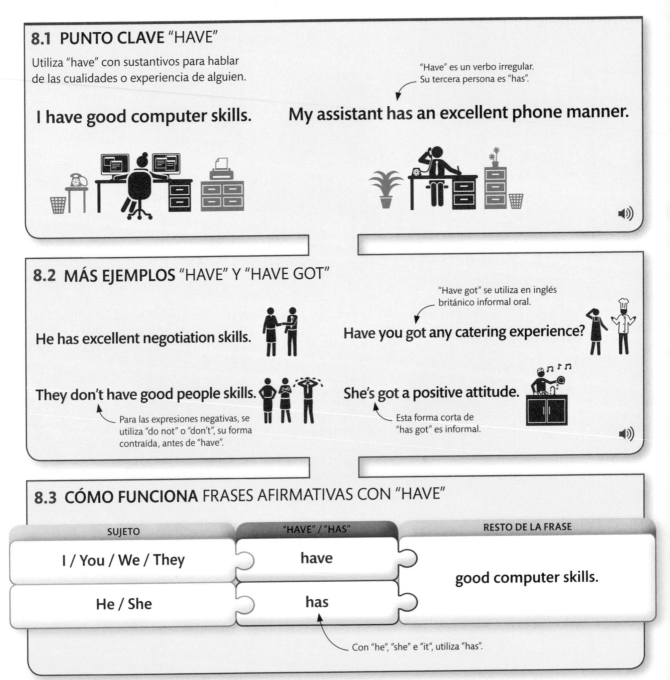

8.4 TACHA LAS PALABRAS INCORRECTAS DE CADA FRASE

He ~~have~~ / **has** excellent typing skills.

① They **don't** / **doesn't** have interviews today.

② He **haven't** / **hasn't** got a diploma.

③ I **don't have** / **don't got** any experience.

④ Do you **has** / **have** good IT skills?

⑤ We **haves** / **have** monthly training sessions.

⑥ He **don't** / **doesn't** have experience with animals.

⑦ He's **have** / **has** a Master's degree.

⑧ They **have** / **got** a lot of inexperienced staff.

⑨ She's **got** / **have** super negotiation skills.

8.5 LEE EL PERFIL EN LÍNEA Y MARCA LAS FRASES QUE SEAN CORRECTAS

Sam Bradley · photographer

HOME | SKILLS | CONTACT

Experience:
I have a lot of experience in digital photography and photo editing. I love working with animals and nature, and I won my first regional competition when I was 13. In college, I chaired the Photography Club and arranged speakers, training, and field trips. I have some experience of working in an office, having spent a summer working for a nature magazine.

Skills:
- I have excellent photography and editing skills learned from my degree and many years of experience.
- I enjoy working in teams, on my own, and with animals.

Qualifications:
- **BA Dance and Drama** (2014)
- **Diploma in Pet Photography** (2016)

Sam has never edited photographs. ☐
Sam has edited photographs. ☑

① Sam loves working with children. ☐
Sam loves working with animals. ☐

② Sam won a regional competition. ☐
Sam won a national competition. ☐

③ Sam didn't organize field trips. ☐
Sam organized field trips at college. ☐

④ Sam worked in an office. ☐
Sam didn't work in an office. ☐

⑤ Sam has excellent photography skills. ☐
Sam has good negotiation skills. ☐

⑥ Sam's degree is in photography. ☐
Sam's degree is in dance and drama. ☐

⑦ Sam has a photography diploma. ☐
Sam has never studied photography. ☐

8.6 PUNTO CLAVE "A / AN / THE"

Utiliza "a" o "an" para hablar de empleos y lugares de trabajo cuando aparecen por primera vez en la conversación. Utiliza "the" para referirte a algo concreto o a algo que ya se ha mencionado antes.

Utiliza "a" porque es la primera vez que aparece el restaurante.

I'm a waiter. I work in a popular restaurant.

The restaurant is always busy.

Utiliza "the" porque el restaurante ya ha aparecido antes.

8.7 MÁS EJEMPLOS "A / AN / THE"

Utiliza "an" antes de una vocal.

I'm an intern at an advertising agency.

The agency is next to a café.

Isaac is a good hairdresser.

The hairdresser who works weekends is terrible.

8.8 COMPLETA LOS ESPACIOS CON "A", "AN" O "THE"

He works in ____*a*____ hotel.

1 Oh, yes. I know _____ hotel you mean.

2 Susan has _____ diploma.

3 Is _____ meeting on the second floor?

4 I work for _____ large recruitment agency.

5 There's _____ ad for a chef here.

6 I hired _____ PA to help me out.

7 He works at _____ hospital down the road.

8 Is there _____ office in Mexico?

8.9 ESCUCHA EL AUDIO Y NUMERA LAS PERSONAS EN EL ORDEN QUE SE DESCRIBEN

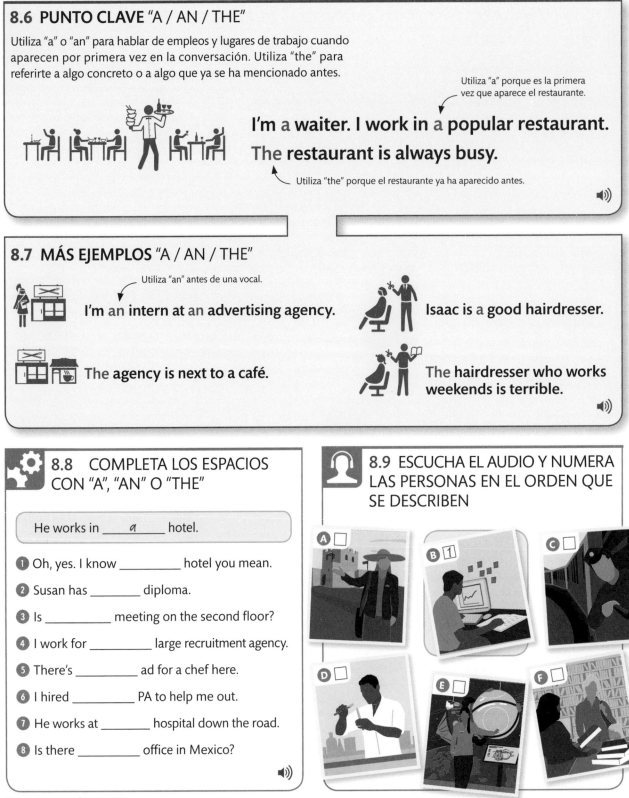

A ☐   B ☐ 1   C ☐

D ☐   E ☐   F ☐

8.10 PUNTO CLAVE OMISIÓN DEL ARTÍCULO

En inglés a veces los sustantivos van sin "a", "an" o "the" antes del nombre. Esto se conoce como omisión del artículo o zero article. Omite el artículo en plurales cuando hables de cosas en general.

Se refiere a entrevistas en general, no a unas en concreto.

I get very nervous before interviews.

We're looking for people who can sell our products.

Se refiere a personas en general, no a individuos concretos.

8.11 MARCA LAS FRASES QUE SEAN CORRECTAS

Online profiles are really useful. ☑
The online profiles are really useful. ☐

① He was out of the office today. ☐
He was out of an office today. ☐

② I have the excellent people skills. ☐
I have excellent people skills. ☐

③ What skills do you need for this job? ☐
What a skills do you need for this job? ☐

④ Have you read the job requirements? ☐
Have you read a job requirements? ☐

⑤ She's a architect for a top company. ☐
She's an architect for a top company. ☐

⑥ The new designer is very good. ☐
A new designer is very good. ☐

8.12 LEE LA CARTA DE PRESENTACIÓN Y TACHA LAS PALABRAS INCORRECTAS

Dear Mr. Baxter,

I am writing to apply for the / a role of Library Assistant, which I saw advertised on your website. I have / got two years' experience working as a part-time assistant in my local library. The / A job involves working with a / the team of people and the public, so I have good people skills / the good people skills.

I do not have / have not a degree in Library and Information Studies, as an / the ad requested, but I have / has a degree in English Literature.

I look forward to hearing from you.
Yours sincerely,

Judy Stein

Judy Stein

9.1 TRABAJOS

businessman

businesswoman

sales manager

sales assistant

receptionist

hairdresser / stylist

gardener

cleaner / janitor

train driver

taxi driver

electrician

construction worker (US) / builder (UK)

plumber

engineer

mechanic

pilot

flight attendant

travel agent

tour guide

journalist

9.2 EMPLEO

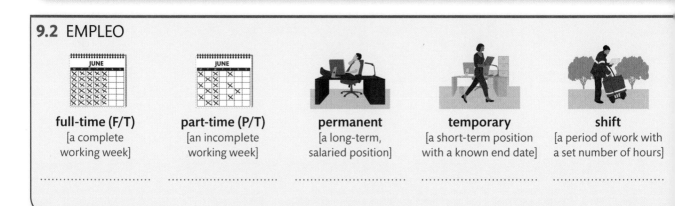

full-time (F/T)
[a complete working week]

part-time (P/T)
[an incomplete working week]

permanent
[a long-term, salaried position]

temporary
[a short-term position with a known end date]

shift
[a period of work with a set number of hours]

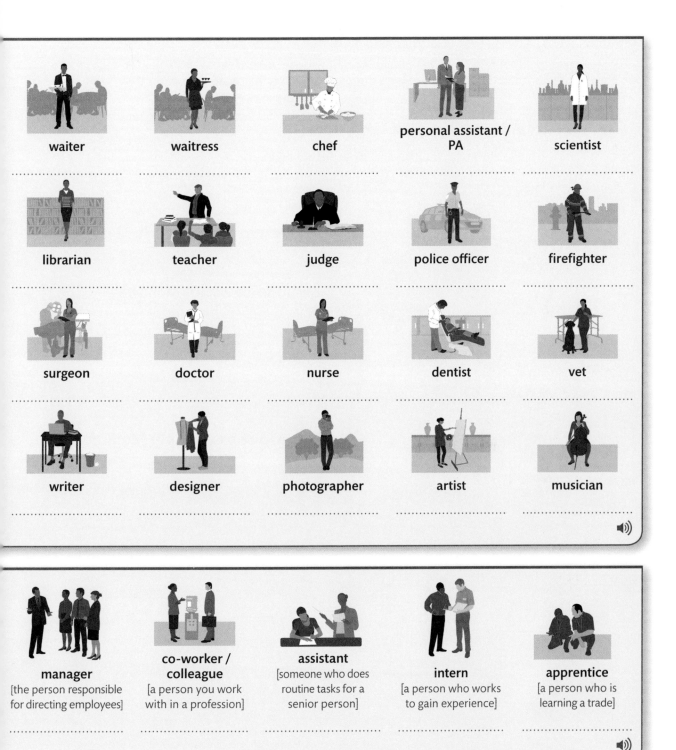

waiter

waitress

chef

personal assistant / PA

scientist

librarian

teacher

judge

police officer

firefighter

surgeon

doctor

nurse

dentist

vet

writer

designer

photographer

artist

musician

manager
[the person responsible for directing employees]

co-worker / colleague
[a person you work with in a profession]

assistant
[someone who does routine tasks for a senior person]

intern
[a person who works to gain experience]

apprentice
[a person who is learning a trade]

41

10 Elegir un trabajo

Los verbos "like", "enjoy" y "hate" expresan sentimientos sobre las cosas. Se utilizan a menudo para hablar sobre qué actividades se quieren desempeñar en el trabajo.

⚙ **Lenguaje** "Like", "enjoy" y "hate"
Aa Vocabulario Actividades del lugar de trabajo
🧩 **Habilidad** Encontrar el trabajo adecuado

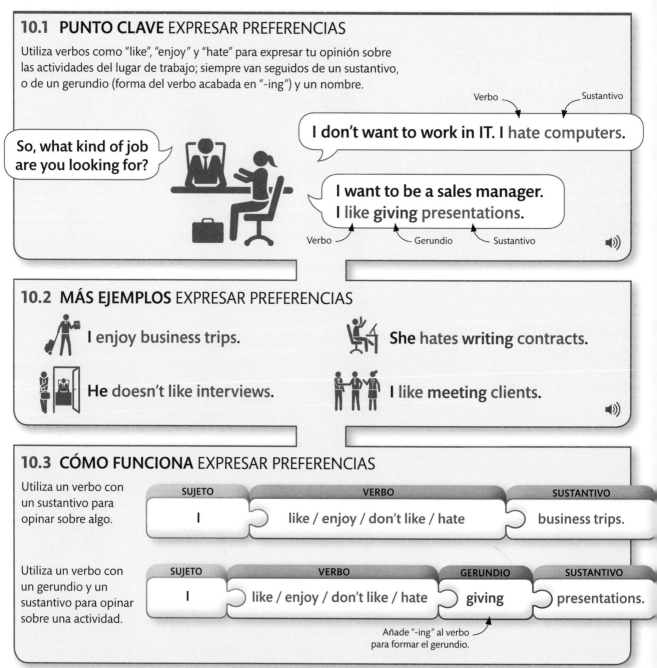

10.1 PUNTO CLAVE EXPRESAR PREFERENCIAS

Utiliza verbos como "like", "enjoy" y "hate" para expresar tu opinión sobre las actividades del lugar de trabajo; siempre van seguidos de un sustantivo, o de un gerundio (forma del verbo acabada en "-ing") y un nombre.

Verbo — Sustantivo

I don't want to work in IT. I hate computers.

So, what kind of job are you looking for?

I want to be a sales manager. I like giving presentations.

Verbo — Gerundio — Sustantivo

10.2 MÁS EJEMPLOS EXPRESAR PREFERENCIAS

I enjoy business trips.

She hates writing contracts.

He doesn't like interviews.

I like meeting clients.

10.3 CÓMO FUNCIONA EXPRESAR PREFERENCIAS

Utiliza un verbo con un sustantivo para opinar sobre algo.

SUJETO	VERBO	SUSTANTIVO
I	like / enjoy / don't like / hate	business trips.

Utiliza un verbo con un gerundio y un sustantivo para opinar sobre una actividad.

SUJETO	VERBO	GERUNDIO	SUSTANTIVO
I	like / enjoy / don't like / hate	giving	presentations.

Añade "-ing" al verbo para formar el gerundio.

42

10.4 TACHA LAS PALABRAS INCORRECTAS DE CADA FRASE

Do you enjoy ~~meet~~ / meeting clients?

❶ She don't like / doesn't like using computers.

❷ He likes training / train new colleagues.

❸ I hates / hate long meetings.

❹ We don't like / doesn't like lazy employees.

❺ She enjoys work / working in a team.

10.5 ESCUCHA EL AUDIO Y MARCA SI A JORDI LE GUSTA O NO LA ACTIVIDAD DE CADA IMAGEN

Le gusta ☐
No le gusta ☑

❶ Le gusta ☐
No le gusta ☐

❷ Le gusta ☐
No le gusta ☐

❸ Le gusta ☐
No le gusta ☐

❹ Le gusta ☐
No le gusta ☐

10.6 LEE LA OFERTA DE EMPLEO Y RESPONDE A LAS PREGUNTAS

The tour guide might work with children. **True** ☑ **False** ☐

❶ Not many tourists go to Notwen Castle. **True** ☐ **False** ☐

❷ The job involves greeting visitors. **True** ☐ **False** ☐

❸ The tour guide must like working alone. **True** ☐ **False** ☐

❹ The tour guide always works inside. **True** ☐ **False** ☐

❺ The job involves weekend work. **True** ☐ **False** ☐

JOBS

Tour Guide
needed for top tourist attraction

Do you love working with people from all ages and backgrounds? Notwen Castle is one of the most popular castles in the country. Every visitor to Notwen Castle is special. It will be your job to welcome them to the castle. You must enjoy working as part of a team and have great customer service skills. The job includes working outside and on weekends.

10 ✔ CHECKLIST

⚙ "Like", "enjoy" y "hate" ☐   **Aa** Actividades del lugar de trabajo ☐   Encontrar el trabajo adecuado ☐

Describir el lugar de trabajo

Para explicar cosas de la empresa puedes utilizar "there is" y "there are". Utiliza "Is there...?" o "Are there...?" para formular preguntas sobre un lugar de trabajo.

⚙ **Lenguaje** "There is" y "there are"

Aa Vocabulario Material de oficina

🧩 **Habilidad** Describir un lugar de trabajo

11.1 PUNTO CLAVE "THERE IS" Y "THERE ARE"

Utiliza "there is" para hablar de una cosa y "there are" para hablar de más de una cosa.

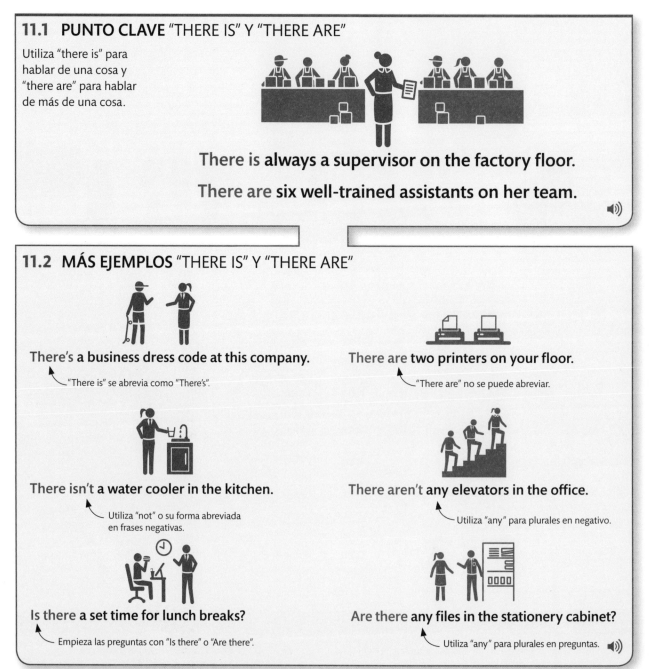

There is always a supervisor on the factory floor.

There are six well-trained assistants on her team.

🔊

11.2 MÁS EJEMPLOS "THERE IS" Y "THERE ARE"

There's a business dress code at this company.

"There is" se abrevia como "There's".

There are two printers on your floor.

"There are" no se puede abreviar.

There isn't a water cooler in the kitchen.

Utiliza "not" o su forma abreviada en frases negativas.

There aren't any elevators in the office.

Utiliza "any" para plurales en negativo.

Is there a set time for lunch breaks?

Empieza las preguntas con "Is there" o "Are there".

Are there any files in the stationery cabinet?

Utiliza "any" para plurales en preguntas. 🔊

11.3 VUELVE A ESCRIBIR LAS FRASES CORRIGIENDO LOS ERRORES

> There is 10 people on the sales team.
> *There are 10 people on the sales team.*

1 There are'nt any bathrooms on this floor.
_____

2 Is there any stationery cabinet in the office?
_____

3 There's staff cafeteria on the third floor.
_____

4 There isnt an elevator in this building.
_____

5 Is there any places to lock my bicycle here?
_____

6 Are there a desk ready for our new designer?
_____

7 There're lots of envelopes in the cabinet.
_____

🔊

11.4 ESCUCHA EL AUDIO Y ESCRIBE RESPUESTAS A LAS PREGUNTAS CON ORACIONES COMPLETAS

Alvita le muestra la oficina a Jonathan, un nuevo compañero de trabajo.

> What happens every Monday afternoon?
> *There is a weekly team meeting.*

1 Where do people leave their wet coats?
_____

2 How many desks are in Jonathan's office?
_____

3 What is across from Jonathan's office?
_____

4 Where do staff sign in every day?
_____

11.5 UTILIZA EL DIAGRAMA PARA CREAR SEIS FRASES CORRECTAS Y DILAS EN VOZ ALTA

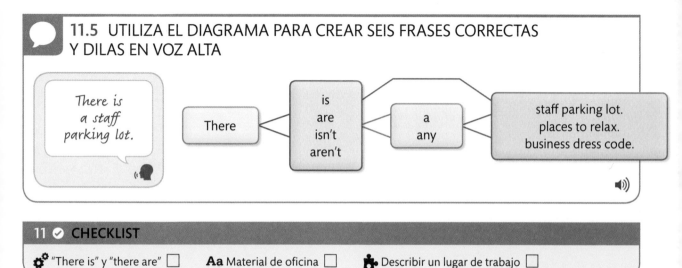

> *There is a staff parking lot.*

There —— is / are / isn't / aren't —— a / any —— staff parking lot. / places to relax. / business dress code.

🔊

---

11 ✓ **CHECKLIST**

⚙️ "There is" y "there are" ☐   **Aa** Material de oficina ☐   🧩 Describir un lugar de trabajo ☐

45

12.1 DINERO

bills (US) / notes (UK)

coins

wallet

wallet (US) / purse (UK)

credit card

debit card

cash machine / ATM

withdraw money

bank

bank statement

online banking

mobile banking

receipt

currency

cash register (US) / till (UK)

safe

invoice

check (US) / cheque (UK)

deposit / pay in money

transfer money

12.2 SALARIO Y CONDICIONES

The company I work for pays an hourly rate of $15.

hourly rate
[the amount of money paid per hour]

The salary for this job is $35,000.

salary
[a fixed, regular payment every month, often expressed as an annual sum]

I work fewer hours now, but I had to take a huge pay cut.

a pay cut
[a reduction in pay]

My annual review was really positive so I'm hoping to get a raise next year.

a raise (US) / a pay rise (UK)
[an increase in pay]

My bonus this year was $2,000 so I'm going to buy a new car.

a bonus
[money added to a person's wages as a reward for good performance]

Benefits include a free gym membership.

benefits
[extras given to employees in addition to their usual pay]

I work extra hours regularly and get overtime pay.

overtime
[additional pay for extra hours worked]

The demand for plumbers has decreased so I earned half as much this year.

to earn
[to receive money in return for labor or services]

The shop has been really busy so our wages are increasing next week.

wage
[the amount of money paid per week or month]

I get 20 days of annual vacation every year.

annual vacation (US) / annual leave (UK)
[paid time off work granted by employers]

13 Cualidades personales

En el trabajo coincidirás con personas con personalidades y habilidades diferentes. Es muy útil poder describir a tus colegas y hablar de sus fortalezas y debilidades.

🔧 **Lenguaje** Adjetivos posesivos
Aa Vocabulario Rasgos de personalidad
🧩 **Habilidad** Describir a los colegas

13.1 PUNTO CLAVE ADJETIVOS

Los adjetivos por lo general se colocan antes de los sustantivos o después de algunos verbos, como "be", "become", "get", "seem" y "look".

El adjetivo se sitúa antes del sustantivo.

El adjetivo se sitúa después del verbo "be".

> I run a great **team**, but John is really **lazy**.
> It's not fair on his **co-workers**.

NOTA
En general, los adjetivos que describen cualidades negativas, como "lazy", se evitan en entornos profesionales.

13.2 MÁS EJEMPLOS ADJETIVOS

Los adjetivos no cambian en femenino.

Chloe is **polite** to clients.

Sally is always **calm** under pressure.

Michael is very **hardworking**.

Fatima is a **creative** designer.

Ben seems very **organized**.

Utiliza "very" o "really" antes de un adjetivo para dar énfasis.

Ruth and Ian always look **great**.

Los adjetivos no cambian en plural.

13.3 ESCUCHA EL AUDIO Y NUMERA LAS PERSONAS EN EL ORDEN QUE SE DESCRIBEN

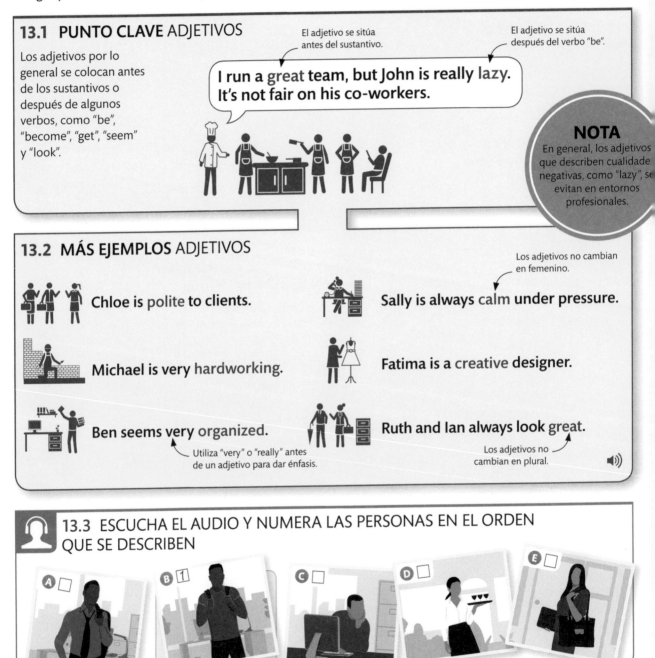

A ☐   B 1   C ☐   D ☐   E ☐

Aa 13.4 LEE EL ARTÍCULO Y ESCRIBE LOS ADJETIVOS MARCADOS EN LOS GRUPOS CORRECTOS

POSITIVOS

motivated

NEGATIVOS

impatient

OUR TEAM

Career climbers who are moving up fast

Meet two of our new employees

A design that inspired Sam Riley

Sam Riley joins Scarlett Fashion Design after a short, steep climb to the top of his career ladder. Sam says, "I've always been an extremely motivated and ambitious person. I am sometimes a little impatient with lazy or impolite people, but I hope my new colleagues will find me to be helpful."

Alik Novozik already has a reputation as a bright and intelligent designer and we are very happy to welcome him to the Scarlett family. Alik says, "I'm looking forward to working with the design team here. Some people say I can be a little nervous. Even if I do get nervous sometimes, I'm definitely not boring."

13.5 VUELVE A ESCRIBIR LAS FRASES CORRIGIENDO LOS ERRORES

> This is a team great. All my colleagues be really hardworkings.
> _This is a great team. All my colleagues are really hardworking._

❶ My team leader impolite is and he is also impatient very.

_____

❷ My co-workers say that I really motivated and ambitious am.

_____

❸ The new young intern seems very intelligent and he really be polite.

_____

❹ I'm very lucky. All my colleagues be hardworking and helpfuls.

_____

13.6 PUNTO CLAVE ADJETIVOS POSESIVOS

Los adjetivos posesivos te dicen de quién es algo. Utilízalos para hablar de colegas, trabajo o la competencia.

Pronombre sujeto.

She looks busy.

Yes. Tamsin takes her work very seriously.

El adjetivo posesivo indica que el trabajo es de Tamsin.

13.7 MÁS EJEMPLOS ADJETIVOS POSESIVOS

Your team is so hardworking.

Pablo is talking to his manager.

My staff is very motivated.

Their products aren't very good.

13.8 CÓMO FUNCIONA ADJETIVOS POSESIVOS

PRONOMBRE SUJETO	I	you	he	she	it	we	they
ADJETIVO POSESIVO	my	your	his	her	its	our	their

13.9 COMPLETA LOS ESPACIOS CONVIRTIENDO LOS PRONOMBRES SUJETO EN ADJETIVOS POSESIVOS

Sophia is so efficient. _____Her_____ (She) desk is always very well organized.

1 Two of the people on _____ (I) team are new to the company, but they're settling in well.

2 _____ (They) manager is very good with people. They enjoy working with him.

3 The company is very proud of _____ (it) reputation and quality products.

4 Is this _____ (you) phone? It doesn't belong to me but I found it on my desk.

13.10 PUNTO CLAVE PRONOMBRES POSESIVOS

Utiliza pronombres posesivos para referirte a tus logros o tus cosas. Si utilizas un pronombre posesivo, no repitas el sustantivo de la pregunta.

"Mine" suena más natural que "my design".

Is that design yours? It looks great!

Yes, it's mine. I'm very proud of it.

13.11 CÓMO FUNCIONA PRONOMBRES POSESIVOS

ADJETIVO POSESIVO	my	your	his	her	its	our	their
	⬇	⬇	⬇	⬇	⬇	⬇	⬇
PRONOMBRE POSESIVO	mine	yours	his	hers	its	ours	theirs

13.12 TACHA LA PALABRA INCORRECTA DE CADA FRASE

This laptop is ~~their~~ / theirs.

1 We hate their product but we love **our** / ours.

2 They are proud of **their** / theirs project.

3 **Our** / Ours clients expect excellent service.

4 This isn't her desk. It's **my** / mine.

5 This is amazing. Is it **her** / hers project?

13.13 ESCRIBE CADA FRASE EN SU FORMA ALTERNATIVA

This is **my** computer.	This computer is mine.
1	I think these files are **yours**.
2 Is this **his** desk?	
3	These pens are **hers**.
4 Are those **their** products?	

13.14 PUNTO CLAVE APÓSTROFO POSESIVO

Añade un apóstrofo y la letra "s" al final de un sustantivo singular para indicar que el sustantivo que le sigue le pertenece.

Un apóstrofo y una "s" indican pertenencia.

Jeremy is Pepe's line manager.

[Jeremy is the line manager of Pepe.]

Si el sustantivo es plural, añade solo un apóstrofo después de la "s".

Añade un apóstrofo sin "s" a los sustantivos plurales.

Jeremy is my colleagues' line manager.

[Jeremy is the line manager of multiple people.]

13.15 ⚠ ERRORES COMUNES APÓSTROFO POSESIVO

No utilices un apóstrofo y una "s" tras un sustantivo plural en una expresión que no denote pertenencia.

"Colleagues" es un sustantivo plural, pero la "s" aquí no indica pertenencia.

My colleagues are late. ✔

My colleagues' are late. ✖

No utilices un apóstrofo porque "late" no pertenece a "colleagues".

My colleague's are late. ✖

13.16 VUELVE A ESCRIBIR LAS FRASES CORRIGIENDO LOS ERRORES

Jasons assistant often works late.

Jason's assistant often works late.

❶ The **intern's** work really hard.

_____

❷ All the team **members'** are intelligent.

_____

❸ This big room is my **boss** office.

_____

❹ All the **bosses'** have parking spaces.

_____

❺ The best thing about this product is **it's** strength.

_____

13.17 VUELVE A ESCRIBIR LAS EXPRESIONES MARCADAS CORRIGIENDO LOS ERRORES

Performance Review:
Jorge Perez

Jorge is very hardworking and he confidence has grown since his joined the company last summer. He writes excellent reports and is polite and friendly with co-workers and customers. Jorges supervisor believes that he will be promoted soon and will have an excellent future in the company. We are very pleased with his work and continued progress here.

Performance Review:
Maria Moran

Maria does not seem to be very happy at work at the moment. She progress is slow and she has not completed a single project yet. Her main problem is that she has difficulties working as part of a team. Co-workers complain that Maria impatient is and also unfriendly. This is a shame as she is obviously intelligent very. We hope that Maria will begin to see how important it is to be a good team player.

his confidence has grown

❶ _____

❷ _____

❸ _____

❹ _____

❺ _____

13.18 UTILIZA EL DIAGRAMA PARA CREAR 14 FRASES CORRECTAS Y DILAS EN VOZ ALTA

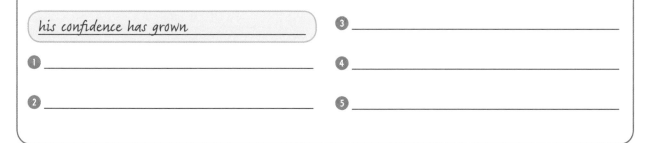

You are my manager.

| You / We / Katy | are / is | my / Sam's / very / really | manager. / assistant. / organized. |

14 Describir tu trabajo

Una manera de explicar cosas de tu trabajo es utilizar adjetivos para describirlo. Los adjetivos te permiten comparar con otros cargos que hayas tenido.

🔧 **Lenguaje** Adjetivos y comparativos
Aa Vocabulario Dinero y salario
🧩 **Habilidad** Describirle tu trabajo a alguien

14.1 PUNTO CLAVE ADJETIVOS CON "-ING" Y "-ED"

Los adjetivos que acaban en "-ing" describen el efecto que tiene algo.
Los adjetivos que acaban en "-ed" describen cómo se ve afectado algo.

El trabajo provoca cansancio.

My job is very tiring.

I am always so tired!

El hombre experimenta cansancio.

🔊

14.2 MÁS EJEMPLOS ADJETIVOS CON "-ING" Y "-ED"

The building is amazing.
The tourists are amazed.

The task is annoying.
She is annoyed.

The meeting was boring.
They were bored.

The vacation is relaxing.
He is relaxed.

🔊

14.3 TACHA LA PALABRA INCORRECTA DE CADA FRASE

That's a very ~~interested~~ / interesting idea.

❶ That meeting was really **bored** / **boring**.

❷ The printer can be **annoyed** / **annoying** at times.

❸ By the end of the week, I'm really **tired** / **tiring**.

❹ The system is **confused** / **confusing** at first.

❺ I'm very **excited** / **exciting** about my project.

❻ The news was **shocked** / **shocking**.

❼ I was very **surprised** / **surprising** by my raise!

🔊

14.4 LEE EL ARTÍCULO Y RESPONDE A LAS PREGUNTAS

> Sven is self-employed.
> **True** ☐ **False** ☐ **Not given** ☑

① Sven wanted to work on a space station.
True ☐ **False** ☐ **Not given** ☐

② Sven's job is based in the US.
True ☐ **False** ☐ **Not given** ☐

③ Sven thinks everyone would like to do his job.
True ☐ **False** ☐ **Not given** ☐

④ Sven works some weekends.
True ☐ **False** ☐ **Not given** ☐

⑤ Sven finds his work annoying.
True ☐ **False** ☐ **Not given** ☐

BUSINESS TODAY

Reach for the stars

This week we talk to
Sven about his work

I was really excited when I first got this job. More than 3,000 people applied for it and I was thrilled to be successful. I do really interesting research on astronauts and space programs. I work in a large office in the United States and analyze data from space stations and satellites. I think the work is really fascinating, although some people might think that looking at screens of statistics from space stations is quite boring. The data arrives all the time, so the work can be quite tiring. We all work quite long hours, but we never get annoyed as we hope that the work we do will be important for scientists and other researchers.

14.5 LEE LAS PISTAS Y ESCRIBE LAS PALABRAS DEL RECUADRO EN EL LUGAR CORRECTO DEL CRUCIGRAMA

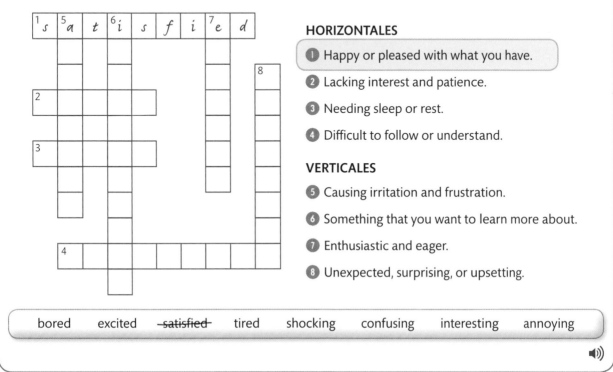

HORIZONTALES

① Happy or pleased with what you have.

② Lacking interest and patience.

③ Needing sleep or rest.

④ Difficult to follow or understand.

VERTICALES

⑤ Causing irritation and frustration.

⑥ Something that you want to learn more about.

⑦ Enthusiastic and eager.

⑧ Unexpected, surprising, or upsetting.

bored   excited   ~~satisfied~~   tired   shocking   confusing   interesting   annoying

14.6 PUNTO CLAVE ADJETIVOS COMPARATIVOS

La mayoría de adjetivos tienen una forma comparativa que
se utiliza para describir la diferencia entre dos cosas.

**Do you like the new job?
I bet the salary is higher!**

Añade "-er" para
formar el comparativo.

**It is, but the hours are much
longer than my old job.**

Utiliza "than" después del
comparativo para comparar
una cosa con otra.

14.7 MÁS EJEMPLOS ADJETIVOS COMPARATIVOS

Si el adjetivo acaba
en "-e", añade "-r".

My new office is closer to the city.

Si el adjetivo acaba en "-y",
quita la "y" y añade "-ier".

I leave the house earlier now.

The New York office is bigger.

Si el adjetivo es monosílabo y acaba
en consonante-vocal-consonante,
dobla la última letra y añade "-er".

Tickets are more expensive.

Si el adjetivo tiene más de dos
sílabas, utiliza "more" para
construir el comparativo.

El adjetivo
no cambia.

14.8 COMPLETA LOS ESPACIOS CON LOS COMPARATIVOS CORRECTOS

My new commute is ___*more expensive*___ (expensive) than before, and it's ___*longer*___ (long).

❶ This printer is _____ (fast) than the other, but that one is _____ (reliable).

❷ This coffee is _____ (strong) than I normally buy, but it is also _____ (tasty).

❸ This building is _____ (new) than my last workplace, and the area is _____ (quiet).

❹ This café is _____ (busy) than the other one, so the service is _____ (slow).

❺ My new uniform is _____ (comfortable) than my old one, but _____ (ugly).

14.9 PUNTO CLAVE ADJETIVOS COMPARATIVOS IRREGULARES

Algunos adjetivos frecuentes (normalmente cortos)
tienen comparativos que no siguen la normativa.

ADJETIVO	bad	good	well	far
COMPARATIVO	worse	better	better	farther (US) / further (UK)

"Well" como adjetivo significa sano; "better"
aquí significa "healthier" o "no longer ill".

14.10 MARCA LAS FRASES QUE SEAN CORRECTAS

Profits are more bad than last year! ☐
Profits are worse than last year! ☑

1. Parking is more expensive this year. ☐
   Parking is expensiver this year. ☐

2. This system is gooder than before. ☐
   This system is better than before. ☐

3. I have much work to do than last year. ☐
   I have more work to do than last year. ☐

4. I arrive much early than my boss. ☐
   I arrive much earlier than my boss. ☐

5. Every year my raise is more smaller. ☐
   Every year my raise is smaller. ☐

6. I feel weller now that I have a new job. ☐
   I feel better now that I have a new job. ☐

7. A digital copy is more useful to me. ☐
   A digital copy is usefuller to me. ☐

8. That meeting was worser than usual. ☐
   That meeting was worse than usual. ☐

14.11 ESCUCHA EL AUDIO Y CONECTA LAS IMÁGENES CON LAS EXPRESIONES CORRECTAS

worse overtime pay

1. longer hours

2. hourly rate is less

3. better salary

4. bigger bonus

5. shorter commute

Aa 14.12 CONECTA CADA PALABRA CON SU OPUESTO

less → more

1. difficult — easy
2. excited — bored
3. weaker — stronger
4. higher — lower
5. expensive — cheap
6. lighter — heavier
7. bigger — smaller
8. little — large
9. better — worse

stronger
worse
more
bored
large
lower
heavier
easy
cheap
smaller

🔊

⚙ 14.13 CORRIGE LOS ERRORES DE LAS EXPRESIONES MARCADAS

Join our team

Are you **more efficienter** than your colleagues? Are you **more friendlier** than others? And do you want to be **more successfuller?** ...then come to work with us at Sandwich Delicious. We sell **morer** sandwiches than any other sandwich bar in the city. We also offer **more good** pay than similar jobs in the area. All our co-workers at Sandwich Delicious deli get **more long** vacations than those working at similar companies. You will get three days off every week.

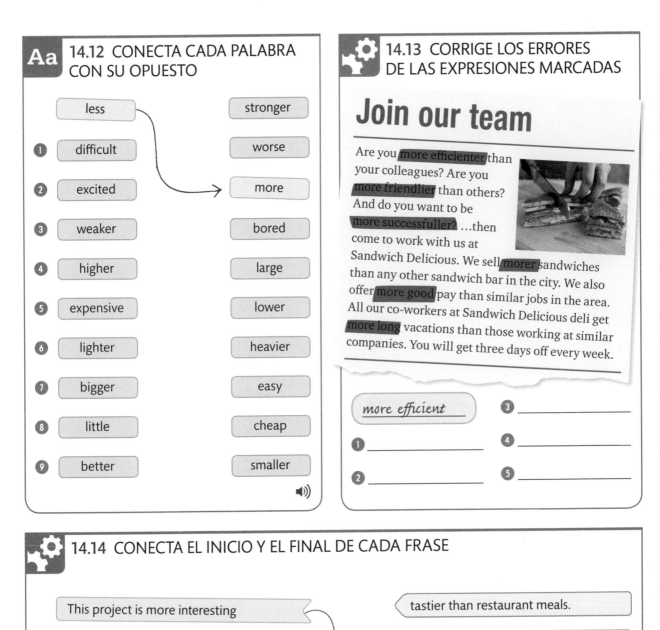

more efficient

1. _____
2. _____
3. _____
4. _____
5. _____

⚙ 14.14 CONECTA EL INICIO Y EL FINAL DE CADA FRASE

This project is more interesting → than the last one.

1. Now, my vacations are longer — than they used to be.
2. This new computer system is more — efficient than the old one.
3. These presentations are making me more — bored than yesterday's.
4. These new laptops are — lighter than the old ones.
5. The cafeteria lunches are — tastier than restaurant meals.

tastier than restaurant meals.
efficient than the old one.
than the last one.
lighter than the old ones.
than they used to be.
bored than yesterday's.

🔊

Joe habla de su nuevo trabajo y lo compara con la última empresa en la que ha trabajado.

Joe says the new company is more modern.
True ☑ **False** ☐ **Not given** ☐

❷ Joe earns more money now than he did before.
True ☐ **False** ☐ **Not given** ☐

❸ Joe spends more time at work now than before.
True ☐ **False** ☐ **Not given** ☐

❹ Joe is bored in his new job.
True ☐ **False** ☐ **Not given** ☐

❺ Joe's new boss has regular meetings with him.
True ☐ **False** ☐ **Not given** ☐

❻ Joe's old workplace was not very organized.
True ☐ **False** ☐ **Not given** ☐

❶ Joe does not enjoy working in social media.
True ☐ **False** ☐ **Not given** ☐

❼ Joe's new workplace is more efficient.
True ☐ **False** ☐ **Not given** ☐

---

14 ✔ CHECKLIST

⚙ Adjetivos y comparativos ☐   **Aa** Dinero y salario ☐   🧩 Describirle tu trabajo a alguien ☐

♻ **REPASA** LO QUE HAS APRENDIDO EN LAS UNIDADES 08–14

NUEVO LENGUAJE	FRASE DE EJEMPLO	☑	UNIDAD
HABLAR DE CAPACIDADES Y EXPERIENCIA	I have **excellent negotiation skills.** I work in **a busy restaurant.**	☐	8.1, 8.6
EXPRESAR PREFERENCIAS	I hate **computers.** He likes giving **presentations.**	☐	10.1, 10.2
DESCRIBIR UN LUGAR DE TRABAJO	There is **a formal dress code at this company.** There are **two printers on your floor.**	☐	11.1, 11.2
DESCRIBIR A LOS COLEGAS	Your new team is really **hardworking.** Jeremy is Pepe's **line manager.**	☐	13.1, 13.14
DESCRIBIR TU TRABAJO	My job is very **tiring.** I am always so **tired!**	☐	14.1
HACER COMPARACIONES	Is the salary **higher** in your new job?	☐	14.6

15 Rutinas del lugar de trabajo

Los empleados tienen agendas y los lugares de trabajo, rutinas y horarios propios. Es útil poder hablar con los colegas sobre cuándo suelen pasar las cosas.

✿ Lenguaje Preposiciones de tiempo
Aa Vocabulario Desplazamientos y transporte
✦ Habilidad Describir rutinas

15.1 PUNTO CLAVE PREPOSICIONES DE TIEMPO

Utiliza preposiciones para proporcionar más información sobre cuándo pasa algo.

"On" se utiliza antes de días y fechas para decir cuándo pasa algo.

"At" se utiliza para decir a qué hora pasa algo.

There is a staff meeting on Mondays at 10 o'clock.

Cuando utilizas "on" seguido de un día de la semana, añade "-s" al día para decir que se produce de manera periódica.

15.2 PUNTO CLAVE MÁS PREPOSICIONES DE TIEMPO

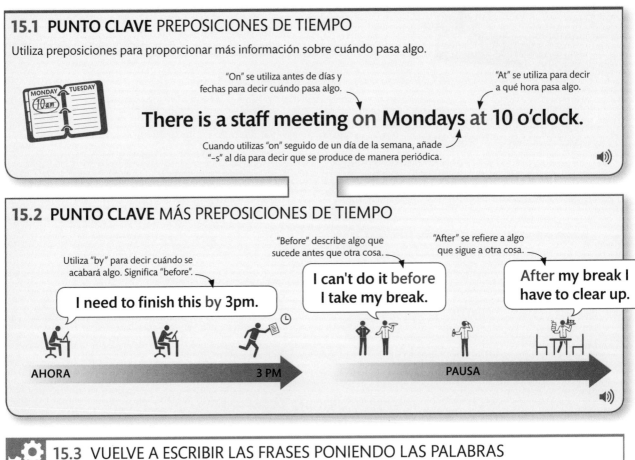

Utiliza "by" para decir cuándo se acabará algo. Significa "before".

I need to finish this by 3pm.

"Before" describe algo que sucede antes que otra cosa.

I can't do it before I take my break.

"After" se refiere a algo que sigue a otra cosa.

After my break I have to clear up.

AHORA   3 PM   PAUSA

15.3 VUELVE A ESCRIBIR LAS FRASES PONIENDO LAS PALABRAS EN SU ORDEN CORRECTO

`I` `home` `work` `Fridays.` `from` `on`
I work from home on Fridays.

2 `leave` `Mr.` `Don't` `Davies.` `before`
_____

1 `served` `is` `at` `noon.` `Lunch`
_____

3 `arrive` `Never` `9am.` `after`
_____

15.4 PUNTO CLAVE PREPOSICIONES DE DURACIÓN

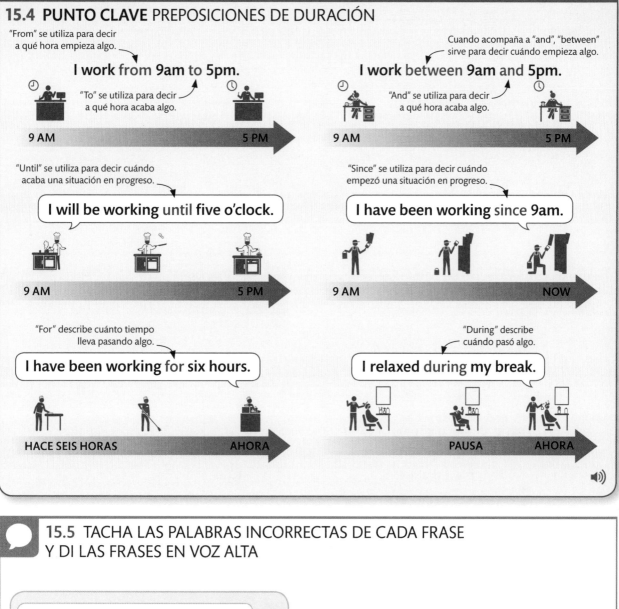

"From" se utiliza para decir a qué hora empieza algo.

I work from 9am to 5pm.

"To" se utiliza para decir a qué hora acaba algo.

9 AM — 5 PM

Cuando acompaña a "and", "between" sirve para decir cuándo empieza algo.

I work between 9am and 5pm.

"And" se utiliza para decir a qué hora acaba algo.

9 AM — 5 PM

"Until" se utiliza para decir cuándo acaba una situación en progreso.

I will be working until five o'clock.

9 AM — 5 PM

"Since" se utiliza para decir cuándo empezó una situación en progreso.

I have been working since 9am.

9 AM — NOW

"For" describe cuánto tiempo lleva pasando algo.

I have been working for six hours.

HACE SEIS HORAS — AHORA

"During" describe cuándo pasó algo.

I relaxed during my break.

PAUSA — AHORA

15.5 TACHA LAS PALABRAS INCORRECTAS DE CADA FRASE Y DI LAS FRASES EN VOZ ALTA

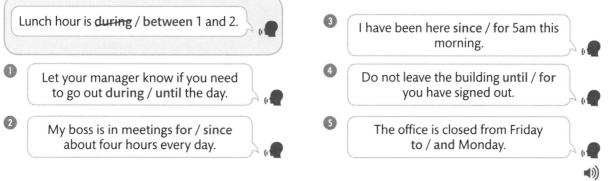

Lunch hour is ~~during~~ / between 1 and 2.

① Let your manager know if you need to go out **during** / **until** the day.

② My boss is in meetings **for** / **since** about four hours every day.

③ I have been here **since** / **for** 5am this morning.

④ Do not leave the building **until** / **for** you have signed out.

⑤ The office is closed from Friday **to** / **and** Monday.

15.6 PUNTO CLAVE LLEGAR AL TRABAJO

Existen diversas maneras para describir cómo vas a trabajar.

Utiliza "take" y "catch" con medios de transporte que no conduces o controlas.

I walk **to work.**

I cycle **to work.**

I drive **to work.**

I take the **metro.**

15.7 CONECTA LAS EXPRESIONES QUE SIGNIFICAN LO MISMO

I drive to work.

Sometimes I ride my bike to work.

1 I take the metro to work.

I go by car.

2 I cycle to work in good weather.

I normally go to work on foot.

3 I commute by train.

I go by metro.

4 I usually walk to work.

Sometimes I take a taxi to work.

5 When it rains, I go by taxi.

I take the bus.

6 I catch the bus to work.

I go by train to work.

15.8 TACHA LA PALABRA INCORRECTA DE CADA FRASE

I usually take / ~~drive~~ the bus to work.

1 I always **catch** / **drive** to work.

2 It's usually quicker to **bike** / **cycle**.

3 When it's sunny, we go on **foot** / **walk**.

4 I don't like taking the **metro** / **cycle**.

5 I **walk** / **foot** to work to stay fit.

6 I read a book when I go **on** / **by** train.

7 I take / walk the bus when it rains.

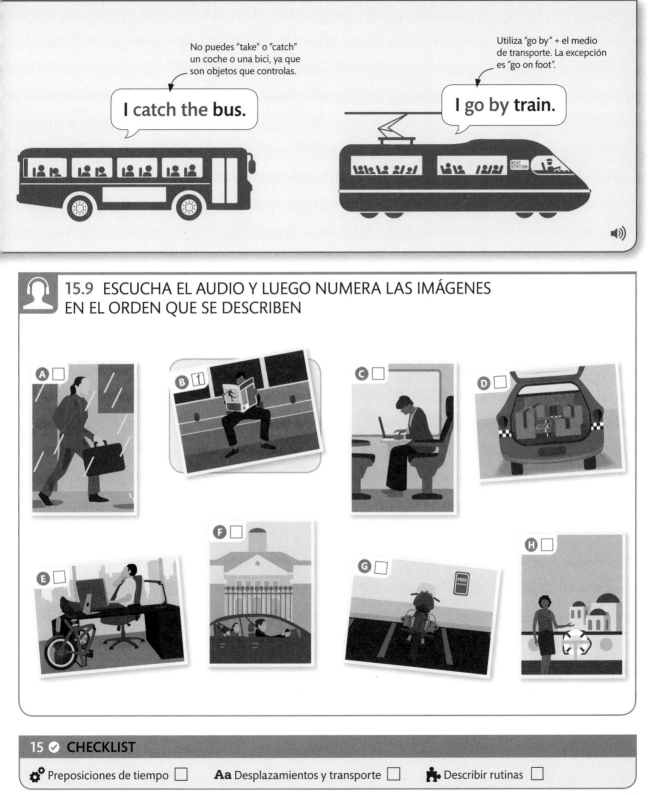

No puedes "take" o "catch" un coche o una bici, ya que son objetos que controlas.

I catch the bus.

Utiliza "go by" + el medio de transporte. La excepción es "go on foot".

I go by train.

15.9 ESCUCHA EL AUDIO Y LUEGO NUMERA LAS IMÁGENES EN EL ORDEN QUE SE DESCRIBEN

15 ✓ CHECKLIST

⚙ Preposiciones de tiempo ☐   Aa Desplazamientos y transporte ☐   🧩 Describir rutinas ☐

16 Vocabulario

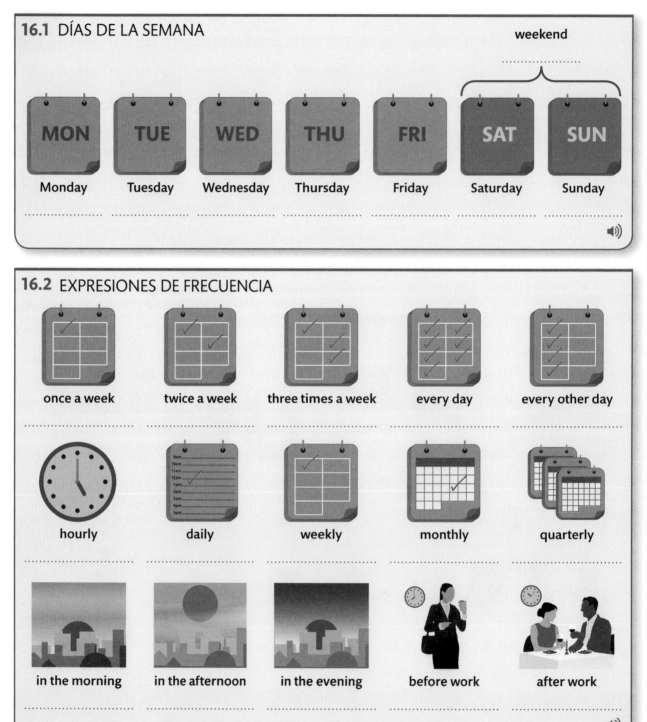

16.1 DÍAS DE LA SEMANA

weekend

MON	TUE	WED	THU	FRI	SAT	SUN
Monday	Tuesday	Wednesday	Thursday	Friday	Saturday	Sunday

16.2 EXPRESIONES DE FRECUENCIA

once a week   twice a week   three times a week   every day   every other day

hourly   daily   weekly   monthly   quarterly

in the morning   in the afternoon   in the evening   before work   after work

16.3 TIEMPO LIBRE

read

draw

write

cook

take photos

stay (at) home

listen to music

watch television

watch a movie

see a play

visit a museum /
an art gallery

meet friends

go out for a meal

go shopping

go to the gym

go cycling

walk / hike

go running

go camping

do exercise

play sports

play board
games

play video
games

play an
instrument

do yoga

17 Aficiones y costumbres

Cuando hables con un colega de aficiones y costumbres, utiliza adverbios de frecuencia para indicar la periodicidad con la que realizas dichas actividades.

⚙ **Lenguaje** Adverbios de frecuencia
Aa Vocabulario Aficiones y costumbres
🧩 **Habilidad** Hablar sobre el tiempo libre

17.1 VOCABULARIO ADVERBIOS DE FRECUENCIA

Algunos adverbios indican la frecuencia con la que pasan las cosas. "Always" y "never" definen casos concretos. Otros, en cambio, como "sometimes", son menos específicos. La posición dentro de la frase depende de los verbos principal y auxiliares.

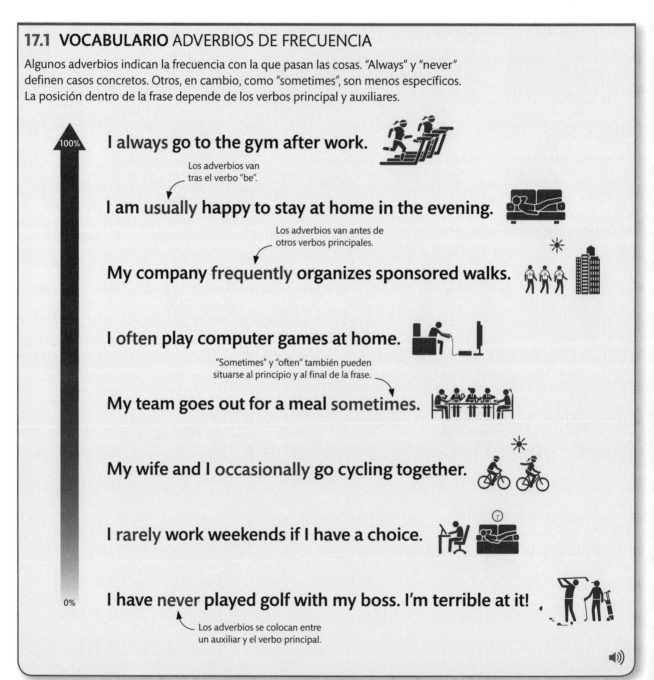

100%

I always go to the gym after work.

Los adverbios van tras el verbo "be".

I am usually happy to stay at home in the evening.

Los adverbios van antes de otros verbos principales.

My company frequently organizes sponsored walks.

I often play computer games at home.

"Sometimes" y "often" también pueden situarse al principio y al final de la frase.

My team goes out for a meal sometimes.

My wife and I occasionally go cycling together.

I rarely work weekends if I have a choice.

0%

I have never played golf with my boss. I'm terrible at it!

Los adverbios se colocan entre un auxiliar y el verbo principal.

🔊

17.2 ESCUCHA EL AUDIO Y CONECTA LAS IMÁGENES CON LOS ADVERBIOS DE FRECUENCIA CORRECTOS

1 **2** **3** **4**

| never | | occasionally | | sometimes |

| always | | frequently |

17.3 VUELVE A ESCRIBIR LAS FRASES PONIENDO LAS PALABRAS EN SU ORDEN CORRECTO

| running | after | I | go | work. | occasionally |

I occasionally go running after work.

1 | often | in | evening. | I | do | yoga | the |

_____

2 | see | go | play. | We | to | occasionally | a |

_____

3 | She | to | at | often | work. | listens | music |

_____

4 | always | go | I | vacation. | when | on | take | I | photos |

_____

17.4 PUNTO CLAVE ADJETIVOS SUPERLATIVOS

Los adjetivos superlativos sirven para comparar dos o más objetos,
personas o lugares. El superlativo describe el grado máximo.

Siempre se utiliza "the"
antes del superlativo.

Friday nights are always the loudest.

This is the most interesting gallery in town.

Los adjetivos largos forman el superlativo con
"the most" o "the least" antes del adjetivo.

17.5 CÓMO FUNCIONA ADJETIVOS SUPERLATIVOS

En la mayoría de adjetivos
cortos añadimos "-est"
para formar el superlativo.
Existen diferentes normas
ortográficas según cómo
acabe la forma simple
del adjetivo.

large

largest

Si el adjetivo
termina en "-e",
se le añade "-st".

easy

easiest

En algunos adjetivos
que terminan en "-y",
se elimina la "-y" y se
añade "-iest".

hot

hottest

En adjetivos que terminan en
consonante-vocal-consonante,
se duplica la última letra y se
añade "-est".

17.6 MÁS EJEMPLOS ADJETIVOS SUPERLATIVOS

That's the longest run I've ever done!

The earliest train is at 4am.

That's the most expensive item!

I go to the newest gym in town.

This is the biggest launch to date.

It's the least exciting party ever.

"The least" es el opuesto
de "the most".

17.7 PUNTO CLAVE ADJETIVOS SUPERLATIVOS IRREGULARES

Determinados adjetivos frecuentes (normalmente cortos) tienen superlativos que no siguen la norma.

ADJETIVO	bad	good	little	much	far
SUPERLATIVO	worst	best	least	most	farthest (US) furthest (UK)

17.8 MARCA LAS FRASES QUE SEAN CORRECTAS

This is the best restaurant in town. ☑
This is the most good restaurant in town. ☐

❶ This is the most good book I've ever read. ☐
This is the best book I've ever read. ☐

❷ The piano is most easy instrument to play. ☐
The piano is the easiest instrument to play. ☐

❸ Yannick listens to the most loud music. ☐
Yannick listens to the loudest music. ☐

❹ Shopping is the expensivest hobby I do. ☐
Shopping is the most expensive hobby I do. ☐

❺ That was the baddest play I have ever seen. ☐
That was the worst play I have ever seen. ☐

❻ Exercising is the more relaxing thing I do. ☐
Exercising is the most relaxing thing I do. ☐

❼ Let's eat at the most close restaurant. ☐
Let's eat at the closest restaurant. ☐

17.9 TACHA LAS PALABRAS INCORRECTAS DE CADA FRASE Y DI LAS FRASES EN VOZ ALTA

The earliest / ~~most early~~ yoga class is at 8am.

❶ The interestingest / most interesting gallery I've been to is in Paris.

❷ I've just finished the worst / most bad book I've ever read.

❸ The most long / longest hike I've ever done is 15km.

❹ The farthest / most far I've ever gone cycling is 50 miles.

❺ I think that hiking is the morest exciting / most exciting hobby.

17 ✓ CHECKLIST

⚙ Adverbios de frecuencia ☐   **Aa** Aficiones y costumbres ☐   🧩 Hablar sobre el tiempo libre ☐

18 Cosas del pasado

A menudo se utiliza el past simple al hablar sobre cosas que empezaron y acabaron en un momento concreto del pasado reciente o distante.

🔧 **Lenguaje** El past simple
Aa Vocabulario Actividades fuera del trabajo
🧩 **Habilidad** Hablar sobre cosas del pasado

18.1 PUNTO CLAVE VERBOS REGULARES EN PAST SIMPLE

El past simple describe cosas que sucedieron en el pasado. Las formas de los verbos regulares en past simple acaban en "-ed". El negativo utiliza "did not" más la forma base del verbo principal.

> I watched the game last night. It was great!

> I didn't watch the game. I stayed late at work.

18.2 CÓMO FUNCIONA VERBOS REGULARES EN PAST SIMPLE

El past simple de la mayoría de los verbos no cambia con el sujeto.

Utiliza la misma forma para todos los sujetos.

SUJETO	PAST SIMPLE	RESTO DE LA FRASE
I You He She We They	watched	the game.
	NEGATIVO + VERBO	
	didn't watch	

La forma de "do not" en past simple es "did not" o "didn't".

Utiliza la forma base del verbo principal.

18.3 MÁS EJEMPLOS VERBOS REGULARES EN PAST SIMPLE

He walked to the office.

They arrived together.

She didn't walk downtown.

We didn't arrive on time.

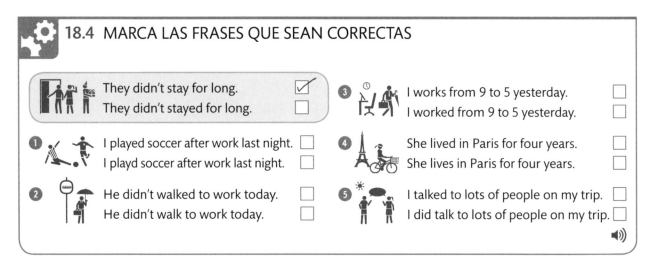

18.4 MARCA LAS FRASES QUE SEAN CORRECTAS

They didn't stay for long. ☑
They didn't stayed for long. ☐

1 I played soccer after work last night. ☐
I playd soccer after work last night. ☐

2 He didn't walked to work today. ☐
He didn't walk to work today. ☐

3 I works from 9 to 5 yesterday. ☐
I worked from 9 to 5 yesterday. ☐

4 She lived in Paris for four years. ☐
She lives in Paris for four years. ☐

5 I talked to lots of people on my trip. ☐
I did talk to lots of people on my trip. ☐

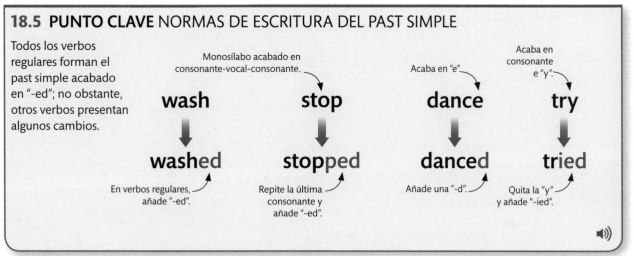

18.5 PUNTO CLAVE NORMAS DE ESCRITURA DEL PAST SIMPLE

Todos los verbos regulares forman el past simple acabado en "-ed"; no obstante, otros verbos presentan algunos cambios.

Monosílabo acabado en consonante-vocal-consonante.

Acaba en "e".

Acaba en consonante e "y".

wash → **washed**
En verbos regulares, añade "-ed".

stop → **stop**ped
Repite la última consonante y añade "-ed".

dance → **danced**
Añade una "-d".

try → **tried**
Quita la "y" y añade "-ied".

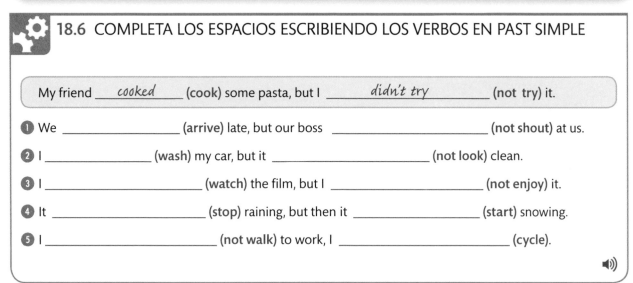

18.6 COMPLETA LOS ESPACIOS ESCRIBIENDO LOS VERBOS EN PAST SIMPLE

My friend ___cooked___ (cook) some pasta, but I ___didn't try___ (not try) it.

1 We _____ (arrive) late, but our boss _____ (not shout) at us.

2 I _____ (wash) my car, but it _____ (not look) clean.

3 I _____ (watch) the film, but I _____ (not enjoy) it.

4 It _____ (stop) raining, but then it _____ (start) snowing.

5 I _____ (not walk) to work, I _____ (cycle).

18.7 CÓMO FUNCIONA PREGUNTAS EN PAST SIMPLE

Utiliza "did" seguido de la forma base del verbo
para formular una pregunta en past simple.

They played tennis after work.

⬇

Did they play tennis after work?

"Did" va antes
del sujeto.

El verbo principal va
en su forma base.

18.8 CÓMO FUNCIONA PREGUNTAS EN PAST SIMPLE

"DID"	SUJETO	FORMA BASE DEL VERBO	RESTO DE LA FRASE
Did	they	play	tennis after work?

18.9 VUELVE A ESCRIBIR LAS FRASES EN FORMA DE PREGUNTA EN PAST SIMPLE

He visited the art gallery with his family yesterday.
Did he visit the art gallery with his family yesterday?

❶ You played board games when you were young.

_____

❷ He cooked some pasta for lunch.

_____

❸ She stayed at home and watched TV last night.

_____

❹ They watched a scary movie at the movie theater.

_____

❺ They walked home from work together.

_____

Dos colegas, Jasmine y Marilyn, hablan sobre cosas que hicieron la semana pasada.

On vacation, Jasmine watched a lot of movies.
True ☐ **False** ☐ **Not given** ☑

❸ Jasmine didn't try yoga.
True ☐ **False** ☐ **Not given** ☐

❶ Jasmine played tennis and volleyball on vacation.
True ☐ **False** ☐ **Not given** ☐

❹ Jasmine liked the local food.
True ☐ **False** ☐ **Not given** ☐

❷ Jasmine played four new sports.
True ☐ **False** ☐ **Not given** ☐

❺ Jasmine and Marilyn often cook for each other.
True ☐ **False** ☐ **Not given** ☐

18.11 DESCRIBE EN VOZ ALTA QUÉ HICIERON UTILIZANDO EN SIMPLE PAST LOS VERBOS DEL RECUADRO

He played soccer.

listen to music   ~~play soccer~~   play a board game   cook a meal   watch TV   visit a museum

---

18 ✓ CHECKLIST

⚙️ El past simple ☐   **Aa** Actividades fuera del trabajo ☐   🧩 Hablar sobre cosas del pasado ☐

19 Fechas y horas

Cuando se hacen planes o se habla de cosas del pasado o del futuro, es importante decir bien la hora. En inglés se puede hacer de diversas maneras.

⚙ **Lenguaje** Cuándo pasan las cosas
Aa Vocabulario Decir la hora
🧩 **Habilidad** Pedir citas

19.1 PUNTO CLAVE DECIR LA HORA

En inglés oral la hora se puede decir con diferentes expresiones concretas.

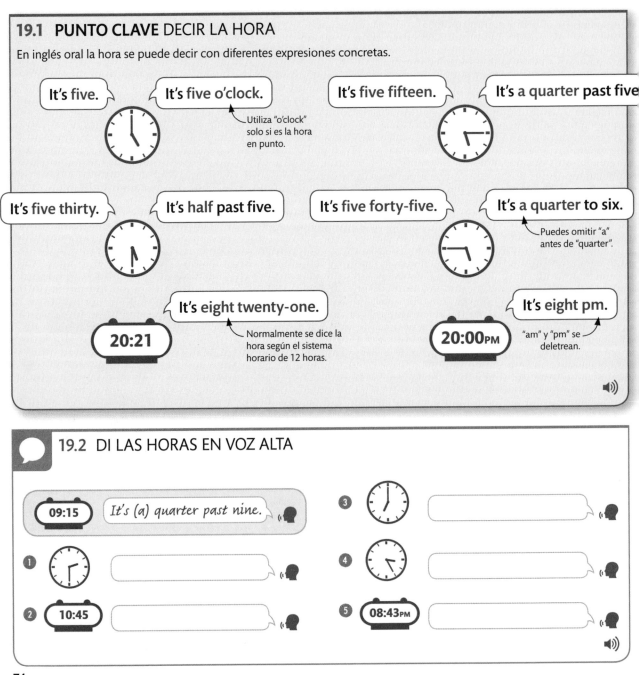

It's five.

It's five o'clock.

Utiliza "o'clock" solo si es la hora en punto.

It's five fifteen.

It's a quarter past five

It's five thirty.

It's half past five.

It's five forty-five.

It's a quarter to six.

Puedes omitir "a" antes de "quarter".

It's eight twenty-one.

20:21

Normalmente se dice la hora según el sistema horario de 12 horas.

It's eight pm.

20:00PM

"am" y "pm" se deletrean.

19.2 DI LAS HORAS EN VOZ ALTA

09:15 — *It's (a) quarter past nine.*

①

② 10:45

③

④

⑤ 08:43PM

19.3 VOCABULARIO MESES DEL AÑO

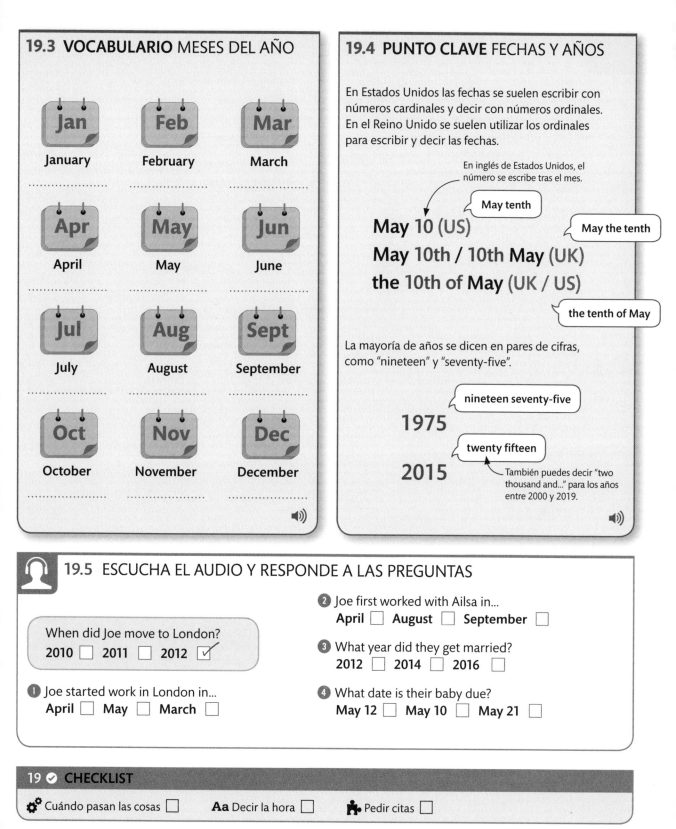

Jan	Feb	Mar
January	February	March

Apr	May	Jun
April	May	June

Jul	Aug	Sept
July	August	September

Oct	Nov	Dec
October	November	December

19.4 PUNTO CLAVE FECHAS Y AÑOS

En Estados Unidos las fechas se suelen escribir con números cardinales y decir con números ordinales. En el Reino Unido se suelen utilizar los ordinales para escribir y decir las fechas.

En inglés de Estados Unidos, el número se escribe tras el mes.

May tenth

May 10 (US)

May the tenth

May 10th / 10th May (UK)

the 10th of May (UK / US)

the tenth of May

La mayoría de años se dicen en pares de cifras, como "nineteen" y "seventy-five".

nineteen seventy-five

1975

twenty fifteen

2015

También puedes decir "two thousand and..." para los años entre 2000 y 2019.

19.5 ESCUCHA EL AUDIO Y RESPONDE A LAS PREGUNTAS

When did Joe move to London?
2010 ☐   2011 ☐   2012 ☑

❶ Joe started work in London in...
April ☐   **May** ☐   **March** ☐

❷ Joe first worked with Ailsa in...
April ☐   **August** ☐   **September** ☐

❸ What year did they get married?
2012 ☐   **2014** ☐   **2016** ☐

❹ What date is their baby due?
May 12 ☐   **May 10** ☐   **May 21** ☐

19 ✓ CHECKLIST

⚙ Cuándo pasan las cosas ☐   **Aa** Decir la hora ☐   👥 Pedir citas ☐

20 Historia laboral

Al conocer nuevos colegas o en una entrevista, puede que te pregunten por trabajos anteriores. Al hablar del pasado es importante que utilices la forma verbal correcta.

⚙ **Lenguaje** Verbos irregulares en past simple
Aa **Vocabulario** Empleos y lugares de trabajo
🧩 **Habilidad** Hablar sobre trabajos anteriores

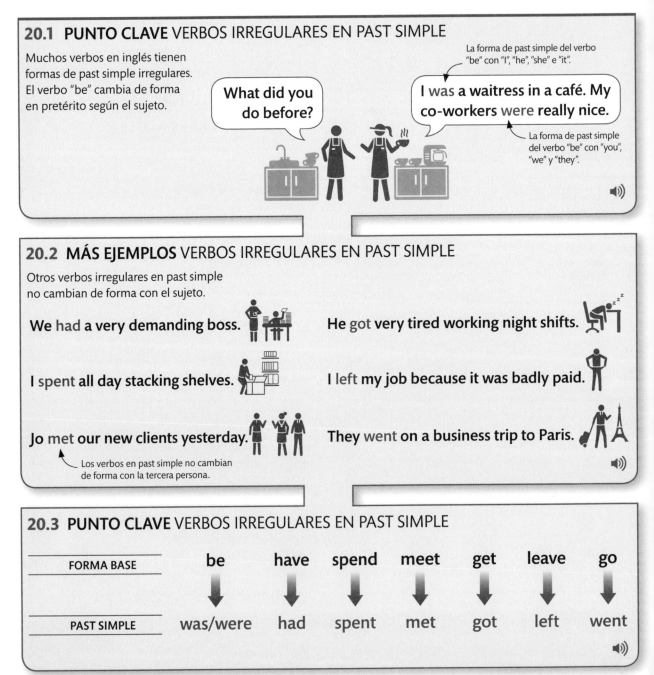

20.1 PUNTO CLAVE VERBOS IRREGULARES EN PAST SIMPLE

Muchos verbos en inglés tienen formas de past simple irregulares. El verbo "be" cambia de forma en pretérito según el sujeto.

La forma de past simple del verbo "be" con "I", "he", "she" e "it".

What did you do before?

I was a waitress in a café. My co-workers were really nice.

La forma de past simple del verbo "be" con "you", "we" y "they".

20.2 MÁS EJEMPLOS VERBOS IRREGULARES EN PAST SIMPLE

Otros verbos irregulares en past simple no cambian de forma con el sujeto.

We had a very demanding boss.

He got very tired working night shifts.

I spent all day stacking shelves.

I left my job because it was badly paid.

Jo met our new clients yesterday.

Los verbos en past simple no cambian de forma con la tercera persona.

They went on a business trip to Paris.

20.3 PUNTO CLAVE VERBOS IRREGULARES EN PAST SIMPLE

FORMA BASE	be	have	spend	meet	get	leave	go
PAST SIMPLE	was/were	had	spent	met	got	left	went

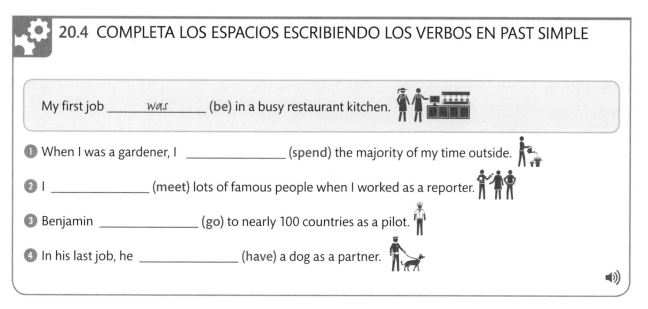

20.4 COMPLETA LOS ESPACIOS ESCRIBIENDO LOS VERBOS EN PAST SIMPLE

My first job _____was_____ (be) in a busy restaurant kitchen.

1 When I was a gardener, I _____ (spend) the majority of my time outside.

2 I _____ (meet) lots of famous people when I worked as a reporter.

3 Benjamin _____ (go) to nearly 100 countries as a pilot.

4 In his last job, he _____ (have) a dog as a partner.

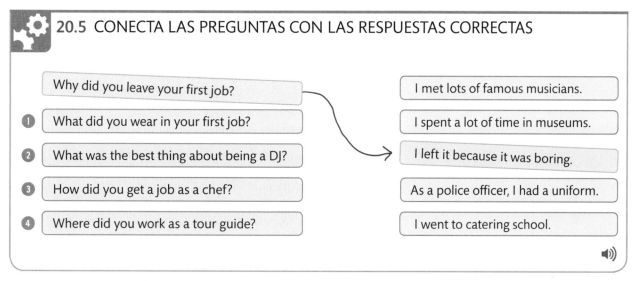

20.5 CONECTA LAS PREGUNTAS CON LAS RESPUESTAS CORRECTAS

Why did you leave your first job? → I left it because it was boring.

I met lots of famous musicians.

1 What did you wear in your first job?

I spent a lot of time in museums.

2 What was the best thing about being a DJ?

3 How did you get a job as a chef?

As a police officer, I had a uniform.

4 Where did you work as a tour guide?

I went to catering school.

20.6 ESCUCHA EL AUDIO Y NUMERA LAS IMÁGENES EN SU ORDEN

A ☐ B 1 C ☐ D ☐ E ☐

BUSINESS BULLETIN

Sadim Nalik: Mailroom to boardroom

He started in the mailroom at his father's company, but Sadim Nalik is now a respected business executive. He tells us what he learned from his first job.

I always wanted to work in my father's company, but my father told me that I had to go to college first. He always said that education was the most important thing in life. He taught himself to read and write and wanted the very best for me. I chose to study engineering in college. When I left college with a top degree, I thought that my father would give me a good job in his company. I remember he sent me an email congratulating me on my university success and offering me a job in the mailroom at the company. I felt really angry at the time because I wanted a better job. I wrote to my father that I would look for a job at another company. He then called me and said I could one day be CEO, but only if I knew the company from top to bottom. After the mailroom, I worked in the kitchen, in the HR department, as a personal assistant, and as his deputy CEO. I finally understood what hard work was like in different areas of the company. The experience taught me to respect all employees and understand that every part of the company must be working well for the whole company to succeed. My father made me CEO five years ago and my daughter, Myra, began working in the mailroom two months ago.

What did Sadim's father tell him to do?

He told Sadim to go to college.

❶ What did Sadim choose to study in college?

_____

❷ What did Sadim think his father would do?

_____

❸ Why did Sadim feel angry?

_____

❹ What did Sadim write to his father?

_____

❺ What did his father say he could be one day?

_____

❻ What did Sadim finally understand?

_____

❼ What did Sadim's work experience teach him?

_____

❽ When did Sadim's father make him CEO?

_____

❾ When did Myra begin working in the mailroom?

_____

20.8 VUELVE A ESCRIBIR LAS FRASES CORRIGIENDO LOS ERRORES

> I choosed to study medical science in college.
> _I chose to study medical science in college._

1 I feeled really happy when I left college with a top degree.

_____

2 My manager sayed that one day I could be CEO of the whole company.

_____

3 My tutor teached me that it was important to check my own work.

_____

4 I maked my girlfriend a big cake to celebrate her new job.

_____

20.9 RESPONDE AL AUDIO EN VOZ ALTA

What was your first job?

I was a sales assistant.

1 How did you get your first job?

2 How did you feel on your first day?

3 Why did you choose your first job?

4 When did you leave your first job?

5 Why did you leave your first job?

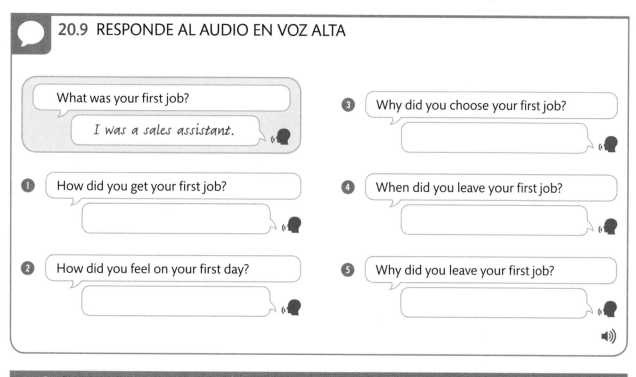

20 ✓ CHECKLIST

⚙ Verbos irregulares en past simple ☐   **Aa** Empleos y lugares de trabajo ☐   🧩 Hablar sobre trabajos anteriores ☐

21 Historia de la empresa

Se puede utilizar el past simple para describir acciones individuales o recurrentes en la historia de una empresa. Estas acciones pueden ser de corta o larga duración.

⚙ **Lenguaje** Past simple con marcadores de tiempo
Aa Vocabulario Describir tendencias
🧩 **Habilidad** Describir la historia de una empresa

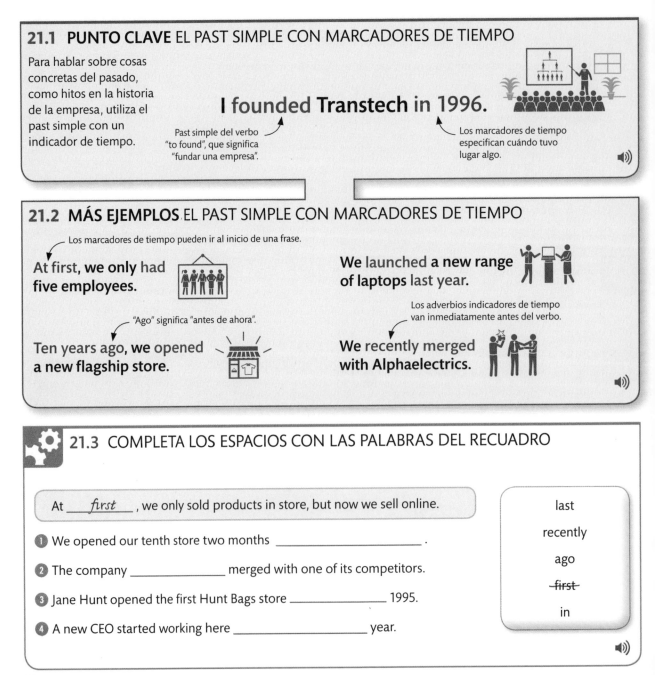

21.1 PUNTO CLAVE EL PAST SIMPLE CON MARCADORES DE TIEMPO

Para hablar sobre cosas concretas del pasado, como hitos en la historia de la empresa, utiliza el past simple con un indicador de tiempo.

I founded Transtech in 1996.

Past simple del verbo "to found", que significa "fundar una empresa".

Los marcadores de tiempo especifican cuándo tuvo lugar algo.

21.2 MÁS EJEMPLOS EL PAST SIMPLE CON MARCADORES DE TIEMPO

Los marcadores de tiempo pueden ir al inicio de una frase.

At first, we only had five employees.

We launched a new range of laptops last year.

"Ago" significa "antes de ahora".

Los adverbios indicadores de tiempo van inmediatamente antes del verbo.

Ten years ago, we opened a new flagship store.

We recently merged with Alphaelectrics.

21.3 COMPLETA LOS ESPACIOS CON LAS PALABRAS DEL RECUADRO

At _____*first*_____ , we only sold products in store, but now we sell online.

1 We opened our tenth store two months _____ .

2 The company _____ merged with one of its competitors.

3 Jane Hunt opened the first Hunt Bags store _____ 1995.

4 A new CEO started working here _____ year.

last
recently
ago
~~first~~
in

21.4 ESCUCHA EL AUDIO Y LUEGO NUMERA LAS FRASES EN EL ORDEN EN QUE APARECEN

 Un director general hace una presentación sobre la historia de la empresa.

A At first, business was quite slow and the salon was often empty. ☐

B They opened a second hair salon in London in 1988. ☐

C By 1995, they were stylists for many top celebrities. ☐

D Brisar Styling was founded by Brian and Sarah Paterson in 1984. ☐ 1

E Five years later, they launched their hair product range. ☐

F Last year, Brisar Styling merged with our beauty product company, Wilson's. ☐

21.5 LEE EL ARTÍCULO Y RESPONDE A LAS PREGUNTAS

> What did Cake & Crumb report last year?
>
> *It reported a record rise in profits.*

❶ When did Ahmed found Cake & Crumb?

_____

❷ Where did Ahmed work at first?

_____

❸ What were sales like in the company's first year?

_____

❹ When did the company open its first store?

_____

❺ When did Cake & Crumb employ 2,000 bakers?

_____

❻ What happened two years ago?

_____

BUSINESS WORLD

A slice of the market

This week, we look at the history of Cake & Crumb

CAKE & CRUMB IS NOW one of the biggest and most popular bakeries in the US. Last year, the company reported a record rise in profits. But Cake & Crumb had much smaller beginnings.

Ahmed Hassan founded the company in 2003. At first, Ahmed worked from his kitchen in his small apartment and sold cakes to customers online. In the company's first year, sales remained steady, but in 2005, sales increased and Ahmed opened the first Cake & Crumb store.

Now, the company has stores all over the US. By 2010, Cake & Crumb employed 2,000 bakers. Two years ago, the company launched a catering service for children's parties. With the launch of this service and rebranding, Cake & Crumb became one of the most successful companies in the catering industry.

21.6 PUNTO CLAVE DESCRIBIR TENDENCIAS

En inglés también se utiliza el past simple con marcadores de tiempo para describir tendencias de la empresa. Ten en cuenta que algunos verbos para describir tendencias tienen formas de past simple irregulares.

Ice cream sales { **increased** / **went up** / **rose** } over the summer.

"Rise" tiene forma de past simple irregular.

House prices { **stayed the same** / **remained steady** / **stabilized** } during the last quarter.

Demand for new cars { **decreased** / **went down** / **fell** } last year.

"Fall" también es un verbo irregular.

21.7 COMPLETA LOS ESPACIOS ESCRIBIENDO LOS VERBOS EN PAST SIMPLE

Visitor numbers at the luxury hotel ___*fell*___ (fall) by 20 percent last year.

1 The number of people going to festivals _____ (go up) last year.

2 Fortunately, the cost of fuel for transportation _____ (stabilize) recently.

3 In the really wet summer of 2010, sales of umbrellas _____ (rise) a lot.

4 The number of people downloading music _____ (stay the same) last month.

5 The numbers of students earning MBAs _____ (remain steady) last year.

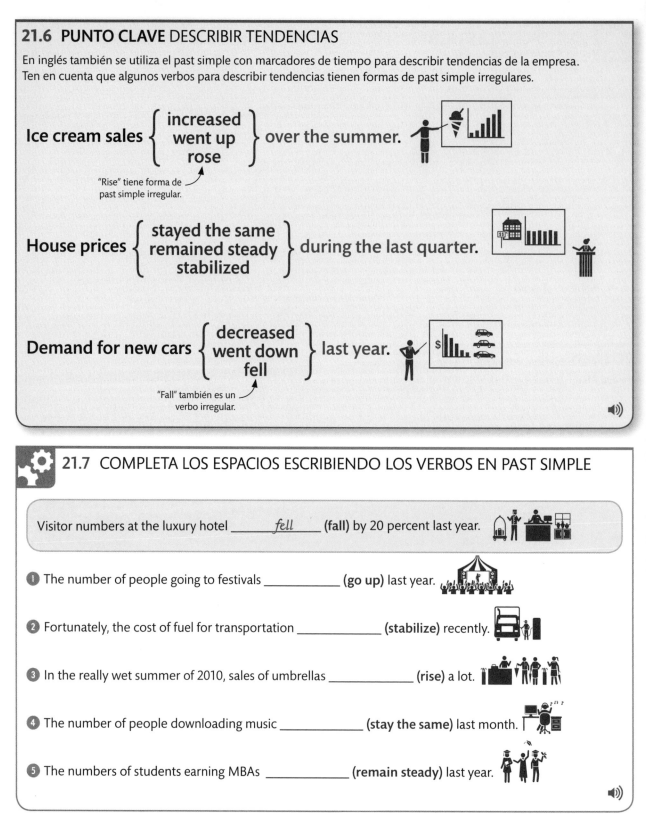

21.8 TACHA LAS PALABRAS INCORRECTAS DE CADA FRASE Y DI LAS FRASES EN VOZ ALTA

Our sales figures ~~increased up~~ / went up in 2011, but ~~falled~~ / fell in 2012.

1. At / In first, the value of the company stayed / stay the same.

2. Marketing costs increasing / increased and sales also rose / rosing.

3. Last / Recent summer, umbrella sales increased / increasing because it was rainy.

4. The number of customers decrease / decreased, but profits go / went up.

5. Two years ago / past, we launched an online delivery service and our sales rised / rose.

♻ REPASA LO QUE HAS APRENDIDO EN LAS UNIDADES 15-21

NUEVO LENGUAJE	FRASE DE EJEMPLO	☑	UNIDAD
PREPOSICIONES DE TIEMPO Y DURACIÓN	There is a staff meeting on Mondays. I work from 9am to 5pm.	☐	15.1, 15.4
ADVERBIOS DE FRECUENCIA	I always go to the gym after work.	☐	17.1
ADJETIVOS SUPERLATIVOS	Friday nights are always the loudest.	☐	17.4
PAST SIMPLE	I watched the game last night. Did they play tennis after work?	☐	18.1, 18.7
VERBOS IRREGULARES EN PAST SIMPLE	I was a waitress. We had a very demanding boss.	☐	20.1, 20.2
PAST SIMPLE CON MARCADORES DE TIEMPO	I founded Transtech in 1996.	☐	21.1, 21.2

22 Vocabulario

22.1 HACER PLANES

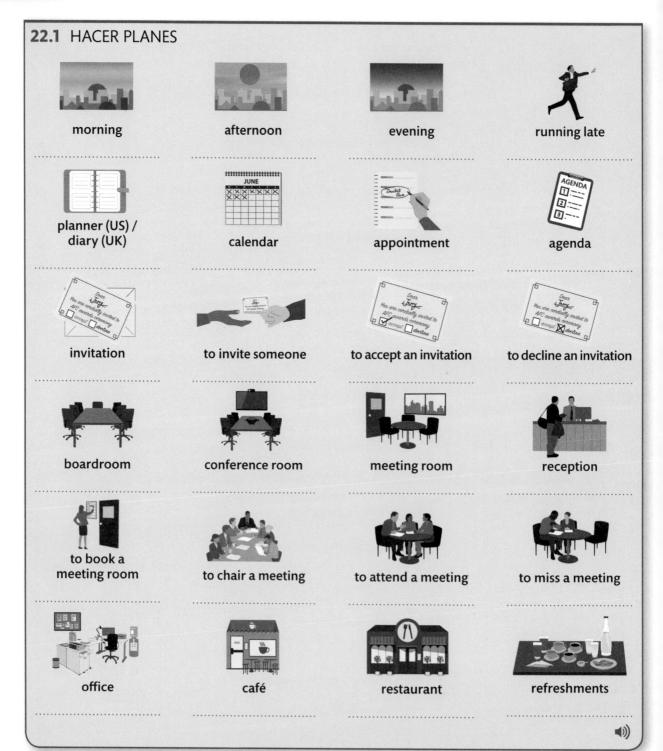

morning

afternoon

evening

running late

planner (US) /
diary (UK)

calendar

appointment

agenda

invitation

to invite someone

to accept an invitation

to decline an invitation

boardroom

conference room

meeting room

reception

to book a
meeting room

to chair a meeting

to attend a meeting

to miss a meeting

office

café

restaurant

refreshments

22.2 ACEPTAR Y DECLINAR

I'm afraid I'm busy today.

to be busy
[to have lots to do]

10am is good for me. See you then!

good for me
[I am free at that time]

Yes, I am free on Wednesday and Thursday this week.

to be free
[to be available]

Yes, the café suits me.

to suit someone
[to be convenient]

I can't make the meeting on Monday. I will reschedule it for Tuesday.

to reschedule
[to decide on a new time and date for a meeting]

2pm is fine. I look forward to meeting you then.

to look forward to
[to be pleased about something that is going to happen]

I'm really busy this morning. Can we postpone the meeting?

to postpone
[to delay a meeting or an event]

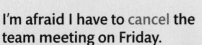

I won't be at the meeting. Something unexpected has come up.

to come up
[to occur unexpectedly]

I'm afraid I have to cancel the team meeting on Friday.

to cancel
[to decide that a planned event will not happen]

Apologies, but I'm unable to attend due to other commitments.

to be unable to attend
[cannot go to]

23 Hablar sobre los planes

Una manera de hacer planes con un compañero de trabajo o un cliente es utilizar el present continuous para hablar de lo que estás haciendo ahora o de los planes de futuro.

⚙ **Lenguaje** El present continuous
Aa Vocabulario Hacer planes
🧩 **Habilidad** Hablar sobre los planes

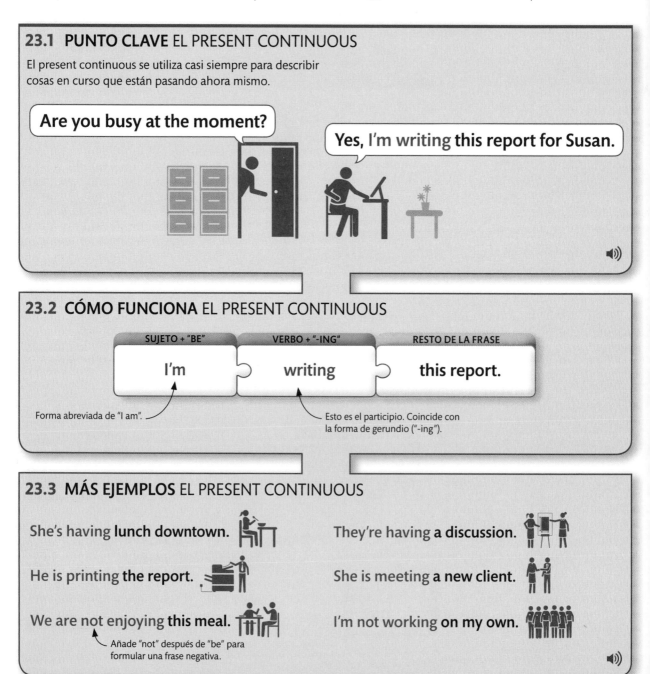

23.1 PUNTO CLAVE EL PRESENT CONTINUOUS

El present continuous se utiliza casi siempre para describir cosas en curso que están pasando ahora mismo.

Are you busy at the moment?

Yes, I'm writing this report for Susan.

23.2 CÓMO FUNCIONA EL PRESENT CONTINUOUS

SUJETO + "BE"	VERBO + "-ING"	RESTO DE LA FRASE
I'm	writing	this report.

Forma abreviada de "I am".

Esto es el participio. Coincide con la forma de gerundio ("-ing").

23.3 MÁS EJEMPLOS EL PRESENT CONTINUOUS

She's having **lunch downtown.**

They're having **a discussion.**

He is printing **the report.**

She is meeting **a new client.**

We are not enjoying **this meal.**

Añade "not" después de "be" para formular una frase negativa.

I'm not working **on my own.**

23.4 ESCUCHA EL AUDIO Y LUEGO NUMERA LAS IMÁGENES EN EL ORDEN EN QUE SE DESCRIBEN

A ☐

B 1

C ☐

D ☐

E ☐

F ☐

G ☐

H ☐

23.5 COMPLETA LOS ESPACIOS ESCRIBIENDO LOS VERBOS EN PRESENT CONTINUOUS

The team _isn't having_ (not have) much success this year, so we _are trying_ (try) new things.

1 Sales _____ (increase) at the moment, so we _____ (get) a bigger bonus.

2 Fashions _____ (change), so we _____ (adapt) to new trends.

3 Travel costs _____ (rise) this year, so we _____ (call) each other more instead.

4 Profits _____ (drop), so we _____ (cut) costs in all areas of the business.

5 We _____ (sell) a lot to Asia, so we _____ (plan) to open an office there next year.

6 I can't believe you _____ (work) late. You _____ (miss) the staff party!

7 I _____ (wait) for my interview to start, and I _____ (feel) nervous.

8 The company _____ (lose) money, so we _____ (consider) a restructure.

◄))

23.6 PUNTO CLAVE PREGUNTAS EN PRESENT CONTINUOUS

Las preguntas en present continuous se forman invirtiendo el sujeto y "be"; si es una pregunta abierta, se añade un pronombre interrogativo.

Para convertir una afirmación en una pregunta, cambia de posición el sujeto y "be".

Se invierten sujeto y "be".

Who are we waiting for?

I'm not sure. Is James coming to this meeting?

Utiliza pronombres interrogativos antes del verbo para formular preguntas abiertas.

23.7 CÓMO FUNCIONA PREGUNTAS EN PRESENT CONTINUOUS

PRONOMBRE INTERROGATIVO	FORMA DE "BE"	SUJETO	VERBO + "-ING"	RESTO DE LA FRASE
Who	**are**	**we**	**waiting**	**for?**

Con un pronombre interrogativo como "where", "what" o "who", la pregunta queda abierta.

23.8 VUELVE A ESCRIBIR LAS FRASES PONIENDO LAS PALABRAS EN SU ORDEN CORRECTO

you   What   writing?   are

What are you writing?

3   we   selling   Are   that?

_____

1   they   this?   Are   buying

_____

4   him?   meeting   Are   you

_____

2   working   now?   it   Is

_____

5   promoting?   Who   they   are

_____

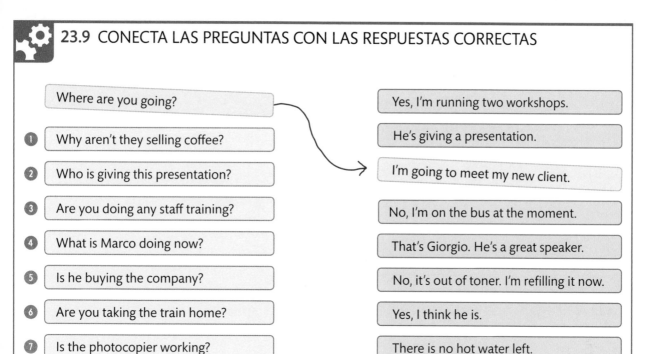

23.9 CONECTA LAS PREGUNTAS CON LAS RESPUESTAS CORRECTAS

Where are you going? — I'm going to meet my new client.

1. Why aren't they selling coffee?
2. Who is giving this presentation?
3. Are you doing any staff training?
4. What is Marco doing now?
5. Is he buying the company?
6. Are you taking the train home?
7. Is the photocopier working?

Yes, I'm running two workshops.

He's giving a presentation.

I'm going to meet my new client.

No, I'm on the bus at the moment.

That's Giorgio. He's a great speaker.

No, it's out of toner. I'm refilling it now.

Yes, I think he is.

There is no hot water left.

23.10 VUELVE A ESCRIBIR LAS AFIRMACIONES COMO PREGUNTAS EN PRESENT CONTINUOUS SIN UTILIZAR PRONOMBRES INTERROGATIVOS

Mariam is working on the new project today.
Is Mariam working on the new project today?

1. The company is buying everyone new laptops.

2. Maria is giving her first presentation at the moment.

3. Rakesh is designing the packaging for the new gadget.

4. We are all going to the team meeting now.

5. They are trying to improve sales in North America.

23.11 PUNTO CLAVE EL PRESENT CONTINUOUS PARA PLANES FUTUROS

También puedes utilizar el present continuous para hablar de planes futuros ya fijados. Normalmente se especifica una fecha, día u hora concretos.

I'm free next week. What are you doing on Monday?

Hace referencia a planes concretos que ya se han realizado.

I'm working from home all day.

Se da una referencia temporal concreta.

23.12 MARCA LAS FRASES QUE SEAN CORRECTAS

What are you doing on Monday? ☑
What are you doing on Mondays? ☐

1. I'm not coming to work tomorrow. ☐
   I not coming to work tomorrow. ☐

2. Are you meeting the team today? ☐
   Is you meeting the team today? ☐

3. I can't go. I'm not leaving until 8pm. ☐
   I can't go. I'm not leave until 8pm. ☐

4. Are we coming back here next year? ☐
   Will we coming back here next year? ☐

5. You are coming to the party later? ☐
   Are you coming to the party later? ☐

6. I'm not taking notes today. Are you? ☐
   I'm not take notes today. Are you? ☐

7. I'm having lunch at noon tomorrow. ☐
   I having lunch at noon tomorrow. ☐

8. Are you going to Asia this winter? ☐
   Will you going to Asia this winter? ☐

23.13 ESCUCHA EL AUDIO Y RESPONDE A LAS PREGUNTAS

Julia llama a Jerome, un cliente, para concertar una reunión.

Who is Julia trying to arrange a meeting for?
Julia and Jerome ☐
Jerome and Sylvie ☐
Jerome and Marie ☑

1. How long is Jerome staying in the city?
   Until Monday ☐
   For 10 days ☐
   He does not say ☐

2. When is Jerome taking Sylvie to the airport?
   Right now ☐
   Next Monday morning ☐
   Every Monday morning ☐

3. Where is the meeting taking place?
   In the bookstore ☐
   At the airport ☐
   In Marie's office ☐

23.14 LEE LA AGENDA Y RESPONDE AL AUDIO EN VOZ ALTA

What are you doing on Monday morning?

> I'm meeting the new client.

1 Who are you meeting on Tuesday afternoon?

2 Where are you going on Wednesday?

3 How are you traveling on Wednesday?

4 When are you getting home on Wednesday?

5 What time are you finishing on Thursday?

6 Who is leaving work on Friday?

MONDAY

10am:
Meet the new client (reception).

TUESDAY

2pm:
Meet HR team.

WEDNESDAY

Train to Paris departs 9am.
Return at 4pm. Home at 7:15pm.

THURSDAY

Finish at 3pm for dentist appointment.

FRIDAY

Lunch break:
Monica's leaving party (cafeteria).

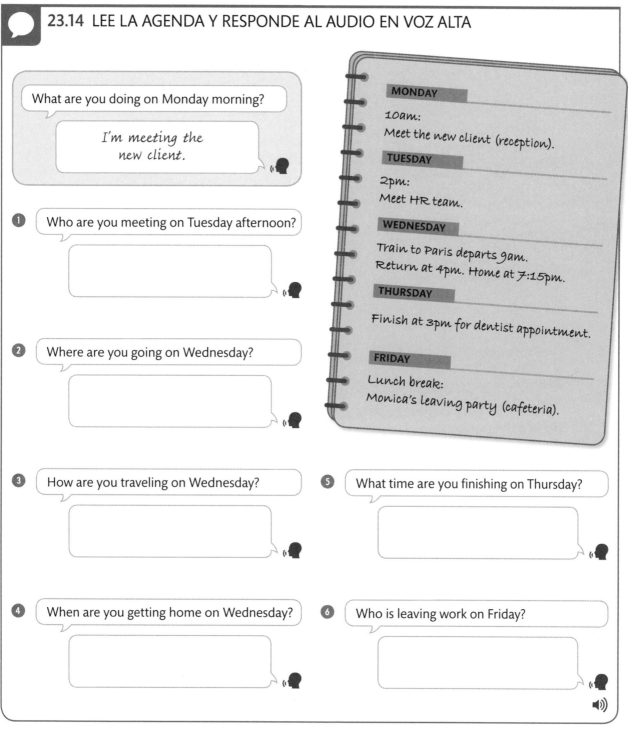

---

23 ✓ CHECKLIST

⚙ El present continuous ☐   **Aa** Hacer planes ☐   👣 Hablar sobre los planes ☐

24 Dar opiniones

En inglés a menudo se utilizan expresiones para indicar que se quiere interrumpir sin ser maleducado. Hay diversas maneras de dar tu opinión de manera educada.

🔧 **Lenguaje** Interrupciones y opiniones
Aa Vocabulario Cuestiones medioambientales
🧩 **Habilidad** Dar opiniones educadamente

24.1 PUNTO CLAVE INTERRUMPIR EDUCADAMENTE

Primero intenta captar la atención del que habla, o levanta la mano.
Si no consigues que te den la palabra, empieza con una de estas expresiones para que la interrupción sea educada.

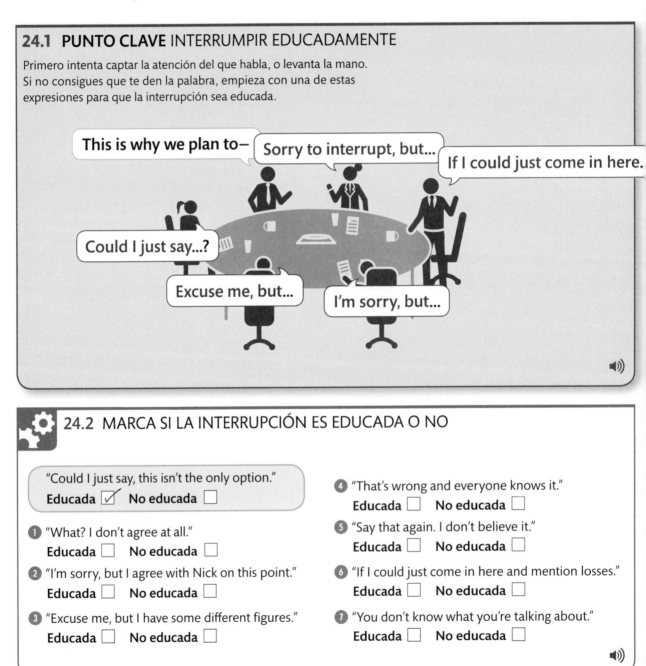

24.2 MARCA SI LA INTERRUPCIÓN ES EDUCADA O NO

"Could I just say, this isn't the only option."
Educada ☑ **No educada** ☐

① "What? I don't agree at all."
Educada ☐ **No educada** ☐

② "I'm sorry, but I agree with Nick on this point."
Educada ☐ **No educada** ☐

③ "Excuse me, but I have some different figures."
Educada ☐ **No educada** ☐

④ "That's wrong and everyone knows it."
Educada ☐ **No educada** ☐

⑤ "Say that again. I don't believe it."
Educada ☐ **No educada** ☐

⑥ "If I could just come in here and mention losses."
Educada ☐ **No educada** ☐

⑦ "You don't know what you're talking about."
Educada ☐ **No educada** ☐

24.3 PUNTO CLAVE INTERCAMBIAR OPINIONES

También es importante introducir tu opinión de manera respetuosa; es de buena educación preguntar la opinión del resto.

Suaviza la interrupción empezando educadamente la intervención.

In my opinion **we need to focus on recycling.**

What do you think?

Pregunta la opinión al público para comprobar que te sigue.

24.4 MÁS EJEMPLOS INTERCAMBIAR OPINIONES

I can see your point, but...

Esta estructura va seguida de un sustantivo o de un gerundio.

What do you think about **doing this?**

What do you think about **this idea?**

I'm not sure I agree. I think...

How about you?

24.5 COMPLETA LOS ESPACIOS CON LAS PALABRAS DEL RECUADRO Y CONTESTA AL AUDIO EN VOZ ALTA

This is clearly the best approach.

I'm sorry, but I'm not sure I _____ *agree* _____ .

1. We will lose thousands of customers.

   Sorry to _____ , but my figures are different.

2. It's the same problem as last year.

   I'm not sure. What do you _____ about new outlets?

3. These will never sell in Asia.

   I'm sorry, but in my _____ they will sell well.

opinion

~~agree~~

interrupt

think

24.6 ESCUCHA EL AUDIO Y RESPONDE A LAS PREGUNTAS

El responsable de política medioambiental de RonMax ha organizado una reunión para hablar de la estrategia medioambiental de la empresa.

The meeting is about past environmental policy. **True** ☐ **False** ☐ **Not given** ☑

① RonMax currently recycles all its waste. **True** ☐ **False** ☐ **Not given** ☐

② RonMax currently pays a company to take away waste paper. **True** ☐ **False** ☐ **Not given** ☐

③ Some rooms will not have lights on all the time. **True** ☐ **False** ☐ **Not given** ☐

④ Everyone agrees with the environmental strategy. **True** ☐ **False** ☐ **Not given** ☐

⑤ RonMax will publicly promote their green policies. **True** ☐ **False** ☐ **Not given** ☐

Aa 24.7 LEE EL ARTÍCULO Y COMPLETA LAS COLOCACIONES

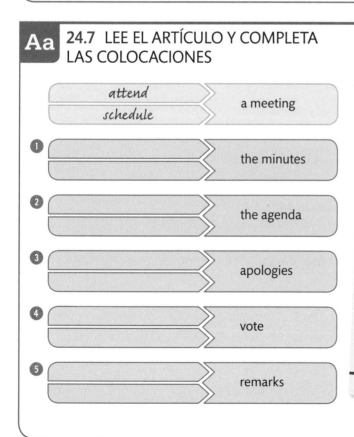

attend / schedule	a meeting
①	the minutes
②	the agenda
③	apologies
④	vote
⑤	remarks

66 **YOUR CAREER**

ATTENDING AND SCHEDULING MEETINGS

During a meeting, someone takes "the minutes" (a record of what was said). You can review these afterward. Before a new meeting, you may be sent an outline ("the agenda"). Make sure to read this beforehand, and follow it as the meeting works through it. If you cannot go to a meeting, send your apologies. These will be announced at the meeting.

Sometimes the person in charge of the meeting ("the chair") takes a vote. He or she may have the casting vote if there is a tie. The best chairs keep the opening and closing remarks short.

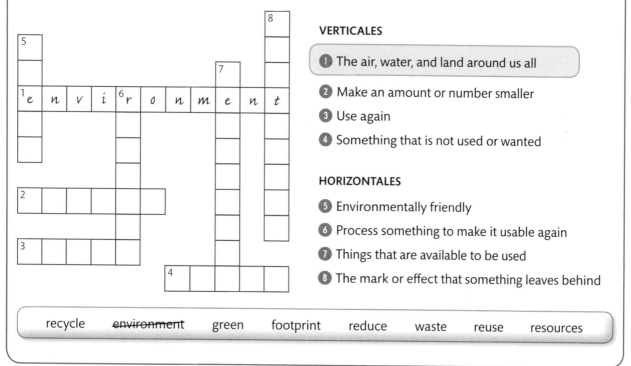

Aa 24.8 LEE LAS PISTAS Y ESCRIBE LAS PALABRAS EN EL LUGAR CORRECTO DEL CRUCIGRAMA

VERTICALES

1. The air, water, and land around us all
2. Make an amount or number smaller
3. Use again
4. Something that is not used or wanted

HORIZONTALES

5. Environmentally friendly
6. Process something to make it usable again
7. Things that are available to be used
8. The mark or effect that something leaves behind

1 → e n v i r o n m e n t

recycle   ~~environment~~   green   footprint   reduce   waste   reuse   resources

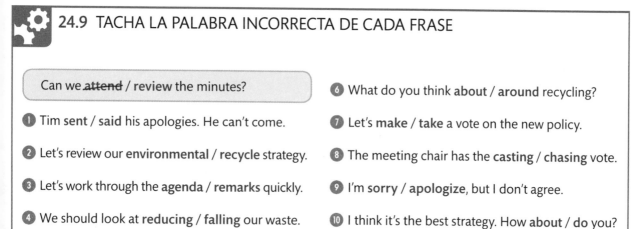

24.9 TACHA LA PALABRA INCORRECTA DE CADA FRASE

Can we ~~attend~~ / **review** the minutes?

1. Tim **sent** / **said** his apologies. He can't come.

2. Let's review our **environmental** / **recycle** strategy.

3. Let's work through the **agenda** / **remarks** quickly.

4. We should look at **reducing** / **falling** our waste.

5. I'm sorry to **interrupt** / **disturb**, but I disagree.

6. What do you think **about** / **around** recycling?

7. Let's **make** / **take** a vote on the new policy.

8. The meeting chair has the **casting** / **chasing** vote.

9. I'm **sorry** / **apologize**, but I don't agree.

10. I think it's the best strategy. How **about** / **do** you?

11. I just have a few **closed** / **closing** remarks.

24 ✓ CHECKLIST

⚙ Interrupciones y opiniones ☐   **Aa** Cuestiones medioambientales ☐   🧩 Dar opiniones educadamente ☐

25 Acuerdos y desacuerdos

Cuando reaccionas a la opinión de alguien, es importante hacerlo de manera educada y respetuosa, especialmente si no estás de acuerdo con esa persona.

🔧 **Lenguaje** Reaccionar a las opiniones
Aa Vocabulario Acuerdos y desacuerdos
🧩 **Habilidad** Debatir opiniones

25.1 PUNTO CLAVE ESTAR DE ACUERDO CON UNA OPINIÓN

Puedes expresar de muchas maneras que estás de acuerdo con alguien. No tienes que decir muchas cosas; a veces, basta con asentir con la cabeza.

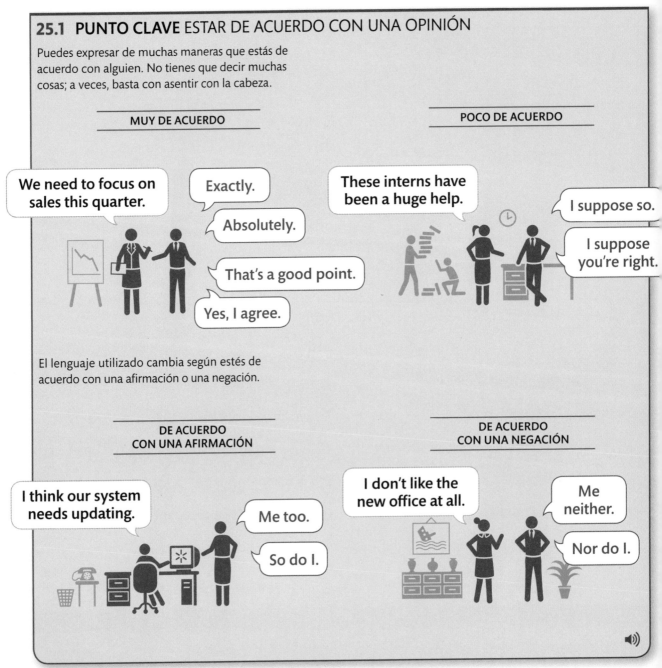

MUY DE ACUERDO

We need to focus on sales this quarter.

Exactly.

Absolutely.

That's a good point.

Yes, I agree.

POCO DE ACUERDO

These interns have been a huge help.

I suppose so.

I suppose you're right.

El lenguaje utilizado cambia según estés de acuerdo con una afirmación o una negación.

DE ACUERDO CON UNA AFIRMACIÓN

I think our system needs updating.

Me too.

So do I.

DE ACUERDO CON UNA NEGACIÓN

I don't like the new office at all.

Me neither.

Nor do I.

25.2 MARCA LA MEJOR RESPUESTA PARA CADA INTERVENCIÓN

25.3 CONECTA LAS INTERVENCIONES CON LAS RESPUESTAS

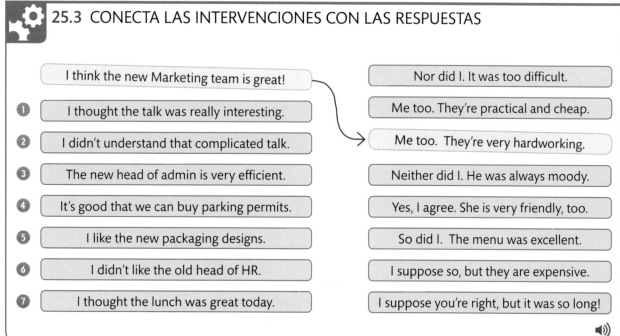

25.4 PUNTO CLAVE ESTAR EN DESACUERDO CON UNA OPINIÓN

En inglés se utilizan diversas frases educadas
para expresar grados de desacuerdo.

DESACUERDO

We should buy more of these new models.

Yes, but

Empieza con "I'm sorry"
o "I'm afraid" para que
suene más educado.

I'm sorry, but I think I disagree.

I'm afraid I don't agree.

POCO EN DESACUERDO

We'll probably finish by 5pm.

I'm not sure about that.

You could be right, but...

MUY EN DESACUERDO

This design is fantastic!

I'm afraid I totally disagree.

I'm sorry, but I don't agree at all.

No significa que tengas miedo o te sepa
mal, sino que sirve para ser más educado.

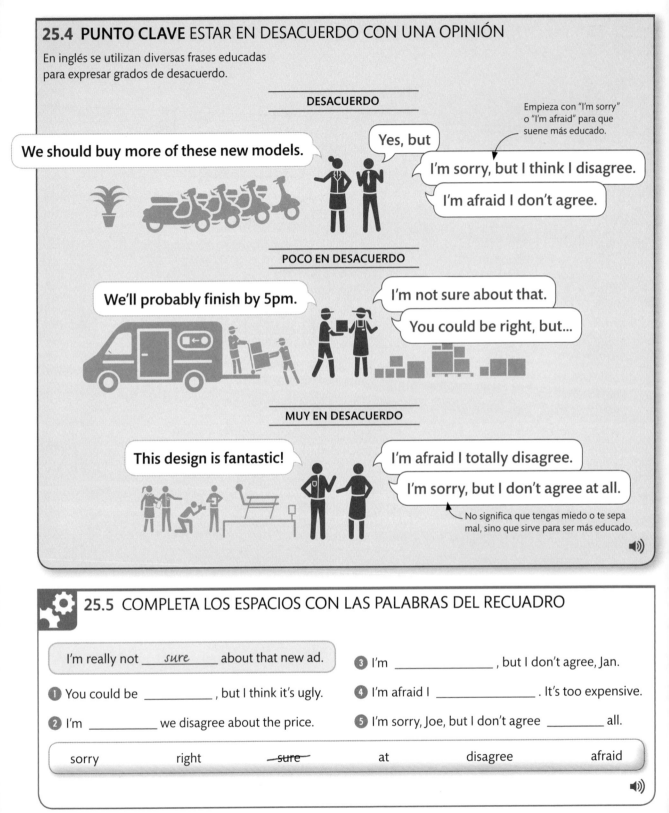

25.5 COMPLETA LOS ESPACIOS CON LAS PALABRAS DEL RECUADRO

I'm really not ___*sure*___ about that new ad.

❶ You could be _____ , but I think it's ugly.

❷ I'm _____ we disagree about the price.

❸ I'm _____ , but I don't agree, Jan.

❹ I'm afraid I _____ . It's too expensive.

❺ I'm sorry, Joe, but I don't agree _____ all.

| sorry | right | ~~sure~~ | at | disagree | afraid |

25.6 ESCUCHA EL AUDIO Y RESPONDE A LAS PREGUNTAS

Jeremy y Sian debaten sobre propuestas de cambio en su lugar de trabajo.

What does Jeremy think about the changes?

He likes all of them ☐
He likes some of them ☑
He dislikes all of them ☐

① Sian loves the idea of shower rooms.

Jeremy strongly agrees with her ☐
Jeremy agrees with her ☐
Jeremy strongly disagrees with her ☐

② Sian is looking forward to a choice of coffees.

Jeremy strongly agrees with her ☐
Jeremy agrees with her ☐
Jeremy strongly disagrees with her ☐

③ Jeremy liked having meetings on Mondays.

Sian strongly agrees with him ☐
Sian agrees with him ☐
Sian disagrees with him ☐

④ Sian is looking forward to the convention in Santiago.

Jeremy strongly agrees with her ☐
Jeremy agrees with her ☐
Jeremy strongly disagrees with her ☐

25.7 TACHA LAS PALABRAS INCORRECTAS DE CADA FRASE Y DI LAS FRASES EN VOZ ALTA

I'm ~~sure~~ / sorry, but I have to disagree with you about that.

① Yes, I suppose your / you're right about the new design.

② You could / should be right, but I need to do more research.

③ I'm sorry, but I don't agree / argue at all with that comment.

④ I'm scared / afraid I don't agree about this one issue.

⑤ I'm not sure / final about that, Sara. I don't like it.

⑥ I'm afraid I totally / finally disagree. That will never work.

25 ✓ CHECKLIST

⚙ Reaccionar a las opiniones ☐   **Aa** Acuerdos y desacuerdos ☐   🧩 Debatir opiniones ☐

26 Salud y seguridad

Muchas empresas tienen directrices para evitar accidentes y trabajar de manera segura. En inglés este tema se trata con vocabulario especializado y pronombres reflexivos.

🔧 **Lenguaje** Pronombres reflexivos
Aa Vocabulario Salud y seguridad en el trabajo
🧩 **Habilidad** Hablar sobre seguridad en el trabajo

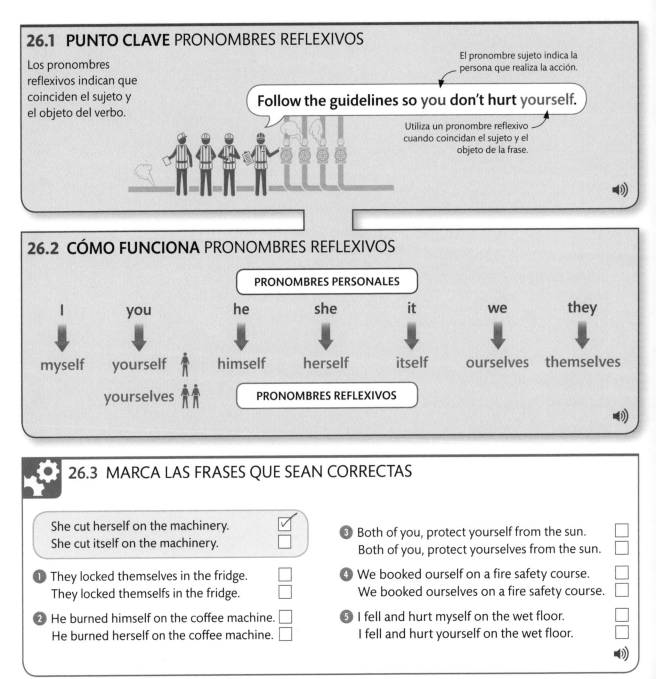

26.1 PUNTO CLAVE PRONOMBRES REFLEXIVOS

Los pronombres reflexivos indican que coinciden el sujeto y el objeto del verbo.

El pronombre sujeto indica la persona que realiza la acción.

Follow the guidelines so you don't hurt yourself.

Utiliza un pronombre reflexivo cuando coincidan el sujeto y el objeto de la frase.

26.2 CÓMO FUNCIONA PRONOMBRES REFLEXIVOS

PRONOMBRES PERSONALES

I	you	he	she	it	we	they
myself	yourself	himself	herself	itself	ourselves	themselves
	yourselves					

PRONOMBRES REFLEXIVOS

26.3 MARCA LAS FRASES QUE SEAN CORRECTAS

She cut herself on the machinery. ✓
She cut itself on the machinery. ☐

① They locked themselves in the fridge. ☐
They locked themselfs in the fridge. ☐

② He burned himself on the coffee machine. ☐
He burned herself on the coffee machine. ☐

③ Both of you, protect yourself from the sun. ☐
Both of you, protect yourselves from the sun. ☐

④ We booked ourself on a fire safety course. ☐
We booked ourselves on a fire safety course. ☐

⑤ I fell and hurt myself on the wet floor. ☐
I fell and hurt yourself on the wet floor. ☐

26.4 LEE EL ARTÍCULO Y RESPONDE A LAS PREGUNTAS

> The author is surprised that accidents happen at work.
> **True** ☐ **False** ☑ **Not given** ☐

❶ The author hurt himself at work last year.
True ☐ **False** ☐ **Not given** ☐

❷ The author does not think health and safety regulations are important.
True ☐ **False** ☐ **Not given** ☐

❸ You should tell your employer if you have an accident at work.
True ☐ **False** ☐ **Not given** ☐

HEALTH AND SAFETY AT J-CORP

Protect yourself at work

How to prevent accidents in the workplace

We spend a lot of our time at work, so it is not surprising that we have accidents there. But what can you do to protect yourself and help your co-workers protect themselves from injury? The first thing is to make sure that your company follows all the sensible health and safety regulations. Most accidents are caused by slips, trips, lifting, and carrying. If you do hurt yourself at work, report it to your employer and don't blame yourself. You could ask to take a first aid course so that you can protect and, if necessary, treat yourself and your co-workers.

26.5 UNE LAS IMÁGENES CON SUS SIGNIFICADOS

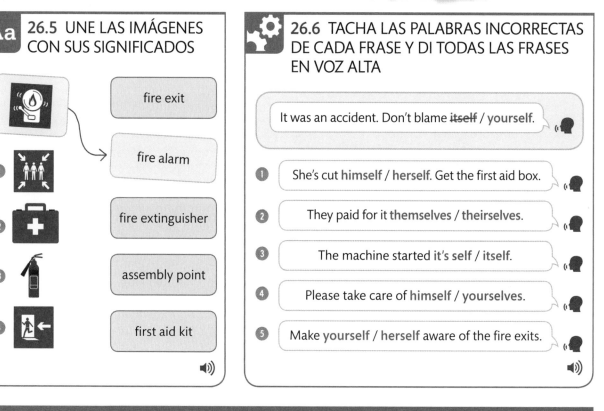

fire exit

fire alarm

fire extinguisher

assembly point

first aid kit

26.6 TACHA LAS PALABRAS INCORRECTAS DE CADA FRASE Y DI TODAS LAS FRASES EN VOZ ALTA

> It was an accident. Don't blame ~~itself~~ / **yourself**.

❶ She's cut **himself** / **herself**. Get the first aid box.

❷ They paid for it **themselves** / **theirselves**.

❸ The machine started **it's self** / **itself**.

❹ Please take care of **himself** / **yourselves**.

❺ Make **yourself** / **herself** aware of the fire exits.

27 Sugerencias y consejos

Cuando aparecen problemas del día a día en el lugar de trabajo, es útil saber cómo realizar sugerencias y ofrecer consejos. En inglés se puede hacer de diversas maneras.

⚙ **Lenguaje** Prefijos y sufijos
Aa Vocabulario Problemas diarios en el trabajo
🧩 **Habilidad** Realizar sugerencias

27.1 PUNTO CLAVE REALIZAR SUGERENCIAS

Existen diversas expresiones para ofrecer consejos o realizar sugerencias. Algunas toman la forma base del verbo, y otras utilizan la forma acabada en "-ing".

"How about" y "what about" precisan de la forma verbal acabada en "-ing".

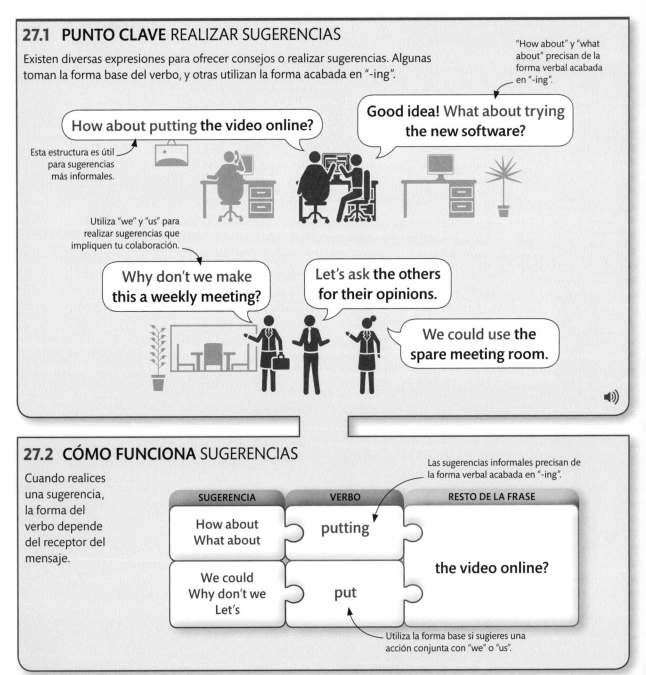

How about putting **the video online?**

Esta estructura es útil para sugerencias más informales.

Good idea! What about trying the new software?

Utiliza "we" y "us" para realizar sugerencias que impliquen tu colaboración.

Why don't we make **this a weekly meeting?**

Let's ask **the others for their opinions.**

We could use **the spare meeting room.**

27.2 CÓMO FUNCIONA SUGERENCIAS

Cuando realices una sugerencia, la forma del verbo depende del receptor del mensaje.

Las sugerencias informales precisan de la forma verbal acabada en "-ing".

SUGERENCIA	VERBO	RESTO DE LA FRASE
How about What about	putting	the video online?
We could Why don't we Let's	put	

Utiliza la forma base si sugieres una acción conjunta con "we" o "us".

27.3 VUELVE A ESCRIBIR LAS FRASES PONIENDO LAS PALABRAS EN SU ORDEN CORRECTO

| building | new | about | a | How | website? |

How about building a new website?

① | Let's | more | media. | on | do | promotion | social |

_____

② | could | the | product. | We | redesign | packaging | this | for |

_____

③ | about | a | consultant? | software | What | hiring |

_____

27.4 PUNTO CLAVE OFRECER CONSEJOS CON "SHOULD" + FORMA BASE

Una manera más convincente de ofrecer consejos es utilizar "should" o "shouldn't", ya que implican consecuencias negativas si se ignoran.

You should try to keep the meeting short.

Forma base del verbo principal

27.5 CONECTA LOS PROBLEMAS DEL TRABAJO CON LAS SUGERENCIAS Y CONSEJOS

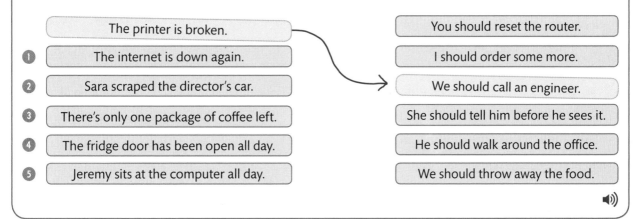

The printer is broken. — You should reset the router.

① The internet is down again. — I should order some more.

② Sara scraped the director's car. — We should call an engineer.

③ There's only one package of coffee left. — She should tell him before he sees it.

④ The fridge door has been open all day. — He should walk around the office.

⑤ Jeremy sits at the computer all day. — We should throw away the food.

27.6 PUNTO CLAVE CAMBIAR DE SIGNIFICADO CON PREFIJOS Y SUFIJOS

Los prefijos y sufijos cambian el significado cuando se añaden a una palabra.
A veces también cambian la categoría de la palabra (por ejemplo, pasa de
sustantivo a adjetivo).

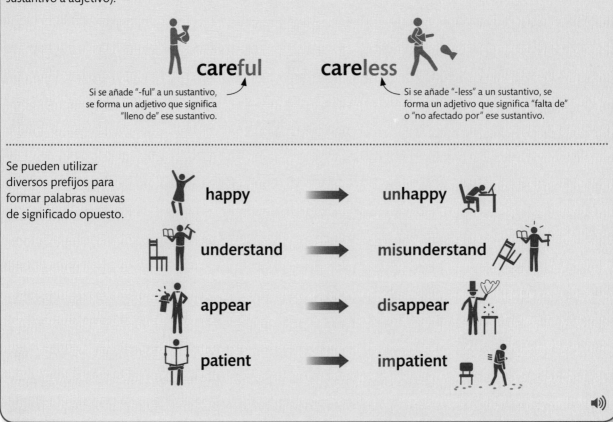

careful

Si se añade "-ful" a un sustantivo,
se forma un adjetivo que significa
"lleno de" ese sustantivo.

careless

Si se añade "-less" a un sustantivo, se
forma un adjetivo que significa "falta de"
o "no afectado por" ese sustantivo.

Se pueden utilizar
diversos prefijos para
formar palabras nuevas
de significado opuesto.

happy ➡ unhappy

understand ➡ misunderstand

appear ➡ disappear

patient ➡ impatient

 ## 27.7 COMPLETA LOS ESPACIOS CON LAS PALABRAS DEL RECUADRO

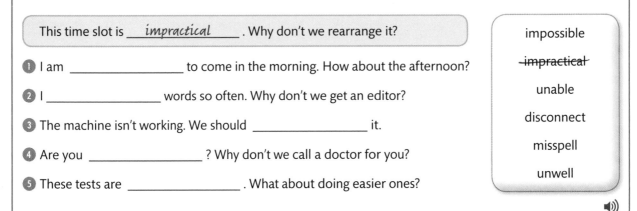

This time slot is ___*impractical*___ . Why don't we rearrange it?

1. I am _____ to come in the morning. How about the afternoon?

2. I _____ words so often. Why don't we get an editor?

3. The machine isn't working. We should _____ it.

4. Are you _____ ? Why don't we call a doctor for you?

5. These tests are _____ . What about doing easier ones?

impossible

~~impractical~~

unable

disconnect

misspell

unwell

ESCUCHA EL AUDIO Y LUEGO NUMERA LAS IMÁGENES EN EL ORDEN EN QUE SE DESCRIBEN

B [1]
C
D
E

27.9 TACHA LAS PALABRAS INCORRECTAS DE CADA FRASE Y DI LAS FRASES EN VOZ ALTA

Why don't we keep notes so we don't **misunderstand** / ~~understand~~ the plan?

1. Let's use our old system again. This new one is so **familiar** / **unfamiliar** and slow.

2. How about changing the time so that more people are **able** / **unable** to come.

3. Let's discuss the negative feedback from people who **agree** / **disagree** with our plan.

4. What about explaining the delay to stop people from becoming so **impatient** / **patient**.

5. I love conventions! It's so easy to **connect** / **disconnect** with new people.

6. I have no idea how to write this report. It seems **possible** / **impossible**!

---

27 ⊘ CHECKLIST

⚙ Prefijos y sufijos ☐   **Aa** Problemas diarios en el trabajo ☐   🧩 Realizar sugerencias ☐

28 Hacer una presentación

Cuando prepares una presentación, asegúrate de que sea clara y fácil de seguir. Puedes utilizar diversas expresiones para que el público te siga durante la charla.

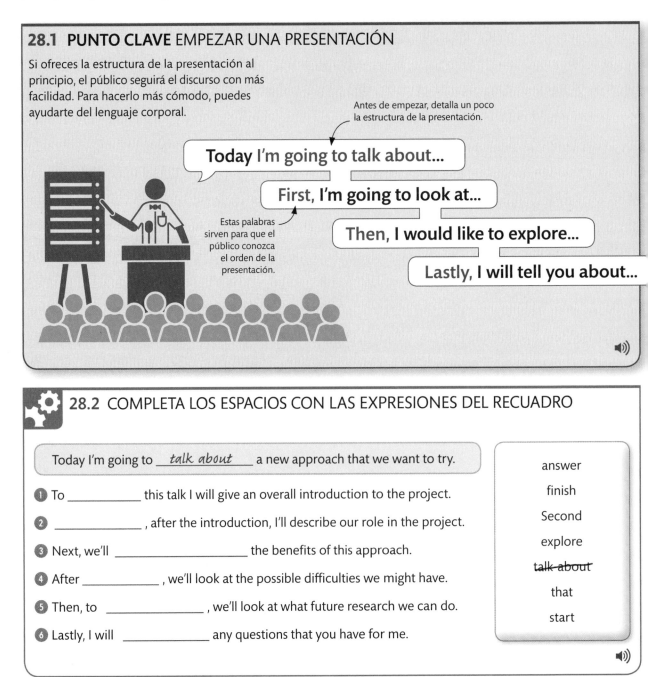

🜚 **Lenguaje** Lenguaje corporal
Aa Vocabulario Material para presentaciones
🧩 **Habilidad** Estructurar un discurso

28.1 PUNTO CLAVE EMPEZAR UNA PRESENTACIÓN

Si ofreces la estructura de la presentación al principio, el público seguirá el discurso con más facilidad. Para hacerlo más cómodo, puedes ayudarte del lenguaje corporal.

Antes de empezar, detalla un poco la estructura de la presentación.

Today I'm going to talk about...

First, I'm going to look at...

Estas palabras sirven para que el público conozca el orden de la presentación.

Then, I would like to explore...

Lastly, I will tell you about...

28.2 COMPLETA LOS ESPACIOS CON LAS EXPRESIONES DEL RECUADRO

Today I'm going to ___*talk about*___ a new approach that we want to try.

1 To _____ this talk I will give an overall introduction to the project.

2 _____ , after the introduction, I'll describe our role in the project.

3 Next, we'll _____ the benefits of this approach.

4 After _____ , we'll look at the possible difficulties we might have.

5 Then, to _____ , we'll look at what future research we can do.

6 Lastly, I will _____ any questions that you have for me.

answer
finish
Second
explore
~~talk about~~
that
start

28.3 PUNTO CLAVE CAMBIAR DE TEMA

También puedes utilizar el lenguaje corporal para pasar de un tema a otro durante la presentación.

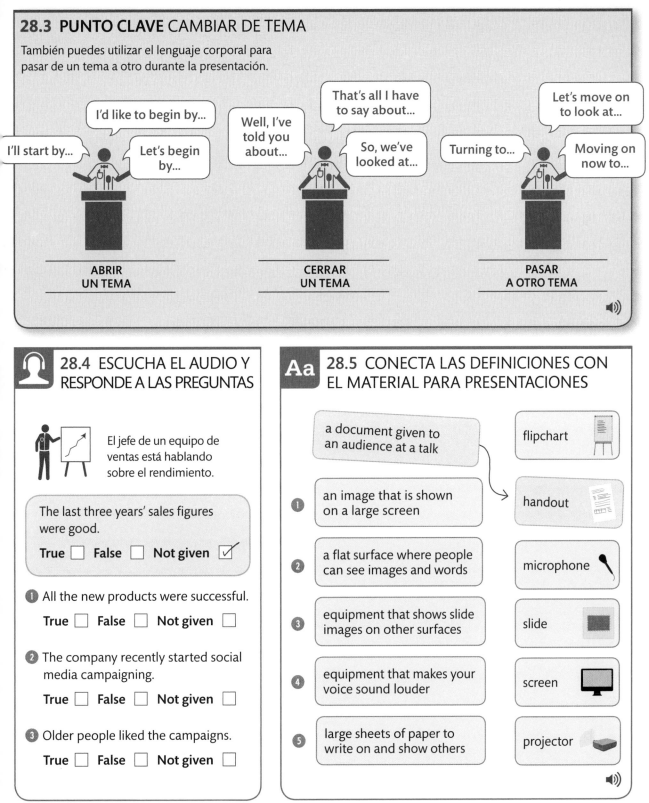

I'll start by...

I'd like to begin by...

Let's begin by...

ABRIR UN TEMA

Well, I've told you about...

That's all I have to say about...

So, we've looked at...

CERRAR UN TEMA

Turning to...

Let's move on to look at...

Moving on now to...

PASAR A OTRO TEMA

28.4 ESCUCHA EL AUDIO Y RESPONDE A LAS PREGUNTAS

El jefe de un equipo de ventas está hablando sobre el rendimiento.

The last three years' sales figures were good.

True ☐   False ☐   Not given ☑

❶ All the new products were successful.

True ☐   False ☐   Not given ☐

❷ The company recently started social media campaigning.

True ☐   False ☐   Not given ☐

❸ Older people liked the campaigns.

True ☐   False ☐   Not given ☐

28.5 CONECTA LAS DEFINICIONES CON EL MATERIAL PARA PRESENTACIONES

a document given to an audience at a talk → handout

flipchart

❶ an image that is shown on a large screen

❷ a flat surface where people can see images and words

❸ equipment that shows slide images on other surfaces

❹ equipment that makes your voice sound louder

❺ large sheets of paper to write on and show others

microphone

slide

screen

projector

28.6 PUNTO CLAVE ACABAR UNA PRESENTACIÓN

Al final de la presentación puedes incluir un breve resumen de lo expuesto
y, si lo deseas, resolver posibles dudas que tenga el público.

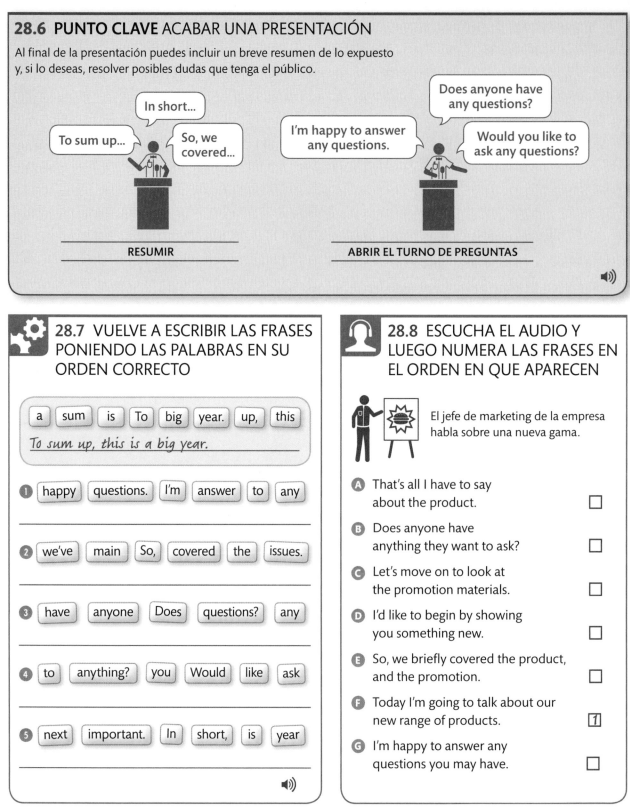

In short...

To sum up...

So, we covered...

Does anyone have any questions?

I'm happy to answer any questions.

Would you like to ask any questions?

RESUMIR

ABRIR EL TURNO DE PREGUNTAS

28.7 VUELVE A ESCRIBIR LAS FRASES PONIENDO LAS PALABRAS EN SU ORDEN CORRECTO

a   sum   is   To   big   year.   up,   this

To sum up, this is a big year.

1 happy   questions.   I'm   answer   to   any

_____

2 we've   main   So,   covered   the   issues.

_____

3 have   anyone   Does   questions?   any

_____

4 to   anything?   you   Would   like   ask

_____

5 next   important.   In   short,   is   year

_____

28.8 ESCUCHA EL AUDIO Y LUEGO NUMERA LAS FRASES EN EL ORDEN EN QUE APARECEN

El jefe de marketing de la empresa habla sobre una nueva gama.

A That's all I have to say about the product. ☐

B Does anyone have anything they want to ask? ☐

C Let's move on to look at the promotion materials. ☐

D I'd like to begin by showing you something new. ☐

E So, we briefly covered the product, and the promotion. ☐

F Today I'm going to talk about our new range of products. 1

G I'm happy to answer any questions you may have. ☐

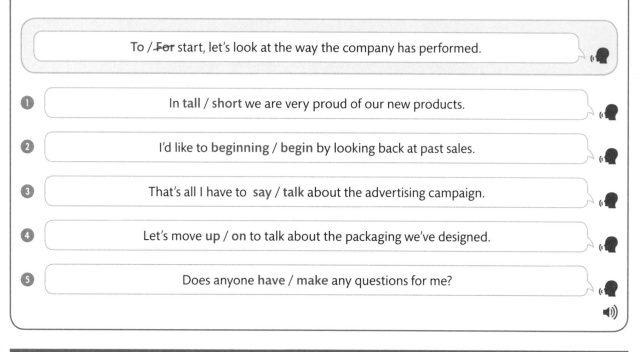

28.9 TACHA LAS PALABRAS INCORRECTAS DE CADA FRASE Y DI LAS FRASES EN VOZ ALTA

To / ~~For~~ start, let's look at the way the company has performed.

1. In **tall** / **short** we are very proud of our new products.

2. I'd like to **beginning** / **begin** by looking back at past sales.

3. That's all I have to **say** / **talk** about the advertising campaign.

4. Let's move **up** / **on** to talk about the packaging we've designed.

5. Does anyone **have** / **make** any questions for me?

---

28 ✓ CHECKLIST

⚙ Lenguaje corporal ☐   **Aa** Material para presentaciones ☐   ✦ Estructurar un discurso ☐

↻ REPASA LO QUE HAS APRENDIDO EN LAS UNIDADES 22-28

NUEVO LENGUAJE	FRASE DE EJEMPLO	✓	UNIDAD
EL PRESENT CONTINUOUS PARA COSAS EN CURSO Y PLANES FUTUROS	I'm finishing **this report.** I'm working **from home on Monday.**	☐	23.1, 23.6, 23.11
INTERRUMPIR EDUCADAMENTE E INTERCAMBIAR OPINIONES	Sorry to interrupt, but... I'm not sure I agree... How about you?	☐	24.1, 24.3
ACUERDOS Y DESACUERDOS	I suppose you're right... I'm afraid I totally disagree.	☐	25.1, 25.4
PRONOMBRES REFLEXIVOS	**Follow the guidelines so you don't hurt** yourself.	☐	26.1
REALIZAR SUGERENCIAS Y OFRECER CONSEJOS	How about putting **the video online?** **You** should try **to keep the meeting short.**	☐	27.1, 27.4
LENGUAJE CORPORAL PARA PRESENTACIONES	First, **I'm going to look at...**	☐	28.1, 28.3, 28.6

29 Normas y peticiones

Utiliza "can" y "have to" para hablar sobre normas en el trabajo, y verbos como "could" para pedir de manera educada a tus colegas que te ayuden con un problema.

⚙ **Lenguaje** Verbos modales
Aa Vocabulario Pedir cosas educadamente
🧩 **Habilidad** Hablar sobre normas y reglas

29.1 PUNTO CLAVE VERBOS MODALES DE PERMISO

Utiliza "can" para dar permiso a un colega para hacer algo.

> You can take your lunch break at 1 o'clock.

Utiliza "can't" para decirle a un colega que no puede hacer algo.

> There's a business dress code here. You can't wear shorts to work.

"Have to" expresa una gran obligación de hacer algo.

> That's the fire alarm! We have to leave the store now.

"Don't have to" significa que algo no es necesario.

> You don't have to stay late tonight. We're not very busy.

🔊

29.2 CONECTA LAS FRASES QUE VAN SEGUIDAS

You can listen to music at work.	It's a special one for fire safety.
1 You have to close that door.	We're meeting clients later this afternoon.
2 You don't have to eat at your desk.	Just make sure it's not too loud.
3 You can't leave early today.	I have saved all the documents.
4 You can shut the computers down.	There's a nice café across the street.

🔊

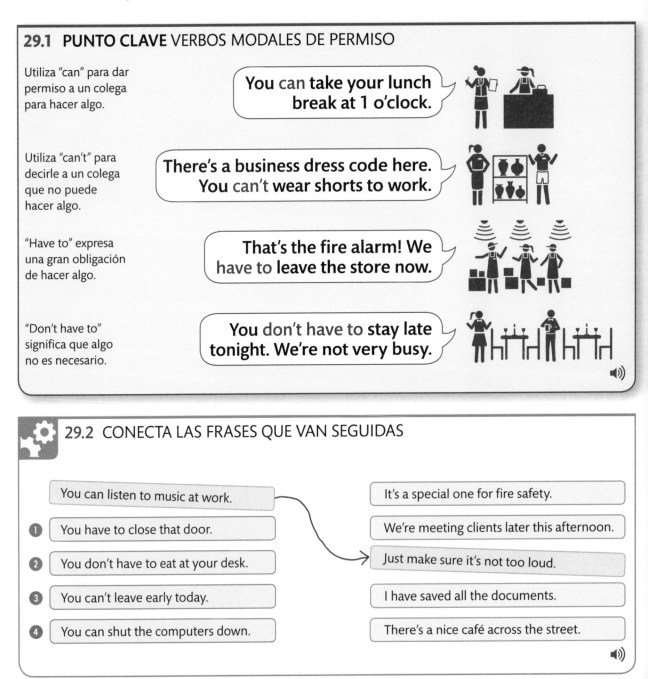

29.3 COMPLETA LOS ESPACIOS CON LAS PALABRAS DEL RECUADRO

You ___can't___ park your car there. It's the CEO's space.

❶ Is your stapler broken? You _____ use mine.

❷ She _____ come to the training session. She did it last year.

❸ You _____ turn off the light if you're the last person to leave the office.

❹ He _____ test the fire alarm every Wednesday morning.

❺ We _____ wear a jacket and tie in the summer months.

| ~~can't~~ | have to | has to | don't have to | can | doesn't have to |

29.4 LEE EL AVISO Y RESPONDE A LAS PREGUNTAS

All staff are allowed to wear jeans to work.
True ☐ False ☐ Not given ☑

❶ Staff get free breakfast at the restaurant.
True ☐ False ☐ Not given ☐

❷ All staff must have short hair.
True ☐ False ☐ Not given ☐

❸ Staff are allowed to keep tips from the clients.
True ☐ False ☐ Not given ☐

❹ Staff are not allowed to leave the kitchen dirty.
True ☐ False ☐ Not given ☐

❺ Staff only wash their hands after touching food.
True ☐ False ☐ Not given ☐

KITCHEN RULES:

- Kitchen staff can wear jeans and sneakers
- Waiting staff have to wear uniform at all times
- All staff can drink free tea, coffee, and soft drinks
- You have to keep cell phones in your locker
- You don't have to cut your hair, but do tie it back
- You don't have to pay for lunch or dinner
- You can keep any tips given by customers
- You can't use bad language in the restaurant
- You have to clean the kitchen before you leave
- And remember that you have to wash your hands before and after touching food

29.5 PUNTO CLAVE VERBOS MODALES PARA PEDIR COSAS EDUCADAMENTE

Utiliza "Could you" con un verbo base o "Would you mind" con un gerundio para pedir ayuda educadamente para cualquier problema del trabajo.

We've run out of hangers.
{ **Could you order**
Would you mind ordering }
some more?

29.6 CÓMO FUNCIONA VERBOS MODALES PARA PEDIR COSAS EDUCADAMENTE

"COULD YOU"	FORMA BASE	RESTO DE LA FRASE
Could you	order	
"WOULD YOU MIND"	GERUNDIO	**some more hangers?**
Would you mind	ordering	

↖ Esta forma es muy educada.

29.7 MÁS EJEMPLOS VERBOS MODALES PARA PEDIR COSAS EDUCADAMENTE

This box is really heavy. Could you help me lift it?

I can't find my stapler. Could you lend me yours, please?

↖ Añade "please" para que suene más educado.

The clients are here early. Would you mind making them tea and coffee?

Our card machine isn't working. Would you mind paying with cash?

29.8 TACHA LA PALABRA INCORRECTA DE CADA FRASE

Would you mind ~~close~~ / **closing** the door?

1 Could you **tell** / telling Jan to call me back?

2 Could you checking / **check** this report?

3 Would you mind **ordering** / order more pens?

4 Could you **mop** / mopping the floor, please?

5 Could you coming / **come** to today's meeting?

6 Would you mind **calling** / call back later?

7 Would you mind turning / **turn** the light off?

8 Could you **wash** / washing these cups, please?

9 Could you passing / **pass** around the reports?

10 Would you mind **book** / booking me a taxi?

11 Could you showing / **show** our clients around?

🔊

29.9 ESCUCHA EL AUDIO Y RESPONDE A LAS PREGUNTAS

Robin le pide a su colega Bruno que le ayude a preparar una reunión complicada con unos proveedores.

Bruno has finished his presentation.
True ✓ **False** ☐

1 Robin doesn't need help with his handout.
True ☐ **False** ☐

2 The suppliers are a new company.
True ☐ **False** ☐

3 Bruno will check Robin's handouts.
True ☐ **False** ☐

4 Robin asks Bruno to call the taxi company.
True ☐ **False** ☐

29.10 UTILIZA EL DIAGRAMA PARA CREAR SEIS FRASES CORRECTAS Y DILAS EN VOZ ALTA

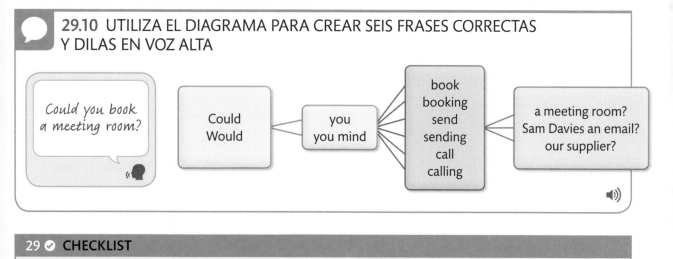

Could you book a meeting room?

| Could Would | you you mind | book booking send sending call calling | a meeting room? Sam Davies an email? our supplier? |

🔊

30.1 MODISMOS EN EL TRABAJO

The road is closed, but it's business as usual in the store.

business as usual
[the normal daily routine at a company]

Spending any more on that useless product would be throwing money down the drain.

throwing money down the drain
[wasting money]

There's so much red tape involved in importing food products.

red tape
[administration, paperwork, or rules and regulations]

You get a free car and the company gets good press. It's a win-win situation.

a win-win situation
[a situation with no negative outcome]

Our sales were poor this year and we're in the red.

to be in the red
[to owe money]

They have to work around the clock to redecorate the shop.

to work around the clock
[to work very long hours]

I can't come home yet, I'm snowed under with work.

to be snowed under
[to have too much work to do]

Sorry, he can't come to the phone. He's tied up with another client.

to be tied up with
[to be busy doing something else]

I hope I can wind down a bit over the weekend.

to wind down
[to gradually relax]

Take it easy! We've got another hour to finish decorating the conference hall.

to take it easy
[to relax or calm down]

Sorry, I'll have to miss lunch. I'm **swamped** with invoices to file.

to be swamped
[to be really busy]

I hate being on the top floor when the elevator is **out of order**.

to be out of order
[to not be working]

She's not a great team member. She doesn't really **pull her weight**.

to pull your weight
[to do a fair share of work]

We've told you our final price. **The ball is in your court** now.

the ball is in your court
[it is your turn to do or say something]

This report is due today. I can't **put it off** any longer.

to put something off
[to delay or avoid something]

Greg is really creative and often **thinks outside the box**.

to think outside the box
[to think about a something in an original way]

They are very difficult clients because they're always **moving the goalposts**.

to move the goalposts
[to change the desired end result]

If we're all here, Marcia, can you **get the ball rolling**?

to get the ball rolling
[to start something]

I don't understand all these error messages. My laptop's **going haywire**!

going haywire
[not acting or behaving as it should]

I want to finish by five o'clock, so let's **get down to business**.

to get down to business
[to start work on something that needs doing]

31 Debatir problemas

Muchos problemas típicos del lugar de trabajo tienen su origen en alguna situación pasada. Utiliza el past continuous para hablar de estos problemas.

⚙ **Lenguaje** Past continuous
Aa Vocabulario Modismos sobre trabajo
🧩 **Habilidad** Describir problemas del trabajo

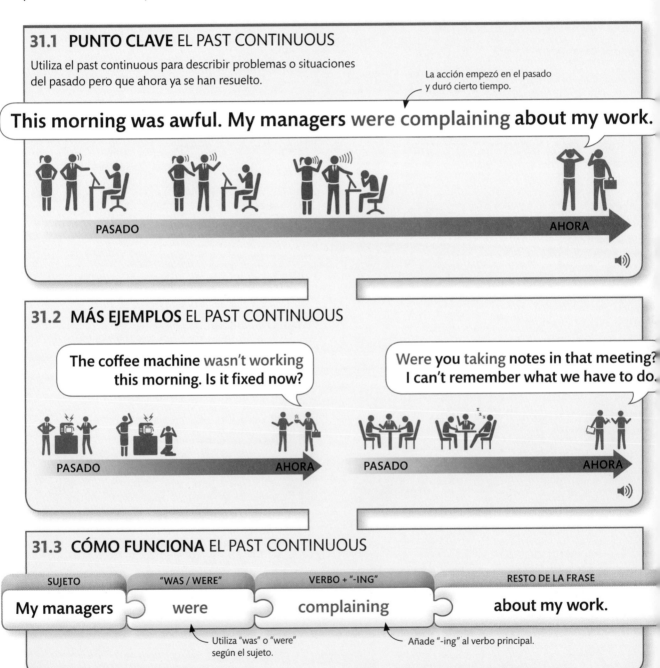

31.1 PUNTO CLAVE EL PAST CONTINUOUS

Utiliza el past continuous para describir problemas o situaciones del pasado pero que ahora ya se han resuelto.

La acción empezó en el pasado y duró cierto tiempo.

This morning was awful. My managers were complaining about my work.

PASADO — AHORA

31.2 MÁS EJEMPLOS EL PAST CONTINUOUS

The coffee machine wasn't working this morning. Is it fixed now?

PASADO — AHORA

Were you taking notes in that meeting? I can't remember what we have to do.

PASADO — AHORA

31.3 CÓMO FUNCIONA EL PAST CONTINUOUS

SUJETO	"WAS / WERE"	VERBO + "-ING"	RESTO DE LA FRASE
My managers	were	complaining	about my work.

Utiliza "was" o "were" según el sujeto.

Añade "-ing" al verbo principal.

31.4 COMPLETA LOS ESPACIOS ESCRIBIENDO LOS VERBOS EN PAST CONTINUOUS

Angel _____was writing_____ (write) his report this morning. He still hasn't finished.

1 Gabino _____ (not listen) during the team meeting this morning.

2 The internet _____ (not work) all day yesterday. I had to call my clients.

3 Hannah and Luke _____ (talk) during the CEO's presentation.

4 I _____ (forget) to do everyday jobs, so I wrote a list.

5 I put you on a new team because you _____ (lose) sales.

31.5 LEE EL ARTÍCULO Y ESCRIBE RESPUESTAS A LAS PREGUNTAS CON ORACIONES COMPLETAS

OUR CAREER

Your problems solved

Our experts are here to help solve your workplace problems

Last week I was reading all your emails about problems with co-workers. Most of us know someone in the office who can be a little bit lazy sometimes, but Maria wrote last week to say that her co-worker was not answering important emails and leaving Maria to reply to all the sales enquiries. Well, my advice, Maria, is to talk to your co-worker first. Perhaps he was going through a difficult time. I know it is difficult if your co-worker is also your friend, but you must make sure that you don't end up doing your work and his as well!

Remember José from last month, who was feeling very tired after lunch every day? Well, he did change his diet so that he ate more salads and vegetables and said last week that he was working until 5pm every day without feeling exhausted. Great news, José!

A healthy lunch will give you more energy at work

What was the author doing last week?
The author was reading emails.

1 What wasn't Maria's co-worker doing?

_____

2 What was he leaving Maria to do?

_____

3 What was the author's advice?

_____

4 What was José's problem last month?

_____

5 What did he do to solve the problem?

_____

6 How late was José working last week?

_____

31.6 ESCUCHA EL AUDIO Y NUMERA LAS IMÁGENES EN EL ORDEN EN QUE SE DESCRIBEN

A ☐

B ①

C ☐

D ☐

E ☐

31.7 VUELVE A ESCRIBIR LAS FRASES CORRIGIENDO LOS ERRORES

> I was **working about** the clock today
> *I was working around the clock today.*

1 Sales were improving. It was **win-win** situation.

_____

2 It's a difficult task. We must think **out** the box.

_____

3 The team was throwing money **up** the drain.

_____

4 Was your assistant **pushing** his weight today?

_____

5 We were working with a lot of **blue** tape.

_____

6 Now we're all here, let's get **in** to business.

_____

31.8 CONECTA LAS IMÁGENES CON SUS DESCRIPCIONES

The printer was going haywire yesterday.

I kept putting off a difficult phone call this morning.

1

The elevator is out of order.

2

I'm tied up with these difficult reports.

3

Our sales fell last year. Now we're in the red.

4

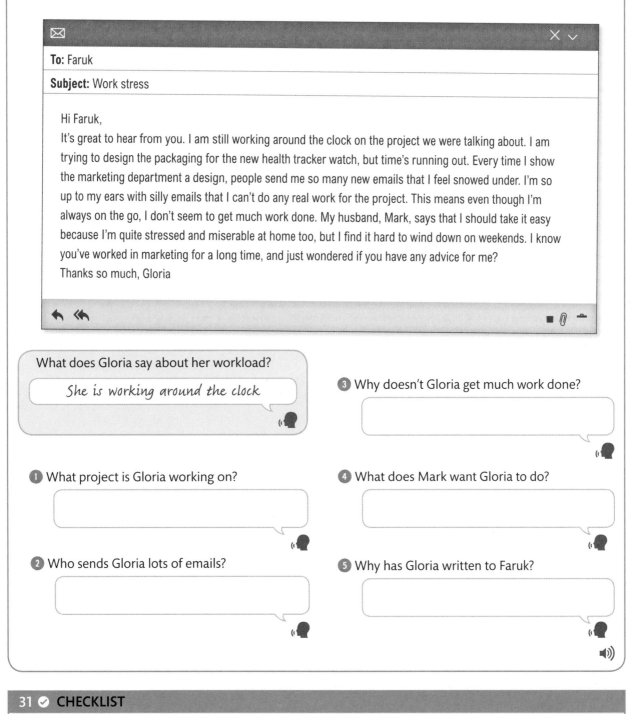

To: Faruk

Subject: Work stress

Hi Faruk,

It's great to hear from you. I am still working around the clock on the project we were talking about. I am trying to design the packaging for the new health tracker watch, but time's running out. Every time I show the marketing department a design, people send me so many new emails that I feel snowed under. I'm so up to my ears with silly emails that I can't do any real work for the project. This means even though I'm always on the go, I don't seem to get much work done. My husband, Mark, says that I should take it easy because I'm quite stressed and miserable at home too, but I find it hard to wind down on weekends. I know you've worked in marketing for a long time, and just wondered if you have any advice for me?

Thanks so much, Gloria

What does Gloria say about her workload?

She is working around the clock

3 Why doesn't Gloria get much work done?

1 What project is Gloria working on?

4 What does Mark want Gloria to do?

2 Who sends Gloria lots of emails?

5 Why has Gloria written to Faruk?

31 ✓ CHECKLIST

⚙ Past continuous ☐   Aa Modismos sobre trabajo ☐   Describir problemas del trabajo ☐

119

32 Disculpas y explicaciones

En inglés dispones de diversas expresiones educadas para disculparte por cualquier error. Utiliza el past continuous y el past simple juntos para dar explicaciones sobre un error.

⚙ Lenguaje Past continuous y past simple
Aa Vocabulario Errores en el lugar de trabajo
🧩 Habilidad Disculparse y dar explicaciones

32.1 PUNTO CLAVE DISCULPAS Y EXPLICACIONES

Existen muchas expresiones formales e informales que puedes utilizar para disculparte y responder a las disculpas de otros. Las respuestas pueden aceptar la disculpa y acabar la conversación o rechazarla y exigir acciones posteriores.

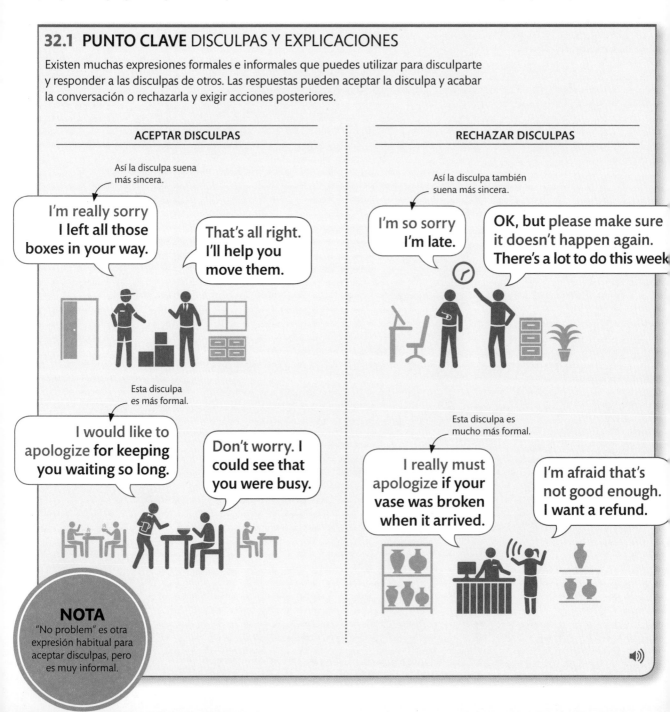

ACEPTAR DISCULPAS

Así la disculpa suena más sincera.

I'm really sorry **I left all those boxes in your way.**

That's all right. I'll help you move them.

Esta disculpa es más formal.

I would like to apologize **for keeping you waiting so long.**

Don't worry. I could see that you were busy.

RECHAZAR DISCULPAS

Así la disculpa también suena más sincera.

I'm so sorry **I'm late.**

OK, but please make sure it doesn't happen again. **There's a lot to do this week.**

Esta disculpa es mucho más formal.

I really must apologize **if your vase was broken when it arrived.**

I'm afraid that's not good enough. I want a refund.

NOTA
"No problem" es otra expresión habitual para aceptar disculpas, pero es muy informal.

🔊

32.2 CONECTA LAS DISCULPAS CON LA RESPUESTA CORRECTA

I'm really sorry I'm late.

Don't worry. I have copies of them here.

① I do apologize. I've left the files at home.

No need. The signal's always bad here.

② I'm sorry. I've forgotten your last name.

That's all right. My train was delayed too.

③ I would like to apologize for the bad line.

Never mind. I've got myself another one.

④ I'm really sorry. I think I'm very early.

No problem. It's Carson.

⑤ I'm so sorry. I took your cup accidentally.

That's OK. We can have coffee first.

🔊

32.3 ESCUCHA EL AUDIO Y MARCA SI KARL ACEPTA LAS DISCULPAS

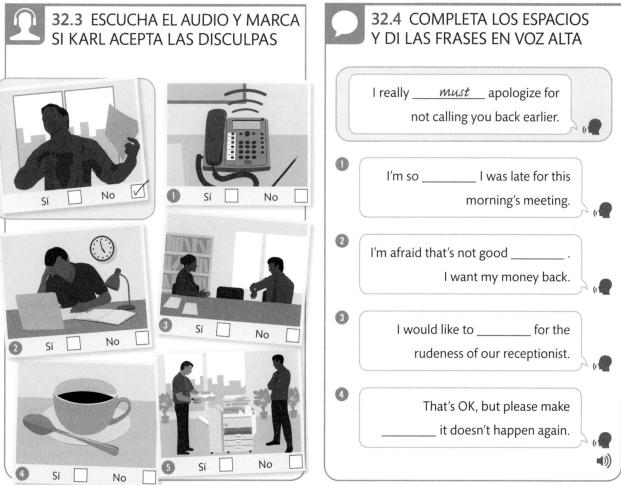

Sí ☐ No ☑

① Sí ☐ No ☐

② Sí ☐ No ☐

③ Sí ☐ No ☐

④ Sí ☐ No ☐

⑤ Sí ☐ No ☐

32.4 COMPLETA LOS ESPACIOS Y DI LAS FRASES EN VOZ ALTA

I really ___*must*___ apologize for not calling you back earlier. 🗣

① I'm so _____ I was late for this morning's meeting. 🗣

② I'm afraid that's not good _____ . I want my money back. 🗣

③ I would like to _____ for the rudeness of our receptionist. 🗣

④ That's OK, but please make _____ it doesn't happen again. 🗣

🔊

32.5 PUNTO CLAVE PAST CONTINUOUS Y PAST SIMPLE

Muchos errores en el lugar de trabajo son por cosas inesperadas
que interrumpen algo. En inglés dispones del past continuous y
past simple juntos para describir esta situación.

Past continuous

Past simple

I'm so sorry. I was writing an email when I spilled water on my keyboard.

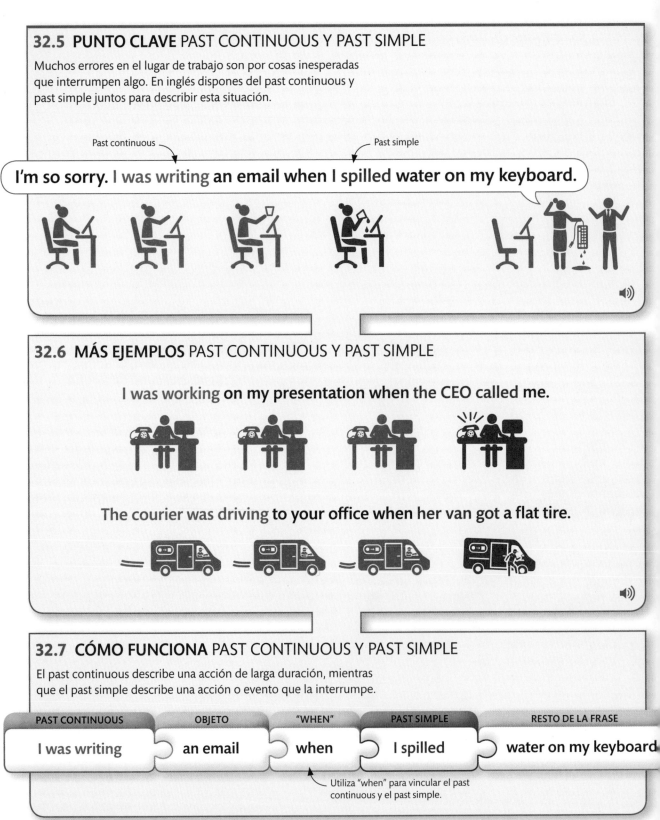

32.6 MÁS EJEMPLOS PAST CONTINUOUS Y PAST SIMPLE

I was working on my presentation when the CEO called me.

The courier was driving to your office when her van got a flat tire.

32.7 CÓMO FUNCIONA PAST CONTINUOUS Y PAST SIMPLE

El past continuous describe una acción de larga duración, mientras
que el past simple describe una acción o evento que la interrumpe.

PAST CONTINUOUS	OBJETO	"WHEN"	PAST SIMPLE	RESTO DE LA FRASE
I was writing	an email	when	I spilled	water on my keyboard

Utiliza "when" para vincular el past
continuous y el past simple.

32.8 TACHA LAS PALABRAS INCORRECTAS DE CADA FRASE

> We ~~signed~~ / were signing the contract when our client ~~was receiving~~ / received a text message.

1. She **was walking** / walked into the room and saw that Clive practiced / **was practicing** his presentation.

2. I tried / **was trying** to make an important point when someone's phone **started** / was starting to ring.

3. The printer worked / **was working** fine when unfortunately the power **went** / was going off.

4. He **opened** / was opening the door and saw that we listened / **were listening** to his conversation.

5. We ate / **were eating** lunch in the cafeteria when we **heard** / were hearing the fire alarm.

32.9 LEE EL CORREO ELECTRÓNICO Y RESPONDE A LAS PREGUNTAS

> Tam accepts that she deleted the document.
> **True** ☑ **False** ☐ **Not given** ☐

1. Tam was working on a presentation.
   True ☐ **False** ☐ **Not given** ☐

2. Tam's computer crashed yesterday.
   True ☐ **False** ☐ **Not given** ☐

3. Tam was only editing a copy of the report.
   True ☐ **False** ☐ **Not given** ☐

4. The company lost a client because of her mistake.
   True ☐ **False** ☐ **Not given** ☐

5. Tam now regularly saves her documents.
   True ☐ **False** ☐ **Not given** ☐

✉

To: Kim May

Subject: Apologies

Dear Kim,

I'm writing to apologize about the season's sales report going missing. It was entirely my fault and I really am sorry for all the disruption it caused to you and our colleagues yesterday.

I was editing the report yesterday when my computer crashed. I thought I was working on a copy of the report, so when my computer restarted, I chose not to save it. Clearly, I was working on the only master copy and accidentally deleted it from all the computers.

I will rewrite the report and now back up all my work to an external hard drive every thirty minutes so that this will not happen again.

Once again, please accept my apologies.

Best wishes,

Tam

---

32 ✔ CHECKLIST

⚙ Past continuous y past simple ☐   **Aa** Errores en el lugar de trabajo ☐   🧩 Disculparse y dar explicaciones ☐

33 Tareas y objetivos

Utiliza el present perfect para que tus compañeros sepan cómo vas de trabajo cuando se acerquen las fechas de entrega y trabajes bajo presión.

⚙ **Lenguaje** Present perfect y past simple
Aa Vocabulario Tareas del trabajo
🧩 **Habilidad** Debatir logros en el trabajo

33.1 PUNTO CLAVE EL PRESENT PERFECT

Utiliza el present perfect para hablar sobre si se han completado las tareas o se han cumplido los objetivos. Utiliza "yet" para cosas que esperas que pasen; utiliza "just" para acontecimientos recientes.

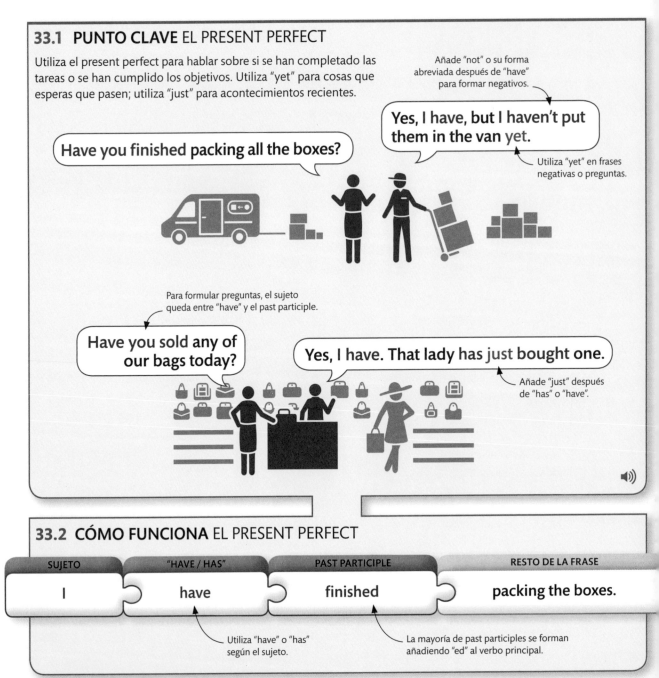

Añade "not" o su forma abreviada después de "have" para formar negativos.

Yes, I have, but I haven't put them in the van yet.

Utiliza "yet" en frases negativas o preguntas.

Have you finished packing all the boxes?

Para formular preguntas, el sujeto queda entre "have" y el past participle.

Have you sold any of our bags today?

Yes, I have. That lady has just bought one.

Añade "just" después de "has" o "have".

33.2 CÓMO FUNCIONA EL PRESENT PERFECT

SUJETO	"HAVE / HAS"	PAST PARTICIPLE	RESTO DE LA FRASE
I	have	finished	packing the boxes.

Utiliza "have" o "has" según el sujeto.

La mayoría de past participles se forman añadiendo "ed" al verbo principal.

33.3 COMPLETA LOS ESPACIOS ESCRIBIENDO LOS VERBOS EN PRESENT PERFECT

We ___have stopped___ (stop) cleaning the windows because it's raining.

1. Adrian _____ (make) three flower arrangements already today.

2. I _____ (start) work on the report, but I won't finish it tonight.

3. Leah _____ (cut) four people's hair so far this afternoon.

4. It's early. We _____ (not speak) to any customers yet.

33.4 TACHA LA PALABRA INCORRECTA DE CADA FRASE

Have you finished the reports just / yet?

1. I've just / yet left work and it's very late.

2. We haven't shown this to the public just / yet.

3. Have you just / yet started selling this product?

4. She hasn't done her training course just / yet.

5. They've just / yet opened the store doors.

33.5 LEE LA LISTA DE COSAS PENDIENTES DE JUAN Y RESPONDE A LAS PREGUNTAS

To do list

- Update timesheets
- File client documents
- Move files across to new server
- Call the engineer
- Book appointment with designer

- Buy coffee and tea
- Update the computer software
- Write training manual
- Renew parking permit
- Call Sam about lunch

Juan has updated his timesheets.
True ☐ False ☑

1. Juan has called the engineer.
True ☐ False ☐

2. Juan has bought tea and coffee.
True ☐ False ☐

3. Juan hasn't written the training manual.
True ☐ False ☐

4. Juan hasn't called Sam about lunch yet.
True ☐ False ☐

33.6 PUNTO CLAVE PRESENT PERFECT Y PAST SIMPLE

Utiliza el present perfect para hablar sobre tareas que has completado hace poco y que aún tienen implicaciones en la actualidad.

No sabemos cuándo se reparó el coche.

Have you fixed Mr. Novak's car?

Yes, I have.

PASADO

AHORA

Utiliza el past simple para especificar cuándo pasó algo en el pasado.

Sabemos cuándo se reparó el coche.

When did you fix it? He's been calling me all day.

I fixed it at 2:30. Sorr for not telling you.

2.30

AHORA

33.7 VUELVE A ESCRIBIR LAS FRASES CORRIGIENDO LOS ERRORES

The courier **has left** the office this morning, and your delivery will arrive today.
The courier left the office this morning, and your delivery will arrive today.

① We've **received** your order two hours ago and sent it about an hour ago.

_____

② I made all those pastries this morning and I **sold** them all now.

_____

③ I've **started** painting Ms. Malone's living room at 7 today, but I haven't finished yet.

_____

④ I emailed the clients yesterday but they **not** replied yet.

_____

33.8 ESCUCHA EL AUDIO Y RESPONDE A LAS PREGUNTAS

Tanya e Imran hablan de una semana muy ocupada en el trabajo.

What has Imran done recently?

Left his job ☐
Started a new job ☑
Won a promotion ☐

1 Imran has met...

some of his new co-workers ☐
all his new co-workers ☐
only his manager ☐

2 What did Imran do on Tuesday?

He had a meeting with his boss ☐
He met some of his co-workers ☐
He went to a conference ☐

3 What did Tanya do this week?

She gave a conference talk ☐
She appeared on TV ☐
She finished her research ☐

4 Where did Imran and Tanya both go?

A meeting for local business ☐
A marketing conference ☐
A talk on local businesses ☐

5 What did they think of the last speaker?

Only Imran liked his talk ☐
Only Tanya liked his talk ☐
They both liked his talk ☐

33.9 COMPLETA LOS ESPACIOS CON LAS PALABRAS DEL RECUADRO Y CONTESTA AL AUDIO EN VOZ ALTA

Have you finished the reports?

No, I haven't finished them___*yet*___ .

1 When did you start working here?

I _____ in January this year.

2 Has Clare explained the task to you?

No, she _____ yet.

3 Have you packed all the boxes yet?

Yes, I've _____ finished.

4 Who has left the meeting room so messy?

Not me. I _____ been in there.

~~yet~~   just   hasn't

haven't   started

34 Tratar las quejas

Si un cliente se queja de un problema, se le puede ofrecer una solución, igual que hacer predicciones o promesas, utilizando el future con "will".

⚙ **Lenguaje** El futuro con "will"
Aa Vocabulario Quejas y disculpas
🧩 **Habilidad** Tratar las quejas

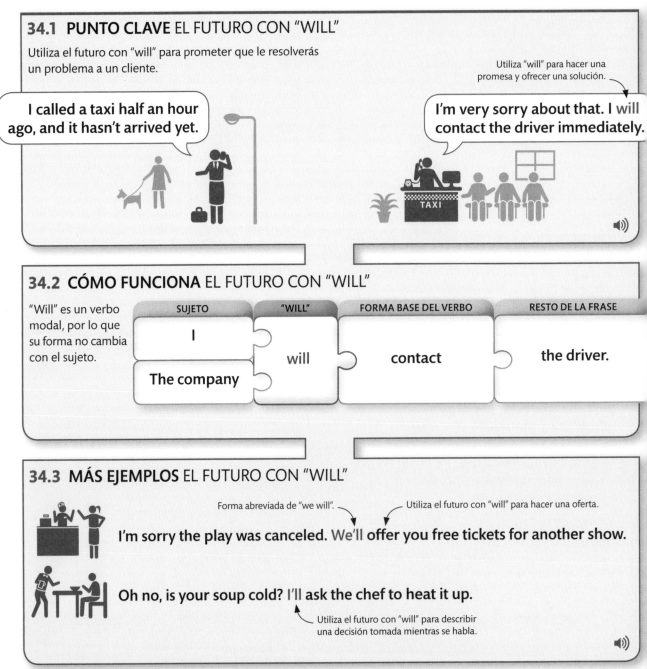

34.1 PUNTO CLAVE EL FUTURO CON "WILL"

Utiliza el futuro con "will" para prometer que le resolverás un problema a un cliente.

Utiliza "will" para hacer una promesa y ofrecer una solución.

I called a taxi half an hour ago, and it hasn't arrived yet.

I'm very sorry about that. I will contact the driver immediately.

34.2 CÓMO FUNCIONA EL FUTURO CON "WILL"

"Will" es un verbo modal, por lo que su forma no cambia con el sujeto.

SUJETO	"WILL"	FORMA BASE DEL VERBO	RESTO DE LA FRASE
I	will	contact	the driver.
The company			

34.3 MÁS EJEMPLOS EL FUTURO CON "WILL"

Forma abreviada de "we will".

Utiliza el futuro con "will" para hacer una oferta.

I'm sorry the play was canceled. We'll offer you free tickets for another show.

Oh no, is your soup cold? I'll ask the chef to heat it up.

Utiliza el futuro con "will" para describir una decisión tomada mientras se habla.

34.4 LEE LA CARTA Y ESCRIBE RESPUESTAS A LAS PREGUNTAS CON ORACIONES COMPLETAS

> What type of vacation did Ms. Chang go on?
>
> *She went on a walking tour.*

1 How did Ms. Chang feel about her vacation?

_____

2 What was Ms. Chang's first complaint about?

_____

3 What will the company do about phone calls?

_____

4 What was Ms. Chang's second complaint?

_____

5 What will the hotel do in the future?

_____

6 What has the company given Ms. Chang?

_____

Dear Ms. Chang,

Thank you very much for your letter of September 24 regarding your walking tour last month. We were very upset to hear that you did not enjoy your vacation, and we take full responsibility for the problems that you experienced.

We were sorry to hear that no one responded to your phone calls on the contact number that you were given when you arrived. We will ensure that every customer is now given a second contact number. Regarding the lack of a vegetarian option in the hotel restaurant, the hotel promises that they will offer both vegetarian and vegan options from now on.

By way of an apology, we have included a voucher worth $200 off your next trip with us.

Yours sincerely,
Dylan Levine

34.5 CONECTA LAS QUEJAS CON LAS RESPUESTAS CORRECTAS

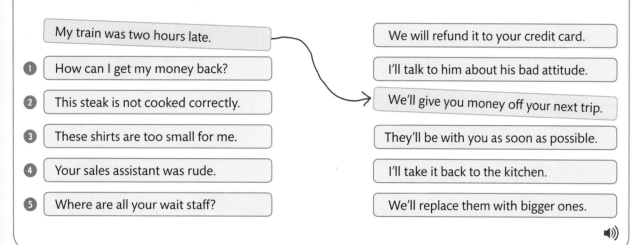

My train was two hours late.

1 How can I get my money back?

2 This steak is not cooked correctly.

3 These shirts are too small for me.

4 Your sales assistant was rude.

5 Where are all your wait staff?

We will refund it to your credit card.

I'll talk to him about his bad attitude.

We'll give you money off your next trip.

They'll be with you as soon as possible.

I'll take it back to the kitchen.

We'll replace them with bigger ones.

34.6 PUNTO CLAVE REALIZAR PREDICCIONES

También puedes utilizar "will" para realizar predicciones de futuro.

Will my taxi arrive in the next five minutes?

Yes, it will. I'm on my way now.

Utiliza "I'm afraid" para pedir disculpas.

Forma abreviada de "will not".

No, I'm afraid it won't. The traffic is terrible.

34.7 COMPLETA LOS ESPACIOS CON LAS PALABRAS DEL RECUADRO

The company will __*offer*__ you a discount.

1. I'm afraid your order _____ arrive today.

2. We'll _____ your appointment now.

3. I'll _____ to my manager for you.

4. We'll _____ you a replacement tomorrow.

5. I _____ contact the courier about the delay.

6. I'll _____ the chef to bring you a new meal.

7. Your delivery will _____ later today.

talk	arrive	won't
~~offer~~		ask
will	change	send

34.8 ESCUCHA EL AUDIO Y MARCA SI CADA SITUACIÓN SE PRODUCIRÁ HOY O NO

Sí ☐   No ✓

1. Sí ☐   No ☐

2. Sí ☐   No ☐

3. Sí ☐   No ☐

4. Sí ☐   No ☐

5. Sí ☐   No ☐

34.9 COMPLETA LOS ESPACIOS CON LAS PALABRAS DEL RECUADRO Y CONTESTA AL AUDIO EN VOZ ALTA

This milk was sour when I bought it.

I'm very ___sorry___ about that. Would you like a ___refund___ ?

afraid

~~refund~~

offer

apologize

won't

discount

replace

~~sorry~~

1. This part is broken and it doesn't work.

   I do _____ . We'll _____ the broken part for you.

2. Can you send the replacement part today?

   I'm _____ it _____ arrive until Wednesday.

3. My train was 90 minutes late!

   We'll _____ you a _____ on your next trip.

---

34 ✓ CHECKLIST

🔧 El futuro con "will" ☐   **Aa** Quejas y disculpas ☐   🧩 Tratar las quejas ☐

🔄 REPASA LO QUE HAS APRENDIDO EN LAS UNIDADES 29-34

NUEVO LENGUAJE	FRASE DE EJEMPLO	☑	UNIDAD
HABLAR SOBRE NORMAS PEDIR COSAS EDUCADAMENTE	You can't **wear jeans to work.** Could you send **your email again, please?**	☐	29.1, 29.5
DESCRIBIR PROBLEMAS DEL TRABAJO	**The printer** wasn't working **today.**	☐	31.1
DISCULPARSE Y DAR EXPLICACIONES	I'm really sorry. I was writing **an email when** I spilled **water on my keyboard.**	☐	32.1, 32.5
HABLAR DE FECHAS DE ENTREGA	I have finished **packing the boxes.**	☐	33.1
TRATAR LAS QUEJAS	We will **investigate this problem, and** we'll **offer you a discount.**	☐	34.1

35.1 TRANSPORTE

car

taxi

bus

coach

plane

train

tram

metro

bicycle

motorcycle (US) /
motorbike (UK)

helicopter

airport

bus stop

train station

taxi stand (US) /
taxi rank (UK)

35.2 VIAJES

one-way ticket

terminal

check-in

boarding pass

first class

round trip ticket (US) / return ticket (UK)

domestic flight

international flight

connecting flight

on time

late

delay

luggage

security

passport

passport control

departure gate

board a plane

seat reservation

aisle seat

window seat

business class

economy

transfer

hotel

36 Planear un viaje

Cuando haces planes de viaje es útil poder hablar sobre los posibles resultados de nuestras acciones o elecciones.

🔧 **Lenguaje** Zero conditional y first conditional
Aa Vocabulario Viajes
🧩 **Habilidad** Hablar sobre acciones y resultados

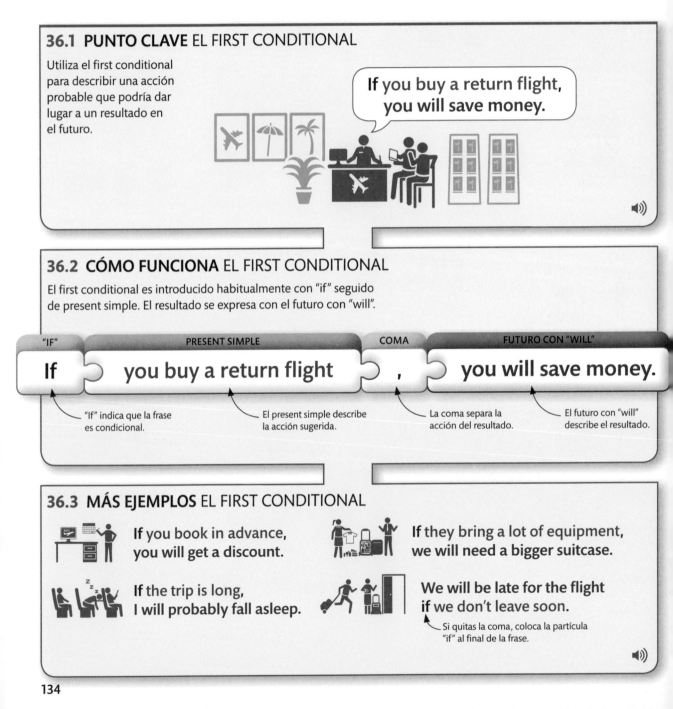

36.1 PUNTO CLAVE EL FIRST CONDITIONAL

Utiliza el first conditional para describir una acción probable que podría dar lugar a un resultado en el futuro.

If you buy a return flight, you will save money.

36.2 CÓMO FUNCIONA EL FIRST CONDITIONAL

El first conditional es introducido habitualmente con "if" seguido de present simple. El resultado se expresa con el futuro con "will".

"IF"	PRESENT SIMPLE	COMA	FUTURO CON "WILL"
If	**you buy a return flight**	**,**	**you will save money.**

"If" indica que la frase es condicional.

El present simple describe la acción sugerida.

La coma separa la acción del resultado.

El futuro con "will" describe el resultado.

36.3 MÁS EJEMPLOS EL FIRST CONDITIONAL

If you book in advance, you will get a discount.

If they bring a lot of equipment, we will need a bigger suitcase.

If the trip is long, I will probably fall asleep.

We will be late for the flight if we don't leave soon.

Si quitas la coma, coloca la partícula "if" al final de la frase.

36.4 CONECTA EL INICIO Y EL FINAL DE CADA FRASE

Will you buy a ticket

① If you go to China for business,

② If I go to China on business,

③ If we win the contract,

④ Will you arrange a taxi

⑤ We won't get a discount

⑥ If you have a lot of luggage,

if we land late at the airport?

you will need a taxi.

if I buy one, too?

will you visit the Great Wall?

if we don't book now.

I won't have time to go sightseeing.

we will go out to celebrate.

🔊

36.5 ESCUCHA EL AUDIO Y RESPONDE A LAS PREGUNTAS

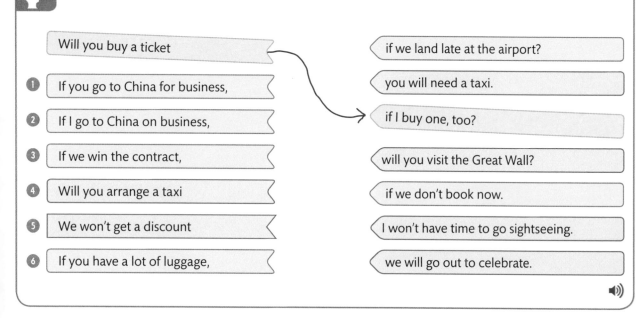

Dan llama a su colega Simon para planear vuelos para asistir a un congreso. Hablan de opciones de viaje.

The person making the booking is...
Dan. ☐
Dan's assistant. ☑
Simon. ☐

① They will travel to the airport...
by train. ☐
by taxi. ☐
by bus. ☐

② Their plane tickets will be...
Economy. ☐
Business Class. ☐
First Class. ☐

③ They will be met in Hanoi by...
a taxi driver. ☐
a former colleague. ☐
nobody. ☐

④ They will travel directly...
to the conference venue. ☐
to the hotel. ☐
to do some sightseeing. ☐

⑤ Dan asks Simon to send him...
the flight tickets. ☐
his passport details. ☐
his presentation. ☐

36.6 PUNTO CLAVE EL ZERO CONDITIONAL

Utiliza el zero conditional para hablar de cosas que suelen ser verdaderas o para describir el resultado directo de una acción.

If your bag weighs too much, we charge a fee.

36.7 CÓMO FUNCIONA EL ZERO CONDITIONAL

El zero conditional utiliza "if" o "when" con el present simple, seguido de otro present simple en la oración principal.

"IF / WHEN"	PRESENT SIMPLE	COMA	PRESENT SIMPLE
If	your bag weighs too much	,	we charge a fee.

También se puede utilizar "when" en algunas frases.

El present simple describe la acción.

La coma separa la acción del resultado.

El resultado va en present simple.

36.8 MÁS EJEMPLOS EL ZERO CONDITIONAL

A veces se puede utilizar "when" en lugar de "if".

If you book online, flights are often cheaper.

When I pack in a hurry, I sometimes forget my passport.

The airport has a shower if you need to freshen up.

Clients get angry if we don't pay their expenses.

The airline offers transfers if you have a connecting flight.

If I don't carry a map, I always get lost in a new city.

36.9 VUELVE A ESCRIBIR LAS FRASES PONIENDO LAS PALABRAS EN SU ORDEN CORRECTO

fly · Business · If · there · Class, · you · a · lounge. · is

If you fly Business Class, there is a lounge.

1 you · transfer, · you. · book · a · When · driver · a · meets

_____

2 get · the · off · Passengers · if · plane · annoyed · takes · late.

_____

3 You · a · meal · vegetarian. · special · can · if · you're · order

_____

36.10 TACHA LAS PALABRAS INCORRECTAS DE CADA FRASE Y DI LAS FRASES EN VOZ ALTA

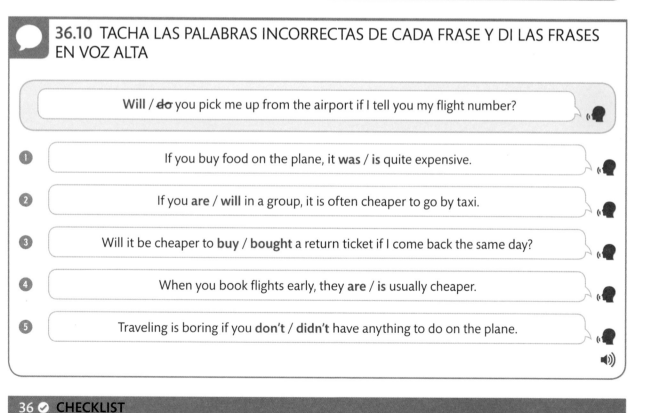

Will / ~~do~~ you pick me up from the airport if I tell you my flight number?

1 If you buy food on the plane, it **was** / **is** quite expensive.

2 If you **are** / **will** in a group, it is often cheaper to go by taxi.

3 Will it be cheaper to **buy** / **bought** a return ticket if I come back the same day?

4 When you book flights early, they **are** / **is** usually cheaper.

5 Traveling is boring if you **don't** / **didn't** have anything to do on the plane.

37 Preguntar direcciones

Cuando viajes a congresos y reuniones es posible que tengas que preguntar direcciones. En tal caso es esencial saber cómo ser educado y claro.

⚙ **Lenguaje** Imperativos, preposiciones de lugar
Aa Vocabulario Direcciones
🧩 **Habilidad** Preguntar y dar direcciones

37.1 PUNTO CLAVE PREGUNTAR Y DAR DIRECCIONES

Cuando preguntes direcciones, sé educado y escucha la respuesta con atención. A veces se utilizan imperativos para dar direcciones.

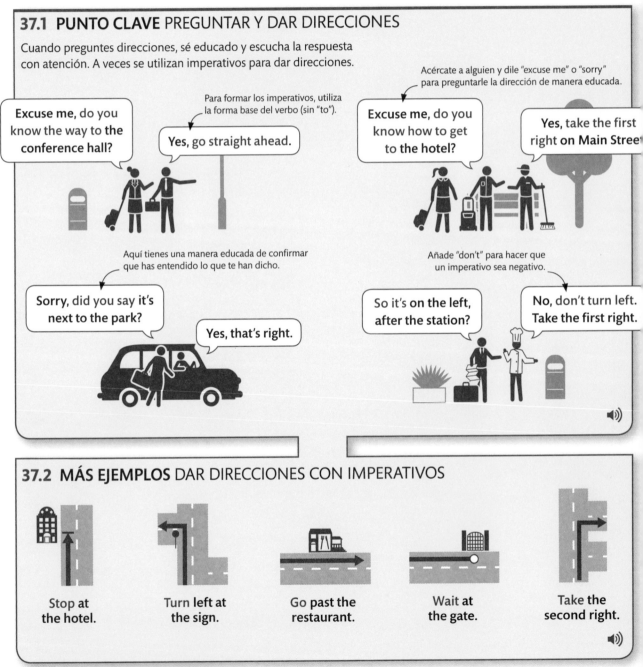

Para formar los imperativos, utiliza la forma base del verbo (sin "to").

Excuse me, do you know the way to **the conference hall**?

Yes, go straight ahead.

Acércate a alguien y dile "excuse me" o "sorry" para preguntarle la dirección de manera educada.

Excuse me, do you know how to get to **the hotel**?

Yes, take the first right **on Main Street**

Aquí tienes una manera educada de confirmar que has entendido lo que te han dicho.

Sorry, did you say **it's next to the park**?

Yes, that's right.

Añade "don't" para hacer que un imperativo sea negativo.

So it's **on the left, after the station**?

No, don't turn left. Take the first right.

37.2 MÁS EJEMPLOS DAR DIRECCIONES CON IMPERATIVOS

Stop at the hotel.

Turn **left** at the sign.

Go **past** the restaurant.

Wait at the gate.

Take the second right.

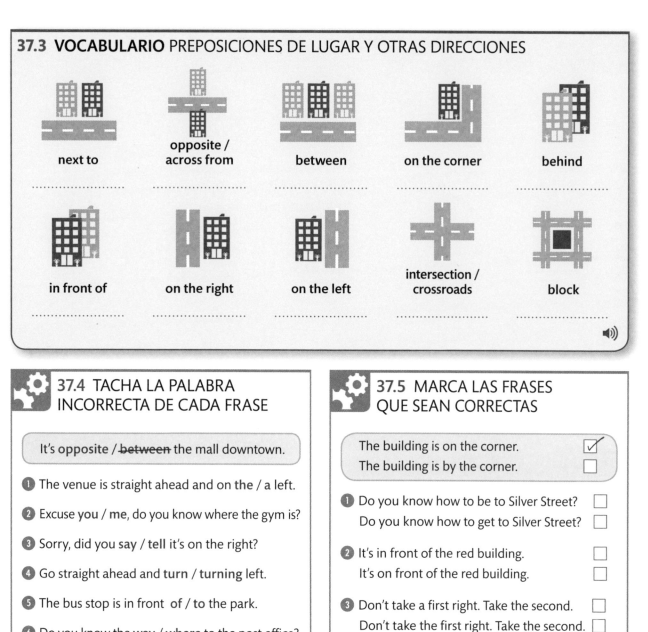

37.3 VOCABULARIO PREPOSICIONES DE LUGAR Y OTRAS DIRECCIONES

next to

opposite / across from

between

on the corner

behind

in front of

on the right

on the left

intersection / crossroads

block

37.4 TACHA LA PALABRA INCORRECTA DE CADA FRASE

It's **opposite** / ~~between~~ the mall downtown.

1 The venue is straight ahead and on **the** / **a** left.

2 Excuse **you** / **me**, do you know where the gym is?

3 Sorry, did you **say** / **tell** it's on the right?

4 Go straight ahead and **turn** / **turning** left.

5 The bus stop is in front **of** / **to** the park.

6 Do you know the **way** / **where** to the post office?

7 The hotel is 50 feet ahead **in** / **on** the right.

8 Do you **think** / **know** the way to the hotel?

9 **Do** / **Go** straight ahead and you'll see the sign.

10 The bus stop is directly opposite **the** / **of** bank.

11 Turn right at the **intersection** / **block**.

37.5 MARCA LAS FRASES QUE SEAN CORRECTAS

The building is on the corner. ☑
The building is by the corner. ☐

1 Do you know how to be to Silver Street? ☐
Do you know how to get to Silver Street? ☐

2 It's in front of the red building. ☐
It's on front of the red building. ☐

3 Don't take a first right. Take the second. ☐
Don't take the first right. Take the second. ☐

4 I'll meet you across from the hotel. ☐
I'll meet you across the hotel. ☐

5 Go straight ahead and turn left at the lights. ☐
Go straight ahead and turn left on lights. ☐

6 The bank is next to the station. ☐
The bank is the next to station. ☐

37.6 VUELVE A ESCRIBIR LAS FRASES PONIENDO LAS PALABRAS EN SU ORDEN CORRECTO

| way | Do | bank? | to | the | know | you | the |

Do you know the way to the bank?

1 | you | Sorry, | opposite | café? | did | say | it's | the |

_____

2 | ahead | right | and | Go | turn | the | straight | at | intersection. |

_____

3 | to | Do | know | to | you | get | the | how | venue? |

_____

4 | past | and | post | Go | on | it's | the | left. | office | the |

_____

37.7 ESCUCHA EL AUDIO Y MARCA LAS DIRECCIONES QUE OIGAS

37.8 MIRA EL MAPA, COMPLETA LOS ESPACIOS Y RESPONDE AL AUDIO EN VOZ ALTA

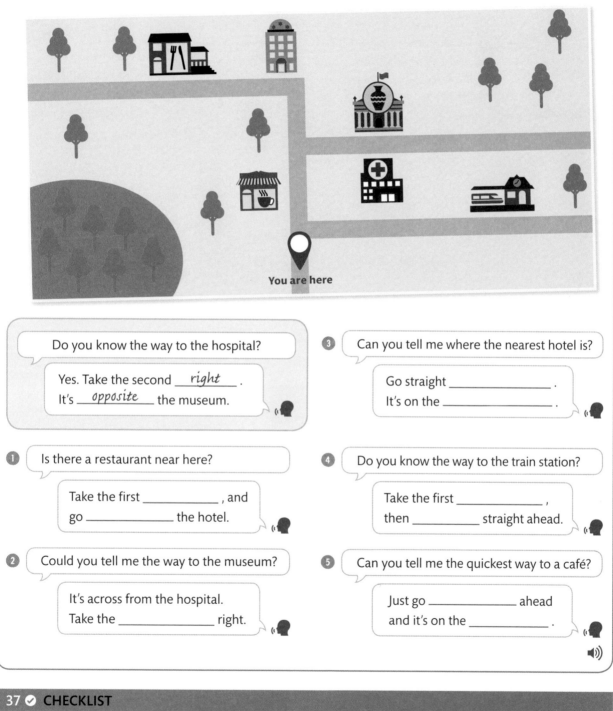

You are here

Do you know the way to the hospital?

Yes. Take the second ___right___ .
It's ___opposite___ the museum.

❸ Can you tell me where the nearest hotel is?

Go straight _____ .
It's on the _____ .

❶ Is there a restaurant near here?

Take the first _____ , and
go _____ the hotel.

❹ Do you know the way to the train station?

Take the first _____ ,
then _____ straight ahead.

❷ Could you tell me the way to the museum?

It's across from the hospital.
Take the _____ right.

❺ Can you tell me the quickest way to a café?

Just go _____ ahead
and it's on the _____ .

37 ✔ CHECKLIST

⚙ Imperativos, preposiciones de lugar ☐   **Aa** Direcciones ☐   🧩 Preguntar y dar direcciones ☐

38 Describir la estancia

Puedes describir acontecimientos con frases activas o pasivas. La frase pasiva sirve para destacar la acción en lugar de lo que la ha causado.

Lenguaje La voz pasiva
Aa Vocabulario Hoteles y alojamiento
Habilidad Uso de la voz pasiva

38.1 PUNTO CLAVE LA VOZ PASIVA

En frases pasivas, la persona o cosa que hace la acción no se conoce, no es importante o es obvia.

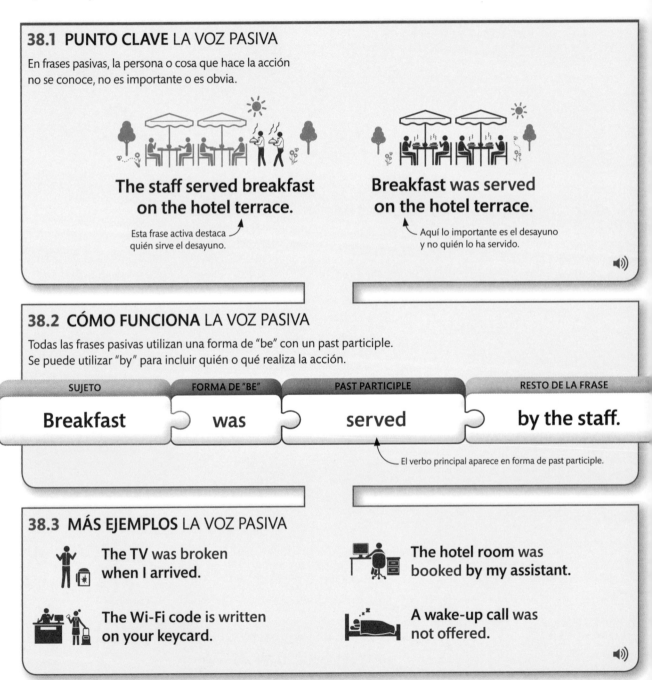

The staff served breakfast on the hotel terrace.

Esta frase activa destaca quién sirve el desayuno.

Breakfast was served on the hotel terrace.

Aquí lo importante es el desayuno y no quién lo ha servido.

38.2 CÓMO FUNCIONA LA VOZ PASIVA

Todas las frases pasivas utilizan una forma de "be" con un past participle.
Se puede utilizar "by" para incluir quién o qué realiza la acción.

SUJETO	FORMA DE "BE"	PAST PARTICIPLE	RESTO DE LA FRASE
Breakfast	**was**	**served**	**by the staff.**

El verbo principal aparece en forma de past participle.

38.3 MÁS EJEMPLOS LA VOZ PASIVA

The TV was broken when I arrived.

The hotel room was booked by my assistant.

The Wi-Fi code is written on your keycard.

A wake-up call was not offered.

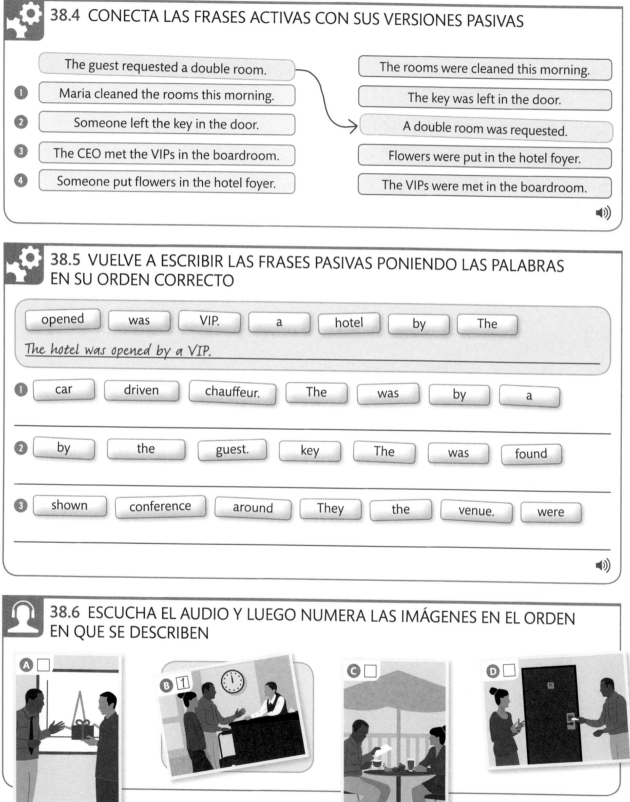

38.4 CONECTA LAS FRASES ACTIVAS CON SUS VERSIONES PASIVAS

The guest requested a double room.

The rooms were cleaned this morning.

❶ Maria cleaned the rooms this morning.

The key was left in the door.

❷ Someone left the key in the door.

A double room was requested.

❸ The CEO met the VIPs in the boardroom.

Flowers were put in the hotel foyer.

❹ Someone put flowers in the hotel foyer.

The VIPs were met in the boardroom.

38.5 VUELVE A ESCRIBIR LAS FRASES PASIVAS PONIENDO LAS PALABRAS EN SU ORDEN CORRECTO

opened | was | VIP. | a | hotel | by | The

The hotel was opened by a VIP.

❶ car | driven | chauffeur. | The | was | by | a

❷ by | the | guest. | key | The | was | found

❸ shown | conference | around | They | the | venue. | were

38.6 ESCUCHA EL AUDIO Y LUEGO NUMERA LAS IMÁGENES EN EL ORDEN EN QUE SE DESCRIBEN

Ⓐ ☐

Ⓑ 1

Ⓒ ☐

Ⓓ ☐

38.7 LEE LAS OPINIONES Y RESPONDE A LAS PREGUNTAS

Hotel Gwesty is not near the airport
True ☐ **False** ☐ **Not given** ☑

① Hugh Jenkins didn't like the hotel staff.
True ☐ **False** ☐ **Not given** ☐

② Hugh Jenkins and his clients ate at the hotel.
True ☐ **False** ☐ **Not given** ☐

③ Hugh Jenkins will go back to Hotel Gwesty.
True ☐ **False** ☐ **Not given** ☐

④ Sue Vardy was impressed by Hotel Plaza.
True ☐ **False** ☐ **Not given** ☐

⑤ The Wi-Fi worked well at Hotel Plaza.
True ☐ **False** ☐ **Not given** ☐

⑥ The furniture at Hotel Plaza was bad.
True ☐ **False** ☐ **Not given** ☐

Which hotel?

HOME | REVIEWS | ABOUT | CONTACT

Hotel Gwesty: Review by Hugh Jenkins, CEO TotalData
The hotel is very conveniently located, less than two miles from the airport. From the moment we checked in, I was impressed by the staff's professional manner. They immediately took us to the meeting room to look around before our clients arrived. The meeting room was comfortable and had all the equipment we needed for presentations and discussions. Throughout the day, we had refreshments provided in the room and an excellent buffet lunch. Our clients were happy and we will be returning here for future meetings.

Hotel Plaza: Review by Sue Vardy, Director Centria32
The best part of our stay here was checking out! We booked this hotel to launch our new product, and it was a disaster. Our conference room was very dark and there was no Wi-Fi or internet connection at all. We could not turn the projector on, the furniture was falling apart, and worst of all, they forgot to pick up our client from the airport! A horrible place!

Aa 38.8 CONECTA LAS DEFINICIONES CON SUS PHRASAL VERBS

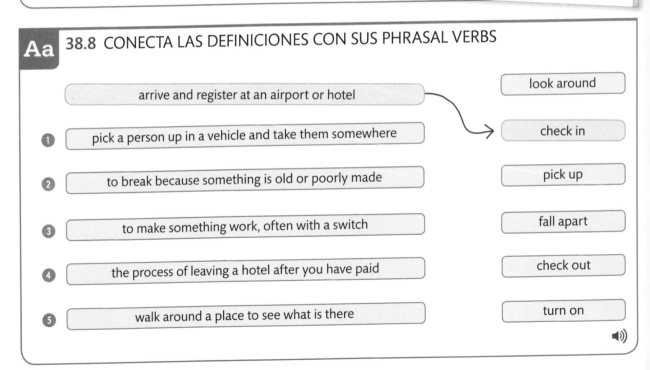

arrive and register at an airport or hotel — check in

look around

① pick a person up in a vehicle and take them somewhere

pick up

② to break because something is old or poorly made

fall apart

③ to make something work, often with a switch

check out

④ the process of leaving a hotel after you have paid

turn on

⑤ walk around a place to see what is there

144

38.9 ESCUCHA EL AUDIO Y LUEGO NUMERA LAS FRASES EN EL ORDEN EN QUE APARECEN

Una secretaria llama a un hotel para reservar una habitación para su jefe.

A How many rooms would you like? ☐

B Could I reserve a parking space for those days? ☐

C Would you like to book breakfast now? ☐

D I'd like to make a reservation, please. ☑1

E Can I have the name, please? ☐

38.10 ESCRIBE LOS VERBOS EN VOZ PASIVA Y CONTESTA AL AUDIO EN VOZ ALTA

What did you think of the meals during your stay?

The hotel food _____was prepared_____ (prepare) very badly.

1 Where did you have breakfast in the morning?

Breakfast _____ (serve) in the main restaurant.

2 Were the rooms clean and tidy?

The rooms _____ (clean) every day.

3 Who reserved your rooms?

The reservation _____ (make) by my assistant.

4 Were the rooms nice?

Yes. Very. They _____ (decorate) beautifully.

38 ✓ CHECKLIST

⚙ La voz pasiva ☐   **Aa** Hoteles y alojamiento ☐   🧩 Uso de la voz pasiva ☐

145

39.1 COMER FUERA

chef	waiter	waitress	make a reservation / booking	menu
appetizer (US) / starter (UK)	entrée (US) / main course (UK)	dessert	check (US) / bill (UK)	receipt
café	restaurant	bar	tip	food allergy / intolerance
breakfast	lunch	dinner	vegan	vegetarian
broil (US) / grill (UK)	bake	roast	boil	fry

food

drinks

fork

knife

spoon

napkin

cup

glass

tea

coffee

water

milk

cream

butter

cheese

meat

fish

seafood

fruit

vegetables

potatoes

rice

pasta

bread

sandwich

soup

salad

cake

chocolate

sugar

40 Congresos y visitantes

Es importante saber interactuar de manera educada en inglés, ya seas tú quien reciba visitas o el que visite otra empresa.

⚙ **Lenguaje** "A", "some", "any"
Aa Vocabulario Hospitalidad
🧩 **Habilidad** Dar la bienvenida a los visitantes

40.1 PUNTO CLAVE DAR LA BIENVENIDA A LOS VISITANTES

Puedes utilizar diversas expresiones para dar la bienvenida a tu empresa a los visitantes.

Welcome **to Hanoi.**

Have you been **to Hanoi before?**

You must be **Mr. Burford.**

Yes, we spoke on the phone.

It's great to meet in person.

Did you have a good flight?

Can I get you anything?

40.2 MARCA LAS FRASES QUE SEAN CORRECTAS

You are Mr. Draper. ☐
You must be Mr. Draper. ☑

1. Yes, we speak on the phone. ☐
   Yes, we spoke on the phone. ☐

2. Have you been to Mexico City before? ☐
   Have you been Mexico City before? ☐

3. I'll let Mrs. Singh know that you're here. ☐
   I'll tell Mrs. Singh know you're here. ☐

4. Would you like some tea or coffee? ☐
   Would you have some tea or coffee? ☐

5. Did you have a good flight? ☐
   Did you have a well flight? ☐

6. I've been looking forward to this visit. ☐
   I've been look forward to this visit. ☐

7. It's great to meet your person. ☐
   It's great to meet you in person. ☐

8. Did you have any trouble getting here? ☐
   Do you have any trouble getting here? ☐

9. Can I get you anything? ☐
   Can I have you anything? ☐

🔊

40.3 PUNTO CLAVE "A", "SOME", "ANY"

En inglés, los sustantivos pueden ser contables (que se pueden contar con facilidad) o incontables (que normalmente no se cuentan de manera individual). Utiliza "a" o "an" con sustantivos contables en singular. Utiliza "some" con sustantivos contables en plural y sustantivos incontables. Utiliza "any" en preguntas y frases en negativo.

Los sustantivos incontables pueden convertirse en contables si se colocan en recipientes.

Would you like a cup of coffee?

Do you have any tea?

Utiliza "any" en preguntas y frases en negativo.

I'm afraid not. Can I get you some water?

Utiliza siempre "some" con sustantivos incontables; nunca "a", "an" o una cifra.

40.4 VUELVE A ESCRIBIR CORRIGIENDO LOS ERRORES

Do you have some luggage?
Do you have any luggage?

① Would you like some cup of tea?

_____

② Do you take a sugar?

_____

③ Did you have any good trip?

_____

④ Could I have any water, please?

_____

⑤ Here are any details about the hotel.

_____

40.5 CONECTA EL INICIO Y EL FINAL DE CADA FRASE

I like to drink   a good flight?

① I didn't bring   any help?

② Did you have   coffee at breakfast.

③ Do you need   any luggage.

④ Would you like to   anything to drink?

⑤ There will be   meet the team?

⑥ Can I get you   seat and wait here.

⑦ Please take a   something to eat.

40.6 ESCUCHA EL AUDIO Y RESPONDE A LAS PREGUNTAS

Dos asistentes hablan sobre productos en un congreso de marketing en Hanoi.

Where has Mr. Park traveled from?

London ☐
Moscow ☑
Seoul ☐

1. When was the conference's opening reception?
   The morning before ☐
   The evening before ☐
   That morning ☐

2. What does Mr. Park want to see at the conference?
   A product launch ☐
   Ms. Lyng's presentation ☐
   The closing session ☐

3. What is Ms. Lyng giving a presentation about?
   Networking at conferences ☐
   Social media and marketing ☐
   A new product launch ☐

40.7 COMPLETA LOS ESPACIOS CON LAS PALABRAS DEL RECUADRO

Collect your lanyard from ___*reception*___ .

1. The _____ speech will start at 10am.

2. The main _____ used a lot of slides.

3. The main sponsor will _____ a new product.

4. Every attendee gets a _____ and a name tag.

5. In a workshop the _____ get involved.

6. There are lots of _____ opportunities.

~~reception~~   keynote

launch   lanyard   networking

delegates   presenter

🔊

40.8 TACHA LAS PALABRAS INCORRECTAS DE CADA FRASE

There is a / ~~any~~ / ~~some~~ workshop at midday.

1. They have a / **some** / **any** free food and drinks.

2. Do you have a / **some** / **any** lanyard already?

3. I have a / **some** / **any** business cards to give people.

4. I'd like to see a / **some** / **any** interesting talks.

5. Are you going to a / **some** / **any** talks today?

6. Do you have a / **some** / **any** business card?

7. Are you staying in a / **some** / **any** hotel?

8. They don't have a / **some** / **any** drinks.

9. I'm giving a / **some** / **any** presentation today.

🔊

1 Use conferences to network.
Dress professionally, act politely,
and tell everyone all about yourself. ☐

2 Use conferences to network. Dress
professionally, act politely, and find out
about the person you are talking to. ☐

3 Use conferences to network.
Dress professionally, act politely,
and tell your clients about yourself. ☐

Conference tips:

Going to a conference is one of the best ways to network and make new business connections.

● It is really important to make a good first impression. Remember, you might be talking to a future client or employer.

● Dress professionally and always behave politely. Most importantly, show an interest in the person you are talking to. Find out their name; ask them what they do and ask about their family. This, in turn, will make them more likely to ask about you.

40.10 COMPLETA LOS ESPACIOS CON LAS PALABRAS DEL RECUADRO Y CONTESTA AL AUDIO EN VOZ ALTA

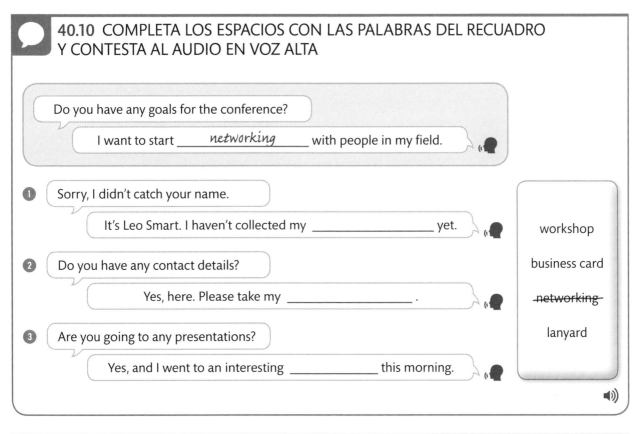

Do you have any goals for the conference?

I want to start ___*networking*___ with people in my field.

1 Sorry, I didn't catch your name.

It's Leo Smart. I haven't collected my _____ yet.

2 Do you have any contact details?

Yes, here. Please take my _____ .

3 Are you going to any presentations?

Yes, and I went to an interesting _____ this morning.

workshop

business card

~~networking~~

lanyard

---

40 ✓ CHECKLIST

⚙ "A", "some", "any" ☐   **Aa** Hospitalidad ☐   Dar la bienvenida a los visitantes ☐

Comidas y hospitalidad

Es importante conocer las costumbres locales en cuanto a comidas y ocio. En las comidas de negocios y congresos, sigue estas costumbres y utiliza un lenguaje adecuado.

⚙ **Lenguaje** "Much / many", "too / enough"
Aa Vocabulario Restaurantes
🧩 **Habilidad** Ofrecer y aceptar hospitalidad

41.1 PUNTO CLAVE COMER EN RESTAURANTES

Cuando comas u ofrezcas tu hospitalidad a los clientes, es importante que te muestres abierto y educado como huésped o anfitrión.

I'd like a table for two, please.

Do you have a reservation?

Yes. My name is Sarah Key.

Do you have any tables free for lunch?

How many people are in your party?

I'm afraid there is a 20-minute wait.

Are you ready to order?

"Could" es más educado que "can".

Could I have the fish?

Do you have any allergies?

Yes. I'm allergic to peanuts.

I'll have the soup, please.

Añade "please" para que suene más educado.

How is everything?

There were lots of bones in my fish.

Could we have the check, please?

En inglés británico se dice "bill".

I don't have enough cash. Can I pay by card?

There is too much cream in my soup.

41.2 VUELVE A ESCRIBIR LAS FRASES PONIENDO LAS PALABRAS EN SU ORDEN CORRECTO

| are | How | there? | many | options | vegetarian |

How many vegetarian options are there?

❶ | like | Would | see | you | to | dessert | menu? | the |

_____

❷ | sparkling | have | water, | Could | some | please? | we |

_____

❸ | have | receipt | this, | I | a | Could | please? | for |

_____

🔊

41.3 COMPLETA LOS ESPACIOS CON LAS PALABRAS DEL RECUADRO Y CONTESTA AL AUDIO EN VOZ ALTA

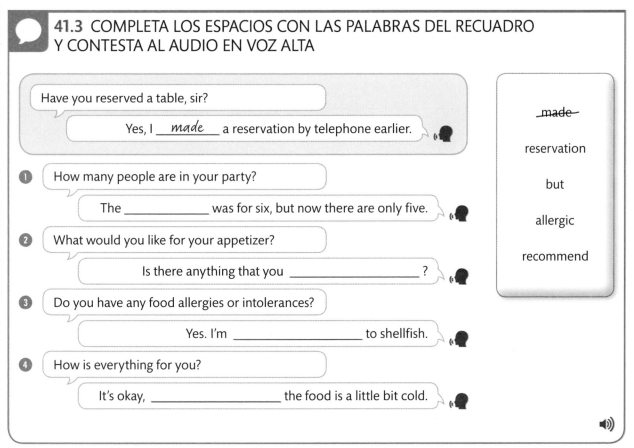

Have you reserved a table, sir?

Yes, I ___made___ a reservation by telephone earlier.

made

reservation

but

allergic

recommend

❶ How many people are in your party?

The _____ was for six, but now there are only five.

❷ What would you like for your appetizer?

Is there anything that you _____?

❸ Do you have any food allergies or intolerances?

Yes. I'm _____ to shellfish.

❹ How is everything for you?

It's okay, _____ the food is a little bit cold.

🔊

41.4 PUNTO CLAVE HABLAR DE CANTIDADES

Utiliza "much", "many" y "enough" para hablar de cantidades. Estas palabras también sirven para mostrar nuestros sentimientos sobre dichas cantidades. Por ejemplo, "too much" es negativo, mientras que "enough" es positivo.

How much time do we have?

Utiliza "much" para formular preguntas sobre cantidades de sustantivos incontables.

How many sides have you ordered?

Utiliza "many" para formular preguntas sobre cantidades de sustantivos contables.

There is too much chili in this!

Utiliza "too much / many" para hablar de cantidades demasiado grandes.

There aren't enough waiters.

Utiliza "enough" y "not enough" para hablar sobre sustantivos contables e incontables.

🔊

41.5 MARCA LAS FRASES QUE SEAN CORRECTAS

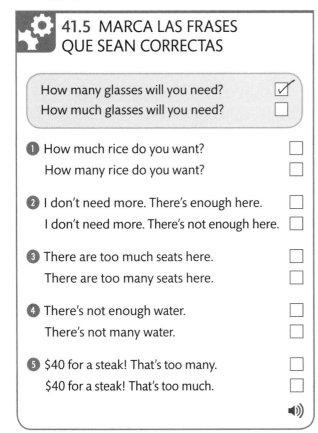

How many glasses will you need? ☑
How much glasses will you need? ☐

1 How much rice do you want? ☐
  How many rice do you want? ☐

2 I don't need more. There's enough here. ☐
  I don't need more. There's not enough here. ☐

3 There are too much seats here. ☐
  There are too many seats here. ☐

4 There's not enough water. ☐
  There's not many water. ☐

5 $40 for a steak! That's too many. ☐
  $40 for a steak! That's too much. ☐

🔊

41.6 COMPLETA LOS ESPACIOS CON LAS PALABRAS DEL RECUADRO

Do you have ____enough____ bread?

1 I've eaten _____ many chocolates.

2 How _____ glasses do we need?

3 There's too _____ sauce on this.

4 How _____ should we tip here?

much	much	many
	too	~~enough~~

🔊

154

41.7 LEE EL ARTÍCULO Y RESPONDE A LAS PREGUNTAS

You should ask all clients to business lunches.
True ☐ False ☐ Not given ☑

1 The author recommends reading about local customs.
True ☐ False ☐ Not given ☐

2 Guests should be given a selection of places to eat.
True ☐ False ☐ Not given ☐

3 You should go outside to answer your phone.
True ☐ False ☐ Not given ☐

4 Guests shouldn't order the most expensive meal.
True ☐ False ☐ Not given ☐

5 The author suggests you shouldn't eat too much.
True ☐ False ☐ Not given ☐

MEALS AND DEALS

Business lunches can be a great way to get to know your clients, but be careful about who you invite to lunch. CEOs, for example, have busy schedules, and it may be better to invite them for coffee. If you do invite someone to lunch, you should read about the local dining etiquette. You could also present your guest with several dining options before making a restaurant reservation. Once you arrive at the restaurant, turn off your phone. Your guests should have all your attention. If you are a guest yourself, arrive on time, and make sure that you do not order the most expensive thing on the menu. Last, as host or guest, try to enjoy yourself.

---

41 ✔ CHECKLIST

⚙ "Much / many", "too / enough" ☐   **Aa** Restaurantes ☐   🧩 Ofrecer y aceptar hospitalidad ☐

♻ REPASA LO QUE HAS APRENDIDO EN LAS UNIDADES 35–41

NUEVO LENGUAJE	FRASE DE EJEMPLO	☑	UNIDAD
EL FIRST CONDITIONAL	If you buy a return flight, you will save money.	☐	36.1
EL ZERO CONDITIONAL	If your bag weighs too much, we charge a fee.	☐	36.6
DAR DIRECCIONES CON IMPERATIVOS	Go straight ahead.	☐	37.1
LA VOZ PASIVA	Breakfast was served on the hotel terrace.	☐	38.1
"A", "SOME", "ANY"	Do you have any tea? Would you like a cup of coffee or some water?	☐	40.3
"MUCH / MANY", "TOO / ENOUGH"	How much time do we have? There are not enough waiters.	☐	41.4

42 Llamadas telefónicas informales

En la mayoría de empresas puedes utilizar lenguaje educado informal al hablar por teléfono con tus colegas. El inglés tiene para ello verbos de dos o tres partes.

Lenguaje Lenguaje telefónico
Aa Vocabulario Números de teléfono y etiqueta
Habilidad Llamar a los compañeros de trabajo

42.1 PUNTO CLAVE HACER LLAMADAS TELEFÓNICAS INFORMALES

Las llamadas telefónicas entre compañeros de trabajo incluyen diversas expresiones adecuadas para abrir y cerrar la llamada e intercambiar información.

Di tu nombre seguido de "speaking" al descolgar el teléfono.

Hello. Miguel speaking.

Hi, Miguel. It's Tana from finance.

Utiliza "Could" en lugar de "Can" para que suene más educado.

Hi. Can I speak to Jan, please?

Significa "I'm Jan".

Speaking. How can I help you?

También puedes identificarte diciendo el nombre del departamento.

Hello, IT department.

Hi. I'm calling because my computer screen has frozen.

Educado, pero mantiene un cierto tono de informalidad.

Can I ask who's calling, please?

Alternativa educada a "yes".

Of course. It's Oliver Timms.

Utilízalo para ofrecer más ayuda o consejos.

Is there anything else I can help you with?

Utilízalo para declinar de manera educada más ayuda y acabar la llamada.

No, that's all, thanks. Goodbye.

Manera informal de terminar una llamada educadamente.

I'd better be going.

También puedes acabar con "Speak to you soon".

OK. Talk to you soon.

42.2 COMPLETA LOS ESPACIOS CON LAS PALABRAS DEL RECUADRO

Can I _____speak_____ to Jan, please?

1 Hi, Karl. It's Katie _____ HR.

2 Hi. I'm _____ about the Wi-Fi.

3 My client is here. I'd _____ be going.

4 Can I ask _____ calling, please?

5 Is there _____ else I can do for you?

6 Hello. Olga _____ .

7 No, thanks. That's _____ . Bye.

better	from	who's
	anything	all
~~speak~~	calling	speaking

🔊

42.3 ESCUCHA EL AUDIO Y LUEGO NUMERA LAS FRASES EN EL ORDEN QUE APARECEN

Danny llama al departamento de informática para explicar qué le pasa a su ordenador.

A Hi, Danny. How can I help? ☐

B Thanks again. Talk to you soon. ☐

C I know it's down. I've just reset the router. ☐

D Hi, Sandra. It's Danny from sales. [1]

E Is there anything else I can help you with? ☐

F I'm calling about the internet. ☐

42.4 CORRIGE LOS ERRORES Y DI LAS FRASES EN VOZ ALTA

I'd better be go. Goodbye.

I'd better be going. Goodbye. 🗣

1 Hi. Can I speak Jacob, please?

_____ 🗣

2 Hello, Sophie. Here Ahmed from sales.

_____ 🗣

3 Could I say who's calling, please?

_____ 🗣

4 Hi. Adam speaks.

_____ 🗣

5 It's Sandy off IT.

_____ 🗣

6 Hi. I call because the elevator is stuck.

_____ 🗣

7 Bye then. Speaking to you soon.

_____ 🗣

8 Can I ask who calls, please?

_____ 🗣

🔊

42.5 PUNTO CLAVE DECIR TU NÚMERO DE TELÉFONO

Puedes decir tu número de teléfono con diversas expresiones habituales.

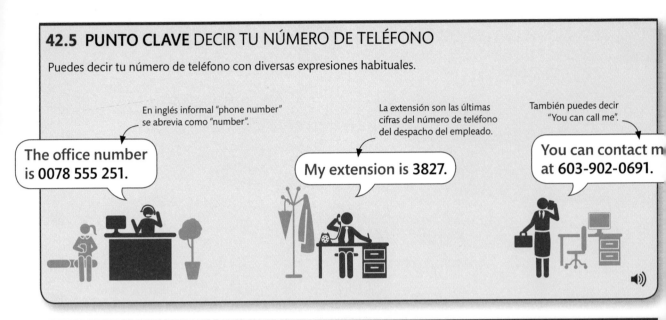

En inglés informal "phone number" se abrevia como "number".

The office number is 0078 555 251.

La extensión son las últimas cifras del número de teléfono del despacho del empleado.

My extension is 3827.

También puedes decir "You can call me".

You can contact m at 603-902-0691.

42.6 PRONUNCIACIÓN NÚMEROS

En inglés de Estados Unidos, el número 0 se pronuncia "zero" y los números iguales seguidos se dicen uno por uno.
En inglés británico existen diversas pronunciaciones diferentes para el número 0 y los números iguales seguidos.

zero — "oh" — **0** — nought

four four — forty-four — **44** — double four

five five five — treble five — **555** — triple five — five double five

42.7 ESCUCHA EL AUDIO Y ANOTA LOS NÚMEROS DE TELÉFONO QUE OIGAS

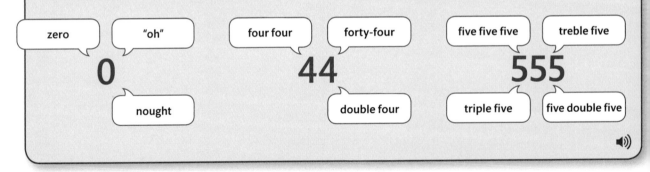

0 7 8 8 4 0 9 6 6 2

1 _____

2 _____

3 _____

4 _____

5 _____

6 _____

7 _____

42.8 TACHA LAS PALABRAS INCORRECTAS DE CADA FRASE Y DI LAS FRASES EN VOZ ALTA

If you want to arrange a meeting, you **can** / ~~will~~ contact me on 0078 555 251.

1. **Can** / **Don't** you call Martin at the office? His number's 902-555-4349.

2. You **can** / **will** call me on my cell phone any time. My number's 03069 991332.

3. Hi, it's Myra. **Can** / **Do** you call me back? My number's 07064 881206.

4. **Would** / **Can** you be able to call me back? I'm at the office. My extension is 8762.

5. If you **want** / **should** to contact Samuel later, his number's 01632 960441.

6. I've got a number for Hanna if you **can** / **want** to contact her. It's 321-554-8933.

42.9 ESCUCHA EL AUDIO Y RESPONDE A LAS PREGUNTAS

Tara llama a su compañero de trabajo Sven para que la ayude con unos problemas de su trabajo.

What department does Sven work in?
Sales ☐
IT ☑
HR ☐

1. What is Tara working on at the moment?
   A project selling mobile devices ☐
   A project selling shoes ☐
   A project selling apps ☐

2. What is her main problem?
   The mobile devices do not work ☐
   The Wi-Fi does not work ☐
   She cannot connect to the Wi-Fi ☐

3. What is Sven's solution?
   Enter a different passcode ☐
   Turn them off and on again ☐
   Come to a different office ☐

4. What is the passcode that Sven gives?
   JG330XS ☐
   GJ330XF ☐
   GJ330XS ☐

5. What does Sven say about Tara's second problem?
   He cannot fix it ☐
   She cannot fix it ☐
   He will fix it ☐

159

42.10 PUNTO CLAVE VERBOS PARA LLAMADAS TELEFÓNICAS

En inglés informal oral, especialmente en el lenguaje telefónico, se utilizan a menudo verbos de dos o tres partes.

> I have to **hang up** now, but I'll **call** you **back** tomorrow.

42.11 MÁS EJEMPLOS VERBOS PARA LLAMADAS TELEFÓNICAS

I'll just **put** you **through** to the IT department.

This line is awful! I just **got cut off**.

Sorry, I'm really busy. Can I **get back to** you in 10 minutes?

Their receptionist never **picks up** the phone.

42.12 TACHA LAS PALABRAS INCORRECTAS DE CADA FRASE

This line is terrible! I hope we don't get cut ~~up~~ / off /~~on.~~

1. Anna, can I call you **off** / **on** / **back** later from the office?

2. Suzanna always takes ages to pick **up** / **on** / **off** the phone.

3. Ethan, I will get back **to** / **with** / **until** you later with an answer.

4. I'll put you **in** / **back** / **through** to Ivor now.

5. If a customer is very rude, you can hang **on** / **off** / **up**.

6. I'll find out the information and get **off** / **back** / **on** to you.

7. I'm busy now, Valeria, but I'll call **you** / **me** / **us** back later.

42.13 VUELVE A ESCRIBIR LAS FRASES PONIENDO LAS PALABRAS EN SU ORDEN CORRECTO

| to | get | later | back | Can | you | today? | I |

Can I get back to you later today?

1 | I'll | through | sales. | you | put | to | Simone | in |

_____

2 | will | you | afternoon. | back | I | call | this | later |

_____

3 | just | were | off. | cut | we | about | Sorry | that; |

_____

Aa 42.14 LEE EL ARTÍCULO Y ESCRIBE LAS EXPRESIONES MARCADAS JUNTO A SUS DEFINICIONES

| end a call | = | *hang up* |

1 have a call interrupted = _____

2 answer the phone = _____

3 talk louder = _____

4 return your call = _____

5 becoming bad quality = _____

6 call them again = _____

Problem phone call?

What to do with people who won't stop talking

We have all wanted to hang up on callers who keep talking when we are really busy at work. Sometimes, the usual, "I'd better be going" does not work. One thing you can do is to say that you have a meeting in another room and that you will get back to them later. Another tactic is to say, "Could you speak up, please? The line keeps breaking up. I hope we don't get cut off." Then put the phone down. If they call you back, don't pick up the phone!

---

43 Llamadas telefónicas formales

Cuando hables con clientes o recepcionistas, utiliza un lenguaje telefónico formal. Quizá también debas dejar o tomar un mensaje telefónico.

⚙ **Lenguaje** Orden de los adjetivos
Aa **Vocabulario** Lenguaje telefónico formal
🧩 **Habilidad** Dejar mensajes en el contestador

43.1 PUNTO CLAVE CONVERSACIONES TELEFÓNICAS FORMALES

Utiliza un lenguaje formal para presentarte, saludar al interlocutor y tomar o dejar un mensaje.

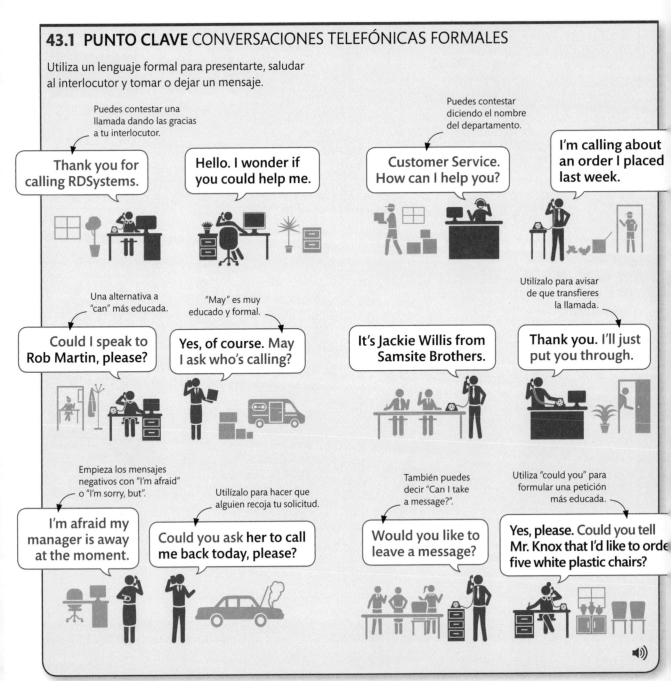

Puedes contestar una llamada dando las gracias a tu interlocutor.

Thank you for calling RDSystems.

Hello. I wonder if you could help me.

Puedes contestar diciendo el nombre del departamento.

Customer Service. How can I help you?

I'm calling about an order I placed last week.

Una alternativa a "can" más educada.

Could I speak to Rob Martin, please?

"May" es muy educado y formal.

Yes, of course. May I ask who's calling?

It's Jackie Willis from Samsite Brothers.

Utilízalo para avisar de que transfieres la llamada.

Thank you. I'll just put you through.

Empieza los mensajes negativos con "I'm afraid" o "I'm sorry, but".

I'm afraid my manager is away at the moment.

Utilízalo para hacer que alguien recoja tu solicitud.

Could you ask her to call me back today, please?

También puedes decir "Can I take a message?".

Would you like to leave a message?

Utiliza "could you" para formular una petición más educada.

Yes, please. Could you tell Mr. Knox that I'd like to order five white plastic chairs?

43.2 MARCA LA MEJOR RESPUESTA PARA CADA INTERVENCIÓN

Could I speak to Jia Li, please?
- May I ask who's calling, please? ✓
- Who are you? ☐

① Would you like to leave a message?
- I'll just put you through to HR. ☐
- Can you say that I'll arrive late? ☐

② Thank you for calling TCE Consulting.
- I want the sales department. ☐
- Could I speak to someone in sales? ☐

③ I'm afraid my manager is out of the office.
- Can I talk to the manager? ☐
- Can I leave a message for her? ☐

④ Could I talk to Myra Singh, please?
- I'll get her now. ☐
- Certainly. I'll just put you through. ☐

⑤ Customer service department. How can I help you?
- Yes, please. ☐
- I have a problem with an order. ☐

⑥ Thank you for calling EcoTech.
- I'll just put you through. ☐
- Hello. I wonder if you could help me. ☐

◀))

43.3 TACHA LA PALABRA INCORRECTA DE CADA FRASE Y DI LAS FRASES EN VOZ ALTA

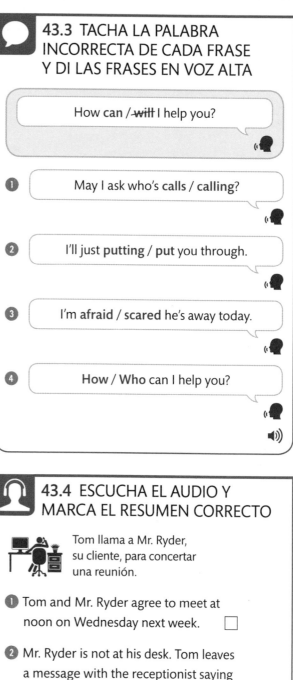

How **can** / ~~will~~ I help you?

① May I ask who's **calls** / **calling**?

② I'll just **putting** / **put** you through.

③ I'm **afraid** / **scared** he's away today.

④ **How** / **Who** can I help you?

◀))

43.4 ESCUCHA EL AUDIO Y MARCA EL RESUMEN CORRECTO

Tom llama a Mr. Ryder, su cliente, para concertar una reunión.

① Tom and Mr. Ryder agree to meet at noon on Wednesday next week. ☐

② Mr. Ryder is not at his desk. Tom leaves a message with the receptionist saying he will call again tomorrow. ☐

③ Mr. Ryder is not at his desk. Tom leaves a message with the receptionist saying he will meet him next week. ☐

43.5 PUNTO CLAVE ORDEN DE LOS ADJETIVOS

Los adjetivos aportan detalles a las descripciones y mensajes. Los adjetivos
se tienen que colocar en un orden concreto antes del sustantivo.

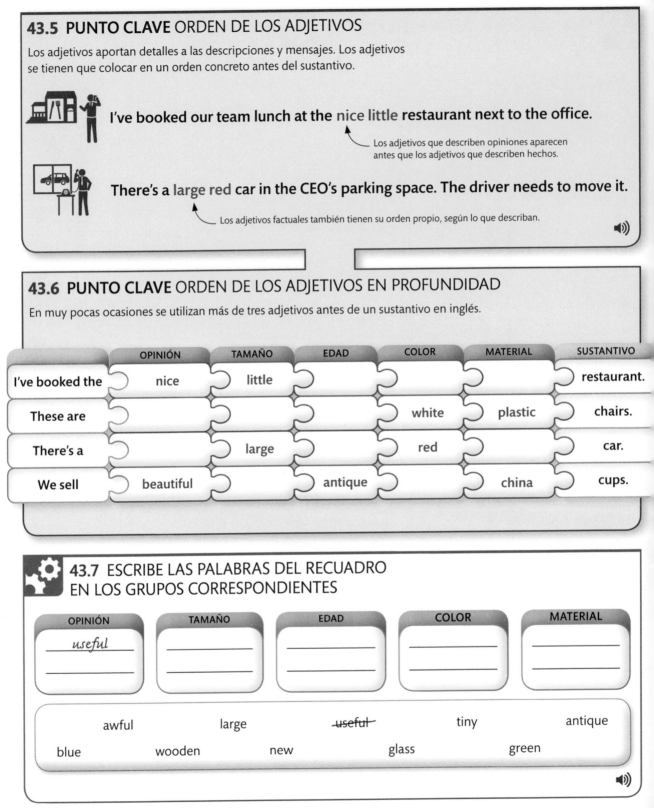

I've booked our team lunch at the nice little restaurant next to the office.

Los adjetivos que describen opiniones aparecen
antes que los adjetivos que describen hechos.

There's a large red car in the CEO's parking space. The driver needs to move it.

Los adjetivos factuales también tienen su orden propio, según lo que describan.

43.6 PUNTO CLAVE ORDEN DE LOS ADJETIVOS EN PROFUNDIDAD

En muy pocas ocasiones se utilizan más de tres adjetivos antes de un sustantivo en inglés.

	OPINIÓN	TAMAÑO	EDAD	COLOR	MATERIAL	SUSTANTIVO
I've booked the	nice	little				restaurant.
These are				white	plastic	chairs.
There's a		large		red		car.
We sell	beautiful		antique		china	cups.

43.7 ESCRIBE LAS PALABRAS DEL RECUADRO EN LOS GRUPOS CORRESPONDIENTES

OPINIÓN	TAMAÑO	EDAD	COLOR	MATERIAL
useful				

awful   large   ~~useful~~   tiny   antique

blue   wooden   new   glass   green

164

43.8 VUELVE A ESCRIBIR LAS FRASES CORRIGIENDO LOS ERRORES

I have a tiny awful old desk in my office.
I have an awful tiny old desk in my office.

1 My boss has a white large friendly cat.

_____

2 My computer is a old white huge desktop from 1995.

_____

3 We're marketing a clever watch tiny new that helps keep you fit.

_____

4 Have you seen the black tiny amazing briefcase she has?

_____

5 The meeting room has a modern painting very large.

_____

43.9 ESCUCHA EL AUDIO Y RESPONDE A LAS PREGUNTAS

Julio atiende una llamada telefónica de Mrs. Garcia, que se queja de un pedido que ha hecho.

Julio's manager isn't at her desk.
True ☑ False ☐ Not given ☐

1 Mrs. Garcia ordered an old coffee pot.
True ☐ False ☐ Not given ☐

2 Mrs. Garcia's items are broken.
True ☐ False ☐ Not given ☐

3 Mrs. Garcia does not like the color purple.
True ☐ False ☐ Not given ☐

4 Julio will send a replacement coffee pot.
True ☐ False ☐ Not given ☐

5 Mrs. Garcia must go to the post office.
True ☐ False ☐ Not given ☐

6 Julio will tell his manager about the call.
True ☐ False ☐ Not given ☐

43 ✓ CHECKLIST

⚙ Orden de los adjetivos ☐ **Aa** Lenguaje telefónico formal ☐ 🧩 Dejar mensajes en el contestador ☐

44 Redactar un currículum

El currículum ("résumé" en EE. UU. y también CV en el Reino Unido) es un resumen de tu carrera profesional. Los verbos de acción en past simple son útiles para describir tus logros.

⚙ **Lenguaje** Verbos de acción sobre logros
Aa Vocabulario Vocabulario de currículum
🧩 **Habilidad** Redactar un currículum

44.1 PUNTO CLAVE ENCABEZAMIENTOS DEL CURRÍCULUM

A continuación aparecen los apartados típicos de un currículum en inglés, así como expresiones útiles para describir tus logros.

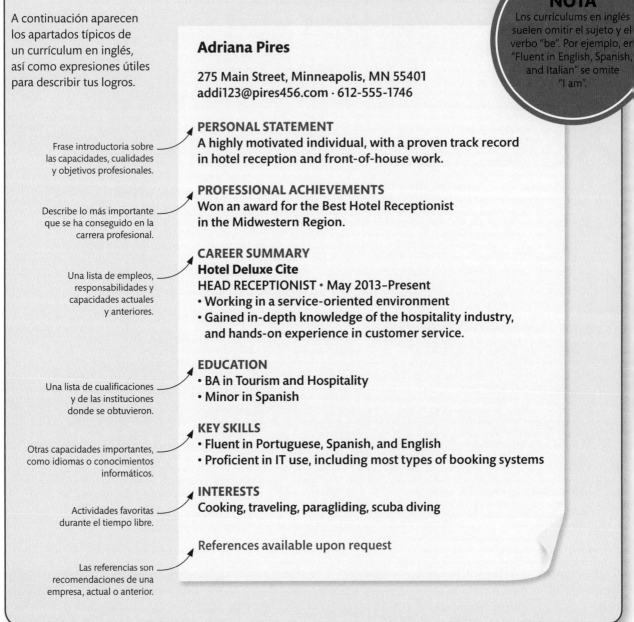

Adriana Pires

275 Main Street, Minneapolis, MN 55401
addi123@pires456.com · 612-555-1746

Frase introductoria sobre las capacidades, cualidades y objetivos profesionales.

PERSONAL STATEMENT
A highly motivated individual, with a proven track record in hotel reception and front-of-house work.

Describe lo más importante que se ha conseguido en la carrera profesional.

PROFESSIONAL ACHIEVEMENTS
Won an award for the Best Hotel Receptionist in the Midwestern Region.

Una lista de empleos, responsabilidades y capacidades actuales y anteriores.

CAREER SUMMARY
Hotel Deluxe Cite
HEAD RECEPTIONIST · May 2013–Present
• Working in a service-oriented environment
• Gained in-depth knowledge of the hospitality industry, and hands-on experience in customer service.

Una lista de cualificaciones y de las instituciones donde se obtuvieron.

EDUCATION
• BA in Tourism and Hospitality
• Minor in Spanish

Otras capacidades importantes, como idiomas o conocimientos informáticos.

KEY SKILLS
• Fluent in Portuguese, Spanish, and English
• Proficient in IT use, including most types of booking systems

Actividades favoritas durante el tiempo libre.

INTERESTS
Cooking, traveling, paragliding, scuba diving

Las referencias son recomendaciones de una empresa, actual o anterior.

References available upon request

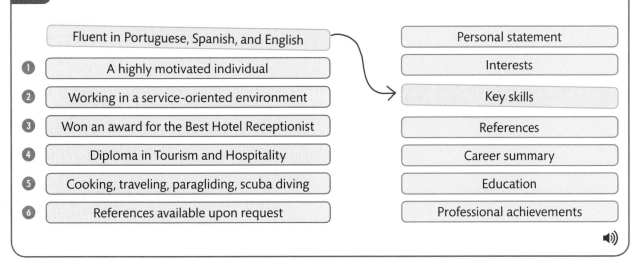

44.2 CONECTA LAS EXPRESIONES CON SUS APARTADOS DEL CURRÍCULUM

Fluent in Portuguese, Spanish, and English

① A highly motivated individual

② Working in a service-oriented environment

③ Won an award for the Best Hotel Receptionist

④ Diploma in Tourism and Hospitality

⑤ Cooking, traveling, paragliding, scuba diving

⑥ References available upon request

Personal statement

Interests

Key skills

References

Career summary

Education

Professional achievements

44.3 COMPLETA LOS ESPACIOS CON LAS PALABRAS DEL RECUADRO

I have a ___*proven*___ track record in the the catering industry.

① I am _____ in Japanese and Mandarin Chinese.

② I have a great deal of _____ experience in the construction industry.

③ I have an _____ knowledge of hair-coloring techniques.

④ As an ex-car salesman, I have a _____ background.

⑤ I am a highly _____ librarian and love reading.

⑥ I am _____ in all major types of accounting software.

service-oriented   ~~proven~~   motivated   fluent   proficient   hands-on   in-depth

44.4 **PUNTO CLAVE** VERBOS DE ACCIÓN EN PAST SIMPLE

Utiliza verbos de acción en past simple en el currículum para hablar
de responsabilidades que tenías y de logros anteriores.

I managed **a successful team of scientists.**

I coordinated **a major product launch.**

I negotiated **a great price for the company's products.**

I volunteered **in a local school.**

I established **a new training program.**

I collaborated **with designers to produce the company logo.**

44.5 TACHA LA PALABRA INCORRECTA DE CADA FRASE

Last year, I **managed** / ~~negotiated~~ a small team of painters.

1. Our teams **established** / **collaborated** to create the packaging design.

2. We **established** / **collaborated** a new headquarters downtown.

3. I **coordinated** / **collaborated** a staff training day for all departments.

4. I **managed** / **volunteered** for a charity and built a classroom.

5. I **established** / **negotiated** with all our suppliers and cut costs by 15 percent.

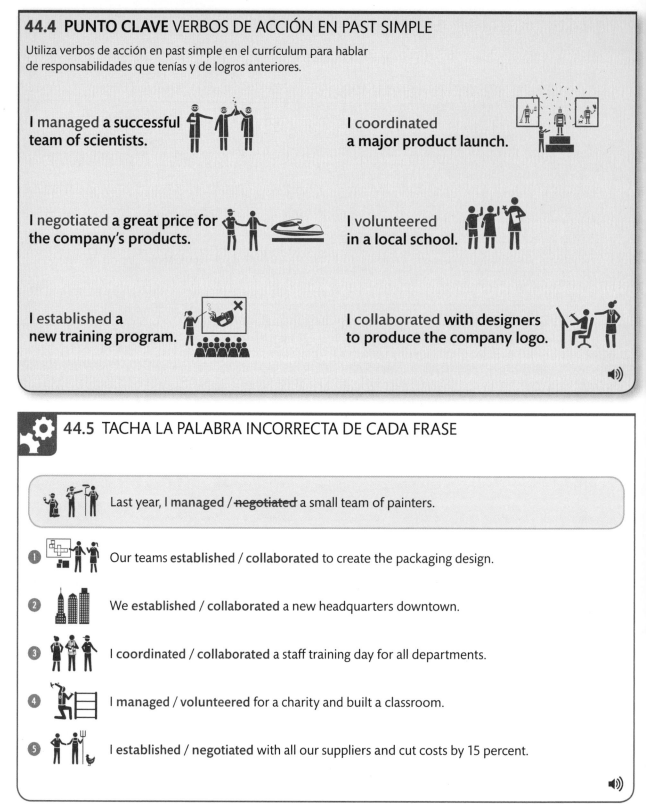

Ela Babinski

7 Gold Street
Perth
1609
elabab765@babela12.com
+61 491 570 156

I am determined and enthusiastic with practical experience in arranging and running sporting and educational activities for young adults. I have organized and supervised a number of overseas activity vacations in various countries and I have numerous health and safety certificates.

Career summary

YLHS Activity Vacations
HEAD OF ACTIVITIES • April 2013–present
YLHS Activity Vacations is a small, successful company, which combines adventure vacations with language education.

Duties:
- I create and supervise safe and exciting activity programs for 14–18 year-olds in three different countries.
- I manage teams of up to 16 activity leaders.

World Youth Language Schools
ACTIVITY LEADER • November 2011–April 2013
World Youth Language Schools run language courses around the world. Each day students have lessons followed by a sports activity.

Duties:
- I supervised up to 15 students at a time for activities.
- I also arranged transportation for students to and from each activity.

Professional achievements
Voted "Activity Leader of the Year" three years in a row by co-workers

Education
- Certificate in Activity Leadership, Level 3
- International Baccalaureate Diploma

Key skills
- Fluent in French and intermediate level Spanish
- First aid qualified
- Excellent organizer and people manager

Interests
Canoeing, climbing, and photography.

All the activities Ela organizes are in France.
True ☐ **False** ☐ **Not given** ☑

❶ Ela currently manages other activity leaders.
True ☐ **False** ☐ **Not given** ☐

❷ Ela's co-workers voted for her to receive an award.
True ☐ **False** ☐ **Not given** ☐

❸ Ela was a language teacher for World Youth.
True ☐ **False** ☐ **Not given** ☐

❹ Ela got her Activity Leadership Certificate last year.
True ☐ **False** ☐ **Not given** ☐

❺ Ela can speak French and Spanish fluently.
True ☐ **False** ☐ **Not given** ☐

---

44 ✓ CHECKLIST

⚙ Verbos de acción sobre logros ☐   **Aa** Vocabulario de currículum ☐   🧩 Redactar un currículum ☐

45 Hacer planes

En inglés se utiliza el futuro con "going to" para hablar sobre planes y decisiones que ya se han tomado. Es útil para informar a los compañeros de trabajo de tus planes.

🔧 **Lenguaje** El futuro con "going to"
Aa Vocabulario Pedir cosas educadamente
🧩 **Habilidad** Hacer planes

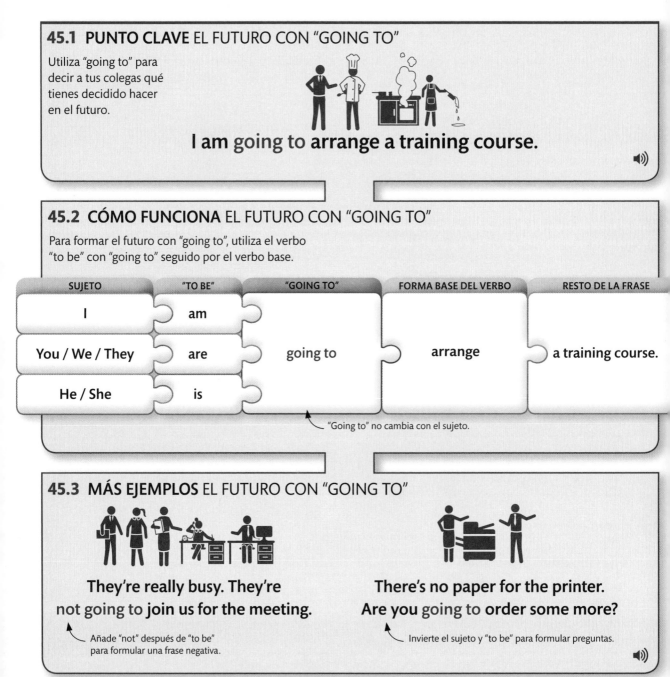

45.1 PUNTO CLAVE EL FUTURO CON "GOING TO"

Utiliza "going to" para decir a tus colegas qué tienes decidido hacer en el futuro.

I am going to arrange a training course.

45.2 CÓMO FUNCIONA EL FUTURO CON "GOING TO"

Para formar el futuro con "going to", utiliza el verbo "to be" con "going to" seguido por el verbo base.

SUJETO	"TO BE"	"GOING TO"	FORMA BASE DEL VERBO	RESTO DE LA FRASE
I	am			
You / We / They	are	going to	arrange	a training course.
He / She	is			

"Going to" no cambia con el sujeto.

45.3 MÁS EJEMPLOS EL FUTURO CON "GOING TO"

They're really busy. They're not going to join us for the meeting.

Añade "not" después de "to be" para formular una frase negativa.

There's no paper for the printer. Are you going to order some more?

Invierte el sujeto y "to be" para formular preguntas.

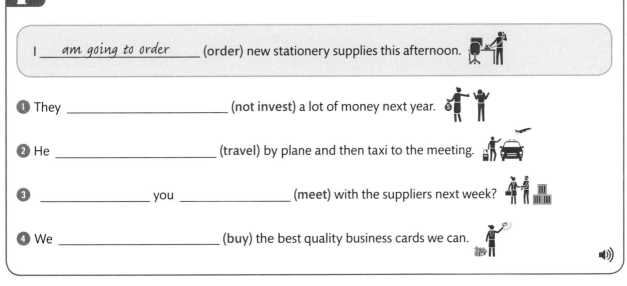

45.4 COMPLETA LOS ESPACIOS UTILIZANDO EL FUTURO CON "GOING TO"

I ___am going to order___ (order) new stationery supplies this afternoon.

1 They _____ (not invest) a lot of money next year.

2 He _____ (travel) by plane and then taxi to the meeting.

3 _____ you _____ (meet) with the suppliers next week?

4 We _____ (buy) the best quality business cards we can.

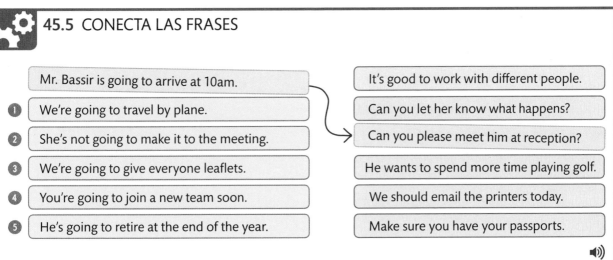

45.5 CONECTA LAS FRASES

Mr. Bassir is going to arrive at 10am.	It's good to work with different people.
1 We're going to travel by plane.	Can you let her know what happens?
2 She's not going to make it to the meeting.	Can you please meet him at reception?
3 We're going to give everyone leaflets.	He wants to spend more time playing golf.
4 You're going to join a new team soon.	We should email the printers today.
5 He's going to retire at the end of the year.	Make sure you have your passports.

45.6 ESCUCHA EL AUDIO Y NUMERA LAS IMÁGENES EN EL ORDEN EN QUE SE DESCRIBEN

A ☐   B 1   C ☐   D ☐   E ☐

45.7 PUNTO CLAVE ALTERNATIVAS EDUCADAS A DAR ÓRDENES

Recuerda que es más educado pedir cosas
con preguntas que con órdenes.

"Can" es más directo que "could",
pero continúa siendo educado.

Añade "please" para que
suene más educado.

Can you **serve the refreshments, please?**

[You have to serve the refreshments.]

Utiliza "we" en lugar de "you" para hacer que
la petición suene especialmente educada.

Could we **possibly move the time of the meeting?**

[Move the time of the meeting.]

45.8 MARCA LAS PETICIONES QUE SEAN EDUCADAS

Please could you call our suppliers? ☑
You must call our suppliers. ☐

1 Come to my office. ☐
Could you come to my office? ☐

2 Why don't we discuss this at the meeting? ☐
I don't have time to discuss this now. ☐

3 Can you tell me when it's finished, please? ☐
When will it be finished? ☐

4 Could we move these files? ☐
Why haven't you moved these files? ☐

5 Could you send the design to the printers? ☐
You should send the printers the design. ☐

6 Can you help me with these figures, please? ☐
I need help with these figures. ☐

45.9 VUELVE A ESCRIBIR CORRIGIENDO LOS ERRORES

Could you to serve the refreshments?
Could you serve the refreshments?

1 Can help you me move this cupboard?
_____

2 Could you being a little neater, please?
_____

3 Can you to finish the design soon, please?
_____

4 Could us meet at 5 instead of 6?
_____

5 Could you possible send me the report today?
_____

6 Can you to clean up the meeting room?
_____

45.10 LEE EL CORREO ELECTRÓNICO Y RESPONDE A LAS PREGUNTAS EN VOZ ALTA

What is Diego going to do?

> *Diego is going to arrange the refreshments for the conference.*

1 Who is Sven going to meet in the afternoon?

2 Who is going to work on the Information Desk?

3 Who is going to wear the lanyards during the conference?

4 What is Simon going to check when he emails the venue?

To: Gylfi Laarson

Subject: Conference preparations

Hello Gylfi,

Following our meeting yesterday, I have some more news about the plans for the sales conference. I spoke to Diego this morning about the refreshments and he's going to call ConCater Ltd today to make arrangements.

Sven is going to meet the printers about the posters and leaflets this afternoon. He's going to email us after the meeting when he has more news about prices. We need to move ahead ASAP on the printing.

I've emailed Diane and she's going to work on the Information Desk during the conference. Agnes is going to organize lanyards for all the delegates to wear. Could you arrange for the names to be printed for the lanyards, please?

I'm just going to email the venue to check that the rooms all have projectors and an internet connection. I'll email you later with a further update.

Best,
Simon

46.1 FORMAS DE COMUNICACIÓN

email	letter	envelope	stamp
internal mail	mail (US) / post (UK)	courier	delivery
telephone call / phone call	voicemail	answering machine	switchboard
transfer a call	text message	formal meeting	informal meeting
presentation	conference call	web conference	online chat
social networking	website	memo	bulletin board (US) / notice board (UK)

46.2 ENVIAR CORREOS ELECTRÓNICOS

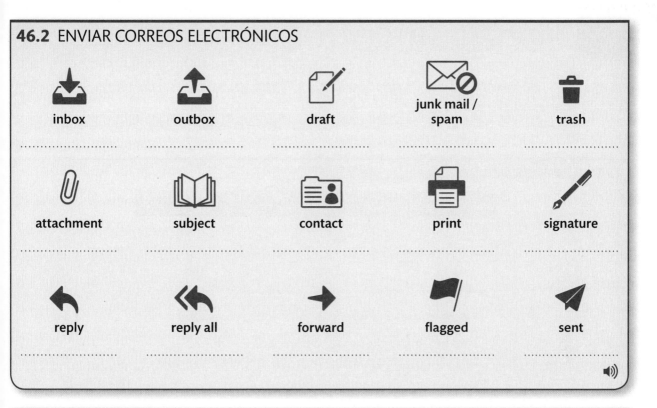

inbox

outbox

draft

junk mail / spam

trash

attachment

subject

contact

print

signature

reply

reply all

forward

flagged

sent

46.3 ABREVIATURAS

I've CC'd Marie as she may have more information.

CC
[copy]

Please BCC everyone on these emails.

BCC
[blind copy]

Could you get those figures to me ASAP?

ASAP
[as soon as possible]

I'm forwarding you their latest comments, just FYI.

FYI
[for your information]

Could you tell me your ETA tomorrow, please?

ETA
[estimated time of arrival]

We think the retail price will be $85, but that's TBC.

TBC
[to be confirmed]

Just a quick note RE order #MYJ497P.

RE
[regarding]

NB I will be out of the office tomorrow morning.

NB
[note]

Please RSVP to your invitations by next week.

RSVP
[respond]

47 Enviar un correo electrónico

Los correos electrónicos a los clientes deben ser educados y detallar claramente los planes e intenciones de futuro. Utiliza el present continuous o "going to" al hablar de planes.

⚙ **Lenguaje** Uso de futuros para planes
Aa Vocabulario Correo electrónico formal
🧩 **Habilidad** Enviar un correo a un cliente

47.1 PUNTO CLAVE CORREO ELECTRÓNICO A UN CLIENTE

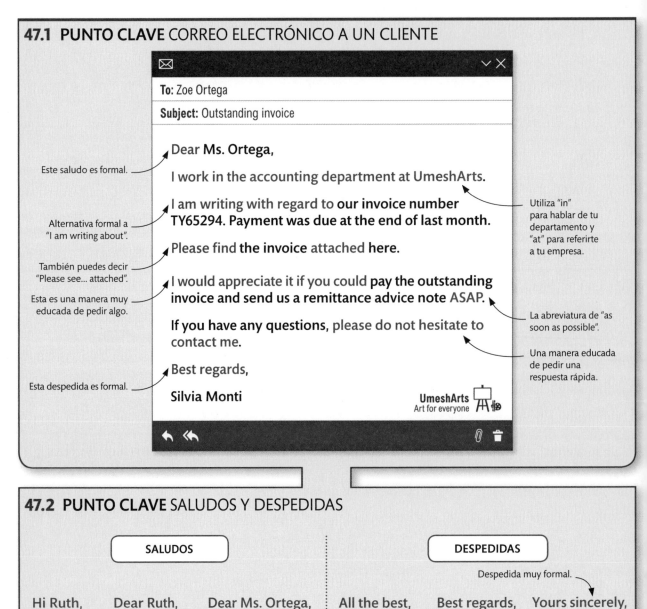

To: Zoe Ortega

Subject: Outstanding invoice

Este saludo es formal. → Dear **Ms. Ortega,**

I work in the accounting department at UmeshArts. → Utiliza "in" para hablar de tu departamento y "at" para referirte a tu empresa.

Alternativa formal a "I am writing about". → I am writing with regard to **our invoice number TY65294. Payment was due at the end of last month.**

También puedes decir "Please see... attached". → Please find **the invoice** attached **here.**

Esta es una manera muy educada de pedir algo. → I would appreciate it if you could **pay the outstanding invoice and send us a remittance advice note** ASAP. → La abreviatura de "as soon as possible".

If you have any questions, please do not hesitate to contact me. → Una manera educada de pedir una respuesta rápida.

Esta despedida es formal. → Best regards,

Silvia Monti

UmeshArts
Art for everyone

47.2 PUNTO CLAVE SALUDOS Y DESPEDIDAS

SALUDOS			DESPEDIDAS		

Despedida muy formal. →

Hi Ruth,   **Dear Ruth,**   **Dear Ms. Ortega,**   **All the best,**   **Best regards,**   **Yours sincerely,**

Esto es muy informal.

Utilizar el apellido es muy formal.

Despedida informal.

También puedes decir "Best wishes" o "Kind regards".

176

47.3 LEE EL CORREO ELECTRÓNICO Y RESPONDE A LAS PREGUNTAS

To: Richard McGrath

Subject: Recycling opportunity

Dear Mr. McGrath,

I work in the recycling department at Science Solutions. I deal with repurposing waste from technology companies.

It has come to our attention that the microchips you no longer deem fit for purpose are being discarded to landfill. I wonder if you are aware that we could purchase this waste from you? Such a proposition would benefit both your company and the environment.

I would welcome the opportunity to discuss this further with you in a meeting.

Best regards,
Zarifa Sahli

Science Solutions

What is the main purpose of Zarifa's job?
Science ☐ **Recycling** ☐ **Technology** ☑

1. What sort of companies does Zarifa work with?
Schools ☐ **Laboratories** ☐ **Technology** ☐

2. Old microchips are currently being...
recycled ☐ **sold** ☐ **discarded to landfill** ☐

3. What does Science Solutions want to do with waste?
Purchase it ☐ **Discard it** ☐ **Sell it** ☐

4. What will benefit from this?
The environment ☐ **Science** ☐ **Nothing** ☐

5. How would Zarifa like to discuss further?
Email ☐ **Telephone** ☐ **In a meeting** ☐

47.4 VUELVE A ESCRIBIR LAS FRASES CORRIGIENDO LOS ERRORES

I am writing with regarding to your damaged packages.
I am writing with regard to your damaged packages.

1. Please find your attached to invoice this email.

2. I am writing to you as the new CEO in Yoghurt500.

3. I would am appreciate it if you could reply by 3 o'clock this afternoon.

4. My name's Scott and I work at the packaging department.

47.5 PUNTO CLAVE HABLAR DE PLANES FUTUROS

Para explicar a los clientes tus planes de futuro, utiliza el present continuous, en especial si has indicado cuándo pasará algo.

I am writing to inform you that we are meeting other suppliers on Monday.

Sabemos cuándo pasará esto.

Present continuous.

Se puede utilizar "going to" con un indicador de tiempo, pero se utiliza más a menudo en lugar del present continuous para hablar sobre planes para un futuro por especificar.

I am writing to inform you that we are going to meet other microchip suppliers.

No sabemos cuándo pasará esto.

Futuro con "going to".

47.6 TACHA LAS PALABRAS INCORRECTAS DE CADA FRASE

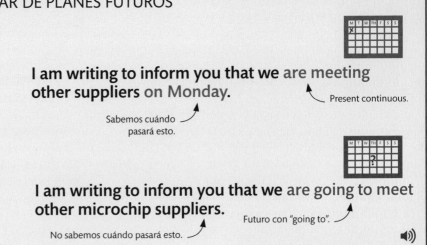

We are ~~paying~~ / going to pay your invoice very soon.

1. He is **emailing** / going to emailing all the clients this afternoon.

2. She is **to sending** / going to send vouchers to all customers.

3. They are **meet** / going to meet in Rome to discuss options.

4. I am **speaking** / going speaking with our couriers tomorrow.

47.7 COMPLETA LOS ESPACIOS CON LAS EXPRESIONES DEL RECUADRO

We _____ *are meeting* _____ our new clients on Friday.

1. We hope they're _____ us a discount.

2. Our CEO is _____ a merger.

3. Simone is _____ your invoice this afternoon.

4. Mark and Johan are _____ the calls later.

going to discuss

going to offer

~~are meeting~~

going to answer

sending

47.8 ESCRIBE LAS EXPRESIONES MARCADAS CORRIGIENDO ERRORES

with regard to the

❶ _____

❷ _____

❸ _____

❹ _____

❺ _____

❻ _____

To: Ian Grant

Subject: Agenda for meeting

Dear Mr. Grant,

I am writing with regard the annual meeting later this week. The meeting is going to taking place in the main boardroom of our Gold Road building at 1:00pm on Thursday. Please find attachment the agenda for the meeting. We is going to discuss the sales figures for the last quarter. Markos Kaloyiannis who works at the design department is also attend the meeting on Thursday. He is going discuss the design for the new coffee jars.

We look forward to seeing you there,

Kind regards,
Anton Schmidt

---

47 ✓ CHECKLIST

⚙️ Uso de futuros para planes ☐   **Aa** Correo electrónico formal ☐   🧩 Enviar un correo a un cliente ☐

♻️ REPASA LO QUE HAS APRENDIDO EN LAS UNIDADES 42-47

NUEVO LENGUAJE	FRASE DE EJEMPLO	☑	UNIDAD
LLAMADAS TELEFÓNICAS INFORMALES	Can I ask who's calling, please? I **have to** hang up **now**. **I'll** call you back **later**.	☐	42.1, 42.10
LLAMADAS TELEFÓNICAS FORMALES	Customer Service. How can I help you? May I ask who's calling?	☐	43.1
ORDEN DE LOS ADJETIVOS	I've booked a nice little **restaurant for lunch.**	☐	43.5
REDACTAR EL CURRÍCULUM	I have a proven track record in sales.	☐	44.1
FUTURO CON "GOING TO"	I am going to arrange a training course.	☐	45.1
CORREO ELECTRÓNICO A UN CLIENTE	I am writing with regard to **our invoice number TY65294.**	☐	47.1
HABLAR DE PLANES FUTUROS	We are meeting **other suppliers** on Monday.	☐	47.5

Respuestas

01

1.2
1. Hello. My **name's** Sebastian.
2. Good **afternoon**. My name is Joe Carr.
3. Hi, Marie. **I'm** Clive.
4. It's great to meet you, **too**, Sven.
5. It's a **pleasure** to meet you.

1.4
1. B 2. A 3. B 4. B 5. A

1.6
1. **It's a pleasure to meet you**, too.
2. Hi, **I'm** Adedeyo. / Hi, **my** name's Adedeyo.
3. **Great** to meet you.
4. This **is** my new colleague, Martin.
5. Marisa, **meet** Roula, my partner.
6. It's good to **meet you**, Katherine.
7. **May I** introduce Claudia Gomez, our new CEO?

1.7
1. Greene
2. 14 years
3. Accountant
4. Jill and Mr. Singh

1.8
1. Hello, Mr. Lucas. It's a **pleasure** to meet **you**.
2. Ashley, **meet** André. André and I work on the **same** project.
3. **Hello**, Sophie. My **name's** Rachel Davies. Great to meet you.
4. **This** is my colleague, Hayley. We went to college **together**.
5. It's **good** to meet you, Cori. **My** name's Angel.
6. Hello, James. **It's** really nice **to** meet you. My name's Alex.

02

2.4
1. He opens all the windows in the afternoon.
2. He brings the team tea and coffee every afternoon.
3. She shouts at the computer every day.
4. She walks around her office every 30 minutes.

2.5
1. She **is** a hairdresser.
2. He **travels** by train every morning.
3. She **leaves** work at 6pm every day.
4. She **drinks** coffee twice a day.
5. He **eats** lunch at a local café.

2.6
1. False
2. True
3. False
4. Not given
5. False

2.8
1. The head of marketing **speaks** for about an hour at every team meeting.
2. Arianna and Gabriel **read** their emails first thing every morning.
3. The photocopier **stops** working if we don't load the paper carefully.
4. The owners of the hotel **visit** it at the end of every month.
5. The cleaner **starts** work at 6am every day. The office is always clean in the mornings.

2.9
1. I work from Monday to Friday.
2. I have a meeting every morning.
3. You work from Monday to Friday.
4. You have a meeting every morning.
5. She works from Monday to Friday.
6. She has a meeting every morning.
7. My manager works from Monday to Friday.
8. My manager has a meeting every morning.

2.10
1. False
2. True
3. True
4. False
5. True
6. False
7. True

04

4.4
1. I'm on the **European** sales team.
2. Our **Chilean** office is in Santiago.
3. We sell leather shoes from **Spain**.
4. My job is to watch the **Asian** markets.
5. Book a trip to **Mexico** with us.

4.5
1. India
2. France
3. Asia
4. Italy
5. Africa

4.7
1. These polo shirts **aren't** made in Vietnam.
2. This restaurant **doesn't** use British meat.
3. The onions in this market **aren't** local.
4. **I'm not** Brazilian, but I work in Brazil.
5. The company **doesn't** have overseas clients.

4.9
1. True
2. False
3. True
4. False
5. False
6. True

06

6.3
1. Are the windows open?
2. Is your phone working?
3. Are these your files?
4. Is that drawer locked?
5. Is his desk clean?

6.6
1. **Does** he have a key for this drawer?
2. **Does** your laptop have a DVD drive?
3. **Do** Jim and Tom have new screens?
4. **Do** you keep pens in your desk drawer?
5. **Does** Sarah write the minutes?
6. **Do** all employees have wall calendars?

6.7

Ⓐ 3 Ⓑ 4 Ⓒ 1 Ⓓ 5 Ⓔ 2

6.10 ◀))

1 **Where** are the cups?
2 **What** is the photocopier code?
3 **How** do I turn off the screen?
4 **Why** is this drawer always locked?
5 **When** does the cafeteria open?
6 **Who** do I ask for printer ink?
7 **What** do you discuss at meetings?

6.11 ◀))

1 You need to talk to Anne in HR.
2 It's always full on weekend evenings.
3 So that Marie can control the stock.
4 Turn it on and then select your drink.
5 At 2 o'clock. We usually start on time.

6.12 ◀))

1 What can I do to help you?
2 Do you know where the key is?
3 When does the store open?
4 How do I connect the keyboard?
5 Why is her desk always a mess?

6.13 ◀))

1 **Where** are the paperclips and pens?
2 **What** is for lunch today?
3 **Why** do we use old computers?
4 **When** do they close the office?

7.4

Ⓐ 2 Ⓑ 5 Ⓒ 3 Ⓓ 1 Ⓔ 4 Ⓕ 6

7.5 ◀))

1 Do you **have** a website I can look up?
2 Your job **title** isn't listed here.
3 Just **drop** me a line for more details.
4 How can I **reach** you to follow up?
5 Is this your phone **number**?
6 Here's my **business** card.
7 **Call** me to arrange a meeting.
8 Drop me a **line** to follow up next week.

7.6

1 True
2 False
3 False

---

4 False
5 False
6 True

7.8 ◀))

1 Yes, it is.
2 Yes, they are.
3 Yes, they do.
4 Yes, it does.
5 No, we don't.

7.9 ◀))

1 No, it isn't.
2 Yes, they are.
3 Yes, I do.
4 No, it doesn't.
5 Yes, they do.
6 Yes, I do.
7 No, I don't.

8.4 ◀))

1 They **don't** have interviews today.
2 He **hasn't** got a diploma
3 I **don't have** any experience.
4 Do you **have** good IT skills?
5 We **have** monthly training sessions.
6 He **doesn't** have experience with animals.
7 He **has** a Master's degree.
8 They **have** a lot of inexperienced staff.
9 She's **got** super negotiation skills.

8.5

1 Sam loves working with animals.
2 Sam won a regional competition.
3 Sam organized field trips at college.
4 Sam worked in an office.
5 Sam has excellent photography skills.
6 Sam's degree is in dance and drama.
7 Sam has a photography diploma.

8.8 ◀))

1 Oh, yes. I know **the** hotel you mean.
2 Susan has **a** diploma.
3 Is **the** meeting on the second floor?
4 I work for **a** large recruitment agency.
5 There's **an** ad for a chef here.
6 I hired **a** PA to help me out.
7 He works at **the** hospital down the road.
8 Is there **an** office in Mexico?

8.9

Ⓐ 4 Ⓑ 1 Ⓒ 5 Ⓓ 2 Ⓔ 6 Ⓕ 3

8.11 ◀))

1 He was out of the office today.
2 I have excellent people skills.
3 What skills do you need for this job?
4 Have you read the job requirements?
5 She's an architect for a top company.
6 The new designer is very good.

8.12

Dear Mr. Baxter,

I am writing to apply for **the** role of Library Assistant, which I saw advertised on your website. I **have** two years' experience working as a part-time assistant in my local library. **The** job involves working with **a** team of people and the public, so I have **good people skills**. I **do not have** a degree in Library and Information Studies, as **the** ad requested, but I **have** a degree in English Literature.

I look forward to hearing from you.

Yours sincerely,
Judy Stein

10.4 ◀))

1 She **doesn't like** using computers.
2 He likes **training** new colleagues.
3 I **hate** long meetings.
4 We **don't like** lazy employees.
5 She enjoys **working** in a team.

10.5

1 No le gusta
2 Le gusta
3 Le gusta
4 Le gusta

10.6

1 False
2 True
3 False
4 False
5 True

181

11.3 🔊
1. There **aren't** any bathrooms on this floor.
2. Is there **a** stationery cabinet in the office?
3. There's **a** staff cafeteria on the third floor.
4. There **isn't** an elevator in this building.
5. **Are** there any places to lock my bicycle here?
6. **Is** there a desk ready for our new designer?
7. **There are** lots of envelopes in the cabinet.

11.4
Respuestas modelo
1. They should leave them in a closet by the main entrance door.
2. There are four desks in Jonathan's office.
3. There is a tea and coffee machine.
4. Staff sign in at reception.

11.5 🔊
1. There is a staff parking lot.
2. There is a business dress code.
3. There are places to relax.
4. There isn't a staff parking lot.
5. There isn't a business dress code.
6. There aren't any places to relax.

13

13.3
Ⓐ 4 Ⓑ 1 Ⓒ 5 Ⓓ 2 Ⓔ 3

13.4
POSITIVOS:
motivated, ambitious, helpful, bright, intelligent
NEGATIVOS:
impatient, lazy, **impolite**, **nervous**, **boring**

13.5 🔊
1. My team leader **is impolite** and he is also **very impatient**.
2. My co-workers say that I **am really motivated and ambitious**.
3. The new young intern seems very intelligent and he **is really** polite.
4. I'm very lucky. All my colleagues **are** hardworking and **helpful**.

13.9 🔊
1. Two of the people on **my** team are new to the company, but they're settling in well.
2. **Their** manager is very good with people. They enjoy working with him.
3. The company is very proud of **its** reputation and quality products.
4. Is this **your** phone? It doesn't belong to me but I found it on my desk.

13.12 🔊
1. We hate their product, but we love **ours**.
2. They are proud of **their** project.
3. **Our** clients expect excellent service.
4. This isn't her desk. It's **mine**.
5. This is amazing. Is it **her** project?

13.13 🔊
1. I think these are your files.
2. Is this desk his?
3. These are her pens.
4. Are those products theirs?

13.16 🔊
1. The **interns** work really hard.
2. All the team **members** are intelligent.
3. This big room is my **boss's** office.
4. All the **bosses** have parking spaces.
5. The best thing about this product is **its** strength.

13.17
1. he joined the company
2. Jorge's supervisor
3. Her progress is slow
4. Maria is impatient
5. very intelligent

13.18 🔊
1. You are my manager.
2. You are my assistant.
3. You are Sam's manager.
4. You are Sam's assistant.
5. You are very organized.
6. You are really organized.
7. We are very organized.
8. We are really organized.
9. Katy is my manager.
10. Katy is Sam's manager.
11. Katy is my assistant.
12. Katy is Sam's assistant.
13. Katy is very organized.
14. Katy is really organized.

14.3 🔊
1. That meeting was really **boring**.
2. The printer can be **annoying** at times.
3. By the end of the week, I'm really **tired**.
4. The system is **confusing** at first.
5. I'm very **excited** about my project.
6. The news was **shocking**.
7. I was very **surprised** by my raise!

14.4
1. Not given
2. True
3. False
4. Not given
5. False

14.5 🔊
1. satisfied
2. bored
3. tired
4. confusing
5. annoying
6. interesting
7. excited
8. shocking

14.8 🔊
1. This printer is **faster** than the other, but that one is **more reliable**.
2. This coffee is **stronger** than I normally buy, but it is also **tastier**.
3. This building is **newer** than my last workplace, and the area is **quieter**.
4. This café is **busier** than the other one, so the service is **slower**.
5. My new uniform is **more comfortable** than my old one, but **uglier**.

14.10 🔊
1. Parking is more expensive this year.
2. This system is better than before.
3. I have more work to do than last year.
4. I arrive much earlier than my boss.
5. Every year my raise is smaller.
6. I feel better now that I have a new job.
7. A digital copy is more useful to me.
8. That meeting was worse than usual.

14.11
1. better salary
2. worse overtime pay
3. hourly rate is less
4. shorter commute
5. bigger bonus

14.12 ◀))
1. easy
2. bored
3. stronger
4. lower
5. cheap
6. heavier
7. smaller
8. large
9. worse

14.13
1. friendlier
2. more successful
3. more
4. better
5. longer

14.14 ◀))
1. Now, my vacations are longer **than they used to be**.
2. This new computer system is more **efficient than the old one**.
3. These presentations are making me more **bored than yesterday's**.
4. These new laptops are **lighter than the old ones**.
5. The cafeteria lunches are **tastier than restaurant meals**.

14.15
1. False
2. Not given
3. True
4. False
5. Not given
6. True
7. True

15.3 ◀))
1. Lunch is served at noon.
2. Don't leave before Mr. Davies.
3. Never arrive after 9am.

15.5 ◀))
1. Let your manager know if you need to go out **during** the day.
2. My boss is in meetings **for** about four hours every day.
3. I have been here **since** 5am this morning.
4. Do not leave the building **until** you have signed out.
5. The office is closed from Friday **to** Monday.

15.7 ◀))
1. I go by metro.
2. Sometimes I ride my bike to work.
3. I go by train to work.
4. I normally go to work on foot.
5. Sometimes I take a taxi to work.
6. I take the bus.

15.8 ◀))
1. I always **drive** to work.
2. It's usually quicker to **cycle**.
3. When it's sunny, we go on **foot**.
4. I don't like taking the **metro**.
5. I **walk** to work to stay fit.
6. I read a book when I go **by** train.
7. I **take** the bus when it rains.

15.9
Ⓐ 8 Ⓑ 1 Ⓒ 3 Ⓓ 7 Ⓔ 2 Ⓕ 5 Ⓖ 4 Ⓗ 6

17.2
1. frequently 2. sometimes
3. occasionally 4. never

17.3 ◀))
1. I often do yoga in the evening.
2. We occasionally go to see a play.
3. She often listens to music at work.
4. I always take photos when I go on vacation.

17.8 ◀))
1. This is the best book I've ever read.
2. The piano is the easiest instrument to play.
3. Yannick listens to the loudest music.
4. Shopping is the most expensive hobby I do.
5. That was the worst play I have ever seen.
6. Exercising is the most relaxing thing I do.
7. Let's eat at the closest restaurant.

17.9 ◀))
1. The **most interesting** gallery I've been to is in Paris.
2. I've just finished the **worst** book I've ever read.
3. The **longest** hike I've ever done is 15km.
4. The **farthest** I've ever gone cycling is 50 miles.
5. I think that hiking is the **most exciting** hobby.

18.4 ◀))
1. I played soccer after work last night.
2. He didn't walk to work today.
3. I worked from 9 to 5 yesterday.
4. She lived in Paris for four years.
5. I talked to lots of people on my trip.

18.6 ◀))
1. We **arrived** late, but our boss **didn't shout** at us.
2. I **washed** my car, but it **didn't look** clean.
3. I **watched** the film, but I **didn't enjoy** it.
4. It **stopped** raining, but then it **started** snowing.
5. I **didn't walk** to work, I **cycled**.

18.9 ◀))
1. Did you play board games when you were young?
2. Did he cook some pasta for lunch?
3. Did she stay at home and watch TV last night?
4. Did they watch a scary movie at the movie theater?
5. Did they walk home from work together?

18.10
1. True
2. Not given
3. False
4. True
5. Not given

18.11 ◀))
1. They visited a museum.
2. She listened to music.
3. He watched TV.
4. They cooked a meal.
5. They played a board game.

19.2 🔊
1. It's two thirty. / It's half past two.
2. It's ten forty-five. / It's (a) quarter to eleven.
3. It's seven. / It's seven o'clock.
4. It's three twenty-five. / It's twenty-five past three.
5. It's eight forty-three pm.

19.5
1. March
2. August
3. 2014
4. May 12

20

20.4 🔊
1. When I was a gardener, I **spent** the majority of my time outside.
2. I **met** lots of famous people when I worked as a reporter.
3. Benjamin **went** to nearly 100 countries as a pilot.
4. In his last job, he **had** a dog as a partner.

20.5 🔊
1. As a police officer, I had a uniform.
2. I met lots of famous musicians.
3. I went to catering school.
4. I spent a lot of time in museums.

20.6
Ⓐ 3   Ⓑ 1   Ⓒ 4   Ⓓ 5   Ⓔ 2

20.7
Respuestas modelo
1. Sadim chose to study engineering in college.
2. Sadim thought his father would give him a good job in his company.
3. Sadim felt angry because he wanted a better job.
4. Sadim wrote to his father that he would look for another job.
5. His father said he could be CEO one day.
6. Sadim finally understood what hard work was like in different areas of the company.
7. Sadim's work experience taught him to respect all employees.

8. Sadim's father made him CEO five years ago.
9. Myra began working in the mailroom two months ago.

20.8 🔊
1. I **felt** really happy when I left college with a top degree.
2. My manager **said** that one day I could be CEO of the whole company.
3. My tutor **taught** me that it was important to check my own work.
4. I **made** my girlfriend a big cake to celebrate her new job.

20.9 🔊
Respuestas modelo
1. I saw an ad for the job in the store window.
2. I felt very excited on my first day.
3. I chose the job because I wanted to work with customers.
4. I left my first job five years ago.
5. I left my first job because the hours were long.

21

21.3 🔊
1. We opened our tenth store two months **ago**.
2. The company **recently** merged with one of its competitors.
3. Jane Hunt opened the first Hunt Bags store **in** 1995.
4. A new CEO started working here **last** year.

21.4
Ⓐ 2   Ⓑ 3   Ⓒ 5   Ⓓ 1   Ⓔ 4   Ⓕ 6

21.5
Respuestas modelo
1. Ahmed founded Cake & Crumb in 2003.
2. At first, he worked from the kitchen in his small apartment.
3. In the company's first year, sales remained steady.
4. The company opened its first store in 2005.
5. Cake & Crumb employed 2,000 bakers by 2010.
6. Two years ago, the company launched a catering service for children's parties.

21.7 🔊
1. The number of people going to festivals **went up** last year.
2. Fortunately, the cost of fuel for transportation **stabilized** recently.
3. In the really wet summer of 2010, sales of umbrellas **rose** a lot.
4. The number of people downloading music **stayed the same** last month.
5. The number of students earning MBAs **remained steady** last year.

21.8 🔊
1. **At** first, the value of the company **stayed** the same.
2. Marketing costs **increased** and sales also **rose**.
3. **Last** summer, umbrella sales **increased** because it was rainy.
4. The number of customers **decreased**, but profits **went** up.
5. Two years **ago**, we launched an online delivery service and our sales **rose**.

23

23.4
Ⓐ 4   Ⓑ 1   Ⓒ 6   Ⓓ 3   Ⓔ 2   Ⓕ 8   Ⓖ 7   Ⓗ 5

23.5 🔊
1. Sales **are increasing** at the moment, so we **are getting** a bigger bonus.
2. Fashions **are changing**, so we **are adapting** to new trends.
3. Travel costs **are rising** this year, so we **are calling** each other more instead.
4. Profits **are dropping**, so we **are cutting** costs in all areas of the business.
5. We **are selling** a lot to Asia, so we **are planning** to open an office there next year.
6. I can't believe you **are working** late. You **are missing** the staff party!
7. I **am waiting** for my interview to start, and I **am feeling** nervous.
8. The company **is losing** money, so we **are considering** a restructure.

23.8 🔊
1. Are they buying this?
2. Is it working now?
3. Are we selling that?
4. Are you meeting him?
5. Who are they promoting?

23.9 🔊
1. There is no hot water left.
2. That's Giorgio. He's a great speaker.
3. Yes, I'm running two workshops.
4. He's giving a presentation.
5. Yes, I think he is.
6. No, I'm on the bus at the moment.
7. No, it's out of toner. I'm refilling it now.

23.10 🔊
1. Is the company buying everyone new laptops?
2. Is Maria giving her first presentation at the moment?
3. Is Rakesh designing the packaging for the new gadget?
4. Are we all going to the team meeting now?
5. Are they trying to improve sales in North America?

23.12 🔊
1. I'm not coming to work tomorrow.
2. Are you meeting the team today?
3. I can't go. I'm not leaving until 8pm.
4. Are we coming back here next year?
5. Are you coming to the party later?
6. I'm not taking notes today. Are you?
7. I'm having lunch at noon tomorrow.
8. Are you going to Asia this winter?

23.13
1. For 10 days
2. Next Monday morning
3. In the bookstore

23.14 🔊 Respuestas modelo
1. I'm meeting the HR team.
2. I'm going to Paris.
3. I'm traveling by train.
4. I'm getting home at 7.15pm.
5. I'm finishing at 3pm.
6. Monica is leaving work on Friday.

24

24.2
1. Impolite
2. Polite
3. Polite
4. Impolite
5. Impolite
6. Polite
7. Impolite

24.5 🔊
1. Sorry to **interrupt**, but my figures are different.
2. I'm not sure. What do you **think** about new outlets?
3. I'm sorry, but in my **opinion** they will sell well.

24.6
1. False
2. Not given
3. True
4. False
5. True

24.7 🔊
1. **take** the minutes, **review** the minutes
2. **read** the agenda, **work through** the agenda
3. **send** apologies, **announce** apologies
4. **take a** vote, **casting** vote
5. **opening** remarks, **closing** remarks

24.8
1. environment
2. reduce
3. reuse
4. waste
5. green
6. recycle
7. resources
8. footprint

24.9 🔊
1. Tim **sent** his apologies. He can't come.
2. Let's review our **environmental** strategy.
3. Let's work through the **agenda** quickly.
4. We should look at **reducing** our waste.
5. I'm sorry to **interrupt**, but I disagree.
6. What do you think **about** recycling?
7. Let's **take** a vote on the new policy.
8. The meeting chair has the **casting** vote.
9. I'm **sorry**, but I don't agree.
10. I think it's the best strategy. How **about** you?
11. I just have a few **closing** remarks.

25

25.2 🔊
1. So did I.
2. Me too.
3. So do I.
4. Me neither.
5. Nor did I.

25.3 🔊
1. I suppose you're right, but it was so long!
2. Nor did I. It was too difficult.
3. Yes, I agree. She is very friendly, too.
4. I suppose so, but they are expensive.
5. Me too. They're practical and cheap.
6. Neither did I. He was always moody.
7. So did I. The menu was excellent.

25.5 🔊
1. You could be **right**, but I think it's ugly.
2. I'm **afraid** we disagree about the price.
3. I'm **sorry**, but I don't agree, Jan.
4. I'm afraid I **disagree**. It's too expensive.
5. I'm sorry, Joe, but I don't agree **at all**.

25.6
1. Jeremy strongly disagrees with her.
2. Jeremy agrees with her.
3. Sian disagrees with him.
4. Jeremy strongly agrees with her.

25.7 🔊
1. Yes, I suppose **you're** right about the new design.
2. You **could** be right, but I need to do more research.
3. I'm sorry, but I don't **agree** at all with that comment.
4. I'm **afraid** I don't agree about this one issue.
5. I'm not **sure** about that, Sara. I don't like it.
6. I'm afraid I **totally** disagree. That will never work.

26.3 ◀))
1 They locked themselves in the fridge.
2 He burned himself on the coffee machine.
3 Both of you, protect yourselves from the sun.
4 We booked ourselves on a fire safety course.
5 I fell and hurt myself on the wet floor.

26.4
1 Not given
2 False
3 True

26.5 ◀))
1 assembly point
2 first aid kit
3 fire extinguisher
4 fire exit

26.6 ◀))
1 She's cut **herself**. Get the first aid box.
2 They paid for it **themselves**.
3 The machine started **itself**.
4 Please take care of **yourselves**.
5 Make **yourself** aware of the fire exits.

27

27.3 ◀))
1 Let's do more promotion on social media.
2 We could redesign the packaging for this product.
3 What about hiring a software consultant?

27.5 ◀))
1 You should reset the router.
2 She should tell him before he sees it.
3 I should order some more.
4 We should throw away the food.
5 He should walk around the office.

27.7 ◀))
1 I am **unable** to come in the morning. How about the afternoon?
2 I **misspell** words so often. Why don't we get an editor?

3 The machine isn't working. We should **disconnect** it.
4 Are you **unwell**? Why don't we call a doctor for you?
5 These tests are **impossible**. What about doing easier ones?

27.8
A 4   B 1   C 2   D 5   E 3

27.9 ◀))
1 Let's use our old system again. This new one is so **unfamiliar** and slow.
2 How about changing the time so that more people are **able** to come.
3 Let's discuss the negative feedback from people who **disagree** with our plan.
4 What about explaining the delay to stop people from becoming so **impatient**.
5 I love conventions! It's so easy to **connect** with new people.
6 I have no idea how to write this report. It seems **impossible**!

28

28.2 ◀))
1 To **start** this talk I will give an overall introduction to the project.
2 **Second**, after the introduction, I'll describe our role in the project.
3 Next, we'll **explore** the benefits of this approach.
4 After **that**, we'll look at the possible difficulties we might have.
5 Then, to **finish** we'll look at what future research we can do.
6 Lastly, I will **answer** any questions that you have for me.

28.4
1 False
2 True
3 Not given

28.5 ◀))
1 slide
2 screen
3 projector
4 microphone
5 flipchart

28.7 ◀))
1 I'm happy to answer any questions.
2 So, we've covered the main issues.
3 Does anyone have any questions?
4 Would you like to ask anything?
5 In short, next year is important.

28.8
A 3   B 7   C 4   D 2   E 5   F 1   G 6

28.9 ◀))
1 In **short** we are very proud of our new products.
2 I'd like to **begin** by looking back at past sales.
3 That's all I have to **say** about the advertising campaign.
4 Let's move **on** to talk about the packaging we've designed.
5 Does anyone **have** any questions for me?

29

29.2 ◀))
1 It's a special one for fire safety.
2 There's a nice café across the street.
3 We're meeting clients later this afternoon.
4 I have saved all the documents.

29.3 ◀))
1 Is your stapler broken? You **can** use mine.
2 She **doesn't have to** come to the training session. She did it last year.
3 You **have to** turn off the light if you're the last person to leave the office.
4 He **has to** test the fire alarm every Wednesday morning.
5 We **don't have to** wear a jacket and tie in the summer months.

29.4
1 Not given
2 False
3 True
4 True
5 False

29.8 ◀))
1 Could you **tell** Jan to call me back?
2 Could you **check** this report?
3 Would you mind **ordering** more pens?
4 Could you **mop** the floor, please?

⑤ Could you **come** to today's meeting?
⑥ Would you mind **calling** back later?
⑦ Would you mind **turning** the light off?
⑧ Could you **wash** these cups, please?
⑨ Could you **pass** around the reports?
⑩ Would you mind **booking** me a taxi?
⑪ Could you **show** our clients around?

29.9
① False
② False
③ True
④ True

29.10 ◄))
1. Could you book a meeting room?
2. Could you send Sam Davies an email?
3. Could you call our supplier?
4. Would you mind booking a meeting room?
5. Would you mind sending Sam Davies an email?
6. Would you mind calling our supplier?

31

31.4 ◄)) Nota: las frases negativas también pueden utilizar la forma larga "was not".
① Gabino **wasn't listening** during the team meeting this morning.
② The internet **wasn't working** all day yesterday. I had to call my clients.
③ Hannah and Luke **were talking** during the CEO's presentation.
④ I **was forgetting** to do everyday jobs, so I wrote a list.
⑤ I put you on a new team because you **were losing** sales.

31.5
Respuestas modelo
① He wasn't answering important emails.
② He was leaving Maria to reply to all the sales enquiries.
③ The author's advice was to talk to the co-worker.
④ José was feeling tired after lunch every day.
⑤ He changed his diet so that he ate more salads and vegetables.
⑥ He was working until 5pm every day last week.

31.6
A 5 **B** 1 **C** 3 **D** 2 **E** 4

31.7 ◄)
① Sales were improving. It was **a win-win** situation.
② It's a difficult task. We must think **outside** the box.
③ The team was throwing money **down** the drain.
④ Was your assistant **pulling** his weight today?
⑤ We were working with a lot of **red** tape.
⑥ Now we're all here, let's get **down** to business.

31.8 ◄)
① The elevator is out of order.
② The printer was going haywire yesterday.
③ Our sales fell last year. Now we're in the red.
④ I'm tied up with these difficult reports.

31.9 ◄)
Respuestas modelo
① Gloria is designing packaging for a health tracker watch.
② The marketing department sends her lots of emails.
③ She doesn't get much work done because she's busy answering emails.
④ Mark wants Gloria to take it easy.
⑤ Gloria has written to Faruk to ask for advice.

32

32.2 ◄)
① Don't worry. I have copies of them here.
② No problem. It's Carson.
③ No need. The signal's always bad here.
④ That's OK. We can have coffee first.
⑤ Never mind. I've got myself another one.

32.3
① Sí **②** Sí **③** Sí
④ Sí **⑤** No

32.4 ◄)
① I'm so **sorry** I was late for this morning's meeting.
② I'm afraid that's not good **enough**. I want my money back.
③ I would like to **apologize** for the rudeness of our receptionist.
④ That's OK, but please make **sure** it doesn't happen again.

32.8 ◄)
① She **walked** into the room and saw that Clive **was practicing** his presentation.
② I **was trying** to make an important point when someone's phone **started** to ring.
③ The printer **was working** fine when unfortunately the power **went** off.
④ He **opened** the door and saw that we **were listening** to his conversation.
⑤ We **were eating** lunch in the cafeteria when we **heard** the fire alarm.

32.9
① False
② True
③ False
④ Not given
⑤ True

33

33.3 ◄)
① Adrian **has made** three flower arrangements already today.
② I **have started** work on the report, but I won't finish it tonight.
③ Leah **has cut** four people's hair so far this afternoon.
④ It's early. We **haven't spoken** to any customers yet.

33.4 ◄)
① I've **just** left work and it's very late.
② We haven't shown this to the public **yet**.
③ Have you **just** started selling this product?
④ She hasn't done her training course **yet**.
⑤ They've **just** opened the store doors.

33.5
① True **②** False
③ False **④** True

33.7 ◄)
① **We received** your order two hours ago and sent it about an hour ago.
② I made all those pastries this morning and **I've sold** them all now.
③ **I started** painting Ms. Malone's living room at 7 today, but I haven't finished yet.
④ I emailed the clients yesterday but they **haven't** replied yet.

33.8

1. Some of his new co-workers
2. He had a meeting with his boss
3. She finished her research
4. A marketing conference
5. They both liked his talk

33.9 🔊

1. I **started** in January this year.
2. No, she **hasn't** yet.
3. Yes, I've **just** finished.
4. Not me. I **haven't** been in there.

34.4

Respuestas modelo

1. She did not enjoy it.
2. No one responded to her phone calls.
3. The company will ensure every customer is given a second contact number.
4. There wasn't a vegetarian option in the hotel restaurant.
5. The hotel will offer vegetarian and vegan options.
6. The company has given Ms. Chang a voucher.

34.5 🔊

1. We will refund it to your credit card.
2. I'll take it back to the kitchen.
3. We'll replace them with bigger ones.
4. I'll talk to him about his bad attitude.
5. They'll be with you as soon as possible.

34.7 🔊

1. I'm afraid your order **won't** arrive today.
2. We'll **change** your appointment now.
3. I'll **talk** to my manager for you.
4. We'll **send** you a replacement tomorrow.
5. I **will** contact the courier about the delay.
6. I'll **ask** the chef to bring you a new meal.
7. Your delivery will **arrive** later today.

34.8

1. Sí
2. No
3. No
4. Sí
5. Sí

34.9 🔊

1. I do **apologize**. We'll **replace** the broken part for you.
2. I'm **afraid** it **won't** arrive until Wednesday.
3. We'll **offer** you a **discount** on your next trip.

36.4 🔊

1. If you go to China for business, will you visit the Great Wall?
2. If I go to China on business, I won't have time to go sightseeing.
3. If we win the contract, we will go out to celebrate.
4. Will you arrange a taxi if we land late at the airport?
5. We won't get a discount if we don't book now.
6. If you have a lot of luggage, you will need a taxi.

36.5

1. by taxi
2. Business Class
3. a former colleague
4. to do some sightseeing
5. his passport details

36.9 🔊

1. When you book a transfer, a driver meets you.
2. Passengers get annoyed if the plane takes off late.
3. You can order a special meal if you're vegetarian.

36.10 🔊

1. If you buy food on the plane, it **is** quite expensive.
2. If you **are** in a group, it is often cheaper to go by taxi.
3. Will it be cheaper to **buy** a return ticket if I come back the same day?
4. When you book flights early, they **are** usually cheaper.
5. Traveling is boring if you **don't** have anything to do on the plane.

37.4 🔊

1. The venue is straight ahead and on **the** left.
2. Excuse **me**, do you know where the gym is?
3. Sorry, did you **say** it's on the right?
4. Go straight ahead and **turn** left.
5. The bus stop is in front **of** the park.
6. Do you know the **way** to the post office?
7. The hotel is 50 feet ahead **on** the right.
8. Do you **know** the way to the hotel?
9. **Go** straight ahead and you'll see the sign.
10. The bus stop is directly opposite **the** bank.
11. Turn right at the **intersection**.

37.5 🔊

1. Do you know how to get to Silver Street?
2. It's in front of the red building.
3. Don't take the first right. Take the second.
4. I'll meet you across from the hotel.
5. Go straight ahead and turn left at the lights.
6. The bank is next to the station.

37.6 🔊

1. Sorry, did you say it's opposite the café?
2. Go straight ahead and turn right at the intersection.
3. Do you know how to get to the venue?
4. Go past the post office and it's on the left.

37.7

1. A 2. B 3. B 4. A 5. A

37.8 🔊

1. Take the first **left**, and go **past** the hotel.
2. It's across from the hospital. Take the **second** right.
3. Go straight **ahead**. It's on the **corner**.
4. Take the first **right**, then **go** straight ahead.
5. Just go **straight** ahead and it's on the **left**.

38.4 🔊

1. The rooms were cleaned this morning.
2. The key was left in the door.
3. The VIPs were met in the boardroom.
4. Flowers were put in the hotel foyer.

38.5 🔊
1 The car was driven by a chauffeur.
2 The key was found by the guest.
3 They were shown around the conference venue.

38.6
Ⓐ 4　Ⓑ 1　Ⓒ 3　Ⓓ 2

38.7
1 False　2 True　3 True
4 False　5 False　6 True

38.8 🔊
1 pick up
2 fall apart
3 turn on
4 check out
5 look around

38.9
Ⓐ 2　Ⓑ 4　Ⓒ 5　Ⓓ 1　Ⓔ 3

38.10 🔊
1 Breakfast **was served** in the main restaurant.
2 The rooms **were cleaned** every day.
3 The reservation **was made** by my assistant.
4 Yes. Very. They **were decorated** beautifully.

40.2 🔊
1 Yes, we spoke on the phone.
2 Have you been to Mexico City before?
3 I'll let Mrs. Singh know that you're here.
4 Would you like some tea or coffee?
5 Did you have a good flight?
6 I've been looking forward to this visit.
7 It's great to meet you in person.
8 Did you have any trouble getting here?
9 Can I get you anything?

40.4 🔊
1 Would you like **a** cup of tea?
2 Do you take **(any)** sugar?
3 Did you have **a** good trip?
4 Could I have **some** water, please?
5 Here are **some** details about the hotel.

40.5 🔊
1 I didn't bring any luggage.
2 Did you have a good flight?
3 Do you need any help?
4 Would you like to meet the team?
5 There will be something to eat.
6 Can I get you anything to drink?
7 Please take a seat and wait here.

40.6
1 The evening before
2 A product launch
3 Social media and marketing

40.7 🔊
1 The **keynote** speech will start at 10am.
2 The main **presenter** used a lot of slides.
3 The main sponsor will **launch** a new product.
4 Every attendee gets a **lanyard** and a name tag.
5 In a workshop the **delegates** get involved.
6 There are lots of **networking** opportunities.

40.8 🔊
1 They have **some** free food and drinks.
2 Do you have **a** lanyard already?
3 I have **some** business cards to give people.
4 I'd like to see **some** interesting talks.
5 Are you going to **any** talks today?
6 Do you have **a** business card?
7 Are you staying in **a** hotel?
8 They don't have **any** drinks.
9 I'm giving **a** presentation today.

40.9
2

40.10 🔊
1 It's Leo Smart. I haven't collected my **lanyard** yet.
2 Yes, here. Please take my **business card**.
3 Yes, and I went to an interesting **workshop** this morning.

41.2 🔊
1 Would you like to see the dessert menu?
2 Could we have some sparkling water, please?
3 Could I have a receipt for this, please?

41.3 🔊
1 The **reservation** was for six, but now there are only five.
2 Is there anything that you **recommend**?
3 Yes. I'm **allergic** to shellfish.
4 It's ok, **but** the food is a little bit cold.

41.5 🔊
1 How much rice do you want?
2 I don't need more. There's enough here.
3 There are too many seats here.
4 There's not enough water.
5 $40 for a steak! That's too much.

41.6 🔊
1 I've eaten **too** many chocolates.
2 How **many** glasses do we need?
3 There's too **much** sauce on this.
4 How **much** should we tip here?

41.7
1 True
2 True
3 False
4 True
5 Not given

42.2 🔊
1 Hi, Karl. It's Katie **from** HR.
2 Hi. I'm **calling** about the Wi-Fi.
3 My client is here. I'd **better** be going.
4 Can I ask **who's** calling, please?
5 Is there **anything** else I can do for you?
6 Hello. Olga **speaking**.
7 No, thanks. That's **all**. Bye.

42.3
Ⓐ 2　Ⓑ 6　Ⓒ 4　Ⓓ 1　Ⓔ 5　Ⓕ 3

42.4 🔊
1. Hi. Can I speak **to** Jacob, please?
2. Hello, Sophie. **It's** Ahmed from sales.
3. Could I **ask** who's calling, please?
4. Hi. Adam **speaking**.
5. It's Sandy **from** IT.
6. Hi. **I'm calling** because the elevator is stuck.
7. Bye then. **Speak** to you soon.
8. Can I ask **who's calling**, please?

42.7
1. 6057700930
2. 03069990555
3. 01632960042
4. 01184962027
5. 07700900844
6. 03069690447
7. 01632960177

42.8 🔊
1. **Can** you call Martin at the office? His number's 902-555-4349.
2. You **can** call me on my cell phone any time. My number's 03069 991332.
3. Hi, it's Myra. **Can** you call me back? My number's 07064 881206.
4. **Would** you be able to call me back? I'm at the office. My extension is 8762.
5. If you **want** to contact Samuel later, his number's 01632 960441.
6. I've got a number for Hanna if you **want** to contact her. It's 321-554-8933.

42.9
1. A project selling shoes
2. She cannot connect to the Wi-Fi
3. Enter a different passcode
4. GJ330XS
5. He will fix it

42.12 🔊
1. Anna, can I call you **back** later from the office?
2. Suzanna always takes ages to pick **up** the phone.
3. Ethan, I will get back **to** you later with an answer.
4. I'll put you **through** to Ivor now.
5. If a customer is very rude, you can hang **up**.
6. I'll find out the information and get **back** to you.
7. I'm busy now, Valeria, but I'll call **you** back later.

42.13 🔊
1. I'll put you through to Simone in sales.
2. I will call you back later this afternoon.
3. Sorry about that; we were just cut off.

42.14 🔊
1. get cut off
2. pick up
3. speak up
4. call you back
5. breaking up
6. get back to them

43

43.2 🔊
1. Can you say that I'll arrive late?
2. Could I speak to someone in sales?
3. Can I leave a message for her?
4. Certainly. I'll just put you through.
5. I have a problem with an order.
6. Hello. I wonder if you could help me.

43.3 🔊
1. May I ask who's **calling**?
2. I'll just **put** you through.
3. I'm **afraid** he's away today.
4. **How** can I help you?

43.4
2.

43.7 🔊
OPINIÓN:
useful, **awful**
TAMAÑO:
large, **tiny**
EDAD:
antique, **new**
COLOR:
blue, **green**
MATERIAL:
wooden, **glass**

43.8 🔊
1. My boss has a **friendly large white** cat.
2. My computer is a **huge old white** desktop from 1995.
3. We're marketing a **clever tiny new** watch that helps keep you fit.
4. Have you seen the **amazing tiny black** briefcase she has?
5. The meeting room has a **very large modern** painting.

43.9
1. False
2. False
3. Not given
4. True
5. False
6. Not given

44

44.2 🔊
1. Personal statement
2. Career summary
3. Professional achievements
4. Education
5. Interests
6. References

44.3 🔊
1. I am **fluent** in Japanese and Mandarin Chinese.
2. I have a great deal of **hands-on** experience in the construction industry.
3. I have an **in-depth** knowledge of hair-coloring techniques.
4. As an ex-car salesman, I have a **service-oriented** background.
5. I am a highly **motivated** librarian and love reading.
6. I am **proficient** in all major types of accounting software.

44.5 🔊
1. Our teams **collaborated** to create the packaging design.
2. We **established** a new headquarters downtown.
3. I **coordinated** a staff training day for all departments.
4. I **volunteered** for a charity and built a classroom.

⑤ I **negotiated** with all our suppliers and cut costs by 15 percent.

44.6
① True
② True
③ False
④ Not given
⑤ False

45.4 ◁»
Nota: las respuestas de **①**, **②** y **④** también pueden redactarse en su forma abreviada.
① They **are not going to** invest a lot of money next year.
② He **is going to travel** by plane and then taxi to the meeting.
③ **Are** you **going to meet** with the suppliers next week?
④ We **are going to buy** the best quality business cards we can.

45.5 ◁»
① Make sure you have your passports.
② Can you let her know what happens?
③ We should email the printers today.
④ It's good to work with different people.
⑤ He wants to spend more time playing golf.

45.6
Ⓐ 2 **Ⓑ** 1 **Ⓒ** 3 **Ⓓ** 5 **Ⓔ** 4

45.8 ◁»
① Could you come to my office?
② Why don't we discuss this at the meeting?
③ Can you tell me when it's finished, please?
④ Could we move these files?
⑤ Could you send the design to the printers?
⑥ Can you help me with these figures, please?

45.9 ◁»
① Can **you help** me move this cupboard?
② Could you **be** a little neater, please?
③ Can you **finish** the design soon, please?
④ Could **we** meet at 5 instead of 6?
⑤ Could you **possibly** send me the report today?
⑥ Can you **clean up** the meeting room?

45.10 ◁»
Respuestas modelo
① Sven is going to meet the printers in the afternoon.
② Diane is going to work on the Information Desk.
③ All the delegates are going to wear lanyards during the conference.
④ Simon is going to check that the rooms all have projectors and an internet connection.

47

47.3
① Technology
② Discarded to landfill
③ Purchase it
④ The environment
⑤ In a meeting

47.4 ◁»
① Please find your **invoice attached to** this email.
② I am writing to you as the new CEO **at** Yogurt500.
③ I **would appreciate** it if you could reply by 3 o'clock this afternoon.
④ My name's Scott and I work **in** the packaging department.

47.6 ◁»
① He is **emailing** all the clients this afternoon.
② She is **going to send** vouchers to all customers.
③ They are **going to meet** in Rome to discuss options.
④ I am **speaking** with our couriers tomorrow.

47.7 ◁»
① We hope they're **going to offer** us a discount.
② Our CEO is **going to discuss** a merger.
③ Simone is **sending** your invoice this afternoon.
④ Mark and Johan are **going to answer** the calls later.

47.8
① is going to take place
② Please find attached
③ We are going to
④ in the
⑤ is also attending
⑥ going to discuss

ENGLISH
FOR EVERYONE

LIBRO DE ESTUDIO **NIVEL ❷**

BUSINESS ENGLISH

Nivel ❷ Contenidos

01 Presentaciones

Tienes muchas expresiones para presentarte cuando entras en una empresa. Los demás también tienen otras expresiones para presentarte.

⚙ **Lenguaje** Present simple y present continuous
Aa Vocabulario Etiqueta de las presentaciones
🧩 **Habilidad** Presentarte a ti mismo y a otros

1.1 PUNTO CLAVE PRESENTARTE A TI MISMO Y A OTROS

Es habitual dar la mano a los nuevos colegas y presentarse.

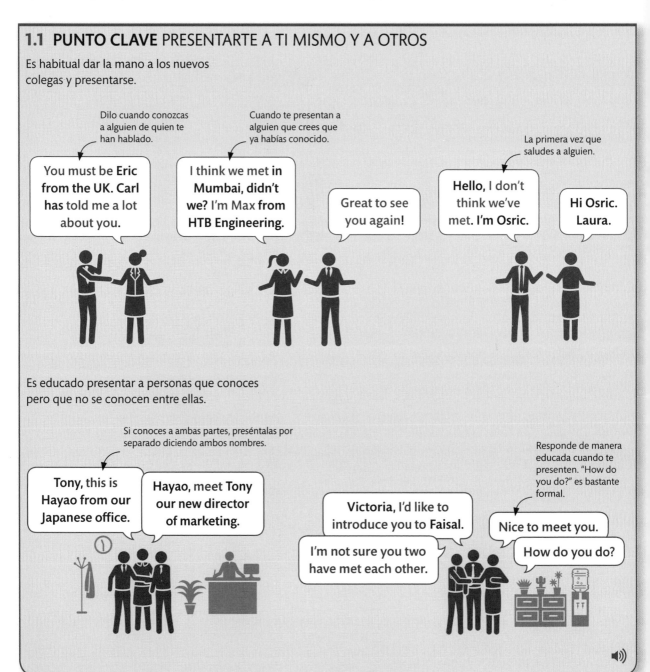

Dilo cuando conozcas a alguien de quien te han hablado.

> You must be **Eric from the UK. Carl has** told me a lot about you.

Cuando te presentan a alguien que crees que ya habías conocido.

> I think we met **in Mumbai, didn't we?** I'm Max **from HTB Engineering.**

> Great to see you again!

La primera vez que saludes a alguien.

> Hello, I don't think we've met. I'm Osric.

> Hi Osric. Laura.

Es educado presentar a personas que conoces pero que no se conocen entre ellas.

Si conoces a ambas partes, preséntalas por separado diciendo ambos nombres.

> Tony, this is Hayao from our Japanese office.

> Hayao, meet **Tony our new director of marketing.**

> Victoria, I'd like to introduce you to **Faisal.**

> I'm not sure you two have met each other.

Responde de manera educada cuando te presenten. "How do you do?" es bastante formal.

> Nice to meet you.

> How do you do?

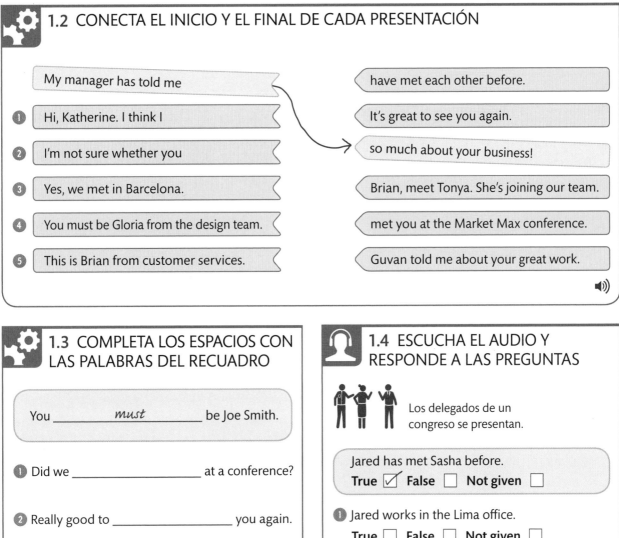

1.2 CONECTA EL INICIO Y EL FINAL DE CADA PRESENTACIÓN

My manager has told me

1. Hi, Katherine. I think I

2. I'm not sure whether you

3. Yes, we met in Barcelona.

4. You must be Gloria from the design team.

5. This is Brian from customer services.

have met each other before.

It's great to see you again.

so much about your business!

Brian, meet Tonya. She's joining our team.

met you at the Market Max conference.

Guvan told me about your great work.

1.3 COMPLETA LOS ESPACIOS CON LAS PALABRAS DEL RECUADRO

You _____must_____ be Joe Smith.

1. Did we _____ at a conference?

2. Really good to _____ you again.

3. Roula, meet Maria, _____ new assistant.

4. I'd like to _____ you to Karl.

5. Have you two _____ each other before?

~~must~~   introduce
meet   our
        met   see

1.4 ESCUCHA EL AUDIO Y RESPONDE A LAS PREGUNTAS

Los delegados de un congreso se presentan.

Jared has met Sasha before.
True ☑ **False** ☐ **Not given** ☐

1. Jared works in the Lima office.
True ☐ **False** ☐ **Not given** ☐

2. Daniel and Sasha have not met before.
True ☐ **False** ☐ **Not given** ☐

3. Daniel shares an office with Jared.
True ☐ **False** ☐ **Not given** ☐

4. Their new product is expensive.
True ☐ **False** ☐ **Not given** ☐

5. Sasha works in Lima.
True ☐ **False** ☐ **Not given** ☐

199

1.5 **PUNTO CLAVE** EL PRESENT SIMPLE Y EL PRESENT CONTINUOUS

Utiliza el present simple para describir algo que pasa en general o que forma parte de algo repetitivo. El present continuous describe algo que pasa ahora mismo y que continuará pasando durante un tiempo determinado.

I don't usually enjoy networking, but I'm enjoying this conference.

El **present simple** se construye con la forma base del verbo sin "to".

El **present continuous** se forma añadiendo "be" antes del verbo e "-ing" después.

1.6 LEE EL ARTÍCULO Y RESPONDE A LAS PREGUNTAS

What word is used for making connections?
Networking ✓ Sharing ☐ Dividing ☐

① What kind of people is the article aimed at?
Shy ☐ Confident ☐ Intelligent ☐

② What types of connections are useful?
New ones ☐ Good ones ☐ Lots of them ☐

③ Who might be useful people to talk to?
Ex-colleagues ☐ Recruiters ☐ Family ☐

④ What do shy people do a lot?
Lie ☐ Say sorry ☐ Say thank you ☐

⑤ What does apologizing a lot make you seem?
Confident ☐ Worried ☐ Unprofessional ☐

⑥ Where should you look when talking to people?
Their eyes ☐ Their feet ☐ Their mouths ☐

⑦ What should you give contacts?
Money ☐ Gifts ☐ Your business card ☐

CAREER LADDER

Making connections

How to network better if you're shy

Networking doesn't necessarily mean talking to hundreds of people at a conference. A few good connections are much better than meeting lots of people who you will never hear from again. Start by chatting to ex-colleagues or old friends. Ask what they are doing now and share your experiences.

One common habit of shy people is to constantly apologize for everything. Apologizing all of the time looks unprofessional and shows a lack of confidence in yourself. Instead of saying sorry, remember to smile, maintain eye contact, ask questions, and, of course, exchange business cards.

1.7 VUELVE A ESCRIBIR LAS FRASES CORRIGIENDO LOS ERRORES

> I am being happy to finally meet you, Zoe.
> *I'm happy to finally meet you, Zoe.*

1 Hi James. I'm Vanisha. I don't think we are meeting before.

_____

2 Ashley, I'd like introduce you to my colleague Neil.

_____

3 I enjoying the presentations. Are you?

_____

4 Nice to meet you Bethany. How do you doing?

_____

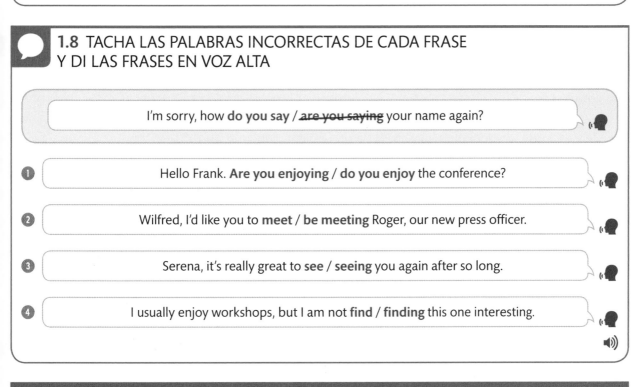

1.8 TACHA LAS PALABRAS INCORRECTAS DE CADA FRASE Y DI LAS FRASES EN VOZ ALTA

> I'm sorry, how **do you say** / ~~are you saying~~ your name again?

1 Hello Frank. **Are you enjoying** / **do you enjoy** the conference?

2 Wilfred, I'd like you to **meet** / **be meeting** Roger, our new press officer.

3 Serena, it's really great to **see** / **seeing** you again after so long.

4 I usually enjoy workshops, but I am not **find** / **finding** this one interesting.

---

01 ✓ CHECKLIST

⚙ Present simple y continuous ☐   **Aa** Etiqueta de las presentaciones ☐   Presentarte a ti mismo y a otros ☐

02 Conocer a los colegas

Hablar de antiguos empleos es una buena manera de conocer a los colegas. Para hacerlo se suelen utilizar el past simple y el past continuous.

🗝 **Lenguaje** Past simple y past continuous
Aa Vocabulario Compartir experiencias anteriores
🧩 **Habilidad** Hablar sobre el pasado

2.1 PUNTO CLAVE EL PAST SIMPLE Y EL PAST CONTINUOUS

Utiliza el past simple para hablar de una acción concreta y finalizada del pasado, costumbres del pasado o un estado que se produjo durante un tiempo en el pasado.

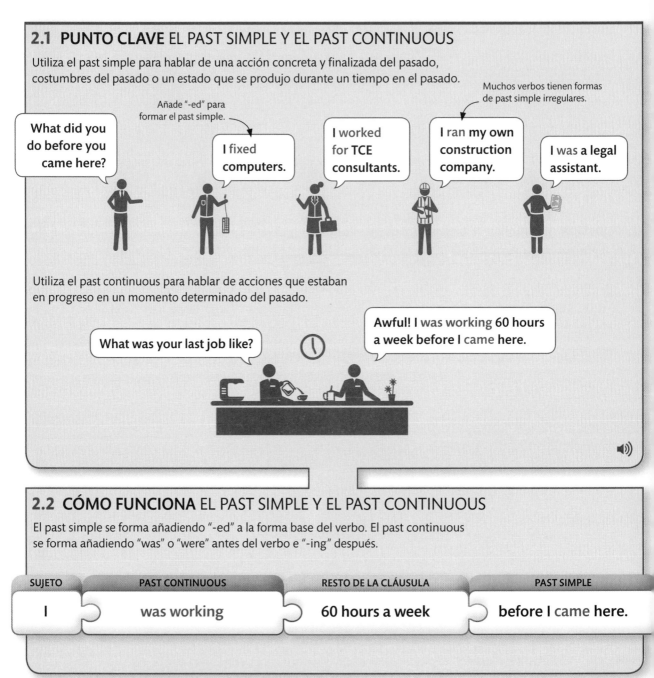

Muchos verbos tienen formas de past simple irregulares.

Añade "-ed" para formar el past simple.

What did you do before you came here?

I fixed computers.

I worked for **TCE** consultants.

I ran **my own construction company.**

I was **a legal assistant.**

Utiliza el past continuous para hablar de acciones que estaban en progreso en un momento determinado del pasado.

What was your last job like?

Awful! I was working 60 hours a week before I came here.

2.2 CÓMO FUNCIONA EL PAST SIMPLE Y EL PAST CONTINUOUS

El past simple se forma añadiendo "-ed" a la forma base del verbo. El past continuous se forma añadiendo "was" o "were" antes del verbo e "-ing" después.

SUJETO	PAST CONTINUOUS	RESTO DE LA CLÁUSULA	PAST SIMPLE
I	was working	60 hours a week	before I came here.

I started / ~~was starting~~ my own printing company more than 10 years ago.

1 They **began** / **were beginning** to sell more when the shop suddenly closed last year.

2 I **lost** / **was losing** my job when the factory closed last December.

3 I was delighted when I **got** / **was getting** promoted to senior manager in 2015.

4 We moved here when my wife **was finding** / **found** a new job two years ago.

5 I **was training** / **trained** to be a chef when I was given this award.

6 When I worked 90 hours a week, I **felt** / **was feeling** exhausted all the time.

7 When I was a photographer, I **was meeting** / **met** a lot of famous people through my work.

🔊

2.4 **PUNTO CLAVE** EL PRETÉRITO Y LA EDUCACIÓN

Es posible que oigas preguntas sobre situaciones actuales en pretérito: así la pregunta suena más educada.

"Do" pasa a "Did" para formular la pregunta en pretérito.

Did you want a tour of the office?

A veces también se utiliza el pretérito para formular una petición más educada.

I wanted **to ask about the company's history.**

🔊

2.5 MARCA LAS FRASES QUE SEAN CORRECTAS

Did you want some more coffee? ☑
Do you wanting some more coffee? ☐

1 I was to look for another job. ☐
I was looking for another job. ☐

2 I was wondering if you could help. ☐
I was wondered if you could help. ☐

3 Were you working as a waiter? ☐
Were you work as a waiter? ☐

4 They weren't employing young people. ☐
They not employing young people. ☐

5 I didn't enjoy my last job. ☐
I didn't enjoying my last job. ☐

6 Did you work in a hotel? ☐
Did you working in a hotel? ☐

🔊

2.6 PUNTO CLAVE EL PRESENT PERFECT SIMPLE

El present perfect simple se utiliza para hablar de acontecimientos del pasado reciente que tienen efecto aún en el momento actual.

No se dice la fecha, por eso se utiliza el present perfect.

Se indica una fecha concreta, por eso se utiliza el past simple.

So, have you worked in a team before?

I have worked **in a few different teams.**

No, I haven't worked **in a team before.**

I worked **in a small team in 2005.**

2.7 CÓMO FUNCIONA EL PRESENT PERFECT SIMPLE

El present perfect simple se construye con "have" y un past participle.

SUJETO	"HAVE / HAS" + PAST PARTICIPLE	RESTO DE LA FRASE
I	**have worked**	**in a few teams.**

2.8 COMPLETA LOS ESPACIOS ESCRIBIENDO LOS VERBOS EN PRESENT PERFECT SIMPLE

Susan ___*has worked*___ (work) here since she graduated from college five years ago.

❶ He _____ (take) 15 days off sick this year and it is only May!

❷ Julia has a lot of experience. She _____ (manage) this department for years.

❸ They _____ (employ) more than 300 people over the years.

❹ John _____ (train) lots of young employees across a few different teams.

❺ I'm so happy! I _____ (finish) my apprenticeship at last.

❻ My manager _____ (approve) my vacation days. I'm going to Italy in July.

2.9 ESCUCHA EL AUDIO Y RESPONDE A LAS PREGUNTAS

Dos colegas hablan sobre trabajos anteriores.

This is Suzi's first day at the company.
True ☐ **False** ✓ **Not given** ☐

❶ Suzi's previous company was smaller.
True ☐ **False** ☐ **Not given** ☐

❷ Suzi has always worked in HR.
True ☐ **False** ☐ **Not given** ☐

❸ Jack has worked for CIE for six years.
True ☐ **False** ☐ **Not given** ☐

❹ Jack has never worked for another company.
True ☐ **False** ☐ **Not given** ☐

❺ Jack and Suzi always work the same days.
True ☐ **False** ☐ **Not given** ☐

2.10 TACHA LAS PALABRAS INCORRECTAS DE CADA FRASE Y DI LAS FRASES EN VOZ ALTA

I ~~worked~~ / ~~was working~~ / have worked in marketing since 1995.

❶ I drove / was driving / **have driven** taxis when I saw this job advertised.

❷ I managed / was managing / **have managed** accounts for this company for seven years.

❸ I bought / was buying / **have bought** my first business in 2009.

❹ I was studying in college when I saw / was seeing / **have seen** this job.

❺ They invested / were investing / **have invested** in this company since 2010.

❻ In 2014, I **sold** / was selling / has sold the company to an investor.

02 ✓ CHECKLIST

⚙ Past simple y past continuous ☐   **Aa** Compartir experiencias anteriores ☐   🧩 Hablar sobre el pasado ☐

3.1 DEPARTAMENTOS

Administration

[deals with organization and internal and external communication]

Production

[ensures all manufacturing stages run smoothly]

Research and Development (R&D)

[deals with researching and developing future products for a company]

Purchasing

[deals with buying goods and raw materials]

Human Resources (HR)

[deals with employee relations and matters such as hiring staff]

Sales

[deals with selling a finished product to outside markets]

Accounts / Finance

[deals with money matters, from paying bills to projecting sales]

Facilities / Office Services

[ensures the smooth day-to-day running of the practical aspects of a company]

Marketing

[deals with promoting products]

Legal

[ensures that all contracts and company activities are legal]

Public Relations (PR)

[deals with maintaining a positive public image for a company]

Information Technology (IT)

[ensures that all technological systems are working and maintained]

3.2 ROLES

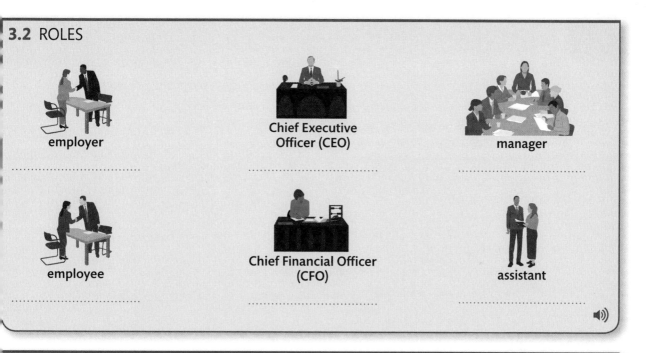

employer

Chief Executive Officer (CEO)

manager

employee

Chief Financial Officer (CFO)

assistant

3.3 DESCRIBIR ROLES

We all work for a large department store.

to work for
[to be employed by a company]

He looks after our salaries and wages.

to look after
[to ensure something runs smoothly]

I work in event management.

to work in
[to be employed in a department or area of an industry]

They are responsible for office maintenance.

to be responsible for
[to have the duty of ensuring something is done effectively]

She works as a fashion designer.

to work as
[to have a particular job or role]

I'm in charge of administration.

to be in charge of
[to have control and authority over something]

04 Hablar de cambios

Puedes hablar de muchas maneras sobre cambios en el trabajo en el pasado y en el presente. Muchas expresiones incluyen "used to", que tiene distintos significados.

🔧 **Lenguaje** "Used to", "be / get used to"
Aa Vocabulario Charla informal
🧩 **Habilidad** Hablar sobre cambios en el trabajo

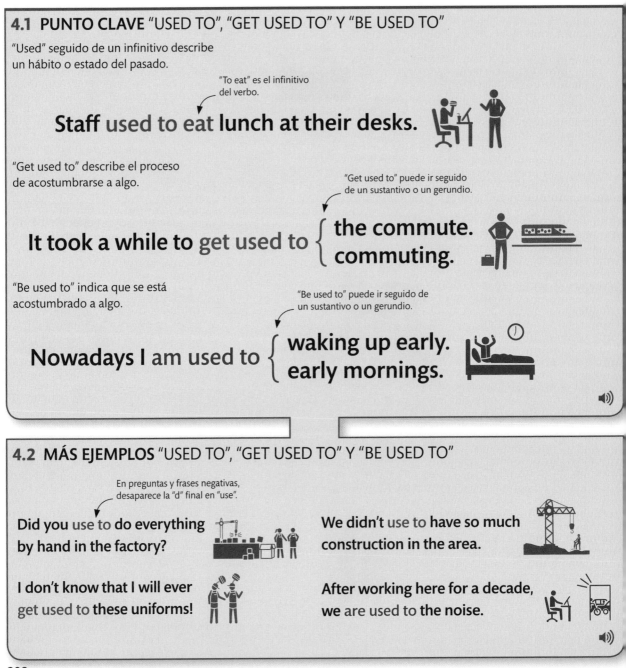

4.1 PUNTO CLAVE "USED TO", "GET USED TO" Y "BE USED TO"

"Used" seguido de un infinitivo describe un hábito o estado del pasado.

"To eat" es el infinitivo del verbo.

Staff used to eat lunch at their desks.

"Get used to" describe el proceso de acostumbrarse a algo.

"Get used to" puede ir seguido de un sustantivo o un gerundio.

It took a while to get used to { **the commute.** **commuting.** }

"Be used to" indica que se está acostumbrado a algo.

"Be used to" puede ir seguido de un sustantivo o un gerundio.

Nowadays I am used to { **waking up early.** **early mornings.** }

4.2 MÁS EJEMPLOS "USED TO", "GET USED TO" Y "BE USED TO"

En preguntas y frases negativas, desaparece la "d" final en "use".

Did you use to do everything by hand in the factory?

We didn't use to have so much construction in the area.

I don't know that I will ever get used to these uniforms!

After working here for a decade, we are used to the noise.

4.3 MARCA LAS FRASES QUE SEAN CORRECTAS

He is used to working from home. ☑
He is use to working from home. ☐

1. I use to travel to work by car. ☐
   I used to travel to work by car. ☐

2. She's used to giving big presentations. ☐
   She's used to give big presentations. ☐

3. I'll get used to my new job eventually. ☐
   I get used my new job eventually. ☐

4. We didn't used to get paid a bonus. ☐
   We didn't use to get paid a bonus. ☐

5. Did he use to work in marketing? ☐
   Did he used to work in marketing? ☐

🔊

4.4 ESCUCHA EL AUDIO Y NUMERA LAS IMÁGENES EN EL ORDEN EN QUE SE DESCRIBEN

Ⓐ ☐

Ⓑ 1

Ⓒ ☐

Ⓓ ☐

4.5 VUELVE A ESCRIBIR LAS FRASES PONIENDO LAS PALABRAS EN SU ORDEN CORRECTO

| to | here? | get | Will | used | we | living | ever |

Will we ever get used to living here?

1. | on | used | finish | Fridays. | at | We | to | noon |

_____

2. | serious. | didn't | to | She | be | use | so |

_____

3. | strict | am | boss. | used | working | I | for | to | a |

_____

4. | to | London? | work | you | Did | use | in |

_____

🔊

209

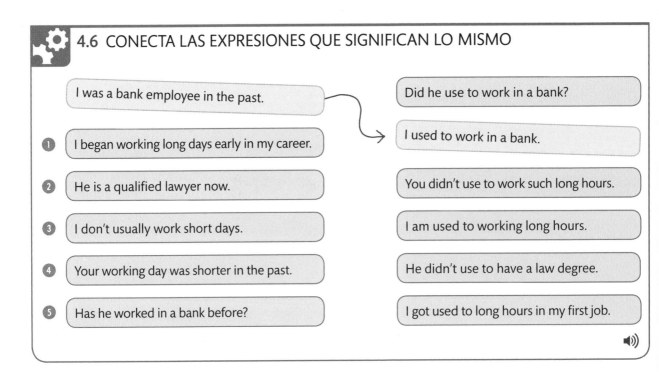

4.6 CONECTA LAS EXPRESIONES QUE SIGNIFICAN LO MISMO

I was a bank employee in the past. → I used to work in a bank.

Did he use to work in a bank?

1. I began working long days early in my career.

2. He is a qualified lawyer now.

3. I don't usually work short days.

4. Your working day was shorter in the past.

5. Has he worked in a bank before?

You didn't use to work such long hours.

I am used to working long hours.

He didn't use to have a law degree.

I got used to long hours in my first job.

4.7 LEE EL ARTÍCULO Y RESPONDE A LAS PREGUNTAS

Weather is a common topic for small talk.
True ☑ False ☐ Not given ☐

1. Being good at small talk can give you an advantage in your job.
True ☐ False ☐ Not given ☐

2. Sports are the most common topic for small talk.
True ☐ False ☐ Not given ☐

3. People who are good at small talk are generally disliked.
True ☐ False ☐ Not given ☐

4. When talking to a colleague, don't look at their face.
True ☐ False ☐ Not given ☐

5. Not every topic is suitable for small talk.
True ☐ False ☐ Not given ☐

WORKPLACE ADVICE

It's good to talk

Small talk—chatting about trivial topics such as the weather

"**M**orning, Sammy. Did you see the game last night?" This kind of small talk happens in every office around the world, every day. People who make an effort to talk to others are more well-liked by their colleagues. When you make small talk, you make the other person feel more relaxed, and form a connection with that person. People who are good at small talk tend to be quick thinkers, and businesses like employees who can think on their feet. So what are the key skills you need to master to be good at small talk? Make eye contact with the other person, and listen. Be interested in what they have to say. Stick to topics such as hobbies, books, films, and the weather. And avoid uncomfortable topics such as politics, religion, and money.

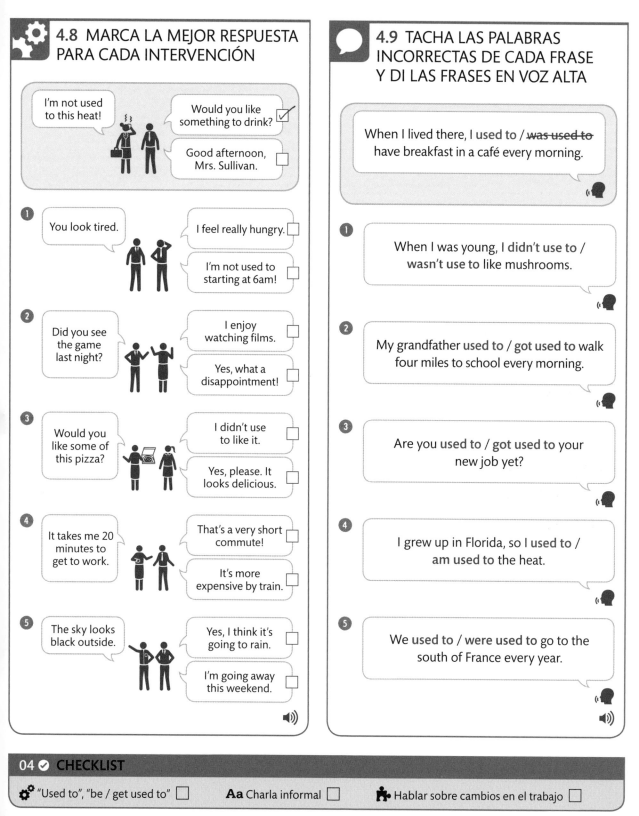

4.8 MARCA LA MEJOR RESPUESTA PARA CADA INTERVENCIÓN

I'm not used to this heat!

Would you like something to drink? ✓

Good afternoon, Mrs. Sullivan. ☐

1 You look tired.

I feel really hungry. ☐

I'm not used to starting at 6am! ☐

2 Did you see the game last night?

I enjoy watching films. ☐

Yes, what a disappointment! ☐

3 Would you like some of this pizza?

I didn't use to like it. ☐

Yes, please. It looks delicious. ☐

4 It takes me 20 minutes to get to work.

That's a very short commute! ☐

It's more expensive by train. ☐

5 The sky looks black outside.

Yes, I think it's going to rain. ☐

I'm going away this weekend. ☐

4.9 TACHA LAS PALABRAS INCORRECTAS DE CADA FRASE Y DI LAS FRASES EN VOZ ALTA

When I lived there, I used to / ~~was used to~~ have breakfast in a café every morning.

1 When I was young, I didn't use to / wasn't use to like mushrooms.

2 My grandfather used to / got used to walk four miles to school every morning.

3 Are you used to / got used to your new job yet?

4 I grew up in Florida, so I used to / am used to the heat.

5 We used to / were used to go to the south of France every year.

---

04 ✔ **CHECKLIST**

⚙ "Used to", "be / get used to" ☐   **Aa** Charla informal ☐   🧩 Hablar sobre cambios en el trabajo ☐

211

05 Delegar tareas

Tal vez quieras delegar tareas a tus colegas cuando haya mucho trabajo. Para ello, en inglés se utilizan varios verbos modales para indicar el nivel de obligación.

⚙ **Lenguaje** Verbos modales de obligación
Aa Vocabulario Delegación y educación
🧩 **Habilidad** Delegar tareas a los colegas

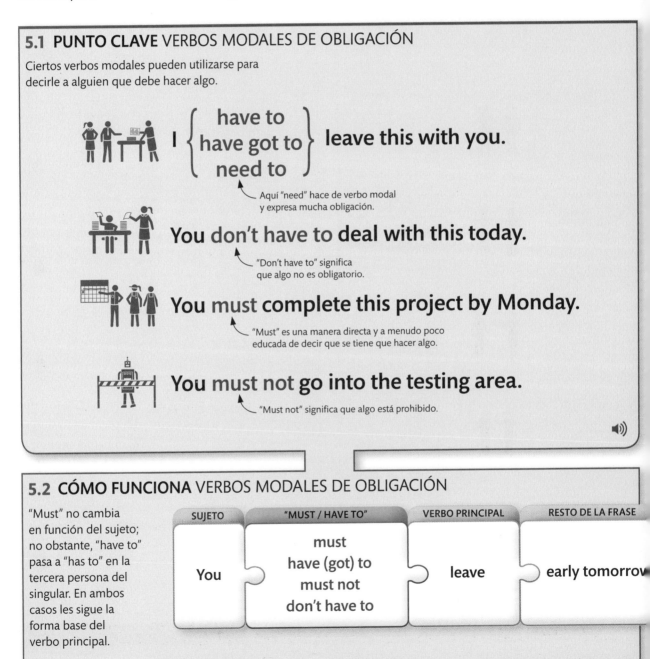

5.1 PUNTO CLAVE VERBOS MODALES DE OBLIGACIÓN

Ciertos verbos modales pueden utilizarse para decirle a alguien que debe hacer algo.

I { have to / have got to / need to } leave this with you.

Aquí "need" hace de verbo modal y expresa mucha obligación.

You don't have to deal with this today.

"Don't have to" significa que algo no es obligatorio.

You must complete this project by Monday.

"Must" es una manera directa y a menudo poco educada de decir que se tiene que hacer algo.

You must not go into the testing area.

"Must not" significa que algo está prohibido.

5.2 CÓMO FUNCIONA VERBOS MODALES DE OBLIGACIÓN

"Must" no cambia en función del sujeto; no obstante, "have to" pasa a "has to" en la tercera persona del singular. En ambos casos les sigue la forma base del verbo principal.

SUJETO	"MUST / HAVE TO"	VERBO PRINCIPAL	RESTO DE LA FRASE
You	must / have (got) to / must not / don't have to	leave	early tomorrow

5.3 CONECTA EL INICIO Y EL FINAL DE CADA FRASE

I need you to —— take care of this project while I'm away.

1. We have got to ask — for some support on this project.

2. You must put the finished — proposal on my desk tomorrow.

3. We must not forget — to complete it today.

4. I have to help Sami produce — a report about recycling.

5. You don't have — to look after this project while he's away.

🔊

5.4 MARCA LAS FRASES QUE SEAN CORRECTAS

You have to do this assignment today. ☑
You has to do this assignment today. ☐

1. We need to increase sales to Europe. ☐
   We need increase sales to Europe. ☐

2. We can't reveal our new product yet. ☐
   We can't to reveal our new product yet. ☐

3. You don't having to work late. ☐
   You don't have to work late. ☐

4. I will need the accounts by tomorrow. ☐
   I need have the accounts tomorrow. ☐

5. We have get to find a new IT manager. ☐
   We have got to find a new IT manager. ☐

6. You must to produce a spreadsheet. ☐
   You need to produce a spreadsheet. ☐

7. We must reaching our sales target. ☐
   We must reach our sales target. ☐

🔊

5.5 ESCUCHA EL AUDIO Y RESPONDE A LAS PREGUNTAS

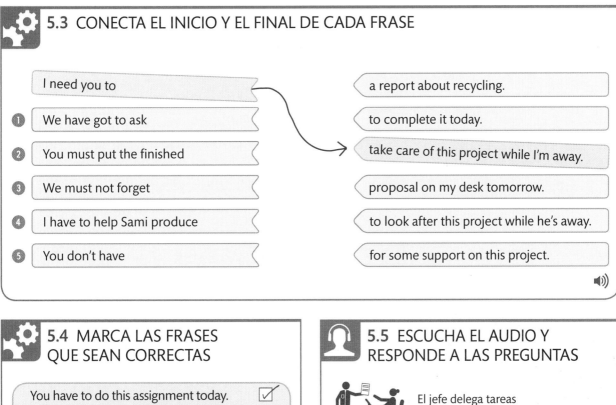

El jefe delega tareas a un empleado de la empresa.

The conference takes place once a year.
True ☐ **False** ☐ **Not given** ☑

1. The conference will take place in August.
   True ☐ **False** ☐ **Not given** ☐

2. The conference will take place at the office.
   True ☐ **False** ☐ **Not given** ☐

3. The manager wants Shona to ask about prices.
   True ☐ **False** ☐ **Not given** ☐

4. Shona must complete the task by tomorrow.
   True ☐ **False** ☐ **Not given** ☐

5. Shona's boss often delegates work to her.
   True ☐ **False** ☐ **Not given** ☐

213

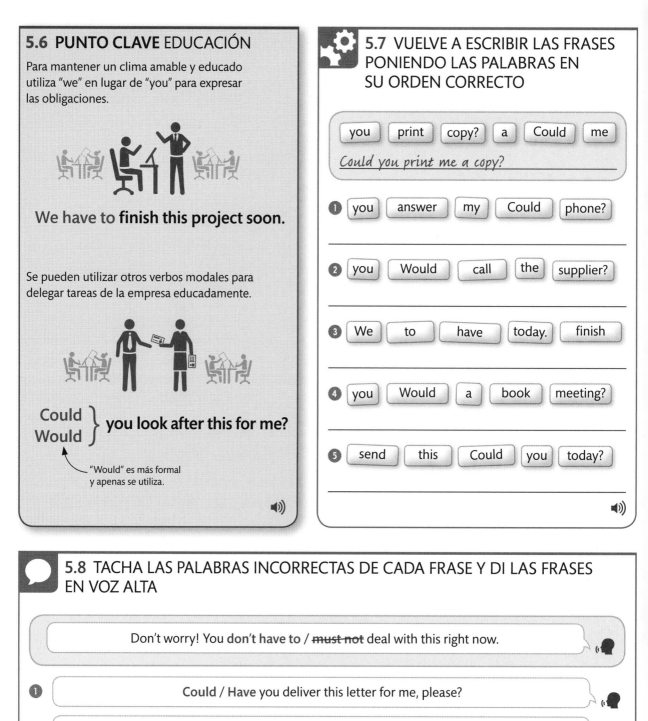

5.6 PUNTO CLAVE EDUCACIÓN

Para mantener un clima amable y educado utiliza "we" en lugar de "you" para expresar las obligaciones.

We have to finish this project soon.

Se pueden utilizar otros verbos modales para delegar tareas de la empresa educadamente.

Could
Would
} **you look after this for me?**

"Would" es más formal y apenas se utiliza.

5.7 VUELVE A ESCRIBIR LAS FRASES PONIENDO LAS PALABRAS EN SU ORDEN CORRECTO

| you | print | copy? | a | Could | me |

Could you print me a copy?

1 | you | answer | my | Could | phone? |

_____

2 | you | Would | call | the | supplier? |

_____

3 | We | to | have | today. | finish |

_____

4 | you | Would | a | book | meeting? |

_____

5 | send | this | Could | you | today? |

_____

5.8 TACHA LAS PALABRAS INCORRECTAS DE CADA FRASE Y DI LAS FRASES EN VOZ ALTA

Don't worry! You **don't have to** / ~~must not~~ deal with this right now.

1 Could / Have you deliver this letter for me, please?

2 Must / Would you show the new employee around the office?

3 Jess, **I have got** / need to leave early today. Could you let Philippe know?

Team leaders should do everyday tasks.
True ☐ False ☑ Not given ☐

1 A routine task is answering customer enquiries.
True ☐ False ☐ Not given ☐

2 People who don't delegate often feel stressed.
True ☐ False ☐ Not given ☐

3 A team leader has to avoid doing everyday tasks.
True ☐ False ☐ Not given ☐

4 Trust in managers is falling in most companies.
True ☐ False ☐ Not given ☐

5 Team leaders should trust their staff.
True ☐ False ☐ Not given ☐

BUSINESS WEEKLY

Sharing the load

Relieve stress by learning to delegate better

Team leaders must think about goals and how to achieve them. This takes time. You won't have this thinking time if you're busy doing routine tasks and you will feel stressed. You have to let your team members handle the everyday tasks. Show your team members you trust them. Ask them if they could show you a plan of how they can manage their work in their own way. This way you will build a better working relationship.

---

05 ✓ CHECKLIST

⚙ Verbos modales de obligación ☐   **Aa** Delegación y educación ☐   🧩 Delegar tareas a los colegas ☐

🔄 **REPASA** LO QUE HAS APRENDIDO EN LAS UNIDADES 01–05

NUEVO LENGUAJE	FRASE DE EJEMPLO	☑	UNIDAD
PRESENTARTE A TI MISMO Y A OTROS	You must be **Eric from the UK.** **Tony, this is Hayao from our Japanese office.**	☐	1.1
EL PAST SIMPLE Y EL PAST CONTINUOUS PARA EXPERIENCIAS ANTERIORES	I was working **60 hours per week when** I came **here.**	☐	2.1
EL PRETÉRITO Y LA EDUCACIÓN	Did **you want a tour of the office?**	☐	2.4
HABLAR DEL PASADO RECIENTE CON EL PRESENT PERFECT SIMPLE	I have worked **in a few different teams.**	☐	2.6
HABLAR DE CAMBIOS CON "USED TO" Y "BE / GET USED TO"	Staff used to **eat lunch at their desks.** It took a while to **get used to the commute.**	☐	4.1
DELEGAR TAREAS CON MODALES	I have to **leave this with you.** Could **you look after this for me?**	☐	5.1, 5.6

6.1 DINERO Y FINANZAS

The company's income fell last year.

income
[money coming into a business]

The initial expenditure on technology was huge, but now we can work faster.

expenditure / outlay
[an amount of money spent]

We have a large budget for this movie, so the effects will be amazing.

a budget
[the amount of money that is available to spend on something]

We must do all we can to avoid getting into debt.

to get into debt
[to get into a situation where you owe people money]

The bank charges for overdrafts now.

an overdraft
[extra money the bank allows you to spend]

The profit margin on these T-shirts is huge!

a profit margin
[the difference between the cost of making or buying something and what it's sold for]

We need to sell two cars to break even.

to break even
[to earn just enough to cover the costs of producing a product]

We haven't sold enough pineapples. We've made a loss.

to make a loss
[to lose money by spending more than you earn]

We need to make sure the accounts are always up to date.

accounts
[records of money paid into and out of a business]

High overheads make this business difficult to run.

overheads
[the regular costs of running a business, such as wages]

I'm selling these earrings at cost to attract customers.

cost (US) / cost price (UK)
[a sales price that covers the costs of producing an item without making a profit]

The prices peaked in June, but they're down now.

to peak
[to reach the highest point]

When the CEO left, the company's value dropped.

to drop
[to fall, especially in worth or value]

Changes in the exchange rate make the market uncertain.

the exchange rate
[the amount of one currency that you get when you change it for another]

Thankfully, there was an upturn in the market.

an upturn in the market
[a change to more positive business conditions]

Our clients need to pay now or we will have a cash flow problem.

cash flow
[the rate at which money comes into and goes out of a business]

It's always hard to see a company go out of business.

to go out of business
[to no longer be able to exist as a business]

VIDEO STORE

We need to undercut our competitors or we will lose customers.

to undercut competitors
[to charge less than others who sell the same goods or services as you]

Our sales figures have improved consistently each year.

sales figures
[the amount or value of total sales over a particular period]

Everyone suffered because of the economic downturn last year.

an economic downturn
[a major decline in economic activity]

Al redactar un informe utiliza diferentes pretéritos para ilustrar el orden de los eventos. También tienes que utilizar expresiones más formales.

⚙ **Lenguaje** Past perfect y past simple
Aa Vocabulario Inglés de negocios formal
🧩 **Habilidad** Redactar informes

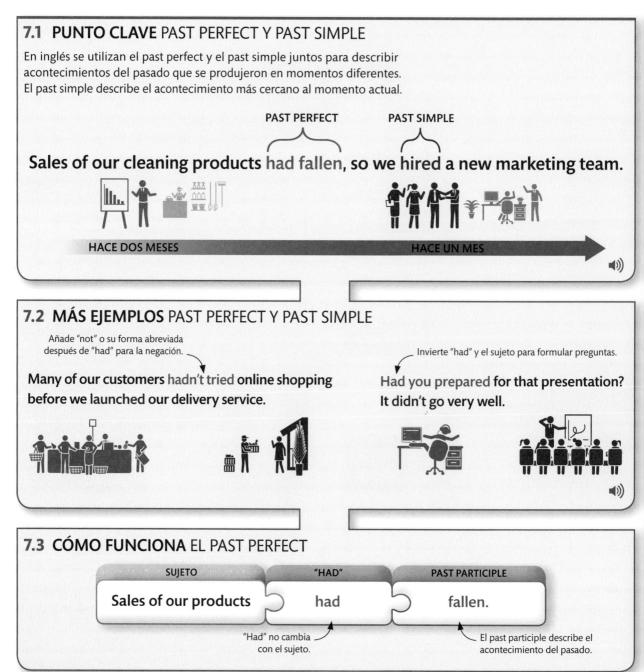

7.1 PUNTO CLAVE PAST PERFECT Y PAST SIMPLE

En inglés se utilizan el past perfect y el past simple juntos para describir acontecimientos del pasado que se produjeron en momentos diferentes. El past simple describe el acontecimiento más cercano al momento actual.

PAST PERFECT   PAST SIMPLE

Sales of our cleaning products had fallen, so we hired a new marketing team.

HACE DOS MESES   HACE UN MES

7.2 MÁS EJEMPLOS PAST PERFECT Y PAST SIMPLE

Añade "not" o su forma abreviada después de "had" para la negación.

Many of our customers hadn't tried online shopping before we launched our delivery service.

Invierte "had" y el sujeto para formular preguntas.

Had you prepared for that presentation? It didn't go very well.

7.3 CÓMO FUNCIONA EL PAST PERFECT

SUJETO	"HAD"	PAST PARTICIPLE
Sales of our products	had	fallen.

"Had" no cambia con el sujeto.

El past participle describe el acontecimiento del pasado.

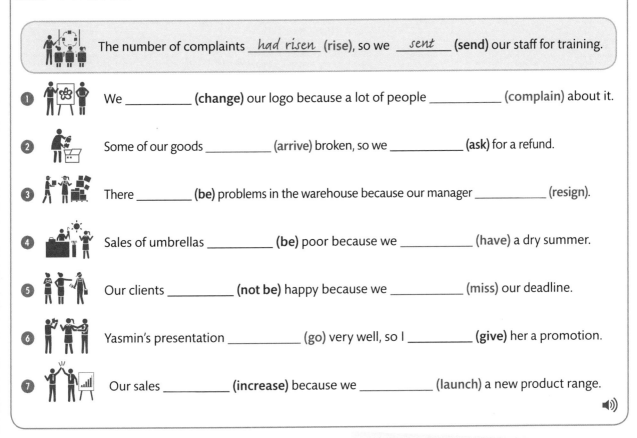

7.4 COMPLETA LOS ESPACIOS ESCRIBIENDO LOS VERBOS EN PAST PERFECT O PAST SIMPLE

The number of complaints _had risen_ (rise), so we _sent_ (send) our staff for training.

1. We _____ (change) our logo because a lot of people _____ (complain) about it.

2. Some of our goods _____ (arrive) broken, so we _____ (ask) for a refund.

3. There _____ (be) problems in the warehouse because our manager _____ (resign).

4. Sales of umbrellas _____ (be) poor because we _____ (have) a dry summer.

5. Our clients _____ (not be) happy because we _____ (miss) our deadline.

6. Yasmin's presentation _____ (go) very well, so I _____ (give) her a promotion.

7. Our sales _____ (increase) because we _____ (launch) a new product range.

7.5 LEE EL INFORME Y MARCA EL RESUMEN CORRECTO

1. The trial had mostly negative results and the report recommends returning to telephone operators only. ☐

2. The trial had both positive and negative results and the report recommends maintaining both systems. ☐

3. The trial had mostly positive results and the report recommends keeping the trial online messaging only. ☐

Replacement of Telephone Operators with Online Messaging

Guil Motors replaced all its telephone operators with online messaging for a trial period.

Benefits:
- Each operator can deal with more than one client
- A written record is kept of each dialogue

Negative effects:
- Significant drop in number of inquiries
- Customer dissatisfaction

Recommendations:
- Offer both phone and online messaging services
- Create positive promotion for online messaging

7.6 PUNTO CLAVE INFORMES DE PROYECTOS

A continuación aparecen algunos ejemplos de lenguaje formal típico de informes de proyectos.

Alternativa formal a "This report shows".

The following report presents the results of a client satisfaction survey.

Alternativa formal a "said".

Our clients stated that they had been disappointed with the sales figures.

Utiliza el infinitivo con "to" para hablar del objetivo.

The purpose of this report is to review our marketing expenditure.

Alternativa formal a "first".

Based on this initial research, we should increase our marketing budget.

Los informes formales se suelen redactar en voz pasiva.

As can be seen in the table, we spent very little on social media marketing.

Alternativa formal a "main".

My principal recommendation is to create and launch a new campaign.

🔊

7.7 VUELVE A ESCRIBIR LAS FRASES CORRIGIENDO LOS ERRORES

> Many of our clients was interviewed for this report.
> _Many of our clients were interviewed for this report._

1 The purpose of this report is review our sales figures for the last quarter.

_____

2 Our principle recommendation is to complete the sale of the downtown store.

_____

3 The follow report presents the results of extensive customer satisfaction research.

_____

4 Our main client state that the recent changes were beneficial for his business.

_____

🔊

220

7.8 CONECTA EL INICIO Y EL FINAL DE CADA FRASE

The following report presents → our staffing plans for the coming year.

1 As can be seen in the table,

2 It is clear from the research

3 A number of focus groups

4 The purpose of this report is

that there were a number of problems.

to present the findings of our survey.

the figures for this period were excellent.

were consulted for this report.

🔊

7.9 COMPLETA LOS ESPACIOS CON LAS PALABRAS DEL RECUADRO

Our clients ___*stated*___ that they had been disappointed with our products.

1 The focus group clients had all _____ both the original and new products.

2 The following chart _____ the sales figures for the two periods.

3 We _____ the customers who had complained why they didn't like the change.

4 The _____ of this report is to present the results of our online trial.

5 We started this online trial after our store costs had _____ by 10 percent.

| compares | ~~stated~~ | asked | risen | used | purpose |

🔊

08 Disculparse

El present perfect continuous habla de algo en progreso del pasado que tiene efecto en el presente. Se utiliza para pedir disculpas y explicar los motivos de un problema.

⚙ Lenguaje Present perfect continuous
Aa Vocabulario Disculpas
🧩 Habilidad Disculparse por teléfono

8.1 PUNTO CLAVE DISCULPAS TELEFÓNICAS

En inglés dispones de diversas expresiones para disculparte, ofrecerte para investigar un problema y dar explicaciones y soluciones.

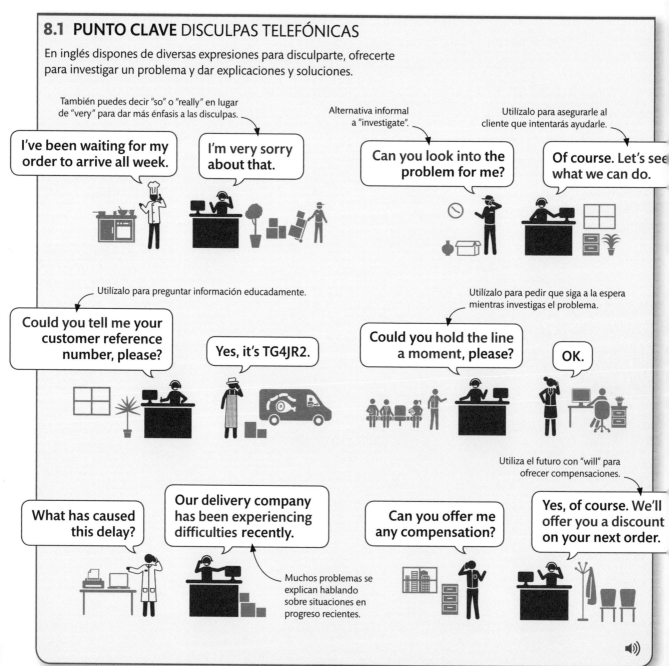

También puedes decir "so" o "really" en lugar de "very" para dar más énfasis a las disculpas.

I've been waiting for my order to arrive all week.

I'm very sorry about that.

Alternativa informal a "investigate".

Can you look into the problem for me?

Utilízalo para asegurarle al cliente que intentarás ayudarle.

Of course. Let's see what we can do.

Utilízalo para preguntar información educadamente.

Could you tell me your customer reference number, please?

Yes, it's TG4JR2.

Utilízalo para pedir que siga a la espera mientras investigas el problema.

Could you hold the line a moment, please?

OK.

Utiliza el futuro con "will" para ofrecer compensaciones.

What has caused this delay?

Our delivery company has been experiencing difficulties recently.

Muchos problemas se explican hablando sobre situaciones en progreso recientes.

Can you offer me any compensation?

Yes, of course. We'll offer you a discount on your next order.

Can you look into the problem for me?

① Could I have a refund?

② Could you tell me your order number?

③ Could you hold the line a moment, please?

④ Why isn't my order here yet?

⑤ My order arrived dirty and broken.

⑥ Will you send me a replacement?

Yes, we'll send you a new one tomorrow.

Our courier has been having difficulties.

Of course. Let's see what we can do.

I'm very sorry to hear that, Mrs. Singh.

Yes, we'll give you a full refund.

OK. No problem.

Yes, it's AMLGW14.

8.3 ESCUCHA EL AUDIO Y LUEGO NUMERA LAS EXPRESIONES EN EL ORDEN EN QUE APARECEN

Ethan atiende por teléfono la queja de una clienta sobre un pedido que ha hecho.

Ⓐ Let's see what I can do. ☐

Ⓑ I'm really sorry to hear that. ☐ 1

Ⓒ We'll offer a discount on your next order. ☐

Ⓓ The driver has been stuck in traffic. ☐

Ⓔ Could you tell me your order number? ☐

Ⓕ Could you hold the line a moment, please? ☐

8.4 TACHA LAS PALABRAS INCORRECTAS DE CADA FRASE Y DI LAS FRASES EN VOZ ALTA

I'm **sorry** / ~~much~~ about the delay.

① We'll **see** / **look** into the problem for you.

② We'll **give** / **giving** you a discount voucher.

③ Could you hold the **phone** / **line** a moment?

④ Let's see **what** / **when** we can do.

8.5 PUNTO CLAVE EL PRESENT PERFECT CONTINUOUS

El present perfect continuous se utiliza para hablar de una situación en progreso del pasado que tiene aún efectos en el presente. Puedes utilizarlo para ofrecer explicaciones a posibles problemas.

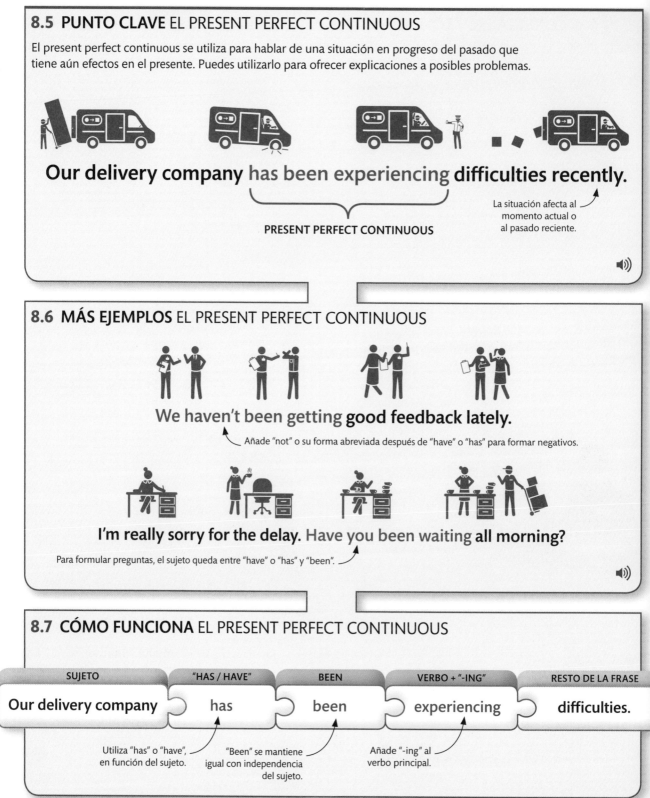

Our delivery company has been experiencing **difficulties recently.**

PRESENT PERFECT CONTINUOUS

La situación afecta al momento actual o al pasado reciente.

8.6 MÁS EJEMPLOS EL PRESENT PERFECT CONTINUOUS

We haven't been getting **good feedback lately.**

Añade "not" o su forma abreviada después de "have" o "has" para formar negativos.

I'm really sorry for the delay. Have you been waiting **all morning?**

Para formular preguntas, el sujeto queda entre "have" o "has" y "been".

8.7 CÓMO FUNCIONA EL PRESENT PERFECT CONTINUOUS

SUJETO	"HAS / HAVE"	BEEN	VERBO + "-ING"	RESTO DE LA FRASE
Our delivery company	has	been	experiencing	difficulties.

Utiliza "has" o "have", en función del sujeto.

"Been" se mantiene igual con independencia del sujeto.

Añade "-ing" al verbo principal.

224

8.8 COMPLETA LOS ESPACIOS ESCRIBIENDO LOS VERBOS EN PRESENT PERFECT CONTINUOUS

Our customers ___*have been complaining*___ (complain) about our poor service recently.

❶ The customers _____ (wait) for us to contact them.

❷ Our engineers _____ (work) on the line for two days.

❸ What _____ you _____ (do) to solve the problem?

❹ I _____ (watch) your program and I want to complain.

❺ We _____ (repair) the broken cables this morning.

❻ They _____ (update) my software and now it doesn't work.

🔊

8.9 LEE EL CORREO ELECTRÓNICO Y RESPONDE A LAS PREGUNTAS

The complaint is about train delays.
True ☑ False ☐ Not given ☐

❶ RailKo says they are sorry about the delay.
True ☐ False ☐ Not given ☐

❷ RailKo says the thieves were found.
True ☐ False ☐ Not given ☐

❸ The problem was unexpected for RailKo.
True ☐ False ☐ Not given ☐

❹ RailKo offers Ms. Pérez a total refund.
True ☐ False ☐ Not given ☐

❺ RailKo will keep passengers up to date with changes.
True ☐ False ☐ Not given ☐

To: Mariana Pérez

Subject: Severe train delay

Dear Ms. Pérez,

Thank you for your email regarding the delay to your trip on July 11th. I've been investigating the problem and see that your train was, indeed, 70 minutes late. We apologize for the inconvenience this caused. We've been upgrading that line for several weeks and unfortunately that morning thieves stole a lot of machinery and it was not safe for trains to travel at their usual speed. As you can imagine, RailKo was unable to predict this event. By way of an apology, however, we'd like to offer you a refund of 50% of the value of your ticket. I've attached the voucher to this email.

Yours sincerely,
Joshua Hawkins

---

08 ✓ CHECKLIST

⚙️ Present perfect continuous ☐   **Aa** Disculpas ☐   🧩 Disculparse por teléfono ☐

9.1 TECNOLOGÍA PARA COMUNICARSE

I can access my work emails from my home computer.

to access
[to enter or connect to something]

I appear to have lost access to the network again!

a network
[a system of interconnected technology]

As a company we always keep our hardware and apps up to date.

up to date
[current and modern]

We have an automated voicemail system.

automated
[computerized; not operated by a human]

My phone is connected to the network so I can receive emails any time.

connected to
[in communication with]

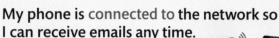

Most people in the office carry a mobile device with them.

a mobile device
[a small computing device, such as a smartphone or tablet, that is easily carried]

For most of the day I have to work online to access the internet and emails.

to work online
[to work with an internet connection]

I work offline when commuting to work because there is no internet on the train.

to work offline
[to work without an internet connection]

If you download the app, you'll get updates about new products.

to download an app
[to get an application from the internet onto a device or computer]

I automatically back up my documents every 15 minutes.

to back up
[to save an extra copy of a document in case the original is lost]

This new program is very user-friendly.

user-friendly
[easy for the operator to use]

I must have the wrong address. My email has bounced.

an email has bounced
[an email has been automatically returned without reaching the intended recipient]

Our new website works on computers and mobile devices.

a website
[a collection of linked pages accessed through the internet]

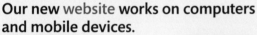

I often use social media to look for job vacancies.

social media
[internet-based tools for communicating with friends and communities]

I'm sorry, I can't hear you properly. You're breaking up.

breaking up
[losing a phone or internet connection]

Can you arrange a videoconference with the clients in Sydney?

a videoconference
[a conference by phone or via the internet in which people can see and talk to each other]

Let's arrange a conference call so we can all catch up.

a conference call
[a group conversation held by phone]

Please could you charge the tablet before the meeting?

to charge
[to connect a mobile device to electricity to give it more power]

Our company always uses the latest software.

software
[computer programs]

When you create your account, you get a username and password.

a username and password
[a name and code used to access an account on a computing device]

10 Planear por correo electrónico

Dispones de diversas formas de hacer planes y comprobar la información por correo electrónico. Asegúrate de que incluso los mensajes informales son educados.

⚙ **Lenguaje** Lenguaje del correo electrónico
Aa Vocabulario Reuniones y talleres
🧩 **Habilidad** Hacer planes

10.1 PUNTO CLAVE CORREOS ELECTRÓNICOS A COLEGAS

En los correos electrónicos profesionales, es importante utilizar un lenguaje educado y claro para intercambiar información con los colegas. Los correos electrónicos para los colegas suelen ser menos formales que los correos electrónicos para los clientes o la directiva.

NOTA
Mantén la coherencia en el estilo. Por ejemplo, si añades una coma tras el saludo, acuérdate de añadir otra tras la despedida.

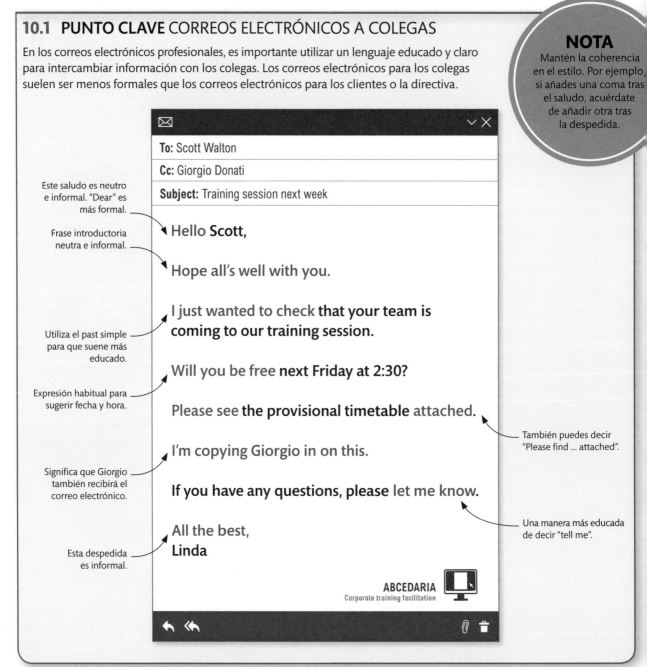

Este saludo es neutro e informal. "Dear" es más formal.

Frase introductoria neutra e informal.

Utiliza el past simple para que suene más educado.

Expresión habitual para sugerir fecha y hora.

Significa que Giorgio también recibirá el correo electrónico.

Esta despedida es informal.

To: Scott Walton
Cc: Giorgio Donati
Subject: Training session next week

Hello **Scott,**

Hope all's well with you.

I just wanted to check **that your team is coming to our training session.**

Will you be free **next Friday at 2:30?**

Please see **the provisional timetable** attached.

I'm copying Giorgio in on this.

If you have any questions, please let me know.

All the best,
Linda

ABCEDARIA
Corporate training facilitation

También puedes decir "Please find ... attached".

Una manera más educada de decir "tell me".

10.2 LEE EL CORREO ELECTRÓNICO Y MARCA EL RESUMEN CORRECTO

To: Catherine Quint

Subject: Sales presentation

Hi Catherine,

Hope all's well with you. I just wanted to check that you got my earlier email about our sales presentation next Friday. Pauline and I are meeting this morning to discuss arrangements. Will you be free to come and join us in Room A at 11:30?

Please find the attached timetable and agenda for the presentation. I've copied Pauline in on this message. If you have any ideas or want to ask any questions, please let me know.

All the best,
Mira

Copy&Print Sprint

1. Mira is emailing Catherine to check that she is coming to a sales presentation in Room A. Pauline is also invited to the presentation. ☐

2. Mira wants to meet next Friday to discuss arrangements for the sales presentation. She has asked Pauline to send her the agenda. ☐

3. Mira is inviting Catherine to a meeting to discuss arrangements for the sales presentation. She has sent Catherine and Pauline the timetable and agenda. ☐

4. Mira is emailing to check that Pauline is coming to the sales presentation. Catherine has sent the timetable and agenda. ☐

10.3 COMPLETA LOS ESPACIOS CON LAS PALABRAS DEL RECUADRO

Please see the timetable for tomorrow's training course ___attached___.

1. I just wanted to _____ that you will be able to make it to the meeting.

2. Don't worry if you have any questions. Just let me _____ .

3. I'm _____ Maxine in on this as she may have some more information.

4. How _____ coming to the restaurant with us this evening?

5. I was _____ if you and Ana could come to the meeting tomorrow.

6. Give me a call if you can't _____ the presentation at 10 o'clock.

know
copying
~~attached~~
wondering
check
about
make

10 ✓ CHECKLIST

⚙ Lenguaje del correo electrónico ☐   **Aa** Reuniones y talleres ☐   🧩 Hacer planes ☐

11 Informar a los clientes

Utiliza el present continuous para informar a los clientes de la situación actual y de los planes de futuro. Los tiempos continuos también suavizan las preguntas y peticiones.

🔧 **Lenguaje** Tiempos continuos
Aa Vocabulario Planes y calendarios
🧩 **Habilidad** Mantener informados a los clientes

11.1 PUNTO CLAVE EL PRESENT CONTINUOUS

Utiliza el present continuous en inglés para describir qué está pasando ahora mismo.

Utiliza "still" para destacar que una situación continúa en progreso.

We are aiming to give you a full progress report.

We are still waiting for a part from our supplier.

En inglés también se utiliza el present continuous para hablar sobre planes para un momento concreto en el futuro.

Utiliza el present continuous con un indicador de tiempo de futuro para hablar de planes futuros.

We are having a meeting with the IT department later today.

Malik is talking to HR next week to discuss the noise issues.

11.2 ESCUCHA EL AUDIO Y MARCA SI LAS ACTIVIDADES DE CADA IMAGEN PASAN EN EL PRESENTE O EL FUTURO

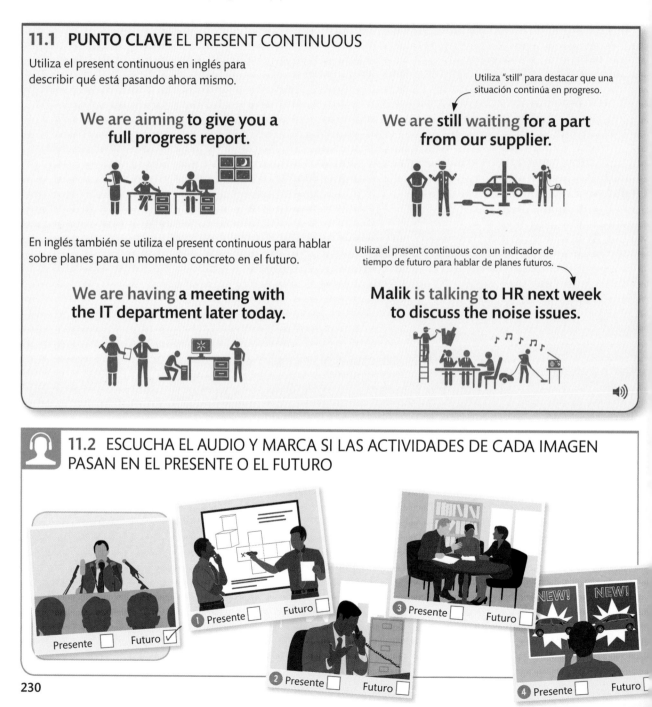

Presente ☐ Futuro ✓

① Presente ☐ Futuro ☐

② Presente ☐ Futuro ☐

③ Presente ☐ Futuro ☐

④ Presente ☐ Futuro ☐

11.3 LEE EL CORREO ELECTRÓNICO Y RESPONDE A LAS PREGUNTAS CON FRASES COMPLETAS

What is Janice informing Yasmin about?

She is informing her that her order is delayed.

1 What happened to the delivery van?

_____

2 When is the company receiving new stock?

_____

3 What is Janice hoping to do next week?

_____

4 How can Yasmin cancel her order?

_____

5 Who should Yasmin contact if she has questions?

_____

To: Yasmin Hendricks

Subject: Delay with order TY309

Dear Ms. Hendricks,

I'm sorry to inform you that our delivery van was involved in an accident yesterday. I've obtained a list of affected customers and unfortunately your order was damaged. We're receiving new stock tomorrow and will contact you with a new delivery date. I'm hoping to confirm a new date next week.

We're very sorry about the inconvenience caused, and would like to assure you that you'll receive your order as soon as possible. If you'd prefer to cancel your order, you can do so online. Do not hesitate to contact me if you have any questions.

Best wishes,

Janice Wright

Aa 11.4 CONECTA LAS DEFINICIONES CON LOS VERBOS CORRECTOS

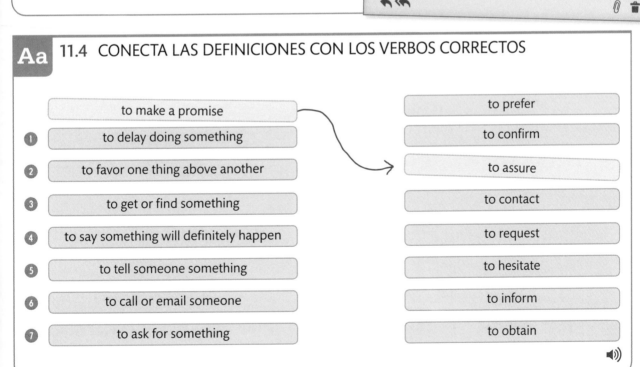

to make a promise

1 to delay doing something

2 to favor one thing above another

3 to get or find something

4 to say something will definitely happen

5 to tell someone something

6 to call or email someone

7 to ask for something

to prefer

to confirm

to assure

to contact

to request

to hesitate

to inform

to obtain

11.5 PUNTO CLAVE TIEMPOS CONTINUOS Y EDUCACIÓN

En la correspondencia con los clientes en inglés, se suelen utilizar tiempos continuos para pedir las cosas de manera más educada o realizar promesas menos concretas.

PRESENT CONTINUOUS

We are hoping to deliver your order next Monday.

[We intend to deliver your order next Monday.]

PAST CONTINUOUS

Aquí el past continuous se utiliza para que suene educado.

I was wondering if we could meet at your office.

[Let's meet at your office.]

FUTURE CONTINUOUS

Utiliza "will", "be" y el verbo acabado en "-ing" para el future continuous.

Will you be attending the launch of our soft drink range?

[We hope you will go to the launch.]

Aa 11.6 VUELVE A ESCRIBIR LAS EXPRESIONES MARCADAS CORRIGIENDO LOS ERRORES

To: Tyson Bailey

Subject: Poster campaign update

Dear Tyson Bailey,
Thanks for your email of December 12th regarding your poster campaign. I aiming to have a final meeting with the designers tomorrow morning, and I is hoping to send you more designs tomorrow afternoon.
We are currently wait for feedback from our focus group, but we expecting to hear from them soon. I was wonder if we could meet at your office to discuss their findings. I ensure you that we doing will be all we can to ensure that the campaign is completed on time. In the meantime, if you have any questions, please do not hesitate contacting me.
Yours,
Darius Gad

I am aiming to have

1. _____
2. _____
3. _____
4. _____
5. _____
6. _____
7. _____

11.7 VUELVE A ESCRIBIR LAS FRASES CORRIGIENDO LOS ERRORES

> Will you attending the launch of the new car this afternoon?
> _Will you be attending the launch of the new car this afternoon?_

1 I was wonder if you would meet the clients at their factory.

_____

2 We is having difficulties with deliveries due to the weather.

_____

3 Will you be pay for the order by bank transfer or credit card?

_____

4 We are aiming finish the redecorating by next Wednesday.

_____

🔊

11.8 VUELVE A ESCRIBIR LAS FRASES PONIENDO LAS PALABRAS EN SU ORDEN CORRECTO

| the | are | job | complete | We | to | aiming | tomorrow. |

We are aiming to complete the job tomorrow.

1 | to | We | from | waiting | supplier. | still | are | our | hear |

_____

2 | wondering | I | could | back. | if | was | me | you | call |

_____

3 | you | meeting | the | be | next | Will | attending | week? | progress |

_____

🔊

---

11 ✔ CHECKLIST

⚙ Tiempos continuos ☐   **Aa** Planes y calendarios ☐   🧩 Mantener informados a los clientes ☐

12 Comunicación informal

Los phrasal verbs se componen de dos o más palabras. Por lo general se utilizan en inglés informal oral y escrito, por ejemplo en mensajes y peticiones a colegas.

⚙ **Lenguaje** Phrasal verbs
Aa Vocabulario Planes
🧩 **Habilidad** Mantener informados a los colegas

12.1 PUNTO CLAVE PHRASAL VERBS

Los phrasal verbs se componen de un verbo seguido de, como mínimo, una partícula. La mayoría de partículas de los phrasal verbs son preposiciones; estas partículas cambian el significado del verbo.

Verbo / Partícula

The paper in the copier has run out.

La partícula cambia a menudo el significado habitual del verbo.

12.2 MÁS EJEMPLOS PHRASAL VERBS

Could you **look into** fixing the coffee machine, please?

Welcome back! When would you like to **catch up**?

Can you **deal with** the overseas orders?

I'm afraid I have to **hang up** now.

12.3 TACHA LAS PALABRAS INCORRECTAS DE CADA FRASE

When should we catch up / ~~off~~ / ~~out~~?

1. I'll look **out / up / into** the problem now.

2. The printer has run **in / out / on** of ink.

3. I need to **catch / deal / look** up with you.

4. Sorry, I have to hang **in / up / into** now.

5. Could you deal **up / out / with** this order?

6. I'll **see / look / watch** into Mr. Li's query.

7. My client just **hung / run / ran** up on me!

12.4 ESCUCHA EL AUDIO Y LUEGO NUMERA LAS FRASES EN EL ORDEN EN QUE APARECEN

Nicky deja un mensaje telefónico para Oscar, su compañero de trabajo.

A I've got lots to do, so I have to hang up now. ☐

B When one printer runs out of ink, all the others stop working, too. ☐

C It would be nice to meet up sometime soon. ☐

D I just wanted to catch up with you about your problem with the printers. ☑1

E I looked into it a bit deeper and discovered the problem. ☐

F It's quite easy to deal with. ☐

Aa 12.5 LEE EL CORREO ELECTRÓNICO Y CONECTA PHRASAL VERBS Y DEFINICIONES

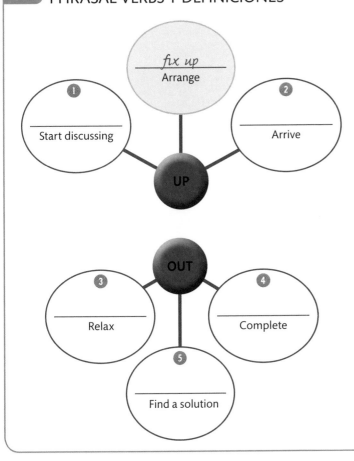

To: André Jennings

Subject: Today

Hi André,

I was just writing to **fix up** a meeting with you to talk about arrangements for next month's sales trip. Maybe we could go for dinner on Friday? We could meet before dinner to **fill out** all the paperwork for the sales meetings and **figure out** the best places to stay during the trip. Then we can **chill out** and eat some food.

We could ask Lucinda to join us. It would be a good opportunity to **bring up** our new sales strategy with her and see what she thinks of it. Hopefully she won't **turn up** late this time!

Let me know your thoughts,
Peter

fix up — Arrange

UP
1 ___ Start discussing
2 ___ Arrive

OUT
3 ___ Relax
4 ___ Complete
5 ___ Find a solution

12.6 PUNTO CLAVE PHRASAL VERBS SEPARABLES

En algunos phrasal verbs, el objeto directo de la oración puede ir entre el verbo y la partícula. Su significado se mantiene.

El objeto puede ir después de la partícula.

Please could you fill out this form?

Please could you fill this form out?

El objeto puede ir también entre el verbo y la partícula.

12.7 MÁS EJEMPLOS PHRASAL VERBS SEPARABLES

We have to back up our files every night.
We have to back our files up every night.

Sue's sick today. Let's call off the meeting.
Sue's sick today. Let's call the meeting off.

They're giving out samples of their products.
They're giving samples of their products out.

Please pass on the message to Jess.
Please pass the message on to Jess.

12.8 VUELVE A ESCRIBIR LAS FRASES CAMBIANDO LA POSICIÓN DE LA PARTÍCULA

Can we **call off** today's meeting?
Can we call today's meeting off?

❶ James, can you **pass** the message **on** to Zane?
_____

❷ Welcome to Jo's. Please **fill out** the visitor's form.
_____

❸ Can you stand at the exit and **hand out** the leaflets?
_____

❹ **Put on** a helmet before entering the site.
_____

❺ Before I update the software, **back up** your files.
_____

12.9 COMPLETA LOS ESPACIOS CON LAS PALABRAS DEL RECUADRO Y DI LAS FRASES EN VOZ ALTA

Every hour I _____back_____ my new files _____up_____ on my computer.

3 Howard, we should really _____ a meeting _____ for this week.

1 Could you please _____ the message _____ to Gary?

4 After a busy day in the office, I usually _____ _____ at home.

2 I have an important meeting, so I _____ a suit _____ this morning.

put	chill	~~back~~	on	out
pass	fix	up	on	~~up~~

---

12 ✓ CHECKLIST

🔩 Phrasal verbs ☐   **Aa** Planes ☐   🧩 Mantener informados a los colegas ☐

♻ REPASA LO QUE HAS APRENDIDO EN LAS UNIDADES 06–12

NUEVO LENGUAJE	FRASE DE EJEMPLO	☑	UNIDAD
PAST PERFECT Y PAST SIMPLE	**Sales of our products** had fallen, **so we** hired **a new marketing team.**	☐	7.1
INFORMES DE PROYECTOS	The following report presents **the results of a client satisfaction survey.**	☐	7.6
DISCULPAS TELEFÓNICAS	I'm very sorry **about the delay.** Let's see what we can do.	☐	8.1
PRESENT PERFECT CONTINUOUS	**Our delivery company** has been experiencing **difficulties recently.**	☐	8.5
CORREOS ELECTRÓNICOS PARA LOS COLEGAS	Please see **the timetable for next week's training course** attached.	☐	10.1
TIEMPOS CONTINUOS	We are hoping **to give you a full update.** I was wondering **if we could meet next week.**	☐	11.1, 11.5
PHRASAL VERBS	**The paper in the copier has** run out. **Please could you** fill **this form** out?	☐	12.1, 12.6

13.1 PRODUCCIÓN

Everyone on the production line starts and finishes work at the same time.

a production line
[a line of people or machinery in a factory, each making a specific part of a product]

These fabrics are much cheaper to manufacture abroad.

to manufacture
[to make a large number of goods, usually in a factory and using machinery]

That car was unique. It was a one-off production for a private customer.

a one-off production
[something that is made or produced only once]

The bags are expensive because they are all handmade.

handmade
[made by a person without the use of a machine]

The price goes up as the cost of raw materials increases.

raw materials
[the basic substances that are used to make a product]

The overproduction of these shirts has meant we need to lower the price.

overproduction
[manufacturing too much of something in relation to demand]

We can make changes. This is just a prototype.

a prototype
[the first form of a design that can be changed, copied, or developed]

All our toys go through a process of product testing.

product testing
[a process to check that goods meet certain standards]

These cars have become much cheaper with mass production.

mass production
[the process of making large numbers of goods, usually in a factory]

We cannot begin manufacture without product approval.

product approval
[a declaration that a product meets certain standards and is suitable for sale]

The packaging of certain goods is vital for sales.

packaging
[the external wrapping of goods before they are sold]

We arrange shipping all over the world for our clients.

shipping
[moving goods from one place to another]

The painting process starts in this room and takes two days.

a process
[a series of actions or steps that are done in a particular order]

These watches are beautiful, but their production is very labor intensive.

labor intensive
[requiring a lot of human effort to make something]

All the ingredients for this product are ethically sourced.

ethically sourced
[found or bought in a morally acceptable way]

Can you ask the warehouse how many we have available to ship today?

a warehouse
[a place where goods are stored before being shipped to customers or sellers]

We have a lot of stock. We need to sell it before we produce any more.

stock
[goods that a company has made but not yet sold]

With food products, quality control is vital.

quality control
[systems that ensure that products are of a high standard]

The factory makes 200,000 bars of chocolate a day.

a factory
[a building or group of buildings where goods are made]

They have been our main supplier of light bulbs for 20 years.

a supplier
[a company that provides or supplies another company with goods and services]

14 Describir un proceso

La voz pasiva es útil para describir el funcionamiento de un proceso, porque destaca la acción en lugar de la persona o la cosa que la hace.

⚙ **Lenguaje** La voz pasiva
Aa Vocabulario Procesos y fabricación
🧩 **Habilidad** Debatir cómo se hacen las cosas

14.1 PUNTO CLAVE HABLAR DE PROCESOS CON LA VOZ PASIVA

El present simple pasivo se forma con "am / is / are" y el past participle.

Our products are designed in London.

El present simple pasivo describe acontecimientos actuales o recurrentes.

El present continuous pasivo se forma con "am / is / are" seguido de "being" y el past participle.

The new models are being released before Christmas.

El present continuous pasivo describe acciones en progreso.

El present perfect pasivo se forma con "have / has" seguido de "been" y el past participle.

All the latest technologies have been used.

El present perfect pasivo describe acontecimientos del pasado que aún tienen efecto en el momento actual.

The past simple pasivo se forma con "was / were" y el past participle.

Our original model was sold worldwide.

El past simple pasivo describe una acción individual y finalizada del pasado.

El past continuous pasivo se forma con "was / were" seguido de "being" y el past participle.

We tested extensively while it was being redesigned.

El past continuous pasivo describe acciones en progreso en el pasado.

El past perfect pasivo describe acontecimientos que pasaron antes que otro acontecimiento pasado.

El past perfect pasivo se forma con "had been" y el past participle.

The media had been notified before we announced the launch.

🔊

14.2 LEE EL ARTÍCULO Y RESPONDE A LAS PREGUNTAS

Potato chips were invented over 100 years ago.
True ☑   False ☐   Not given ☐

1 Chosen potatoes are kept at a steady temperature.
True ☐   False ☐   Not given ☐

2 The biggest potatoes make the best potato chips.
True ☐   False ☐   Not given ☐

3 Potato chips have never come in plastic packaging.
True ☐   False ☐   Not given ☐

4 Chip companies make more money now than ever.
True ☐   False ☐   Not given ☐

5 Chip companies do not monitor packaging styles.
True ☐   False ☐   Not given ☐

BUSINESS TODAY

A slice of history

The essential potato chip:
How did we get here?

It is believed that the first potato chips were created at the end of the 19th century. But how are they made? First, golf-ball-sized potatoes are chosen and stored at a constant temperature. The potatoes are then sliced and fried, and additives are used to keep the chips fresh. Potato-chip packaging has been constantly changing. Packets have been made from paper, foil, plastic, and newer, composite materials. The quality of modern packaging is our main focus and is constantly being monitored.

14.3 TACHA LAS PALABRAS INCORRECTAS DE CADA FRASE

We make everything on site at the Imagicorp plant. All of our products are **built** / ~~build~~ in Europe.

1 Over the last year, an exciting new line has been **developed** / **develop**.

2 This design **has been** / **was** patented in 1938. Nobody has ever managed to make a better product!

3 Their new line **is being** / **have been** launched next Saturday. Everyone is talking about it.

4 Our factory floor **was** / **is being** cleaned before the CEO visited. He was happy things looked good!

5 You don't need to worry about dinner. The food **is** / **had been** cooked to order so that it is fresh.

6 The first cars made in this factory **were** / **was** sold in the UK in 1972, and worldwide the next year.

7 Our original designers **has been** / **were** influenced by Japanese artists.

8 To prepare for the launch, advertising posters **are** / **are being** put up around town as we speak.

🔊

14.4 PUNTO CLAVE AGENTES EN LA VOZ PASIVA

Se puede utilizar "by" para indicar
quién o qué realiza la acción.

Our CEO will announce the launch soon.

Esta frase activa destaca quién
realiza la acción ("our CEO").

The launch will be announced soon.

En la frase pasiva se destaca la acción.
Aquí el sujeto es "the launch".

The launch will be announced soon by our CEO.

Se añade "by" para indicar quién hace la acción; no
obstante, esta acción es la que recibe el énfasis.

14.5 CÓMO FUNCIONA AGENTES EN LA VOZ PASIVA

SUJETO	FORMA DE "BE"	PAST PARTICIPLE	RESTO DE LA FRASE	"BY"
The launch	will be	announced	soon	by our CEO.

14.6 COMPLETA LOS ESPACIOS CON LAS EXPRESIONES PASIVAS DEL RECUADRO

How many new models _____*are being produced*_____ ?

① Their new products _____ on TV now.

② 80,000 packets _____ in the factory each week.

③ A thousand new cars _____ next week.

④ Our latest gadget _____ by Ronnie Angel.

⑤ The production line _____ during the summer.

⑥ Great advances in design _____ recently.

are being promoted

~~are being produced~~

are produced

is stopped

will be sold

have been made

was invented

14.7 VUELVE A ESCRIBIR LAS FRASES EN VOZ PASIVA, INCLUYENDO "BY" PARA QUE APAREZCA EL AGENTE

> Our promotions team markets the product worldwide.
> *The product is marketed worldwide by our promotions team.*

❶ Someone checks all the cars before they leave the factory.

_____

❷ Maxine invented the new photo app for professional artists.

_____

❸ Customers bought all Carl Osric's books on the publication date.

_____

❹ Ron buys all our vegetarian ingredients from the market.

_____

❺ Samantha checks all of the invoices before they are sent out.

_____

14.8 ESCUCHA EL AUDIO Y LUEGO NUMERA LAS IMÁGENES EN EL ORDEN EN QUE SE DESCRIBEN

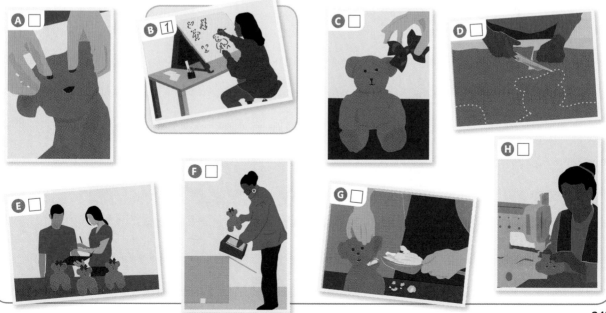

14.9 PUNTO CLAVE MODALES EN LA VOZ PASIVA

Se pueden utilizar algunos modales en expresiones concretas en voz pasiva para expresar ideas de posibilidad, capacidad, probabilidad y obligación.

The importance of product testing can't be overestimated.

[Product testing is very important.]

All products must be approved before leaving the factory.

[Products have to meet certain standards before they leave the factory.]

The product must have been damaged before it was shipped.

[It seems very likely that the product was broken before it was shipped.]

The shipment could have been packaged more carefully.

[The shipment was not packed as carefully as it should have been.]

This device couldn't have been tested before it went on sale.

[It seems impossible that the device was tested before it was sold.]

◀))

14.10 CONECTA LAS FRASES ACTIVAS CON LAS FRASES PASIVAS QUE SIGNIFIQUEN LO MISMO

We must not ignore the costs.	This picture couldn't have been drawn by Sanjit.
❶ Tim must have bought these flowers today.	The price shouldn't have been accepted.
❷ You can't mark these down yet. They're new.	The costs can't be ignored.
❸ Sanjit could not have drawn this picture.	These glasses must be packaged carefully.
❹ Niamh shouldn't have accepted the price.	They can't be marked down yet! They're new.
❺ You should package these glasses carefully.	The oven has been turned up.
❻ Nobody should ignore faults in the products.	These flowers must have been bought today.
❼ Someone has turned the oven up.	Faults in the product shouldn't be ignored.

◀))

How It's Made

A look at an electric car assembly line.

First, the component parts _____are delivered_____ to separate parts of the factory.

① The chassis parts are placed on the _____ .

② The engine and radiator _____ by a robot as they are very heavy.

③ The engine and radiator _____ to the chassis by an assembly worker.

④ The bodywork is fully _____ on a separate line.

⑤ The assembled bodywork is inspected before _____ by a robot.

⑥ The chassis and bodywork are joined together before the vehicle _____ .

being painted	is checked	~~are delivered~~	assembly line
assembled and welded		are secured	are lifted

15 Describir un producto

Al describir un producto, lo más habitual es utilizar adjetivos. Se puede emplear más de uno, pero deben ir siempre en un orden concreto.

⚙ **Lenguaje** Orden de los adjetivos
Aa Vocabulario Adjetivos de opinión y factuales
🧩 **Habilidad** Describir un producto

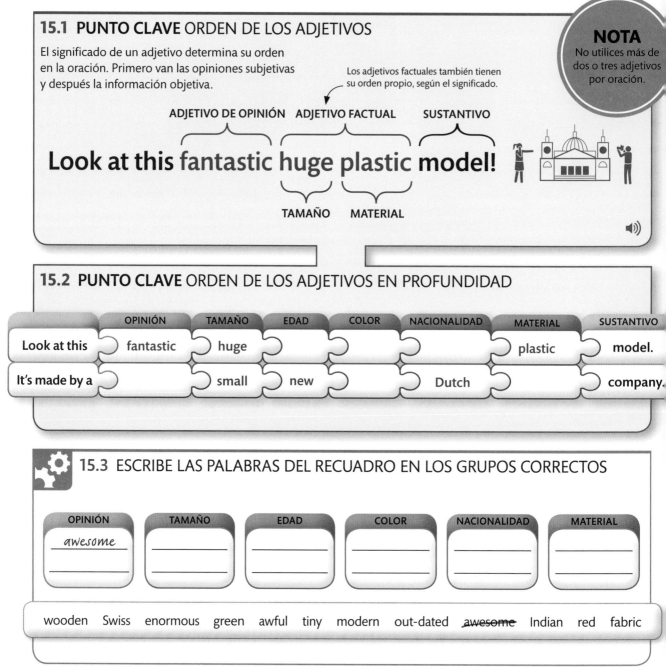

15.1 PUNTO CLAVE ORDEN DE LOS ADJETIVOS

El significado de un adjetivo determina su orden en la oración. Primero van las opiniones subjetivas y después la información objetiva.

Los adjetivos factuales también tienen su orden propio, según el significado.

NOTA
No utilices más de dos o tres adjetivos por oración.

ADJETIVO DE OPINIÓN ADJETIVO FACTUAL SUSTANTIVO

Look at this **fantastic huge plastic model!**

TAMAÑO MATERIAL

15.2 PUNTO CLAVE ORDEN DE LOS ADJETIVOS EN PROFUNDIDAD

	OPINIÓN	TAMAÑO	EDAD	COLOR	NACIONALIDAD	MATERIAL	SUSTANTIVO
Look at this	fantastic	huge				plastic	model.
It's made by a		small	new		Dutch		company.

15.3 ESCRIBE LAS PALABRAS DEL RECUADRO EN LOS GRUPOS CORRECTOS

OPINIÓN	TAMAÑO	EDAD	COLOR	NACIONALIDAD	MATERIAL
awesome					

wooden   Swiss   enormous   green   awful   tiny   modern   out-dated   ~~awesome~~   Indian   red   fabric

15.4 VUELVE A ESCRIBIR LAS FRASES PONIENDO LAS PALABRAS EN SU ORDEN CORRECTO

| I | this | blue | version! | new, | love |

I love this new, blue version!

1 | the | you | plastic | seen | Have | desks? | ugly, |

_____

2 | metallic | We're | range | new, | launching | the | tomorrow. |

_____

3 | you | Would | diamond | prefer | ones? | these | tiny, |

_____

🔊

15.5 ESCUCHA EL AUDIO Y MARCA LAS COSAS QUE SE DESCRIBEN

15.6 PUNTO CLAVE OPINIONES ESPECÍFICAS Y GENERALES

Los adjetivos de opinión general siempre aparecen antes que los de opinión específica. Los de opinión general pueden describir muchas cosas diferentes. Los de opinión específica, en cambio, solo pueden describir un tipo concreto de cosas.

ADJETIVOS DE OPINIÓN

ADJETIVO FACTUAL

What a nice, friendly new team!

"Nice" es un adjetivo de opinión general. Puede describir cosas diferentes.

"Friendly" es un adjetivo de opinión específica. Normalmente solo describe personas o animales.

15.7 TACHA LA PALABRA INCORRECTA DE CADA FRASE

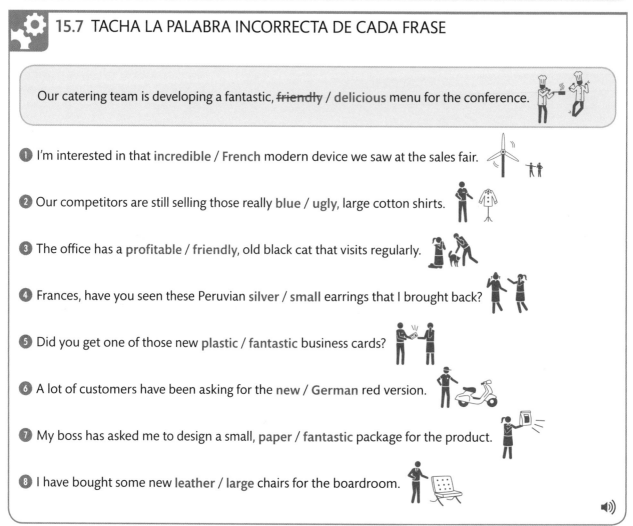

Our catering team is developing a fantastic, ~~friendly~~ / delicious menu for the conference.

① I'm interested in that incredible / French modern device we saw at the sales fair.

② Our competitors are still selling those really blue / ugly, large cotton shirts.

③ The office has a profitable / friendly, old black cat that visits regularly.

④ Frances, have you seen these Peruvian silver / small earrings that I brought back?

⑤ Did you get one of those new plastic / fantastic business cards?

⑥ A lot of customers have been asking for the new / German red version.

⑦ My boss has asked me to design a small, paper / fantastic package for the product.

⑧ I have bought some new leather / large chairs for the boardroom.

15.8 LEE EL ARTÍCULO Y RESPONDE A LAS PREGUNTAS

White guest towels are cheaper this year.
True ☐ **False** ☐ **Not given** ☑

❶ The Festival towel range is colorful.
True ☐ **False** ☐ **Not given** ☐

❷ There is a discount on Festival towels.
True ☐ **False** ☐ **Not given** ☐

❸ Black tablecloths are a new product.
True ☐ **False** ☐ **Not given** ☐

❹ The kitchen towels are made of paper.
True ☐ **False** ☐ **Not given** ☐

❺ The kitchen towels are made in Egypt.
True ☐ **False** ☐ **Not given** ☐

LARA'S LINEN

We have everything your hotel or restaurant needs, from guest towels through to tablecloths. We are keeping our wonderful, best-selling white guest towels at the same fantastic price as last year. But this year we are also adding a range of stunning, multicolored "Festival" towels to our Hotel range. We are also adding to our wonderful Egyptian cotton tableware range. As well as the usual black and white ranges, we now offer burgundy, brown, and olive-colored tablecloths and napkins. Don't forget to check out our hard-wearing, Turkish, cotton kitchen towels and aprons in the Kitchen section of the brochure.

15.9 COMPLETA LOS ESPACIOS CON LAS PALABRAS DEL RECUADRO Y DI LAS FRASES EN VOZ ALTA

His marketing strategy is a
fantastic , intelligent idea.

❶ We offer great, _____ food that people can afford.

❷ Look at that _____ new billboard across the street.

❸ I love buying _____ wooden furniture for the office.

❹ My boss drives a tiny _____ car to work. It's definitely easy to spot!

❺ We aim to offer awesome, _____ customer service at all times.

| delicious | enormous | ~~fantastic~~ |
| friendly | green | antique |

16.1 MARKETING Y PUBLICIDAD

advertising agency

advertisement / ad

copywriter

write copy

brand

logo

slogan / tagline

unique selling point / USP

promote

publicity

press release

door-to-door sales

poster

billboard

sponsor

merchandise

consumer

market research

sales pitch

free sample

special offer

leaflet / flyer

direct mail

coupons

online marketing

online survey

social media

word of mouth

television advertising

radio advertising

telemarketing

small ads / personal ads

Promocionar un producto

Se pueden utilizar diversos adjetivos y adverbios al describir las características principales de un producto o servicio para promocionarlo. No todos los adjetivos se modifican igual.

⚙ **Lenguaje** Adjetivos y adverbios
Aa Vocabulario Adjetivos descriptivos
🧩 **Habilidad** Modificar descripciones de productos

17.1 PUNTO CLAVE ADJETIVOS NO GRADUABLES

La mayoría de los adjetivos son lo que se conoce como "graduables": se pueden modificar con adverbios de grado, como "slightly", "very" y "extremely". Los adjetivos no graduables no admiten este tipo de modificaciones.

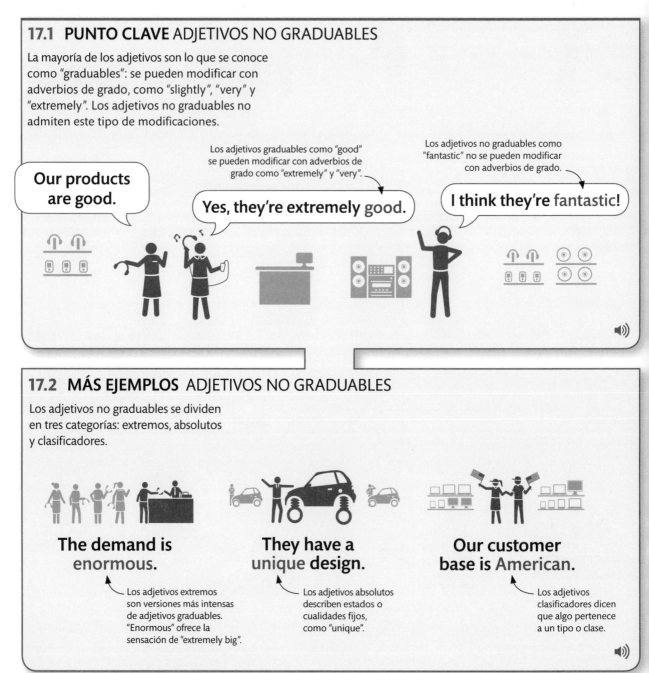

Los adjetivos graduables como "good" se pueden modificar con adverbios de grado como "extremely" y "very".

Los adjetivos no graduables como "fantastic" no se pueden modificar con adverbios de grado.

Our products are good.

Yes, they're extremely good.

I think they're fantastic!

17.2 MÁS EJEMPLOS ADJETIVOS NO GRADUABLES

Los adjetivos no graduables se dividen en tres categorías: extremos, absolutos y clasificadores.

The demand is enormous.

Los adjetivos extremos son versiones más intensas de adjetivos graduables. "Enormous" ofrece la sensación de "extremely big".

They have a unique design.

Los adjetivos absolutos describen estados o cualidades fijos, como "unique".

Our customer base is American.

Los adjetivos clasificadores dicen que algo pertenece a un tipo o clase.

17.3 ESCRIBE LOS ADJETIVOS DEL RECUADRO EN LAS CATEGORÍAS CORRESPONDIENTES

EXTREMOS	ABSOLUTOS	CLASIFICADORES
awful	_unique_	_organic_
_____ _____	_____ _____	_____ _____
_____ _____	_____ _____	_____ _____

fantastic   ~~awful~~   impossible   tiny   right   digital   ~~organic~~   disgusting

perfect   industrial   wrong   electronic   ~~unique~~   enormous   chemical

🔊

17.4 LEE EL ARTÍCULO Y RESPONDE A LAS PREGUNTAS

The author owns his own marketing company.
True ☐   **False** ☐   **Not given** ☑

① Give readers a reason for buying your product.
True ☐   **False** ☐   **Not given** ☐

② Deals of the Day can encourage people to buy.
True ☐   **False** ☐   **Not given** ☐

③ Put key words in a different color text.
True ☐   **False** ☐   **Not given** ☐

④ The article only talks about newsletters.
True ☐   **False** ☐   **Not given** ☐

⑤ Readers do not trust the words "Free" and "New."
True ☐   **False** ☐   **Not given** ☐

⑥ The article recommends setting up a website.
True ☐   **False** ☐   **Not given** ☐

MARKETING WEEKLY

Writing for buyers

Rachid Barbery talks about writing effective marketing texts

Research has shown that there are certain techniques you can use to turn your readers into buyers. First, repeat the positive facts about the product to make them more believable. Make sure you explain why readers would benefit from buying your product compared to others. For example, say that your digital camera weighs 100g less than similar ones and has a unique rubber grip because it makes it easier to carry when traveling. Use the word "you" a lot to help make the connection between the reader and the product. It's also a good idea to promote limited time offers or limited editions as these create an extra reason to buy your product now. This could be a Deal of the Day or Special Edition Color. Using key words in your newsletters and the front pages of your websites or leaflets, such as "Free" and "New" always creates interest and a positive response in readers.

17.5 PUNTO CLAVE ADVERBIOS NO DE GRADO

Algunos adverbios se utilizan para calificar adjetivos no graduables.
Se trata de los "adverbios no de grado" y a menudo significan "entirely"
o "almost entirely". Normalmente no pueden utilizarse con
adjetivos graduables.

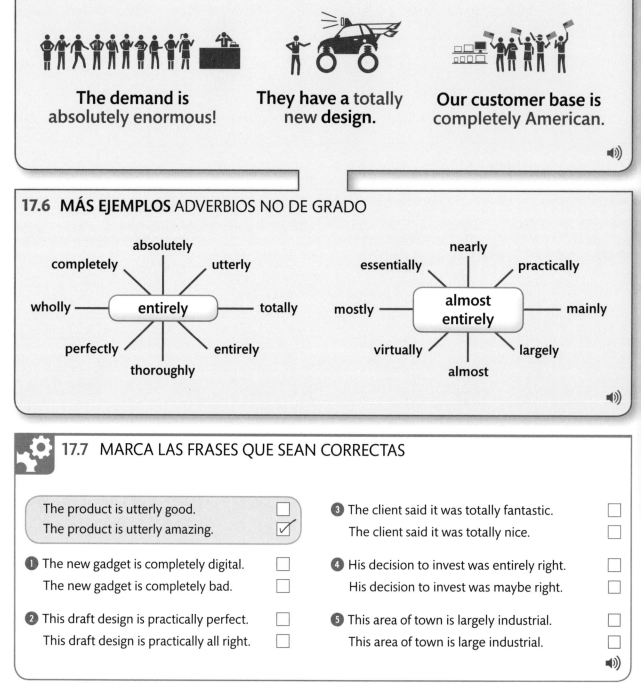

The demand is absolutely enormous!

They have a totally new design.

Our customer base is completely American.

17.6 MÁS EJEMPLOS ADVERBIOS NO DE GRADO

absolutely
completely · utterly
wholly — **entirely** — totally
perfectly · entirely
thoroughly

nearly
essentially · practically
mostly — **almost entirely** — mainly
virtually · largely
almost

17.7 MARCA LAS FRASES QUE SEAN CORRECTAS

The product is utterly good. ☐
The product is utterly amazing. ☑

❶ The new gadget is completely digital. ☐
The new gadget is completely bad. ☐

❷ This draft design is practically perfect. ☐
This draft design is practically all right. ☐

❸ The client said it was totally fantastic. ☐
The client said it was totally nice. ☐

❹ His decision to invest was entirely right. ☐
His decision to invest was maybe right. ☐

❺ This area of town is largely industrial. ☐
This area of town is large industrial. ☐

17.8 PUNTO CLAVE "REALLY", "FAIRLY" Y "PRETTY"

Ciertos adverbios pueden utilizarse con adjetivos graduables y no graduables.
Se trata de "really" (en el sentido de "very much"), y "pretty" y "fairly" (ambos
en el sentido de "quite a lot, but not very").

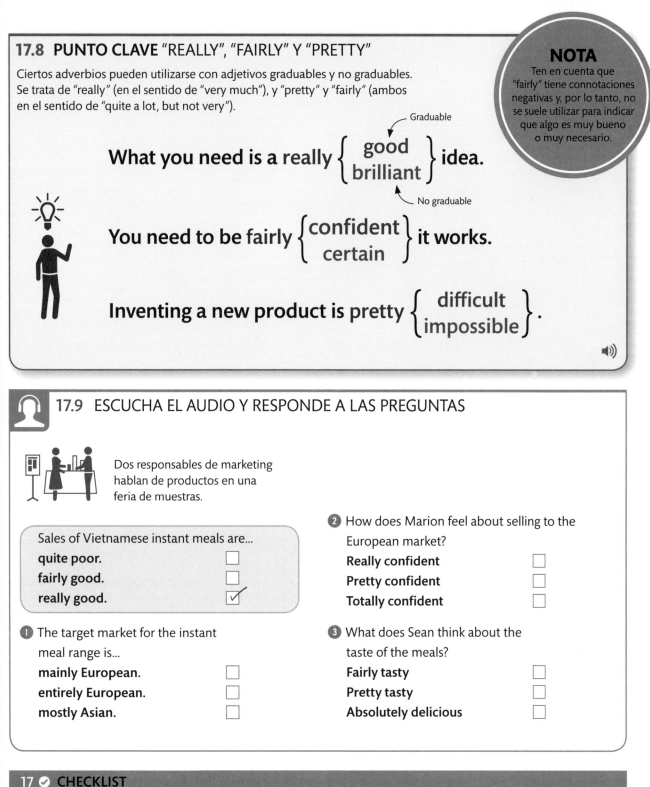

Graduable

What you need is a really { good / brilliant } idea.

No graduable

You need to be fairly { confident / certain } it works.

Inventing a new product is pretty { difficult / impossible }.

NOTA
Ten en cuenta que
"fairly" tiene connotaciones
negativas y, por lo tanto, no
se suele utilizar para indicar
que algo es muy bueno
o muy necesario.

17.9 ESCUCHA EL AUDIO Y RESPONDE A LAS PREGUNTAS

Dos responsables de marketing
hablan de productos en una
feria de muestras.

Sales of Vietnamese instant meals are...
quite poor.	☐
fairly good.	☐
really good.	☑

1 The target market for the instant
meal range is...
mainly European.	☐
entirely European.	☐
mostly Asian.	☐

2 How does Marion feel about selling to the
European market?
Really confident	☐
Pretty confident	☐
Totally confident	☐

3 What does Sean think about the
taste of the meals?
Fairly tasty	☐
Pretty tasty	☐
Absolutely delicious	☐

---

17 ✓ CHECKLIST

✿ Adjetivos y adverbios ☐　　　**Aa** Adjetivos descriptivos ☐　　　🧩 Modificar descripciones de productos ☐

18 Publicidad y marca

El uso de intensificadores como "enough", "too", "so" y "such" ayudan a comunicar mejor tus ideas cuando quieras explicar cosas de tu empresa, productos o marca.

⚙ **Lenguaje** Intensificadores

Aa Vocabulario "Enough", "too", "so" y "such"

🧩 **Habilidad** Añadir énfasis a las descripciones

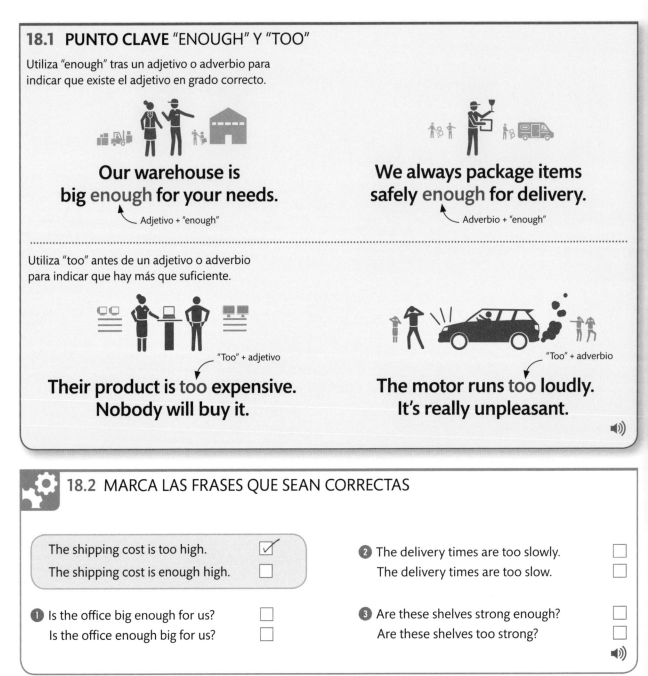

18.1 PUNTO CLAVE "ENOUGH" Y "TOO"

Utiliza "enough" tras un adjetivo o adverbio para indicar que existe el adjetivo en grado correcto.

Our warehouse is big enough for your needs.

Adjetivo + "enough"

We always package items safely enough for delivery.

Adverbio + "enough"

Utiliza "too" antes de un adjetivo o adverbio para indicar que hay más que suficiente.

Their product is too expensive. Nobody will buy it.

"Too" + adjetivo

The motor runs too loudly. It's really unpleasant.

"Too" + adverbio

18.2 MARCA LAS FRASES QUE SEAN CORRECTAS

The shipping cost is too high. ☑
The shipping cost is enough high. ☐

❷ The delivery times are too slowly. ☐
The delivery times are too slow. ☐

❶ Is the office big enough for us? ☐
Is the office enough big for us? ☐

❸ Are these shelves strong enough? ☐
Are these shelves too strong? ☐

18.3 ESCUCHA EL AUDIO Y MARCA LAS COSAS QUE SE DESCRIBEN

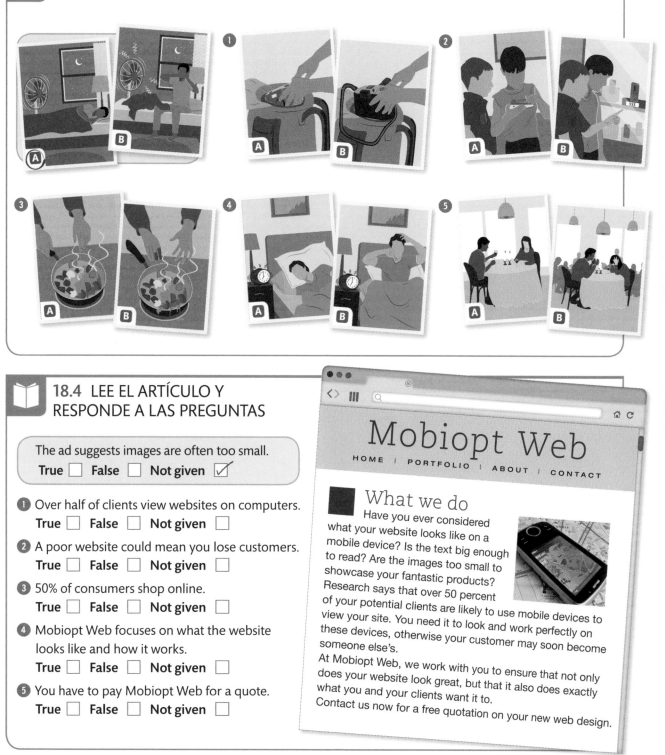

18.4 LEE EL ARTÍCULO Y RESPONDE A LAS PREGUNTAS

The ad suggests images are often too small.
True ☐ False ☐ Not given ☑

❶ Over half of clients view websites on computers.
True ☐ False ☐ Not given ☐

❷ A poor website could mean you lose customers.
True ☐ False ☐ Not given ☐

❸ 50% of consumers shop online.
True ☐ False ☐ Not given ☐

❹ Mobiopt Web focuses on what the website looks like and how it works.
True ☐ False ☐ Not given ☐

❺ You have to pay Mobiopt Web for a quote.
True ☐ False ☐ Not given ☐

Mobiopt Web

HOME | PORTFOLIO | ABOUT | CONTACT

What we do

Have you ever considered what your website looks like on a mobile device? Is the text big enough to read? Are the images too small to showcase your fantastic products? Research says that over 50 percent of your potential clients are likely to use mobile devices to view your site. You need it to look and work perfectly on these devices, otherwise your customer may soon become someone else's.

At Mobiopt Web, we work with you to ensure that not only does your website look great, but that it also does exactly what you and your clients want it to.

Contact us now for a free quotation on your new web design.

257

18.5 PUNTO CLAVE "SO" Y "SUCH"

Añade "such" antes de un sustantivo para enfatizarlo. También puedes añadirlo antes de una combinación de adjetivo y sustantivo.

NOTA

"Such" + "a / an" + sustantivo es más habitual con sustantivos extremos como "success" que con sustantivos neutros como "event".

The new model was such a success.

"Such" + "a / an" + sustantivo

It was such an important meeting.

"Such" + "a / an" + adjetivo + sustantivo

Añade "so" antes de un adjetivo o adverbio para darle más énfasis.

Initial reviews are so important.

"So" + adjetivo

The product launch went so well!

"So" + adverbio

18.6 VUELVE A ESCRIBIR LAS FRASES PONIENDO LAS PALABRAS EN SU ORDEN CORRECTO

price · The · high! · so · is

The price is so high!

❶ such · It's · a · product. · great

_____

❷ boring. · was · so · meeting · The

_____

❸ such · His · was · surprise. · news · a

_____

❹ My · so · is · ambitious. · boss

_____

❺ phones · so · cheap. · Their · are

_____

❻ so · Her · is · company · big!

_____

❼ surprise! · was · such · Our · launch · a

_____

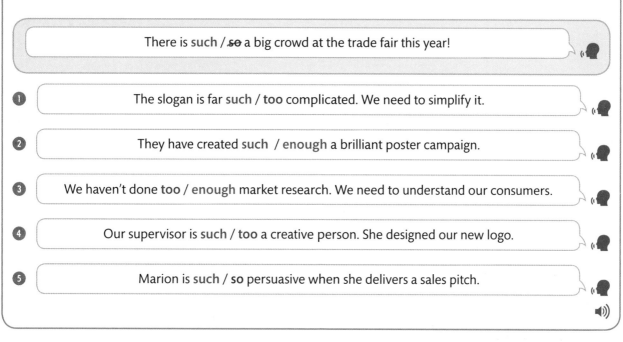

18.7 TACHA LAS PALABRAS INCORRECTAS DE CADA FRASE Y DI LAS FRASES EN VOZ ALTA

There is **such** / ~~so~~ a big crowd at the trade fair this year!

1 The slogan is far **such** / **too** complicated. We need to simplify it.

2 They have created **such** / **enough** a brilliant poster campaign.

3 We haven't done **too** / **enough** market research. We need to understand our consumers.

4 Our supervisor is **such** / **too** a creative person. She designed our new logo.

5 Marion is **such** / **so** persuasive when she delivers a sales pitch.

---

18 ✓ CHECKLIST

⚙ Intensificadores ☐   **Aa** "Enough", "too", "so" y "such" ☐   👤 Añadir énfasis a las descripciones ☐

♻ REPASA LO QUE HAS APRENDIDO EN LAS UNIDADES 13–18

NUEVO LENGUAJE	FRASE DE EJEMPLO	☑	UNIDAD
DESCRIBIR UN PROCESO CON LA VOZ PASIVA	**Our products** are designed **in London.** **Our original model** was sold **worldwide.**	☐	14.1
DESCRIBIR UN PRODUCTO CON LOS ADJETIVOS EN EL ORDEN CORRECTO	**Look at this** fantastic, huge plastic **model!**	☐	15.1, 15.2
OPINIONES ESPECÍFICAS Y GENERALES	**What a** nice, friendly **new team!**	☐	15.6
ADJETIVOS NO GRADUABLES Y ADVERBIOS NO DE GRADO	**They have a** new **design.** **They have a** totally **new design.**	☐	17.1 17.5
"ENOUGH" Y "TOO"	**Our warehouse is big** enough **for your needs.** **Their product is** too **expensive.**	☐	18.1
"SO" Y "SUCH" PARA ENFATIZAR	**The new model was** such **a success.** **Initial reviews are** so **important.**	☐	18.5

19 Consejos y sugerencias

Los verbos modales como "could", "should" y "must" pueden utilizarse para dar consejos y sugerencias. Utilízalos para ayudar a tus colegas en situaciones complicadas o estresantes.

⚙ **Lenguaje** Verbos modales para aconsejar
Aa Vocabulario Presiones en el lugar de trabajo
🧩 **Habilidad** Aconsejar

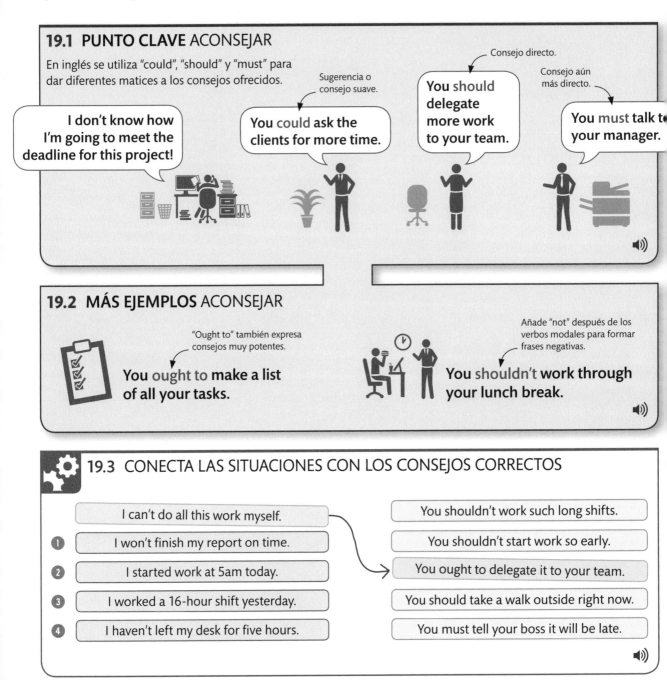

19.1 PUNTO CLAVE ACONSEJAR

En inglés se utiliza "could", "should" y "must" para dar diferentes matices a los consejos ofrecidos.

I don't know how I'm going to meet the deadline for this project!

Sugerencia o consejo suave.

You could ask the clients for more time.

Consejo directo.

You should delegate more work to your team.

Consejo aún más directo.

You must talk to your manager.

19.2 MÁS EJEMPLOS ACONSEJAR

"Ought to" también expresa consejos muy potentes.

You ought to make a list of all your tasks.

Añade "not" después de los verbos modales para formar frases negativas.

You shouldn't work through your lunch break.

19.3 CONECTA LAS SITUACIONES CON LOS CONSEJOS CORRECTOS

I can't do all this work myself.

1. I won't finish my report on time.

2. I started work at 5am today.

3. I worked a 16-hour shift yesterday.

4. I haven't left my desk for five hours.

You shouldn't work such long shifts.

You shouldn't start work so early.

You ought to delegate it to your team.

You should take a walk outside right now.

You must tell your boss it will be late.

19.4 COMPLETA LOS ESPACIOS CON LAS EXPRESIONES DEL RECUADRO

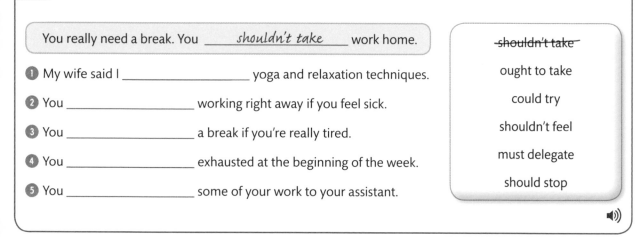

> You really need a break. You _____*shouldn't take*_____ work home.

~~shouldn't take~~
ought to take
could try
shouldn't feel
must delegate
should stop

1 My wife said I _____ yoga and relaxation techniques.

2 You _____ working right away if you feel sick.

3 You _____ a break if you're really tired.

4 You _____ exhausted at the beginning of the week.

5 You _____ some of your work to your assistant.

◀))

19.5 VUELVE A ESCRIBIR LAS FRASES CORRIGIENDO LOS ERRORES

> You **ought** talk to your manager.
> *You ought to talk to your manager.*

1 You **are ought** to relax more.

_____

2 You **must to stop** taking work home every day.

_____

3 He **could trying** to delegate more tasks.

_____

4 You **shouldn't to worry** so much about work.

_____

5 She **shoulds talk** to her colleagues.

_____

6 He **ought to quits** his job if he hates it.

_____

◀))

19.6 ESCUCHA EL AUDIO Y MARCA SI KATE LE ACONSEJA A GIORGIOS QUE HAGA O NO LA ACTIVIDAD DE CADA IMAGEN

Sí ☑   No ☐

1 Sí ☐   No ☐

2 Sí ☐   No ☐

3 Sí ☐   No ☐

4 Sí ☐   No ☐

261

19.7 PUNTO CLAVE HACER SUGERENCIAS

Utiliza "What about...?" seguido de un gerundio o "Why don't we...?" con un verbo base para realizar sugerencias.

What about hiring
Why don't we hire } **more staff?**

19.8 CÓMO FUNCIONA SUGERENCIAS

"WHAT ABOUT"	GERUNDIO	RESTO DE LA FRASE
What about	hiring	**more staff?**

"WHY DON'T WE"	VERBO BASE	
Why don't we	hire	

19.9 MÁS EJEMPLOS REALIZAR SUGERENCIAS

What about working from home on Fridays?

Why don't we organize a team lunch?

What about opening a new store?

Why don't we file these documents?

19.10 UTILIZA EL DIAGRAMA PARA CREAR SEIS FRASES CORRECTAS Y DILAS EN VOZ ALTA

What about taking a break?

What	about	taking	a break?
Why	don't we	take	better equipment?
		buying	new employees?
		buy	
		training	
		train	

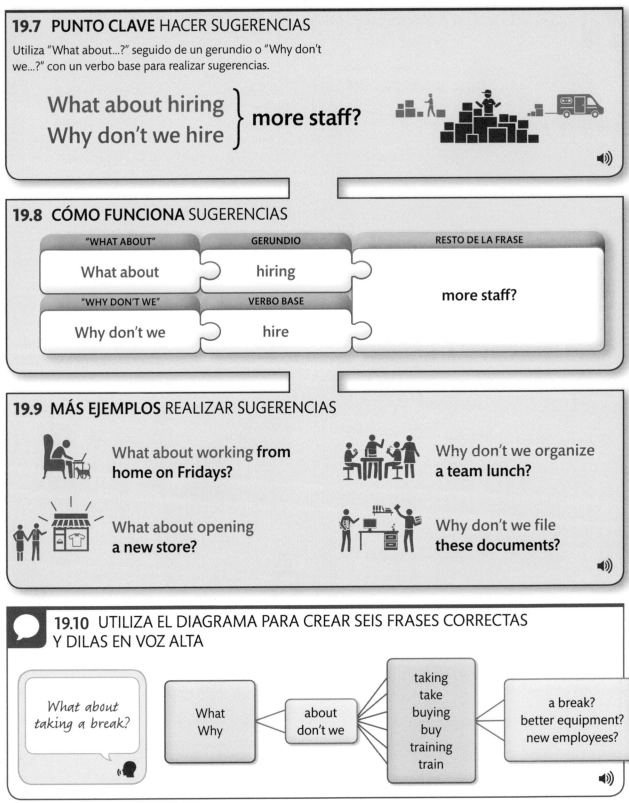

19.11 TACHA LA PALABRA INCORRECTA DE CADA FRASE

What about ~~train~~ / training our staff better?

1 Why don't we buy / buying new chairs?

2 Why don't we go / going for a walk outside?

3 What about drink / drinking less coffee?

4 Why don't we provide / providing free fruit?

5 What about make / making a list of your tasks?

6 What about delegate / delegating this to Jo?

7 Why don't we ask / asking Paul to help us?

19.12 LEE EL ARTÍCULO Y RESPONDE A LAS PREGUNTAS

A heavy workload can affect your health.
True ☑ **False** ☐

1 You must find out what makes you stressed.
True ☐ **False** ☐

2 When you are stressed, you can concentrate.
True ☐ **False** ☐

3 Exercise can help you deal with stress.
True ☐ **False** ☐

4 You should work through your lunch break.
True ☐ **False** ☐

5 It's important to get a good night's sleep.
True ☐ **False** ☐

6 You shouldn't tell people how you feel.
True ☐ **False** ☐

YOUR HEALTH

Stressed out at work?

Our experts give advice about coping with a busy workload

To protect your health from the effects of a heavy workload, you must discover why you feel stressed at work. Then you should learn to recognize signs of excessive stress, such as:
- feeling depressed
- problems sleeping
- difficulty concentrating
- headaches.

Next, you ought to develop positive coping strategies such as exercising and eating well. Have a real break at lunchtime. This in turn will help you sleep better and longer. What about making your night-time routine and your bedroom more relaxing? Sleep is very important, so you shouldn't miss out on it. Finally, you should talk to others about your feelings.

---

19 ⊘ CHECKLIST

⚙ Verbos modales para aconsejar ☐   **Aa** Presiones en el lugar de trabajo ☐   🧩 Aconsejar ☐

20 Vocabulario

20.1 DIRECCIÓN Y LIDERAZGO

Every year I have an appraisal **with my manager.**

an appraisal / a performance review
[an interview to discuss an employee's performance]

We get a $500 sales bonus **if we meet our targets.**

a bonus
[money added to a person's wages as a reward for good performance]

I was promoted **this year, so I have my own office.**

to be promoted
[to be given a more senior position within a company]

My boss is really pleased with my performance **this year.**

performance
[how well a person carries out tasks]

20.2 CAPACIDADES Y HABILIDADES

organization

IT / computing

administration

problem-solving

numeracy

customer service

interpersonal skills

leadership

public speaking

written communication

initiative

telephone manner

Our manager has to approve this before it goes to the client.

to approve
[to officially confirm something meets the required standards]

I like to delegate tasks to give my co-workers a variety of work.

to delegate
[to give work or tasks to a person in a position junior to you]

My team leader allocates tasks at the beginning of each week.

to allocate a task
[to give a task to somebody]

I have to designate a colleague as the main first aider in the office.

to designate
[to choose somebody to take on a particular role]

data analysis

decision-making

teamwork

fast learner

research

fluent in languages

attention to detail

negotiating

work well under pressure

able to drive

project management

time management

21 Hablar sobre capacidades

Para hablar sobre las capacidades de otros, por ejemplo en una evaluación de rendimiento, utiliza verbos modales para expresar capacidades pasadas, presentes y futuras.

⚙ **Lenguaje** Verbos modales de capacidades
Aa Vocabulario Capacidades del lugar de trabajo
🧩 **Habilidad** Describir capacidades

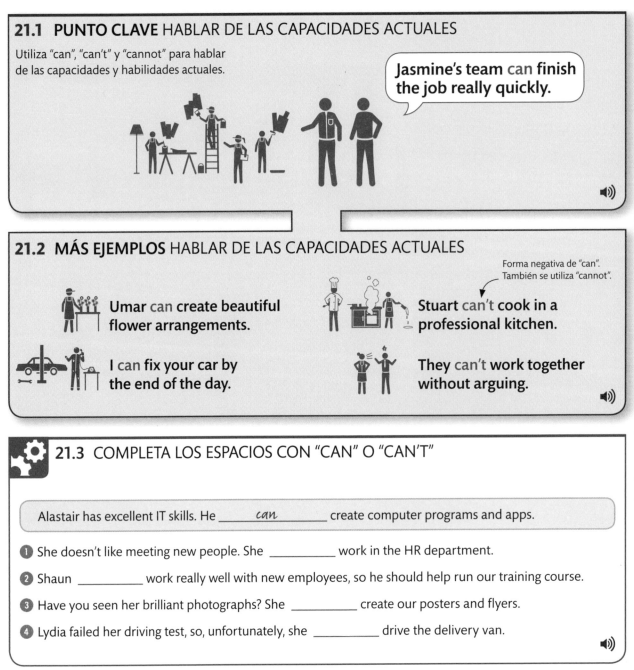

21.1 PUNTO CLAVE HABLAR DE LAS CAPACIDADES ACTUALES

Utiliza "can", "can't" y "cannot" para hablar de las capacidades y habilidades actuales.

> Jasmine's team **can finish** the job really quickly.

21.2 MÁS EJEMPLOS HABLAR DE LAS CAPACIDADES ACTUALES

Forma negativa de "can". También se utiliza "cannot".

Umar **can create** beautiful flower arrangements.

Stuart **can't cook** in a professional kitchen.

I **can fix** your car by the end of the day.

They **can't work** together without arguing.

21.3 COMPLETA LOS ESPACIOS CON "CAN" O "CAN'T"

Alastair has excellent IT skills. He _____*can*_____ create computer programs and apps.

① She doesn't like meeting new people. She _____ work in the HR department.

② Shaun _____ work really well with new employees, so he should help run our training course.

③ Have you seen her brilliant photographs? She _____ create our posters and flyers.

④ Lydia failed her driving test, so, unfortunately, she _____ drive the delivery van.

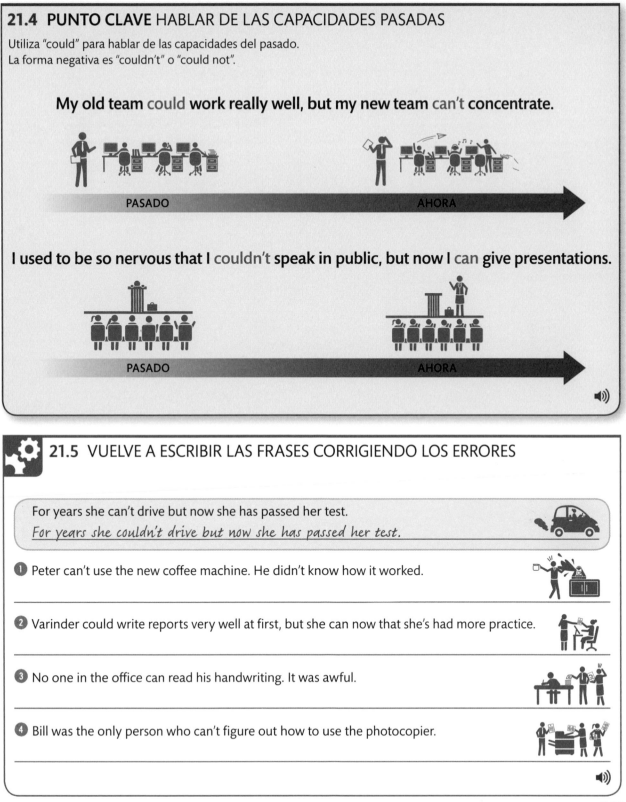

21.4 PUNTO CLAVE HABLAR DE LAS CAPACIDADES PASADAS

Utiliza "could" para hablar de las capacidades del pasado.
La forma negativa es "couldn't" o "could not".

My old team could work really well, but my new team can't concentrate.

PASADO

AHORA

I used to be so nervous that I couldn't speak in public, but now I can give presentations.

PASADO

AHORA

21.5 VUELVE A ESCRIBIR LAS FRASES CORRIGIENDO LOS ERRORES

For years she can't drive but now she has passed her test.

For years she couldn't drive but now she has passed her test.

❶ Peter can't use the new coffee machine. He didn't know how it worked.

❷ Varinder could write reports very well at first, but she can now that she's had more practice.

❸ No one in the office can read his handwriting. It was awful.

❹ Bill was the only person who can't figure out how to use the photocopier.

21.6 PUNTO CLAVE HABLAR DE POTENCIALES FUTUROS

En inglés se utiliza "could" para hablar de capacidades y potenciales futuros de alguien. En este contexto, después de "could" pueden aparecer la mayoría de verbos en inglés.

Utiliza "could" antes de la mayoría de verbos para hablar de posibles situaciones futuras.

If Felipe keeps on working hard, he could become head chef.

Jenny could reach the top of our company's sales rankings.

También puedes utilizar "would" seguido de "do", "make" o "be" para hablar de potenciales futuros. "Would" es más potente que "could" y sugiere que es más probable que algo se produzca.

Utiliza "do" o "make" después de "would" para hablar de potenciales futuros.

Kim is good at training people. She would make an excellent team leader.

Liz is really polite. She would do well in the customer services department.

21.7 MARCA SI LAS AFIRMACIONES SE REFIEREN A UNA CAPACIDAD PASADA O FUTURA

You could be head of your department.
Pasada ☐ **Futura** ☑

① She would make a great team leader.
Pasada ☐ **Futura** ☐

② He couldn't cook before his training.
Pasada ☐ **Futura** ☐

③ He would do well in a smaller team.
Pasada ☐ **Futura** ☐

④ Ray could get along with the old CEO.
Pasada ☐ **Futura** ☐

⑤ Fiona could do better if she tried.
Pasada ☐ **Futura** ☐

Shona y su jefe hablan de la evaluación de rendimiento anual de ella.

Shona's manager wants to talk about her past.
True ☐ **False** ☐ **Not given** ☑

❶ Nick is pleased with Shona's work.
True ☐ **False** ☐ **Not given** ☐

❷ Shona has worked there for five years.
True ☐ **False** ☐ **Not given** ☐

❸ Shona will get a $500 bonus.
True ☐ **False** ☐ **Not given** ☐

❹ Shona can't work well with new staff.
True ☐ **False** ☐ **Not given** ☐

❺ Shona wouldn't be a good team leader.
True ☐ **False** ☐ **Not given** ☐

💬 **21.9** TACHA LAS PALABRAS INCORRECTAS DE CADA FRASE Y DI LAS FRASES EN VOZ ALTA

You're an excellent sales assistant, and you ~~can't~~ / **would** do well in the marketing team.

❶ James's team was weak, but he's trained them well and now they **can** / **can't** do anything.

❷ We think that you are really creative and **couldn't** / **would** make a great addition to the PR team.

❸ I don't know what is wrong with me today. I **can** / **can't** get anything finished.

❹ My confidence is much better now. Before, I **would** / **couldn't** talk in public.

🔊

21 ✔ **CHECKLIST**

⚙️ Verbos modales de capacidades ☐   **Aa** Capacidades del lugar de trabajo ☐   🧩 Describir capacidades ☐

22 Comparar y contrastar

En las discusiones de equipo, los marcadores del discurso facilitan la conversación, pues ayudan a unir ideas similares u opuestas, o conectan una acción con su resultado.

⚙ **Lenguaje** Marcadores del discurso

Aa Vocabulario Trabajo en equipo y cohesión

🧩 **Habilidad** Expresar tus ideas

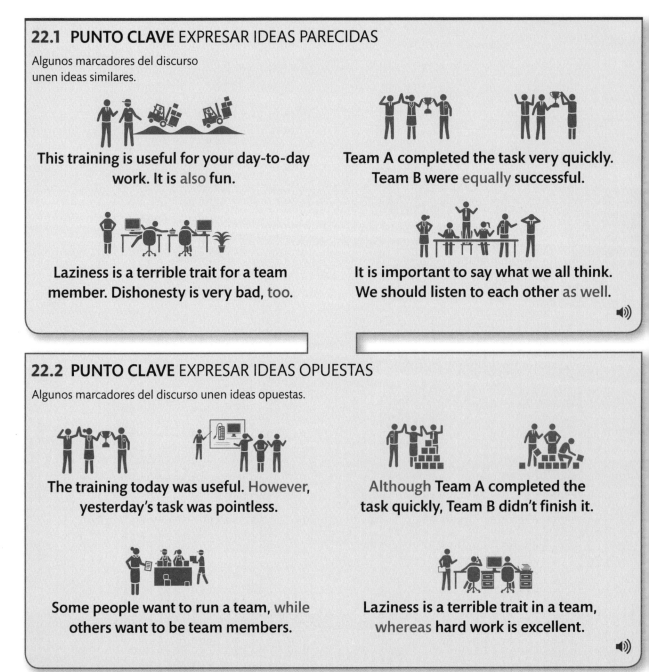

22.1 PUNTO CLAVE EXPRESAR IDEAS PARECIDAS

Algunos marcadores del discurso unen ideas similares.

This training is useful for your day-to-day work. It is also fun.

Team A completed the task very quickly. Team B were equally successful.

Laziness is a terrible trait for a team member. Dishonesty is very bad, too.

It is important to say what we all think. We should listen to each other as well.

22.2 PUNTO CLAVE EXPRESAR IDEAS OPUESTAS

Algunos marcadores del discurso unen ideas opuestas.

The training today was useful. However, yesterday's task was pointless.

Although Team A completed the task quickly, Team B didn't finish it.

Some people want to run a team, while others want to be team members.

Laziness is a terrible trait in a team, whereas hard work is excellent.

22.3 TACHA LA PALABRA INCORRECTA DE CADA FRASE

All staff should follow the dress code for the training. Please be on time, ~~while~~ / too.

1. **Although** / **Equally** I attended the training session, I'm not sure I learned very much.

2. You got a high score for the IT test, and you've done **equally** / **while** well on the team-building course.

3. Team A built a small boat out of plastic bottles, **as well** / **whereas** Team B used wood to make theirs.

4. The training day is a great way to learn new skills. It's **also** / **however** a good way to get to know people.

22.4 ESCUCHA EL AUDIO Y RESPONDE A LAS PREGUNTAS

Un coach explica cómo lo han hecho dos equipos.

The coach says the team-building days are...
challenging and tiring. ☐
challenging but rewarding. ☐
challenging and fun. ☑

1. At the beginning of the team-building day, the participants...
walked across bridges over a river. ☐
walked across bridges high in the air. ☐
made ladders to climb up trees. ☐

2. This task challenged the participants to...
overcome fear and help each other. ☐
deal with a fear of heights. ☐
learn how to build rope bridges. ☐

3. Members of Team Bear were...
the tallest and the quickest. ☐
the tallest and the most scared. ☐
the tallest, whereas Team Lion were slowest. ☐

4. Members of Team Bear helped each other while members of Team Lion...
disagreed with each other. ☐
worked too slowly. ☐
raced each other to the finish. ☐

5. In the future, Team Lion should...
help Team Bear to be less afraid. ☐
argue less and work faster. ☐
work more slowly and listen to their teammates. ☐

22.5 PUNTO CLAVE HABLAR DE RESULTADOS

Algunos marcadores del discurso unen una acción o situación con su resultado.

Marcadores del discurso menos formales.

The training days are useful.

- As a result,
- For this reason,
- Consequently,
- As a consequence,

everyone attends them.

Marcadores del discurso más formales.

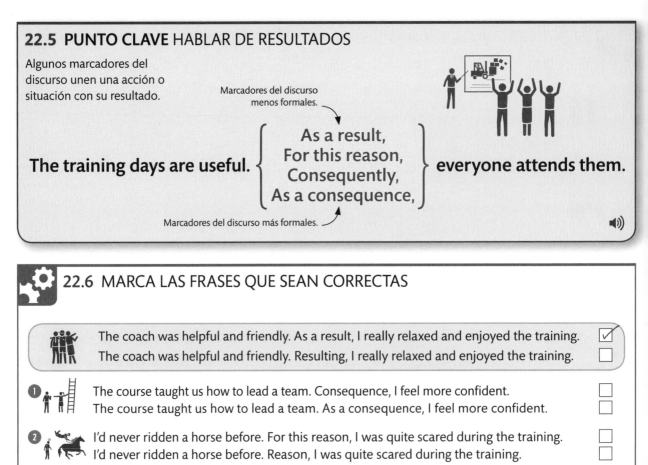

22.6 MARCA LAS FRASES QUE SEAN CORRECTAS

The coach was helpful and friendly. As a result, I really relaxed and enjoyed the training. ☑

The coach was helpful and friendly. Resulting, I really relaxed and enjoyed the training. ☐

1. The course taught us how to lead a team. Consequence, I feel more confident. ☐

   The course taught us how to lead a team. As a consequence, I feel more confident. ☐

2. I'd never ridden a horse before. For this reason, I was quite scared during the training. ☐

   I'd never ridden a horse before. Reason, I was quite scared during the training. ☐

3. Team Lion completed the challenge first. Consequently, they all received medals. ☐

   Team Lion completed the challenge first. Consequent, they all received medals. ☐

22.7 CONECTA EL INICIO Y EL FINAL DE CADA AFIRMACIÓN

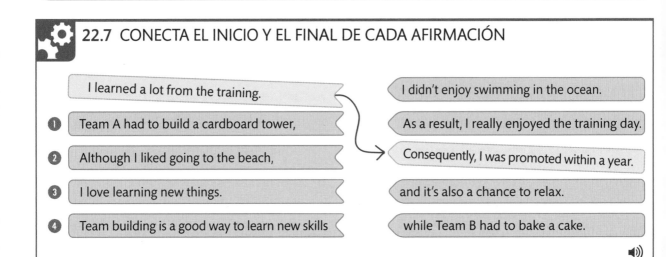

I learned a lot from the training.

1. Team A had to build a cardboard tower,

2. Although I liked going to the beach,

3. I love learning new things.

4. Team building is a good way to learn new skills

I didn't enjoy swimming in the ocean.

As a result, I really enjoyed the training day.

Consequently, I was promoted within a year.

and it's also a chance to relax.

while Team B had to bake a cake.

BUILDING A TEAM

CEO Lucia Gomez talks to us about team building

We send all our employees on team-building courses at least once a year. Our staff have gone on team-building treasure hunts, and they've also completed obstacle courses. However, what activity they do isn't so important. What matters is that they get out of the office and do something that requires them to communicate effectively, and support and help each other, too. It's quite easy to spot employees who are natural-born leaders during these activities. We sometimes identify future managers in this way and put them on our fast-track management-training program.

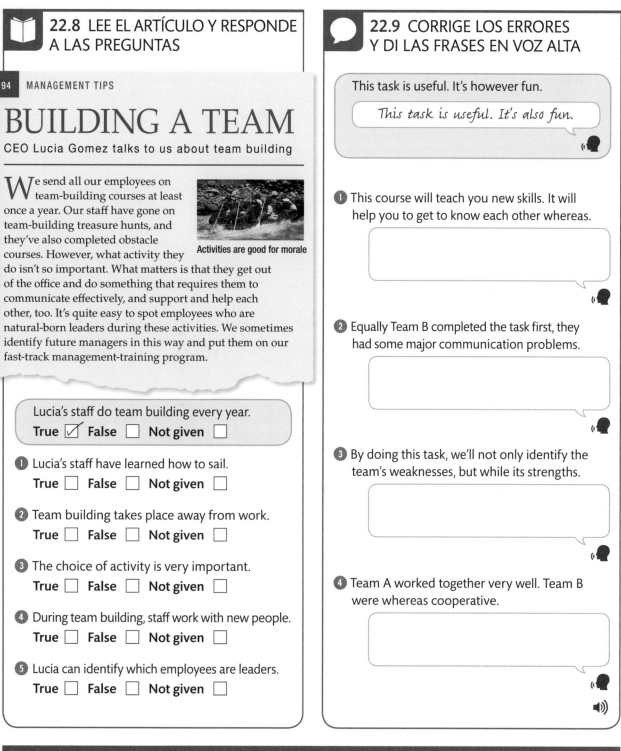

Activities are good for morale

Lucia's staff do team building every year.
True ☑ **False** ☐ **Not given** ☐

❶ Lucia's staff have learned how to sail.
True ☐ **False** ☐ **Not given** ☐

❷ Team building takes place away from work.
True ☐ **False** ☐ **Not given** ☐

❸ The choice of activity is very important.
True ☐ **False** ☐ **Not given** ☐

❹ During team building, staff work with new people.
True ☐ **False** ☐ **Not given** ☐

❺ Lucia can identify which employees are leaders.
True ☐ **False** ☐ **Not given** ☐

22.9 CORRIGE LOS ERRORES Y DI LAS FRASES EN VOZ ALTA

This task is useful. It's however fun.

> This task is useful. It's also fun.

❶ This course will teach you new skills. It will help you to get to know each other whereas.

❷ Equally Team B completed the task first, they had some major communication problems.

❸ By doing this task, we'll not only identify the team's weaknesses, but while its strengths.

❹ Team A worked together very well. Team B were whereas cooperative.

22 ✅ CHECKLIST

⚙️ Marcadores del discurso ☐   **Aa** Trabajo en equipo y cohesión ☐   🧩 Expresar tus ideas ☐

23 Planear eventos

Muchos verbos ingleses que se utilizan para dar opiniones o hablar sobre planes e intenciones van seguidos por un gerundio o un infinitivo.

🗘 **Lenguaje** Patrones verbales
Aa Vocabulario Ocio corporativo
🧩 **Habilidad** Hablar sobre eventos de la empresa

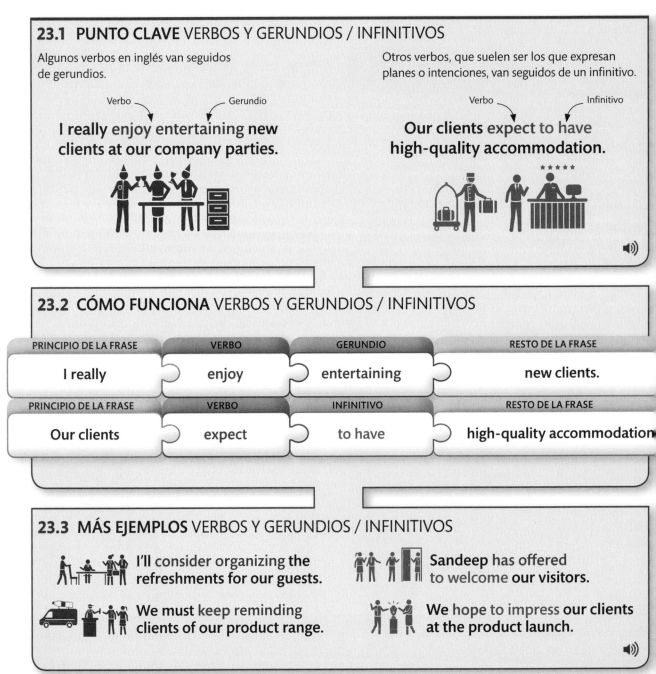

23.1 PUNTO CLAVE VERBOS Y GERUNDIOS / INFINITIVOS

Algunos verbos en inglés van seguidos de gerundios.

Verbo — Gerundio

I really enjoy entertaining new clients at our company parties.

Otros verbos, que suelen ser los que expresan planes o intenciones, van seguidos de un infinitivo.

Verbo — Infinitivo

Our clients expect to have high-quality accommodation.

23.2 CÓMO FUNCIONA VERBOS Y GERUNDIOS / INFINITIVOS

PRINCIPIO DE LA FRASE	VERBO	GERUNDIO	RESTO DE LA FRASE
I really	enjoy	entertaining	new clients.

PRINCIPIO DE LA FRASE	VERBO	INFINITIVO	RESTO DE LA FRASE
Our clients	expect	to have	high-quality accommodation

23.3 MÁS EJEMPLOS VERBOS Y GERUNDIOS / INFINITIVOS

I'll consider organizing the refreshments for our guests.

Sandeep has offered to welcome our visitors.

We must keep reminding clients of our product range.

We hope to impress our clients at the product launch.

23.4 TACHA LAS PALABRAS INCORRECTAS DE CADA FRASE

You need ~~being~~ / **to be** very organized to plan a successful business event.

1. Mara has offered **organizing** / **to organize** the accommodation for our guests.

2. I keep **suggesting** / **to suggest** that our company should organize a golf day, but my boss disagrees.

3. We like **offering** / **to offer** our clients a wide range of food at our conferences.

4. I enjoy **helping** / **to help** out at company open days because I get to meet lots of people.

5. Before I start planning, I usually make a list of all the customers I want **inviting** / **to invite**.

6. I expect **staying** / **to stay** late tonight to help Martina decorate the conference hall.

23.5 LEE EL ANUNCIO Y ESCRIBE RESPUESTAS A LAS PREGUNTAS CON ORACIONES COMPLETAS

Which city is the SmartTech Fair in?

The SmartTech Fair is in Tokyo.

1. What year did the SmartTech Fair open?

_____

2. What is smart health technology helping to do?

_____

3. What could self-driving cars do?

_____

4. How can you show interest in attending an event?

_____

5. How can you buy tickets in advance?

_____

23.6 PUNTO CLAVE VERBOS Y GERUNDIO O INFINITIVO (CAMBIO DE SIGNIFICADO)

Algunos verbos cambian de significado según
la forma del verbo que tienen detrás.

You remember meeting David, don't you? He's the CEO of Unodom.

[You have met David before. Do you remember?]

You must remember to meet David to make plans for the conference.

[You must remember that you have to meet David.]

23.7 MÁS EJEMPLOS VERBOS Y GERUNDIO O INFINITIVO (CAMBIO DE SIGNIFICADO)

En general, el gerundio se suele utilizar para una acción que pasa antes o
simultáneamente a la del verbo principal. El infinitivo se utiliza para describir
una acción que pasa después de la acción del verbo principal.

VERBO + GERUNDIO	VERBO + INFINITIVO

I stopped reading the timetable because my manager called me.

[I was reading the timetable, but then I stopped.]

I stopped to read the timetable for our team training day.

[I stopped what I was doing to read the timetable.]

Sally went on talking all evening. I hope you weren't bored.

[Sally was talking for a long time.]

Sally prepared her presentation, and went on to talk about the company's new branding.

[Sally gave the talk after she had prepared it.]

I regret telling you that I can't come to dinner with the clients. I can see that you're angry.

[I wish I hadn't told you that I can't come to dinner.]

I regret to tell you that I can't come to dinner with the clients. I'm really sorry.

[I'm sorry, but I can't come to dinner.]

23.8 CONECTA EL INICIO Y EL FINAL DE CADA FRASE

I really regret making → that mistake at the conference.

1 We stopped holding breakfast meetings — because few people attended them.

2 We regret to announce — that there will be some job losses.

3 I'm sure Shona will remember — to book the conference room.

4 Sahib went on working — until midnight in order to finish the report.

23.9 ESCUCHA EL AUDIO Y RESPONDE A LAS PREGUNTAS

Sunita y Darren preparan la visita de algunos clientes extranjeros a su oficina.

Two clients are visiting the office next week.
True ☑ **False** ☐ **Not given** ☐

1 Darren is not going to the meetings.
True ☐ **False** ☐ **Not given** ☐

2 The conference is about healthcare products.
True ☐ **False** ☐ **Not given** ☐

3 The conference is on Thursday.
True ☐ **False** ☐ **Not given** ☐

4 Sunita's boss expects her to impress the clients.
True ☐ **False** ☐ **Not given** ☐

5 It is Mr. Yamada's first visit to the US.
True ☐ **False** ☐ **Not given** ☐

6 They may go sightseeing with the clients.
True ☐ **False** ☐ **Not given** ☐

23.10 UTILIZA EL DIAGRAMA PARA CREAR NUEVE FRASES CORRECTAS Y DILAS EN VOZ ALTA

I remember meeting him in Tokyo.

| I / She / We / They | remember / was supposed / wanted | meeting / to book | him in Tokyo. / a nice hotel room. |

277

23.11 PUNTO CLAVE VERBO + OBJETO + INFINITIVO

Algunos verbos, especialmente los que expresan órdenes o peticiones, pueden ir seguidos de un objeto y otro verbo en infinitivo.

We expect **all our staff** to attend **a party with our clients.**

Verbo / Objeto / Infinitivo

23.12 CÓMO FUNCIONA VERBO + OBJETO + INFINITIVO

SUJETO	VERBO	OBJETO	INFINITIVO	RESTO DE LA FRASE
We	expect	all our staff	to attend	a party with our client

23.13 MÁS EJEMPLOS VERBO + OBJETO + INFINITIVO

I've invited **our new clients** to have **lunch with us.**

My manager asked **me** to book **the conference room.**

23.14 COMPLETA LOS ESPACIOS CON LAS EXPRESIONES DEL RECUADRO

We ___*want all our staff*___ to feel happy at work.

1 My boss asked me _____ a meeting with our clients.

2 Our clients _____ to visit them in Paris.

3 We expect all our staff _____ on time.

4 We _____ to attend our end-of-year party.

5 I expect my manager _____ me a promotion soon.

asked us

to arrange

to give

~~want all our staff~~

invited all our clients

to arrive

278

23.15 VUELVE A ESCRIBIR LAS FRASES PONIENDO LAS PALABRAS EN SU ORDEN CORRECTO

| me | book | hotel. | the | The | to | asked | CEO |

The CEO asked me to book the hotel.

1 | excellent | expect | clients | to | Our | receive | service. |

_____

2 | invited | My | a | me | boss | to | conference. | attend |

_____

3 | My | degree | to | me | business | this | allowed | get | job. |

_____

🔊

---

23 ✓ CHECKLIST

⚙️ Patrones verbales ☐   **Aa** Ocio corporativo ☐   🧩 Hablar sobre eventos de la empresa ☐

♻ REPASA LO QUE HAS APRENDIDO EN LAS UNIDADES 19–23

NUEVO LENGUAJE	FRASE DE EJEMPLO	☑	UNIDAD
ACONSEJAR	You should **ask the clients for more time.** You must **talk to your manager.**	☐	19.1
REALIZAR SUGERENCIAS	What about hiring **more staff?** Why don't we open **a new store?**	☐	19.7
HABLAR SOBRE CAPACIDADES	Jasmine's team **can finish the job quickly.** I couldn't **give presentations five years ago.**	☐	21.1, 21.4, 21.6
COMPARAR Y CONTRASTAR IDEAS	This task is useful. It is also fun. Team A won the task, whereas Team B lost.	☐	22.1, 22.2
VERBOS CON GERUNDIOS E INFINITIVOS	I really enjoy entertaining **clients.** Sandeep has offered to welcome **our guests.**	☐	23.1, 23.3, 23.6
VERBO + OBJETO + INFINITIVO	We expect all our staff to attend **the party.**	☐	23.11

24.1 REUNIONES

Lee, could you send out the agenda for Friday's meeting, please?

to send out an agenda
[to send a plan for what will be discussed]

The main objective of this meeting is to agree on a budget.

main objective
[the primary aim]

Yolanda is sick, so she will be absent from the meeting today.

to be absent
[to be not present]

Can we have a show of hands for those who agree with the proposal?

a show of hands
[a vote made by raising hands in the air to show agreement]

Francesca will give a presentation on health and safety.

to give a presentation
[to present information to a group of people]

Today we need to look at our sales figures for the last year.

to look at
[to consider or focus on something]

If we can't reach a consensus, we will have a vote.

to reach a consensus
[to come to an agreement about an issue]

We reached a unanimous agreement on the plan.

unanimous agreement
[when everyone agrees]

We will have another meeting next week because we have run out of time.

to run out of time
[to have no more time left to do something]

We will take questions at the end of the meeting.

to take questions
[to answer questions]

We need someone to take minutes during the meeting.

to take minutes
[to write a record of what was said during a meeting]

Did you manage to review the minutes from the last meeting?

to review the minutes
[to look again at the written record of a past meeting]

Please can you send the minutes to all attendees after the meeting?

attendees
[people who have been to or are going to a meeting]

We need a strategy for increasing sales to young buyers.

a strategy
[a plan for achieving a particular goal]

Let's discuss the options for the new logo.

to discuss
[to talk about something]

I suggest that we use this new design.

to suggest / propose
[to put forward an idea or plan for others to discuss]

It's nearly lunchtime. Let's wrap up the meeting.

to wrap up
[to conclude or finish something]

I'm sorry to interrupt, but I have some more recent figures.

to interrupt
[to say something before someone else has finished speaking]

So to sum up, we really need to increase sales next month.

to sum up
[to conclude]

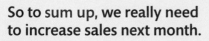

Excellent, we have three clear action points to work on.

action points
[proposals for specific action to be taken]

25 Lo que han dicho otros

Cuando expliques a los colegas lo que alguien ha dicho, puedes tomar sus palabras (direct speech) y referirlas con claridad y precisión: es lo que se llama reported speech.

⚙️ **Lenguaje** Reported speech
Aa Vocabulario Reuniones
🧩 **Habilidad** Decir lo que dijo alguien

25.1 PUNTO CLAVE REPORTED SPEECH

El verbo principal en el reported speech suele ser "said". El verbo que se cita normalmente va en un tiempo distinto al del direct speech.

El direct speech utiliza el present simple.

I can't come to the meeting. I'm too busy.

Luke said that he was too busy to come to the meeting.

"That" suele añadirse después de "said" en reported speech.

El reported speech utiliza el past simple para el verbo que se cita.

25.2 PUNTO CLAVE REPORTED SPEECH EN DISTINTOS TIEMPOS

El tiempo verbal que se utiliza en el reported speech suele ser el anterior temporalmente respecto del tiempo del direct speech.

I'm working in New York.

She said she was working in New York.
El past continuous sustituye al present continuous.

I've been to China twice.

He said that he'd been to China twice.
El past perfect sustituye al present perfect.

I will call you soon.

He said he would call them soon.
"Would" sustituye a "will".

We can speak Japanese.

They said that they could speak Japanese.
"Could" sustituye a "can".

25.3 PUNTO CLAVE REPORTED SPEECH Y EL PAST SIMPLE

El past simple en direct speech puede quedarse igual o cambiar a past perfect en reported speech. El significado es el mismo.

I arrived in Delhi on Saturday.

He said { he arrived / he'd arrived } in Delhi on Saturday.

25.4 CONECTA EL DIRECT SPEECH CON SU REPORTED SPEECH

I'm working on the accounts. ──→ He said he was working on the accounts.

1. I paid the invoice.
2. I will pay the invoice.
3. I will arrange a meeting.
4. I'm arranging a meeting.
5. I've finished writing the report.
6. I'll finish writing the report.

She said she had finished writing the report.

He said he was arranging a meeting.

He said he would pay the invoice.

He said he would arrange a meeting.

She said she paid the invoice.

She said she would finish writing the report.

25.5 VUELVE A ESCRIBIR LAS FRASES EN REPORTED SPEECH

I need to send an email.
He _said that he needed to send an email._

1. I will interview the candidates.
She _____

2. I met the CEO on Monday.
He _____

3. I can book the meeting room.
He _____

4. I'm writing a press release.
She _____

5. I can use design software.
He _____

25.6 PUNTO CLAVE REFERENCIAS DE TIEMPO Y LUGAR

Si se cita algo un tiempo después de que se haya dicho, las palabras utilizadas para hablar de fechas y lugares pueden tener que cambiarse.

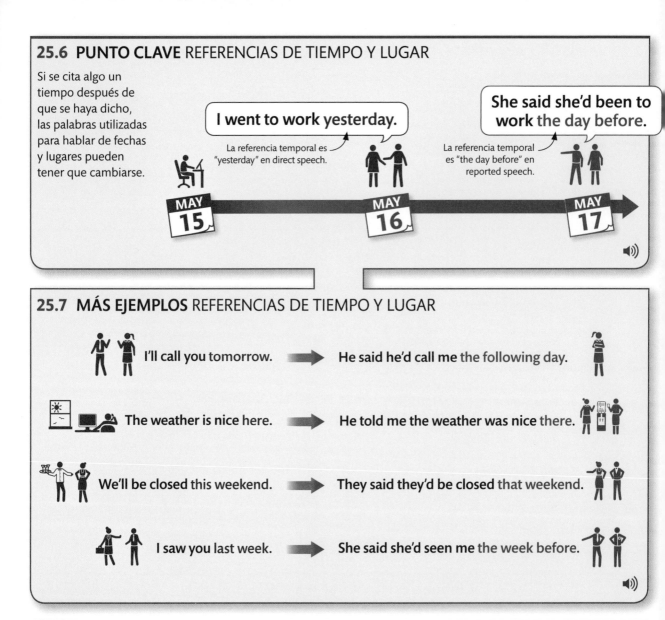

I went to work yesterday.

La referencia temporal es "yesterday" en direct speech.

She said she'd been to work the day before.

La referencia temporal es "the day before" en reported speech.

MAY 15

MAY 16

MAY 17

25.7 MÁS EJEMPLOS REFERENCIAS DE TIEMPO Y LUGAR

I'll call you tomorrow. ➡ He said he'd call me the following day.

The weather is nice here. ➡ He told me the weather was nice there.

We'll be closed this weekend. ➡ They said they'd be closed that weekend.

I saw you last week. ➡ She said she'd seen me the week before.

25.8 ESCUCHA EL AUDIO Y LUEGO NUMERA LAS FRASES EN REPORTED SPEECH EN EL ORDEN QUE APARECEN EN DIRECT SPEECH

A Jack said he would send me the proposal the following day. ☐

B Jack said he had got promoted the week before. ☐

C Jack said he enjoyed working there. ☐

D Jack said he'd be going to Dubai the following weekend. ☐ 1

E Jack said he had gone to the London office the day before. ☐

25.9 PUNTO CLAVE OTROS CAMBIOS EN REPORTED SPEECH

En reported speech, es posible que haya que cambiar los pronombres
para asegurarnos de que se refieren a la persona o a la cosa correctas.

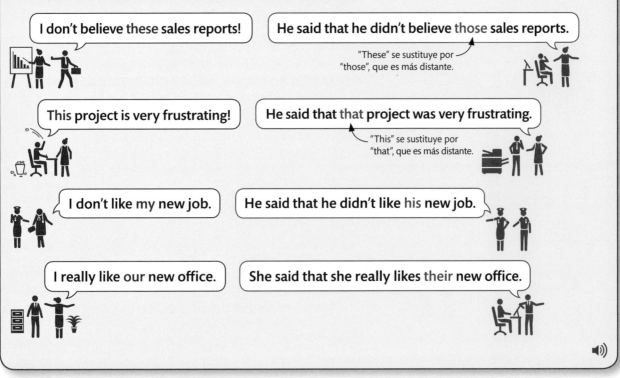

I don't believe these sales reports!

He said that he didn't believe those sales reports.

"These" se sustituye por
"those", que es más distante.

This project is very frustrating!

He said that that project was very frustrating.

"This" se sustituye por
"that", que es más distante.

I don't like my new job.

He said that he didn't like his new job.

I really like our new office.

She said that she really likes their new office.

25.10 VUELVE A ESCRIBIR LAS FRASES PONIENDO LAS PALABRAS EN SU ORDEN CORRECTO

| their | January | positive. | were | sales | He | said | figures | for |

He said their sales figures for January were positive.

① | email. | she | understand | that | She | didn't | the | said |

_____

② | was | said | a | with | He | his | problem | computer. | there |

_____

③ | those | customers. | to | to | said | She | we | need | reply |

_____

25.11 PUNTO CLAVE "TELL" EN REPORTED SPEECH

En reported speech también puede utilizarse "tell" como verbo principal.
Debe ir seguido de un objeto que indique con quién se habla.

I have to change the meeting date.

He told me that he had to change the meeting date

Al contrario que "say", "tell"
debe ir seguido de un objeto.

25.12 PUNTO CLAVE VERBOS DE REPORTED SPEECH CON "THAT"

"Say" y "tell" no dan
información alguna sobre
el tono de quien habla.
Pueden reemplazarse
con otros verbos que
sugieren el ánimo o
las razones de aquel.

I'm not very good at sales.

Neil admitted that he wasn't very good at sales.

"Admit" sugiere una
confesión por parte
del hablante.

25.13 MÁS EJEMPLOS VERBOS DE REPORTED SPEECH CON "THAT"

We have to close the
building for security tests.

They explained that the building
had to be closed for security tests.

Your office is huge!
It has a nice view, too.

Rohit admired our office, and
added that it had a nice view.

That's right! Our profits have risen this year.

Jeremy confirmed that our profits had risen this year.

25.14 COMPLETA LOS ESPACIOS CON LAS PALABRAS DEL RECUADRO PASANDO EL DIRECT SPEECH A REPORTED SPEECH Y DI LAS FRASES EN ALTO

I am not the person in charge of this project.

He _____*denied*_____ that he was the person in charge of that project.

1 Yes, that's right. The sales figures will be ready by 5pm.

Sharon _____ that the sales figures would be ready by 5pm.

2 Don't worry. I'll definitely stay late to help you finish the report.

Lilia _____ that she would stay late to help me finish the report.

3 We have beaten our sales target for the year.

Mr. Lee _____ that we had beaten our sales target for the year.

4 The coffee from the machine tastes awful.

Ben _____ that the coffee from the machine tasted awful.

5 Perhaps you could ask your boss about a raise.

She _____ that I could ask my boss about a raise.

complained   announced   confirmed   suggested   ~~denied~~   promised

25 ✓ CHECKLIST

⚙ Reported speech ☐   **Aa** Reuniones ☐   Decir lo que dijo alguien ☐

26 Lo que han preguntado otros

El reported speech se utiliza a veces para citar lo que preguntó alguien. Las preguntas en direct y en reported speech ordenan las palabras de maneras diferentes.

⚙ **Lenguaje** Preguntas en reported speech
Aa Vocabulario "Have", "make", "get", "do"
🧩 **Habilidad** Decir lo que preguntó alguien

26.1 PUNTO CLAVE REPORTED SPEECH DE PREGUNTAS ABIERTAS

Las preguntas abiertas se citan en reported speech invirtiendo el orden de verbo y sujeto y cambiando el tiempo verbal.

Where is my laptop?

Adam asked me where his laptop was. Have you seen it?

26.2 CÓMO FUNCIONA REPORTED SPEECH DE PREGUNTAS ABIERTAS

SUJETO	VERBO DE REPORTED	OBJETO	PRON. INTERROGATIVO	SUJETO	VERBO
Adam	**asked**	**me**	**where**	**his laptop**	**was.**

El verbo principal en las preguntas en reported speech suele ser "ask".

Podemos prescindir del objeto.

El sujeto va antes del verbo en el reported speech de preguntas.

El tiempo en reported speech es un grado anterior al de la pregunta original.

26.3 MÁS EJEMPLOS REPORTED SPEECH DE PREGUNTAS ABIERTAS

Why can't you come to the meeting?

He asked me why I couldn't come to the meeting.

Puede incluirse un objeto para indicar a quién se hizo la pregunta.

What do you think about the suggestions?

They asked me what I thought about the suggestions.

Cuando la pregunta original utiliza el verbo "do", se prescinde de este en la pregunta en reported speech.

| me | where | was. | Sasha | the | asked | conference |

Sasha asked me where the conference was.

1 | asked | me | I | late | again. | why | was | He |

_____

2 | was. | me | Lara | asked | the | meeting | where |

_____

3 | asked | interview. | I | me | missed | She | the | why | had |

_____

4 | asked | who | had | minutes. | taken | He | me | the |

_____

26.5 ESCUCHA EL AUDIO Y RESPONDE A LAS PREGUNTAS

Dos compañeras de trabajo, Krista y Mandy, hablan de un lanzamiento.

Krista said they're launching a new phone.
True ☐ **False** ☐ **Not given** ☑

1 Krista asked Mandy about the press release.
True ☐ **False** ☐ **Not given** ☐

2 Mandy hasn't finished writing the press release.
True ☐ **False** ☐ **Not given** ☐

3 Journalists are coming to the press launch.
True ☐ **False** ☐ **Not given** ☐

4 Mandy has a good relationship with ABC TV.
True ☐ **False** ☐ **Not given** ☐

5 Mandy asked what to do with the speech.
True ☐ **False** ☐ **Not given** ☐

6 Krista told Mandy to email the speech to her.
True ☐ **False** ☐ **Not given** ☐

7 Mandy usually makes a lot of changes.
True ☐ **False** ☐ **Not given** ☐

26.6 LEE EL ARTÍCULO Y RESPONDE A LAS PREGUNTAS

You must have meetings in order to do business.
True ☐ **False** ☐ **Not given** ☑

1 You should limit the number of things to discuss.
True ☐ **False** ☐ **Not given** ☐

2 There is no need to share the agenda.
True ☐ **False** ☐ **Not given** ☐

3 Let attendees know how long the lunch break is.
True ☐ **False** ☐ **Not given** ☐

4 People tend to take a long break after a meeting.
True ☐ **False** ☐ **Not given** ☐

5 People rarely forget to organize the meeting location.
True ☐ **False** ☐ **Not given** ☐

6 A good meeting room has plenty of light.
True ☐ **False** ☐ **Not given** ☐

BUSINESS TIPS

Preparation is key

CEO David Moss explains how to have successful meetings

It is important to decide your main objectives before the meeting. Create an agenda and send it to all attendees so they can prepare in advance. Set a date and time for your meeting. Decide when you will have a break, and how long you will give attendees to have lunch. If you don't do this, people might take long breaks, reducing your meeting time! Last of all, this sounds simple, but it's easy to forget to make arrangements for the meeting location, especially if you're very busy. Get the room ready with the right amount of chairs and refreshments, and your laptop or any other necessary equipment.

Aa 26.7 COMPLETA LOS ESPACIOS CON LAS PALABRAS DEL RECUADRO PARA CREAR MÁS COLOCACIONES CON "HAVE", "MAKE", "GET" Y "DO"

Suzi suggested that in a couple of years, I could [get *a job*] in the Paris office.

1 The boss is angry with Max. He told him to [do] before he leaves.

2 Mr. Tan promised that I would [get] to manager if I worked hard.

3 Could you [do] ? Could you make 20 copies of this, please?

4 Can I [make] ? Finish the proposal first, then work on the spreadsheet.

5 Paola said that she usually [gets] from work at 6:30pm.

6 Paul said that he [had] with his boss, but he was really late.

his work   a suggestion   ~~a job~~   me a favor   an appointment   home   promoted

🔊

26.8 PUNTO CLAVE REPORTED SPEECH DE PREGUNTAS CERRADAS

Si la respuesta a una pregunta en direct speech es "sí" o "no", se utilizan "if" o "whether" en el reported speech.

Pregunta original.

Are you meeting your sales targets?

La pregunta en reported speech utiliza "if" o "whether".

My boss asked me if I was meeting my sales targets.

Podemos prescindir del objeto que sigue a "asked".

Will you be at the meeting on Monday?

Kara asked whether I would be at the meeting on Monday.

26.9 DI LAS FRASES EN VOZ ALTA COMO PREGUNTAS EN REPORTED SPEECH

Why is the delivery late?

He asked why the delivery was late.

❶ What is the consumer feedback?

❷ Do you have a strategy?

❸ Who is getting promoted?

❹ What are the main points?

❺ Is he the new marketing manager?

27 Informar de cantidades

En presentaciones e informes, quizá tengas que hablar sobre qué cantidad hay de algo. Las palabras que utilices dependen de lo que describas.

🔧 **Lenguaje** "Few", "little" y "all"
Aa Vocabulario Reuniones
🧩 **Habilidad** Hablar sobre cantidades

27.1 PUNTO CLAVE "FEW" PARA CANTIDADES PEQUEÑAS

"Few" se utiliza con sustantivos contables en plural para indicar que hay poco de algo. Enfatiza lo pequeña que es la cantidad.

"A few" se utiliza con sustantivos contables con el significado de "some". Enfatiza que la cantidad, aunque sea pequeña, es suficiente.

few = not many

There have been few new customers this quarter.

a few = some

I have a few suggestions for how to improve sales.

"Few" puede utilizarse también como pronombre con el significado de "not many".

So few are willing to spend money for the deluxe range.

Puede utilizarse "very" para enfatizar que la cantidad de algo es incluso más pequeña.

We have very few items left in stock.

🔊

27.2 MARCA LAS FRASES QUE SEAN CORRECTAS

You'll be glad to hear that we still have a few options available to us this year. ☑

You'll be glad to hear that we still have few options available to us this year. ☐

① We'll have to reduce the price. A few customers have bought our new jeans. ☐

We'll have to reduce the price. Very few customers have bought our new jeans. ☐

② So few people pay by check these days that we no longer accept this form of payment. ☐

A few people pay by check these days that we no longer accept this form of payment. ☐

③ Unfortunately, we've had a few inquiries about our new spa treatments. ☐

Unfortunately, we've had few inquiries about our new spa treatments. ☐

🔊

27.3 PUNTO CLAVE "LITTLE" PARA CANTIDADES PEQUEÑAS

"Little" se utiliza en inglés británico con sustantivos incontables para decir que no hay mucho de algo. Enfatiza lo pequeña que es la cantidad.

"A little" se utiliza con sustantivos incontables con el significado de "some". Enfatiza que la cantidad, aunque sea pequeña, es suficiente.

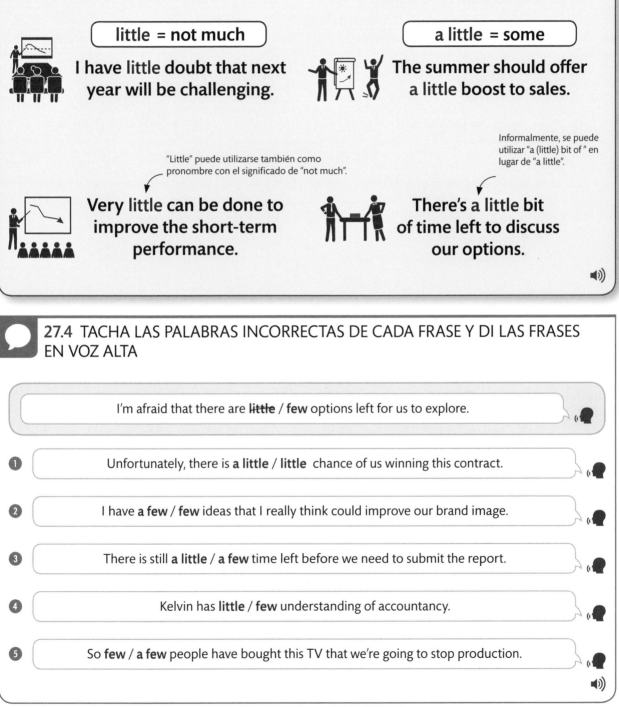

little = not much

I have little doubt that next year will be challenging.

a little = some

The summer should offer a little boost to sales.

"Little" puede utilizarse también como pronombre con el significado de "not much".

Very little can be done to improve the short-term performance.

Informalmente, se puede utilizar "a (little) bit of " en lugar de "a little".

There's a little bit of time left to discuss our options.

27.4 TACHA LAS PALABRAS INCORRECTAS DE CADA FRASE Y DI LAS FRASES EN VOZ ALTA

I'm afraid that there are ~~little~~ / **few** options left for us to explore.

1. Unfortunately, there is **a little** / little chance of us winning this contract.

2. I have **a few** / few ideas that I really think could improve our brand image.

3. There is still **a little** / a few time left before we need to submit the report.

4. Kelvin has **little** / few understanding of accountancy.

5. So **few** / a few people have bought this TV that we're going to stop production.

293

27.5 PUNTO CLAVE "ALL" COMO PRONOMBRE

"All" se utiliza a veces como pronombre con el significado de "everything" o "the only thing".

all = everything	all = the only thing

I hope all goes well in the presentation.

All we can do is hope that they like the product.

27.6 VUELVE A ESCRIBIR LAS FRASES PONIENDO LAS PALABRAS EN SU ORDEN CORRECTO

about | told | all | you | I | know | have | it. | I

I have told you all I know about it.

① do | can | is | your | mistake. | apologize | All | for | you

_____

② expect | I | is | tasks. | to | All | complete | for | staff | their

_____

③ sure | be | the | I'm | will | interview. | well | in | all

_____

④ I | is | All | raise. | want | a

_____

⑤ all | have | information | We | the | need. | we

_____

294

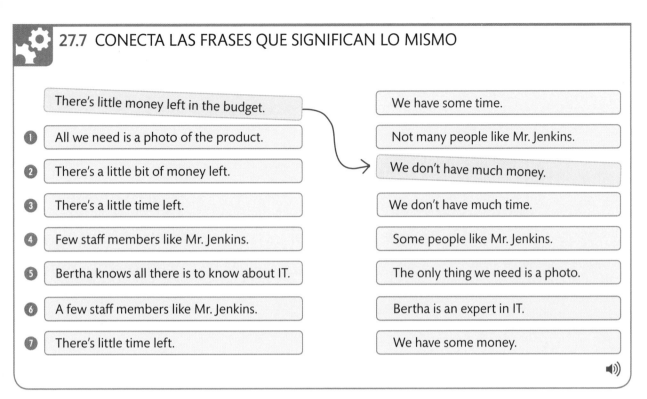

27.7 CONECTA LAS FRASES QUE SIGNIFICAN LO MISMO

There's little money left in the budget.

1. All we need is a photo of the product.

2. There's a little bit of money left.

3. There's a little time left.

4. Few staff members like Mr. Jenkins.

5. Bertha knows all there is to know about IT.

6. A few staff members like Mr. Jenkins.

7. There's little time left.

We have some time.

Not many people like Mr. Jenkins.

We don't have much money.

We don't have much time.

Some people like Mr. Jenkins.

The only thing we need is a photo.

Bertha is an expert in IT.

We have some money.

27.8 ESCUCHA EL AUDIO Y RESPONDE A LAS PREGUNTAS

Un agente de ventas habla con su superior de los resultados del último trimestre.

There are very few dog toys left.
True ☑ **False** ☐ **Not given** ☐

1. The Woof Doggy toy is a new product.
True ☐ **False** ☐ **Not given** ☐

2. It'll be easy to get the supplier to deliver more toys.
True ☐ **False** ☐ **Not given** ☐

3. The boss suggests asking for part of an order.
True ☐ **False** ☐ **Not given** ☐

4. There are no princess costumes left.
True ☐ **False** ☐ **Not given** ☐

5. The princess dress will be delivered next quarter.
True ☐ **False** ☐ **Not given** ☐

6. The camping kit has been very popular.
True ☐ **False** ☐ **Not given** ☐

27 ✓ CHECKLIST

⚙ "Few", "little" y "all" ☐   **Aa** Reuniones ☐   🧩 Hablar sobre cantidades ☐

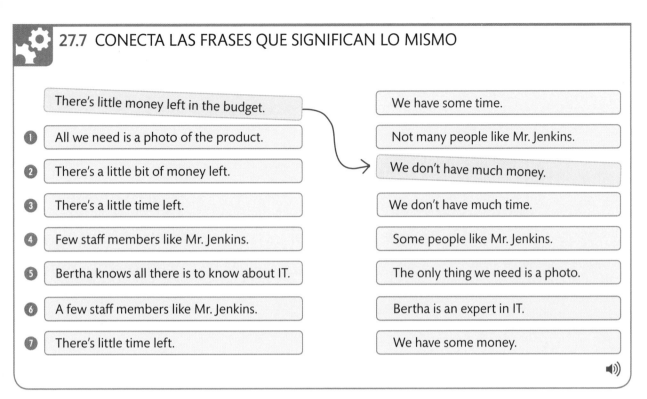

A veces es necesario aclarar si se ha entendido un punto. Hay diversas maneras de comprobar educadamente la información en una conversación.

⚙ **Lenguaje** Preguntas de sujeto, question tags
Aa Vocabulario Comprobaciones y preguntas eco
🧩 **Habilidad** Comprobar la información

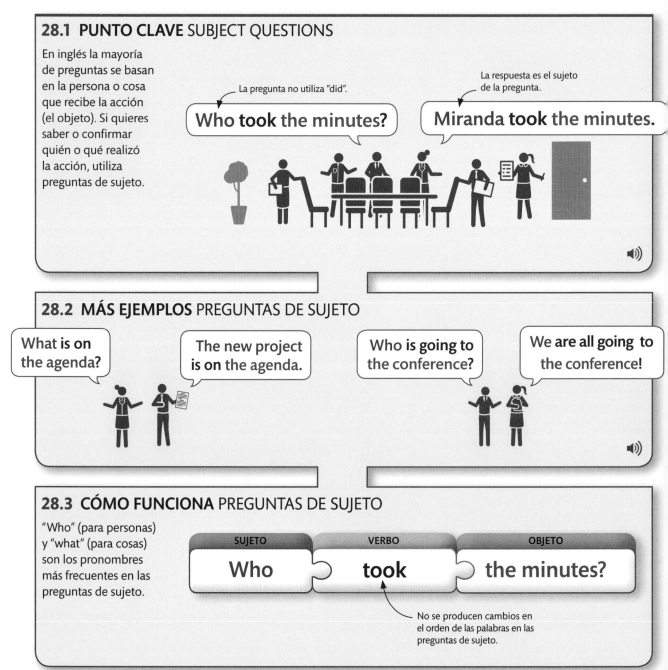

28.1 PUNTO CLAVE SUBJECT QUESTIONS

En inglés la mayoría de preguntas se basan en la persona o cosa que recibe la acción (el objeto). Si quieres saber o confirmar quién o qué realizó la acción, utiliza preguntas de sujeto.

La pregunta no utiliza "did".

Who took the minutes?

La respuesta es el sujeto de la pregunta.

Miranda took the minutes.

28.2 MÁS EJEMPLOS PREGUNTAS DE SUJETO

What is on the agenda?

The new project is on the agenda.

Who is going to the conference?

We are all going to the conference!

28.3 CÓMO FUNCIONA PREGUNTAS DE SUJETO

"Who" (para personas) y "what" (para cosas) son los pronombres más frecuentes en las preguntas de sujeto.

SUJETO	VERBO	OBJETO
Who	took	the minutes?

No se producen cambios en el orden de las palabras en las preguntas de sujeto.

28.4 VUELVE A ESCRIBIR LAS PREGUNTAS ORDENANDO LAS PALABRAS CORRECTAMENTE

| the | is | problem? | What |

What is the problem?

1 | manager? | Who | the | is |

_____

2 | the | What's | in | report? |

_____

3 | answers | telephone? | Who | the |

_____

4 | approves | Who | annual | vacation? |

_____

5 | is | What | deadline? | the |

_____

6 | wrote | the | ad? | Who |

_____

7 | take | Who | questions? | will |

_____

8 | are | the | What | objectives? |

_____

9 | the | What's | about? | complaint |

_____

◄))

28.5 MARCA LA MEJOR PREGUNTA PARA CADA SITUACIÓN

☑ Who called the bank?

☐ Did Joe call the bank?

Joe called the bank.

1
☐ What are our most popular products?
☐ Are our denim jeans popular?

Denim jeans are our most popular product.

2
☐ Do you need to book the meeting?
☐ What do you need to do?

Yes, I do.

3
☐ Does Rhia answer customer emails?
☐ Who answers customer emails?

Rhia answers customer emails.

4
☐ Who wrote this report?
☐ Did Savannah write this report?

No, she didn't.

5
☐ What is our lowest price?
☐ Is our lowest price 49 euros?

Our lowest price is 49 euros.

6
☐ Is James on vacation next week?
☐ Who is on vacation next week?

Yes, he is.

◄))

28.6 PUNTO CLAVE QUESTION TAGS

Otra manera de comprobar la información es utilizar las question tags. Las question tags más simples utilizan el verbo "be" con un pronombre que concuerda con el sujeto de la frase.

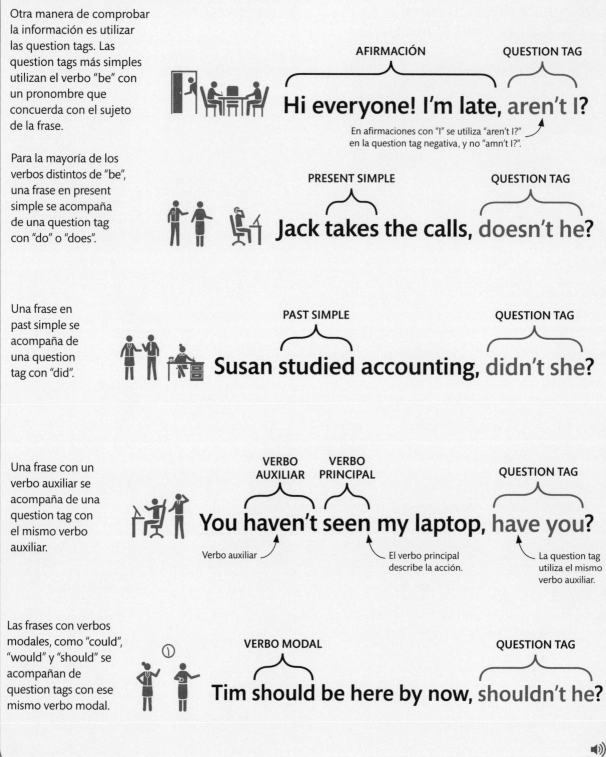

AFIRMACIÓN   **QUESTION TAG**

Hi everyone! I'm late, aren't I?

En afirmaciones con "I" se utiliza "aren't I?" en la question tag negativa, y no "amn't I?".

Para la mayoría de los verbos distintos de "be", una frase en present simple se acompaña de una question tag con "do" o "does".

PRESENT SIMPLE   **QUESTION TAG**

Jack takes the calls, doesn't he?

Una frase en past simple se acompaña de una question tag con "did".

PAST SIMPLE   **QUESTION TAG**

Susan studied accounting, didn't she?

Una frase con un verbo auxiliar se acompaña de una question tag con el mismo verbo auxiliar.

VERBO AUXILIAR   **VERBO PRINCIPAL**   **QUESTION TAG**

You haven't seen my laptop, have you?

Verbo auxiliar

El verbo principal describe la acción.

La question tag utiliza el mismo verbo auxiliar.

Las frases con verbos modales, como "could", "would" y "should" se acompañan de question tags con ese mismo verbo modal.

VERBO MODAL   **QUESTION TAG**

Tim should be here by now, shouldn't he?

28.7 CÓMO FUNCIONA QUESTION TAGS

Una frase afirmativa se acompaña de una question tag negativa,
y una frase negativa se acompaña de una question tag positiva.

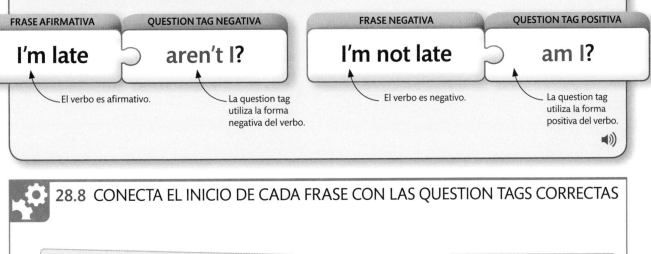

FRASE AFIRMATIVA — **I'm late**
El verbo es afirmativo.

QUESTION TAG NEGATIVA — **aren't I?**
La question tag utiliza la forma negativa del verbo.

FRASE NEGATIVA — **I'm not late**
El verbo es negativo.

QUESTION TAG POSITIVA — **am I?**
La question tag utiliza la forma positiva del verbo.

28.8 CONECTA EL INICIO DE CADA FRASE CON LAS QUESTION TAGS CORRECTAS

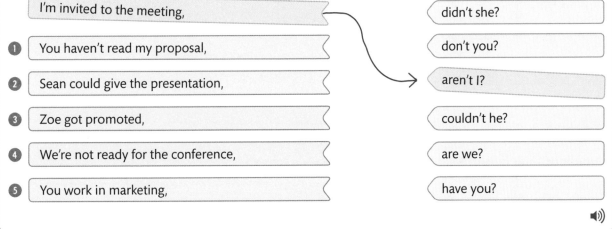

I'm invited to the meeting, —————→ aren't I?

didn't she?

don't you?

1. You haven't read my proposal,

2. Sean could give the presentation,

3. Zoe got promoted,

couldn't he?

4. We're not ready for the conference,

are we?

5. You work in marketing,

have you?

28.9 COMPLETA LOS ESPACIOS CON LAS QUESTION TAGS CORRECTAS

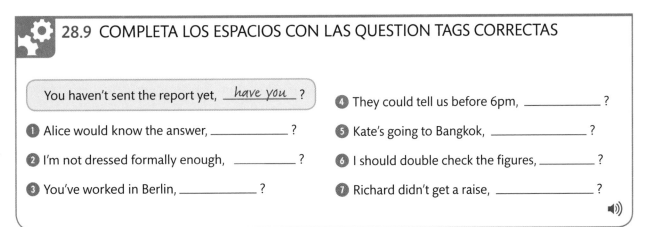

You haven't sent the report yet, _*have you*_ ?

1. Alice would know the answer, _____ ?

2. I'm not dressed formally enough, _____ ?

3. You've worked in Berlin, _____ ?

4. They could tell us before 6pm, _____ ?

5. Kate's going to Bangkok, _____ ?

6. I should double check the figures, _____ ?

7. Richard didn't get a raise, _____ ?

28.10 VOCABULARIO COMPROBACIONES EDUCADAS Y PREGUNTAS ECO

Tienes diversas expresiones concretas para comprobar la información de manera educada.

Pardon?

Could you say that again? I didn't catch it.

What was the last figure? I didn't hear it.

Sorry, I missed that.

Intenta no decir "What?" de manera directa, es de mala educación.

También puedes repetir la palabra o expresión importante que quieras comprobar, o repetir la oración, en parte o entera, con un pronombre interrogativo o expresión interrogativa al final.

We sold $40,000 of stock to Japan last month.

To Japan?

We sold $40,000 of stock to where?

28.11 ESCUCHA EL AUDIO Y RESPONDE A LAS PREGUNTAS

Una agente de ventas llama a su superior para comprobar unos detalles y confirmar la información.

The standard discount offered is 30%.
True ☐ False ☐ Not given ☑

1 Discounts are offered to long-term customers.
True ☐ False ☐ Not given ☐

2 If a customer buys 1,000 units, they get 15% off.
True ☐ False ☐ Not given ☐

3 A new customer in Thailand sent an inquiry.
True ☐ False ☐ Not given ☐

4 They already work with companies in Asia.
True ☐ False ☐ Not given ☐

5 Maxine wants a report about the new customer.
True ☐ False ☐ Not given ☐

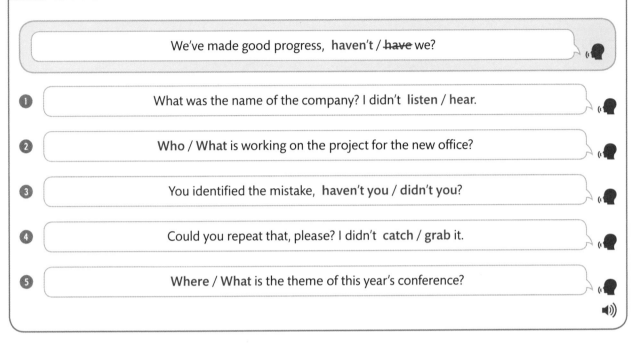

28.12 TACHA LAS PALABRAS INCORRECTAS DE CADA FRASE Y DI LAS FRASES EN VOZ ALTA

We've made good progress, haven't / ~~have~~ we?

1. What was the name of the company? I didn't listen / hear.

2. Who / What is working on the project for the new office?

3. You identified the mistake, haven't you / didn't you?

4. Could you repeat that, please? I didn't catch / grab it.

5. Where / What is the theme of this year's conference?

28 ✓ CHECKLIST

⚙ Preguntas de sujeto, question tags ☐   **Aa** Comprobaciones y preguntas eco ☐   Comprobar la información ☐

↻ REPASA LO QUE HAS APRENDIDO EN LAS UNIDADES 24–28

NUEVO LENGUAJE	FRASE DE EJEMPLO	☑	UNIDAD
REPORTED SPEECH	Luke said that he felt sick. She said she'd been to work the day before.	☐	25.1, 25.6, 25.9
VERBOS DE REPORTED SPEECH	Jeremy confirmed that our profits had risen.	☐	25.12
PREGUNTAS EN REPORTED SPEECH	Adam asked me where his laptop was.	☐	26.1, 26.8
"FEW", "LITTLE" Y "ALL"	I have a few suggestions. Very little can be done. I hope all goes well.	☐	27.1, 27.3, 27.5
COMPROBAR INFORMACIÓN CON PREGUNTAS DE SUJETO Y QUESTION TAGS	Who took the minutes? I'm late, aren't I?	☐	28.1, 28.6
COMPROBACIONES EDUCADAS Y PREGUNTAS ECO	Sorry, I missed that. We sold $40,000 of stock to where?	☐	28.10

29.1 SECTORES

education

healthcare

catering / food

chemical

construction

agriculture / farming

energy

electronics

entertainment

fashion

finance

fishing

hospitality

journalism

manufacturing

advertising

mining

petroleum

pharmaceutical

real estate (US) / property (UK)

recycling

shipping

tourism

transportation

29.2 ATRIBUTOS PROFESIONALES

accurate

adaptable

ambitious

calm

confident

creative

customer-focused

determined

efficient

energetic

flexible

hardworking

honest

independent

innovative

motivated

organized

patient

practical

professional

punctual

reliable

responsible

team player

30 Describir un puesto

Utiliza "a" o "an" en las descripciones de trabajo y para nueva información. No utilices artículo cuando hables de cosas generales; utiliza "the" para referirte a cosas concretas.

⚙ **Lenguaje** Artículos
Aa Vocabulario Describir y solicitar un puesto
🧩 **Habilidad** Describir un puesto

30.1 PUNTO CLAVE "A" Y "AN"

Utiliza "a" o "an" para introducir información nueva. Utiliza "the" cuando el lector u oyente ya conozca de lo que hablas.

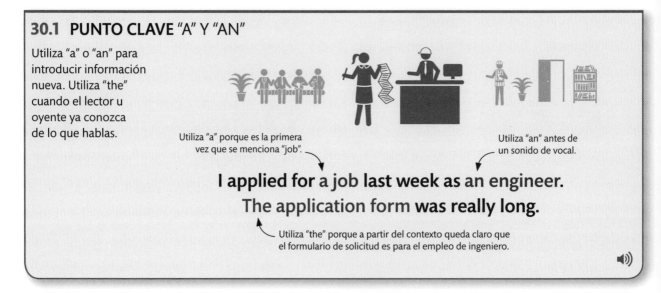

Utiliza "a" porque es la primera vez que se menciona "job".

Utiliza "an" antes de un sonido de vocal.

**I applied for a job last week as an engineer.
The application form was really long.**

Utiliza "the" porque a partir del contexto queda claro que el formulario de solicitud es para el empleo de ingeniero.

30.2 TACHA LAS PALABRAS INCORRECTAS DE CADA FRASE

~~A~~ / ~~An~~ / The salary for this job is really good.

1 A / An / The deadline for applications is Friday.

2 This job is based in a / an / the Berlin office.

3 We are recruiting a / an / the new designer.

4 I've got a / an / the interview for a new job.

5 A / An / The application form for this job is long.

6 Please complete a / an / the form on our website.

7 A / An / The ideal candidate enjoys teamwork.

8 There's an ad for a / an / the English teacher.

30.3 ESCUCHA EL AUDIO Y NUMERA LAS IMÁGENES EN EL ORDEN EN QUE SE DESCRIBEN

30.4 PUNTO CLAVE ZERO ARTICLE Y ARTÍCULOS DEFINIDOS (PLURALES)

En inglés no se utiliza artículo (zero article) en plural al hablar sobre cosas en general. Utiliza "the" (artículo definido) para hablar sobre cosas concretas.

General

Catering jobs are very well paid at the moment.

Específico

The catering jobs at this café are really well paid.

🔊

30.5 MÁS EJEMPLOS ZERO ARTICLE Y ARTÍCULOS DEFINIDOS (PLURALES)

Accountants have to work very hard.
The accountants at my office work long hours.

Managers don't always listen to their staff.
The managers here can't run a team.

Noriko loves giving presentations.
The presentations she gave last week were great.

🔊

⚙ 30.6 MARCA LAS FRASES QUE SEAN CORRECTAS

Most doctors have to work long hours. They are very dedicated people.	☑
Most the doctors have to work long hours. They are the very dedicated people.	☐

1 The jobs I'm really interested in are based in Los Angeles. They're in IT. ☐
Jobs I'm really interested in are based in Los Angeles. They're in the IT. ☐

2 People who interviewed me for the job were really nice. They were managers. ☐
The people who interviewed me for the job were really nice. They were the managers. ☐

3 Clients can be very demanding. The clients I met today had lots of complaints. ☐
The clients can be very demanding. Clients I met today had lots of the complaints. ☐

🔊

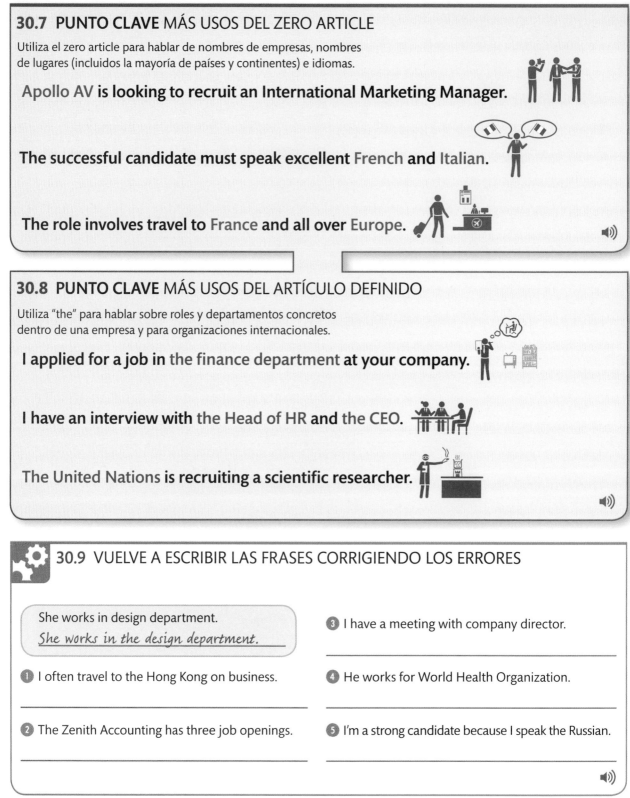

30.7 PUNTO CLAVE MÁS USOS DEL ZERO ARTICLE

Utiliza el zero article para hablar de nombres de empresas, nombres de lugares (incluidos la mayoría de países y continentes) e idiomas.

Apollo AV is looking to recruit an International Marketing Manager.

The successful candidate must speak excellent French and Italian.

The role involves travel to France and all over Europe.

30.8 PUNTO CLAVE MÁS USOS DEL ARTÍCULO DEFINIDO

Utiliza "the" para hablar sobre roles y departamentos concretos dentro de una empresa y para organizaciones internacionales.

I applied for a job in the finance department at your company.

I have an interview with the Head of HR and the CEO.

The United Nations is recruiting a scientific researcher.

30.9 VUELVE A ESCRIBIR LAS FRASES CORRIGIENDO LOS ERRORES

She works in design department.
She works in the design department.

1 I often travel to the Hong Kong on business.

2 The Zenith Accounting has three job openings.

3 I have a meeting with company director.

4 He works for World Health Organization.

5 I'm a strong candidate because I speak the Russian.

30.10 CORRIGE LOS ERRORES DE LAS EXPRESIONES MARCADAS

Golden Wings Ltd.

1. _____

2. _____

3. _____

4. _____

5. _____

FLIGHT ATTENDANT

The Golden Wings Ltd. is hiring! Our airline flies throughout the Europe and Asia, and we have a opening for a bright, enthusiastic flight attendant. Have you go what it takes? A Flight attendants must be polite, hard-working and presentable. If this sounds like you, then we'd love to hear from you. An hours can be long, but the job is well paid, and you will have the

chance to stay in the best hotels and locations across the world. This is a once-in-a-lifetime opportunity to see the world and build the career. Apply now!

30.11 TACHA LAS PALABRAS INCORRECTAS DE CADA FRASE Y DI LAS FRASES EN VOZ ALTA

~~Salary in this job~~ / **The salary in this job** is really good.

1. Your meeting is with **HR manager** / **the HR manager**.

2. We're recruiting more staff in **France** / **the France**.

3. I'm looking for a job as **education consultant** / **an education consultant**.

4. We need someone who can speak **the Italian** / **Italian**.

5. **Omnitech** / **The Omnitech** is advertising several vacancies in its marketing department.

6. I work in **sales department** / **the sales department** of a large company.

---

30 ✓ CHECKLIST

⚙ Artículos ☐   **Aa** Describir y solicitar un puesto ☐   Describir un puesto ☐

31 Solicitar un puesto

Una carta de presentación para solicitar un puesto debe mostrar naturalidad y confianza. Utiliza las preposiciones adecuadas detrás de cada verbo, sustantivo y adjetivo.

⚙️ **Lenguaje** Preposiciones dependientes
Aa Vocabulario Léxico de cartas de presentación
🧩 **Habilidad** Redactar una carta de presentación

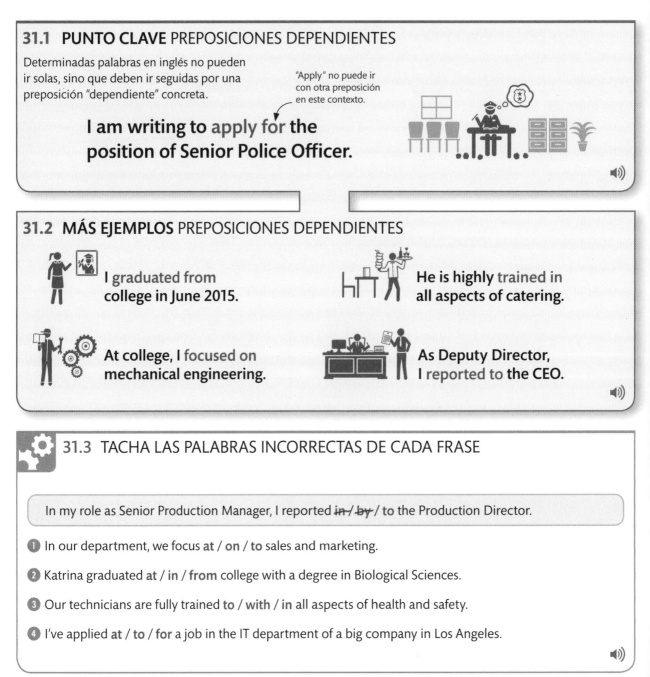

31.1 PUNTO CLAVE PREPOSICIONES DEPENDIENTES

Determinadas palabras en inglés no pueden ir solas, sino que deben ir seguidas por una preposición "dependiente" concreta.

"Apply" no puede ir con otra preposición en este contexto.

I am writing to apply for the position of Senior Police Officer.

31.2 MÁS EJEMPLOS PREPOSICIONES DEPENDIENTES

I graduated from college in June 2015.

He is highly trained in all aspects of catering.

At college, I focused on mechanical engineering.

As Deputy Director, I reported to the CEO.

31.3 TACHA LAS PALABRAS INCORRECTAS DE CADA FRASE

In my role as Senior Production Manager, I reported ~~in~~ / ~~by~~ / **to** the Production Director.

① In our department, we focus **at** / **on** / **to** sales and marketing.

② Katrina graduated **at** / **in** / **from** college with a degree in Biological Sciences.

③ Our technicians are fully trained **to** / **with** / **in** all aspects of health and safety.

④ I've applied **at** / **to** / **for** a job in the IT department of a big company in Los Angeles.

31.4 LEE LA CARTA DE PRESENTACIÓN Y RESPONDE A LAS PREGUNTAS

> Sasha heard about the job on the radio.
> **True** ☐ **False** ☑ **Not given** ☐

1 Sasha is currently a senior travel executive.
True ☐ **False** ☐ **Not given** ☐

2 She has worked for the same company for 10 years.
True ☐ **False** ☐ **Not given** ☐

3 She is responsible for travel to Southeast Asia.
True ☐ **False** ☐ **Not given** ☐

4 She is tired of working in the travel industry.
True ☐ **False** ☐ **Not given** ☐

5 She would like to learn new skills.
True ☐ **False** ☐ **Not given** ☐

6 She has provided written recommendations with her application.
True ☐ **False** ☐ **Not given** ☐

Dear Mr. Goméz,

I am writing to apply for the position of Senior Travel Representative, as advertised in Go Travel! magazine.

I have worked in the travel industry for more than 10 years, and have experience handling both package vacations and tailor-made trips. In my current position, I am responsible for travel to Southeast Asia, and last year I was responsible for more than 15,000 customers. My sales figures amounted to more than $12 million.

I am passionate about working in the travel industry and would welcome the opportunity to learn new skills and broaden my experience. I'm extremely reliable and hard-working.

Please find attached my résumé and references. I look forward to hearing from you.

Yours sincerely,

Sasha Mailovitch

Aa 31.5 CONECTA LAS EXPRESIONES CON EL MISMO SIGNIFICADO

to have a job in a particular industry → to work in

1 to look after something — to be responsible for something
2 to be excited about a future event — to be passionate about
3 to equal a total number — experience in something
4 to make an official request for a job — to amount to
5 to have strong enthusiasm for — to look forward to something
6 skill gained through time spent in a job — to apply for a job

31.6 PUNTO CLAVE PREPOSICIONES DEPENDIENTES (CAMBIO DE SIGNIFICADO)

Algunas palabras pueden ir con diferentes preposiciones dependientes, cuyo significado cambia según la preposición utilizada.

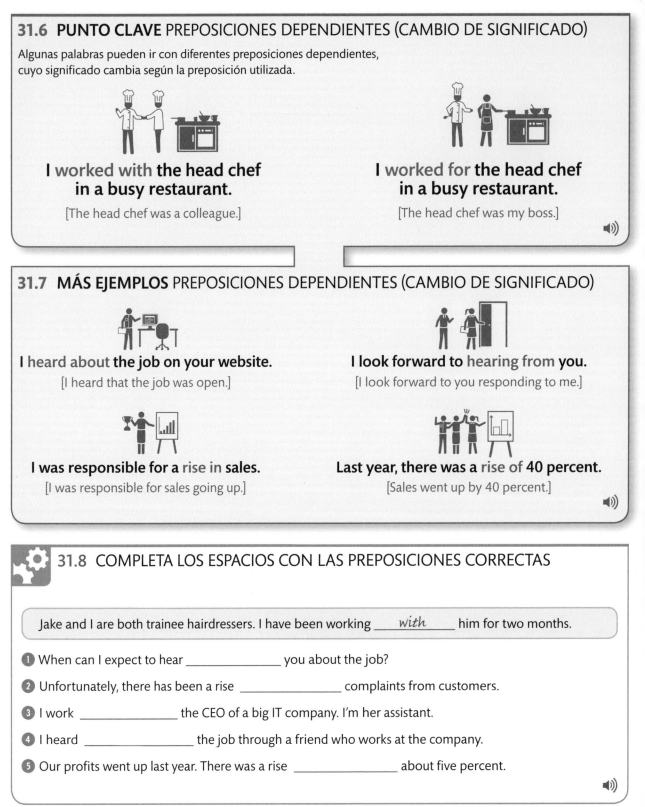

I worked with the head chef in a busy restaurant.

[The head chef was a colleague.]

I worked for the head chef in a busy restaurant.

[The head chef was my boss.]

31.7 MÁS EJEMPLOS PREPOSICIONES DEPENDIENTES (CAMBIO DE SIGNIFICADO)

I heard about the job on your website.

[I heard that the job was open.]

I look forward to hearing from you.

[I look forward to you responding to me.]

I was responsible for a rise in sales.

[I was responsible for sales going up.]

Last year, there was a rise of 40 percent.

[Sales went up by 40 percent.]

31.8 COMPLETA LOS ESPACIOS CON LAS PREPOSICIONES CORRECTAS

Jake and I are both trainee hairdressers. I have been working ___*with*___ him for two months.

1. When can I expect to hear _____ you about the job?

2. Unfortunately, there has been a rise _____ complaints from customers.

3. I work _____ the CEO of a big IT company. I'm her assistant.

4. I heard _____ the job through a friend who works at the company.

5. Our profits went up last year. There was a rise _____ about five percent.

Aa 31.9 LEE LAS PISTAS Y ESCRIBE LAS PALABRAS DEL RECUADRO EN EL LUGAR CORRECTO DE LA PARRILLA

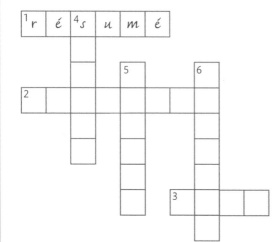

HORIZONTALES

1 A document detailing your qualifications

2 Honest and trustworthy

3 The group of people you work with

VERTICALES

4 A set of abilities resulting from experience

5 A fixed regular payment

6 A person who gives a formal recommendation

skills   salary   ~~résumé~~

team   referee   reliable

31.10 LEE LA CARTA DE PRESENTACIÓN Y TACHA LAS PALABRAS INCORRECTAS

64 Elm Tree Way
West Clinton
PO13 4JS

Dear Mr. Khan,
I am writing to apply for / apply with the position / positioning of head web designer with your company.

I have experience at / experience in managing large commercial websites. Last year, sales from the website that I designed for a major online store amounted at / amounted to more than $6 million.

I am eager to develop my skilful / skills and broaden my knowledge of other industries / industrial.
I believe this job would be a fantastic opponent / opportunity for me, and I'd add a great deal to your company. I am enthusiastic and passionate for / passionate about being at the cutting edge of web development. I'm also very reliability / reliable and I enjoy working in a team.

I have attached my résumé / cover letter and details of my referees. I look forward to hearing to / hearing from you.

Yours sincerely,
Amy Quah

32 Entrevistas de trabajo

En una entrevista de trabajo es importante que describas tus logros de una manera concreta y detallada. Utiliza cláusulas relativas para hacerlo.

⚙ **Lenguaje** Cláusulas relativas
Aa Vocabulario Entrevistas de trabajo
🧩 **Habilidad** Describir detalladamente tus logros

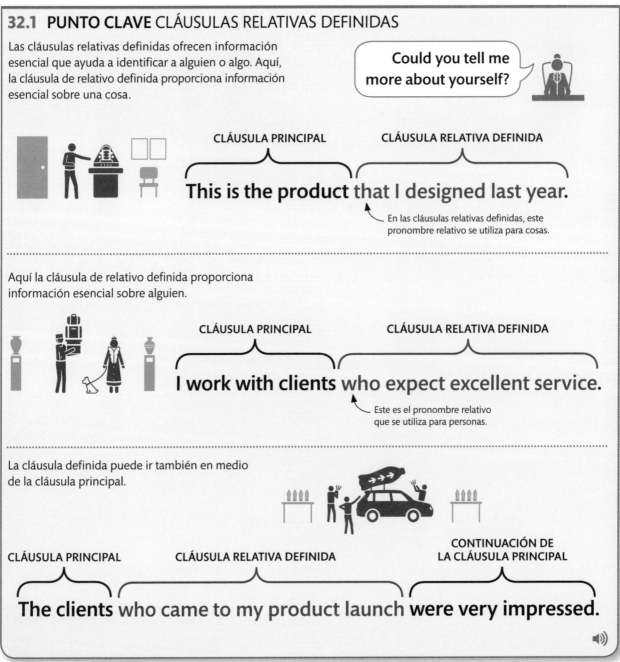

32.1 PUNTO CLAVE CLÁUSULAS RELATIVAS DEFINIDAS

Las cláusulas relativas definidas ofrecen información esencial que ayuda a identificar a alguien o algo. Aquí, la cláusula de relativo definida proporciona información esencial sobre una cosa.

Could you tell me more about yourself?

CLÁUSULA PRINCIPAL   CLÁUSULA RELATIVA DEFINIDA

This is the product that I designed last year.

En las cláusulas relativas definidas, este pronombre relativo se utiliza para cosas.

Aquí la cláusula de relativo definida proporciona información esencial sobre alguien.

CLÁUSULA PRINCIPAL   CLÁUSULA RELATIVA DEFINIDA

I work with clients who expect excellent service.

Este es el pronombre relativo que se utiliza para personas.

La cláusula definida puede ir también en medio de la cláusula principal.

CLÁUSULA PRINCIPAL   CLÁUSULA RELATIVA DEFINIDA   CONTINUACIÓN DE LA CLÁUSULA PRINCIPAL

The clients who came to my product launch were very impressed.

32.2 CONECTA EL INICIO Y EL FINAL DE CADA FRASE

The main thing that I enjoy → about my job is my wonderful team.

① The office that I work in — is modern and open-plan.

② The customers who gave us — say they enjoy working with me.

③ One thing that I don't like — is already selling very well.

④ The people who are on my team — feedback were all very positive.

⑤ The product that we've just launched — about my job is the long hours.

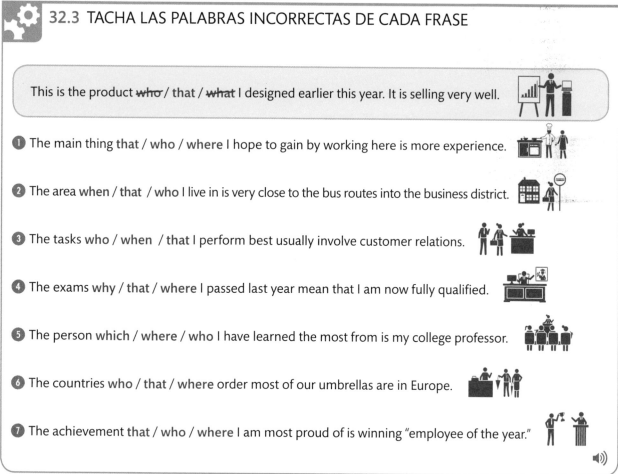

32.3 TACHA LAS PALABRAS INCORRECTAS DE CADA FRASE

This is the product ~~who~~ / that / ~~what~~ I designed earlier this year. It is selling very well.

① The main thing that / who / where I hope to gain by working here is more experience.

② The area when / that / who I live in is very close to the bus routes into the business district.

③ The tasks who / when / that I perform best usually involve customer relations.

④ The exams why / that / where I passed last year mean that I am now fully qualified.

⑤ The person which / where / who I have learned the most from is my college professor.

⑥ The countries who / that / where order most of our umbrellas are in Europe.

⑦ The achievement that / who / where I am most proud of is winning "employee of the year."

32.4 PUNTO CLAVE CLÁUSULAS RELATIVAS INDEFINIDAS

Las cláusulas relativas indefinidas dan información adicional sobre situaciones, personas o cosas.

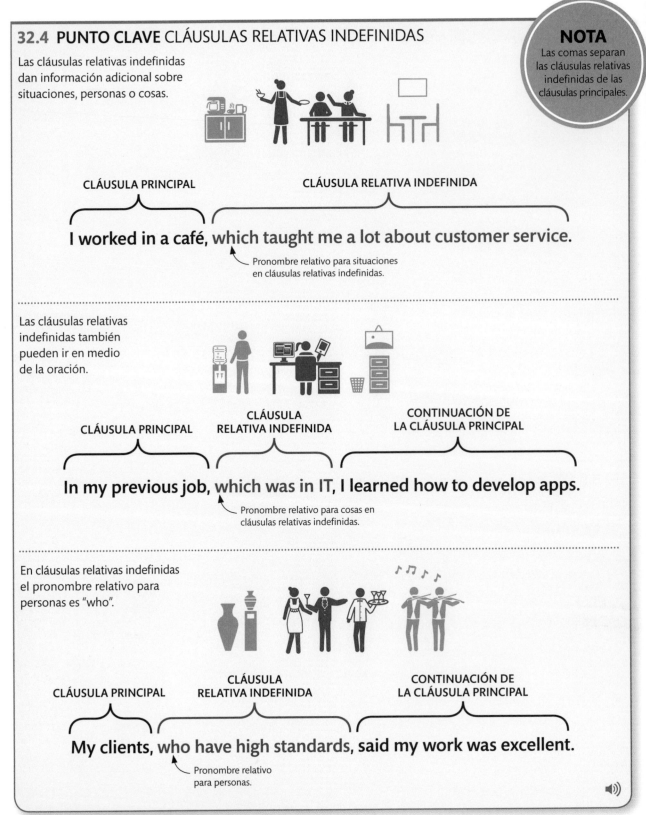

NOTA
Las comas separan las cláusulas relativas indefinidas de las cláusulas principales.

CLÁUSULA PRINCIPAL   CLÁUSULA RELATIVA INDEFINIDA

I worked in a café, which taught me a lot about customer service.

Pronombre relativo para situaciones en cláusulas relativas indefinidas.

Las cláusulas relativas indefinidas también pueden ir en medio de la oración.

CLÁUSULA PRINCIPAL   CLÁUSULA RELATIVA INDEFINIDA   CONTINUACIÓN DE LA CLÁUSULA PRINCIPAL

In my previous job, which was in IT, I learned how to develop apps.

Pronombre relativo para cosas en cláusulas relativas indefinidas.

En cláusulas relativas indefinidas el pronombre relativo para personas es "who".

CLÁUSULA PRINCIPAL   CLÁUSULA RELATIVA INDEFINIDA   CONTINUACIÓN DE LA CLÁUSULA PRINCIPAL

My clients, who have high standards, said my work was excellent.

Pronombre relativo para personas.

32.5 VUELVE A ESCRIBIR LAS FRASES CORRIGIENDO LOS ERRORES

> In my current job which I have been in for three years I often give presentations.
> *In my current job, which I have been in for three years, I often give presentations.*

1 I have completed all the training, who means you wouldn't need to train me.

_____

2 My boss, which is very talented, always encourages me not to work too late.

_____

3 IT development, what is my favorite part of the job, is very fast-paced.

_____

4 My co-workers who are all older than me, have taught me a lot.

_____

5 I worked at the reception desk, that taught me how to deal with customers.

_____

6 I take my job very seriously which means I always follow the company dress code.

_____

7 In my last job, who was in Paris, I learned to speak French fluently.

_____

32.6 ESCUCHA LA ENTREVISTA Y LUEGO NUMERA LAS FRASES EN EL ORDEN EN QUE APARECEN

A I work about 35 hours a week, and I love it. ☐

B I think I'm really good at understanding people's goals and aims. ☐

C I'd like to join a bigger gym so I have the opportunity to build my career. ☐

D I have 40 regular clients, who I spend 30–60 minutes with each session. ☐

E I can see you have some experience already. ☐ 1

F There are only about 100 clients, so there are only two trainers. ☐

32.7 PUNTO CLAVE MÁS PRONOMBRES RELATIVOS

Las cláusulas relativas pueden utilizar otros pronombres relativos, según el sustantivo al que se refieran.

Last summer, when I had just graduated, I did an internship at a law firm.

Utiliza "when" para referirte a un momento.

The fashion industry is where I would hope to expand your client base.

Utiliza "where" para referirte a un lugar o sector.

My team, whose members are very motivated, always meet their targets.

Utiliza "whose" para referirte a una persona, empresa o departamento.

32.8 COMPLETA LOS ESPACIOS CON LAS PALABRAS DEL RECUADRO

My apprenticeship, _____*which*_____ I completed in 2016, was in car manufacturing.

① The place _____ I can concentrate the best is at home.

② The person _____ career inspires me the most is Muhammad Ali.

③ Last year, _____ I was an intern, I learned how to give presentations.

④ My parents, _____ are both doctors, inspired me to study medicine.

where	when	~~which~~	who	whose

32.9 COMPLETA LOS ESPACIOS CON LAS EXPRESIONES DEL RECUADRO Y CONTESTA AL AUDIO EN VOZ ALTA

What would you say is your biggest weakness?

People _____*who know*_____ me well say that I'm sometimes impatient.

1 What do you think of your current salary?

My current salary, _____ $20,000 a year, is not very high.

2 What do you like most about your job?

The thing _____ me excited about my job is seeing our products on sale.

3 Do you think you are a good team leader?

Yes. I always know _____ the responsibility for getting a task done on my team.

4 What benefits do you think you would bring to our company?

I can identify things _____ to change, to make your business more efficient.

5 How soon can you start, supposing we offer you the job?

My boss, _____ quite flexible, would allow me to leave after six weeks' notice.

| that need | that gets | who is | ~~who know~~ | which is | who has |

---

32 ✓ **CHECKLIST**

⚙ Cláusulas relativas ☐   **Aa** Entrevistas de trabajo ☐   🧩 Describir detalladamente tus logros ☐

33 Vocabulario

33.1 MODISMOS DE EMPRESA

Our company is always ahead of the game **in the latest technology.**

to be ahead of the game
[to be ahead of your competitors in a certain field]

This is a big contract. Make sure you do everything by the book.

to do something by the book
[to do something strictly according to the rules]

I just want to check that we are all on the same page.

to be on the same page
[to be in agreement about something]

There's been a change of pace **in the company since our product launch.**

a change of pace
[an increase or decrease in speed from what is normal]

I know it's always difficult to fill someone's shoes.

to fill someone's shoes
[to start doing a job or role that someone else has just left]

The design is flawed. We'll have to go back to square one.

to go back to square one
[to return to the start position]

They haven't signed the contract yet, but at least I have a foot in the door.

to get / have a foot in the door
[to gain a small initial advantage at the beginning of a longer process]

Don't complicate things. Tell me the facts in a nutshell.

in a nutshell
[simply and succinctly]

It's important to go the extra mile **for these customers.**

to go the extra mile
[to make more effort than is usually expected]

It's essential that we get the campaign up and running **this week.**

up and running
[operating properly]

I need an update on this project. Let's touch base next week.

to touch base
[to talk to someone briefly in order to catch up or get an update]

Everyone was pleased when Simon clinched the deal last week.

to clinch the deal
[to confirm or settle an agreement or contract]

I don't know the exact price, but I can give you a ballpark figure.

a ballpark figure
[a rough estimate]

We're not sure which new product to launch this month. It's all up in the air.

up in the air
[uncertain and undecided]

My boss and I see eye to eye on most things.

to see eye to eye
[to agree totally]

It's getting late. I think we should call it a day.

to call it a day
[to stop the current activity]

We want to corner the market in street fashion by next year.

to corner the market
[to have control of a particular market]

Food quality is extremely important in this restaurant. We can't cut corners.

to cut corners
[to do something in a cheaper or easier way, at the expense of high standards]

We're really behind on this project now, Tony. What's the game plan?

a game plan
[a strategy worked out beforehand]

This chair design is totally groundbreaking, Ceri.

groundbreaking
[original and a big departure from what was there before]

34 Relaciones laborales

A menudo se utilizan phrasal verbs para hablar de la relación con los colegas y los clientes. Es importante utilizar el orden adecuado de las palabras con los phrasal verbs.

⚙ **Lenguaje** Phrasal verbs de tres palabras
Aa Vocabulario Redes sociales
🧩 **Habilidad** Redes sociales y contactos

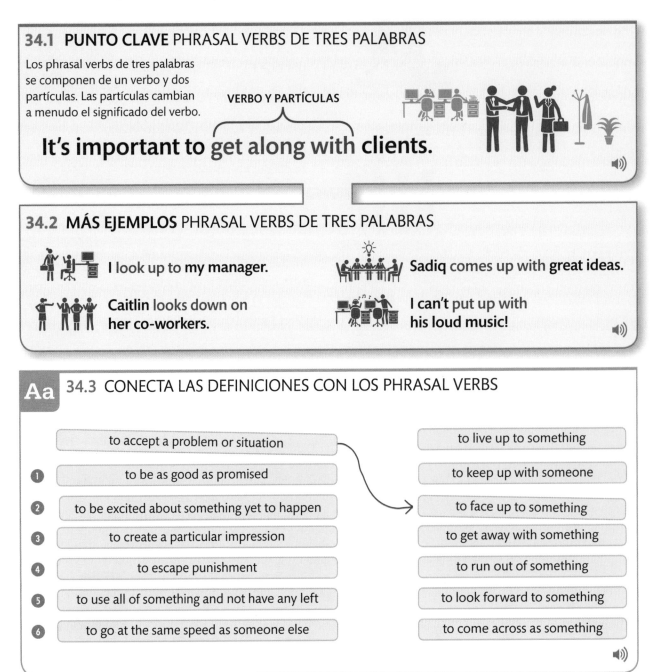

34.1 PUNTO CLAVE PHRASAL VERBS DE TRES PALABRAS

Los phrasal verbs de tres palabras se componen de un verbo y dos partículas. Las partículas cambian a menudo el significado del verbo.

VERBO Y PARTÍCULAS

It's important to **get along with** clients.

34.2 MÁS EJEMPLOS PHRASAL VERBS DE TRES PALABRAS

I **look up to** my manager.

Sadiq **comes up with** great ideas.

Caitlin **looks down on** her co-workers.

I can't **put up with** his loud music!

Aa 34.3 CONECTA LAS DEFINICIONES CON LOS PHRASAL VERBS

to accept a problem or situation

1 to be as good as promised

2 to be excited about something yet to happen

3 to create a particular impression

4 to escape punishment

5 to use all of something and not have any left

6 to go at the same speed as someone else

to live up to something

to keep up with someone

to face up to something

to get away with something

to run out of something

to look forward to something

to come across as something

34.4 LEE EL ARTÍCULO Y RESPONDE A LAS PREGUNTAS

The benefits of social media were recognized quickly.
True ☐ False ☐ Not given ☑

1 Not all companies think social media is useful.
True ☐ False ☐ Not given ☐

2 Some companies think social media costs too much.
True ☐ False ☐ Not given ☐

3 Companies who don't use social media can compete.
True ☐ False ☐ Not given ☐

4 Customers are irritated by ads on social media.
True ☐ False ☐ Not given ☐

5 Social media increases awareness of brands.
True ☐ False ☐ Not given ☐

6 It doesn't matter if customers aren't loyal.
True ☐ False ☐ Not given ☐

BUSINESS FORUM

Using social media
How social networking can benefit your company

Some companies have been slow to recognize the benefits of social media in business. Some even look down on social media, and doubt that it has any serious purpose or value. But ignore social media at your peril, because you can be sure your competitors are using it. And if you don't keep up with the competition, you'll never corner the market.

Using social media platforms can increase awareness of your company. Your brand becomes more familiar and more recognizable. If customers feel that they are keeping up with all your news and developments, they feel like they have a relationship with the company. As a result they become more loyal, and loyal customers make repeat purchases.

34.5 COMPLETA LOS ESPACIOS CON LAS PALABRAS DEL RECUADRO

I look up _____*up*_____ to Yohann. He works hard and always goes the extra mile.

1 Please could you _____ up with a proposal on how to improve punctuality?

2 I can't _____ up with Thom when he goes through the accounts. He's too quick.

3 Liza comes _____ as very serious, but outside of work she's a lot of fun.

4 The two interns don't get _____ with each other very well. They don't see eye to eye.

5 I'm really looking _____ to welcoming our new clients to London.

| come | ~~up~~ | across | keep | forward | along |

◀))

34.6 PUNTO CLAVE PHRASAL VERBS SEPARABLES CON PRONOMBRES

Algunos phrasal verbs son separables, es decir, la partícula no tiene que situarse inmediatamente después del verbo. Si el objeto de la oración con un phrasal verb separable es un pronombre, este tiene que ir entre el verbo y la partícula.

NOTA
Todos los phrasal verbs de tres palabras son inseparables.

I'm looking up our competitors on social media. ✅

I'm looking them up on social media. ✅

I'm looking our competitors up on social media. ✅

I'm looking up them on social media. ❌

34.7 MÁS EJEMPLOS PHRASAL VERBS SEPARABLES CON PRONOMBRES

Here's a new form.
Please can you fill it in?

This is a difficult task.
Can you take it on?

They have a great website.
You must check it out.

Our clients are relying on you.
Don't let them down.

34.8 VUELVE A ESCRIBIR LAS FRASES CON PRONOMBRES DE OBJETO

Jayne really let her co-workers down.
Jayne really let them down.

❶ Can you take on the presentation?
_____

❷ We're giving away free bags.
_____

❸ Let's look up this company on social media.
_____

❹ I think we should call off the meeting.
_____

❺ Can we talk over your sales proposal?
_____

34.9 ESCUCHA EL AUDIO Y RESPONDE A LAS PREGUNTAS

Leah y Tariq hablan de cómo promocionar sus productos en las redes sociales.

Tariq's idea involves...
a sports event. ☑
an online survey. ☐
an advertising campaign. ☐

1. Tariq says the company...
should spend more on advertising. ☐
needs a modern image. ☐
needs to employ more people. ☐

2. The company could use social media to...
increase awareness of health. ☐
tell people about their products. ☐
advertise the event. ☐

3. The event would...
encourage people to become fitter. ☐
benefit the local environment. ☐
increase awareness of the company. ☐

4. Who will take on the work?
Tariq volunteers to do it. ☐
Leah will find a team to work on it. ☐
Leah will do the organizing. ☐

34.10 CORRIGE LOS ERRORES Y DI LAS FRASES EN VOZ ALTA

This is a difficult task. Can you take on it?

This is a difficult task. Can you take it on?

1. I need the report today. Please don't let down me.

2. Josef complains a lot. I can't put with it.

3. I'm looking forward finishing my training.

4. If you have a problem, we can talk over.

5. Don't look down to Rachel. She's still new.

6. Our company is giving off three cars.

34 ✓ CHECKLIST

⚙️ Phrasal verbs de tres palabras ☐ **Aa** Redes sociales ☐ 🧩 Redes sociales y contactos ☐

35 Futuro profesional

Para hablar de posibles acontecimientos futuros, como el desarrollo profesional, utiliza "will", "might" y "won't" para indicar qué probabilidad existe de que algo se produzca.

🜚 **Lenguaje** Verbos modales de posibilidad
Aa Vocabulario Desarrollo profesional
🧩 **Habilidad** Hablar del futuro

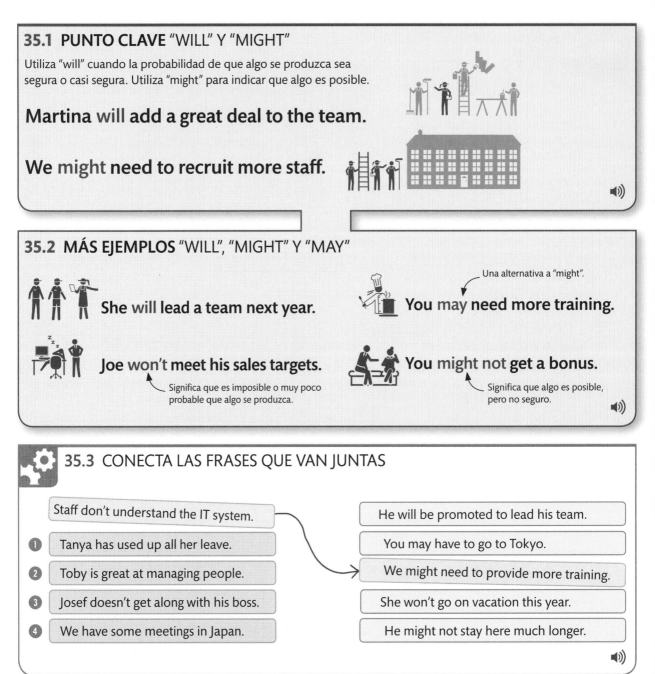

35.1 PUNTO CLAVE "WILL" Y "MIGHT"

Utiliza "will" cuando la probabilidad de que algo se produzca sea segura o casi segura. Utiliza "might" para indicar que algo es posible.

Martina will add a great deal to the team.

We might need to recruit more staff.

35.2 MÁS EJEMPLOS "WILL", "MIGHT" Y "MAY"

She will lead a team next year.

Una alternativa a "might".
You may need more training.

Joe won't meet his sales targets.

Significa que es imposible o muy poco probable que algo se produzca.

You might not get a bonus.

Significa que algo es posible, pero no seguro.

35.3 CONECTA LAS FRASES QUE VAN JUNTAS

Staff don't understand the IT system.

He will be promoted to lead his team.

❶ Tanya has used up all her leave.

You may have to go to Tokyo.

❷ Toby is great at managing people.

We might need to provide more training.

❸ Josef doesn't get along with his boss.

She won't go on vacation this year.

❹ We have some meetings in Japan.

He might not stay here much longer.

35.4 MARCA LAS FRASES QUE SEAN CORRECTAS

Pam has more than 10 years' experience and she wills lead our sales department. ☐
Pam has more than 10 years' experience and she will lead our sales department. ☑

① We can't hire any staff at the moment, so you don't might get an assistant until May. ☐
We can't hire any staff at the moment, so you might not get an assistant until May. ☐

② You're great with new staff, so we may ask you to become a mentor. ☐
You're great with new staff, so we ask may you to become a mentor. ☐

③ It's been a bad year for the company, so you won't get a raise. ☐
It's been a bad year for the company, so you not will get a raise. ☐

④ This report needs to be finished by Friday. You need might to work overtime. ☐
This report needs to be finished by Friday. You might need to work overtime. ☐

⑤ If Lucinda's work doesn't improve, we may have to fire her. ☐
If Lucinda's work doesn't improve, we won't have to fire her. ☐

◀))

35.5 LEE LA EVALUACIÓN DE RENDIMIENTO Y RESPONDE A LAS PREGUNTAS

Performance Review:
Paula Stannard

Paula has worked in our customer relations department for two years. She will be promoted to assistant manager at the beginning of next year.

After her promotion, Paula will be in charge of about 45 people. We may need to give her additional training, but I am confident that she will perform well in this role. Paula will receive a 10 percent raise in her new position. We might consider providing her with a company car, as she will need to go out and visit clients.

Paula works in accounts. **True** ☐ **False** ☑

① Paula will be promoted next year. **True** ☐ **False** ☐

② Paula will be head of her department. **True** ☐ **False** ☐

③ Paula will manage more than 40 people. **True** ☐ **False** ☐

④ She won't need any extra training. **True** ☐ **False** ☐

⑤ Her boss thinks she will perform well. **True** ☐ **False** ☐

⑥ Paula's salary will not increase. **True** ☐ **False** ☐

⑦ Paula may get a company car. **True** ☐ **False** ☐

⑧ Paula will stay in the office all the time. **True** ☐ **False** ☐

35.6 PUNTO CLAVE "DEFINITELY" Y "PROBABLY"

Utiliza "definitely" con "will" y "won't" para hablar de cosas que seguro que pasarán; utiliza "probably" para cosas que sea probable que pasen.

NOTA
"Definitely" y "probably" aparecen después de "will" en la oración, pero antes de "won't".

What are my chances of being promoted this year?

You will definitely **be promoted.**

You will probably **be promoted.**

You probably won't **be promoted.**

You definitely won't **be promoted.**

35.7 VUELVE A ESCRIBIR LAS FRASES CORRIGIENDO LOS ERRORES

You will **probable** move to the new office.
You will probably move to the new office.

❶ He **don't definitely** get the job.

_____

❷ You probably **don't will need** any training.

_____

❸ We **will hire probably** some more staff soon.

_____

❹ She will **definite** get a raise.

_____

❺ I **definitely not will** move to the head office.

_____

❻ I **not probably will** go on vacation this year.

_____

35.8 COLOCA EL MODIFICADOR EN EL LUGAR CORRECTO Y DI LAS FRASES EN VOZ ALTA

You won't get a new laptop. [definitely]

You definitely won't get a new laptop.

❶ We will get a thank-you gift. [probably]

_____

❷ I won't change jobs this year. [definitely]

_____

❸ You will get a bonus. [definitely]

_____

❹ We won't invite him to the meeting. [probably]

_____

326

35.9 ESCUCHA EL AUDIO Y CONECTA LAS IMÁGENES CON LAS EXPRESIONES CORRECTAS

| definitely won't happen | will definitely happen | may happen | might not happen | probably won't happen |

---

35 ✓ CHECKLIST

⚙️ Verbos modales de posibilidad ☐   **Aa** Desarrollo profesional ☐   🧩 Hablar del futuro ☐

♻️ REPASA LO QUE HAS APRENDIDO EN LAS UNIDADES 29-35

NUEVO LENGUAJE	FRASE DE EJEMPLO	☑	UNIDAD
"A" Y "THE"	I applied for a job as a nurse. The application form was really long.	☐	30.1
ZERO ARTICLE Y ARTÍCULOS DEFINIDOS EN PLURALES	Accountants work very hard. The accountants in my office work long hours.	☐	30.4, 30.5
PREPOSICIONES DEPENDIENTES	I worked with the head chef in a restaurant.	☐	31.1, 31.6
CLÁUSULAS RELATIVAS	This is the product that I designed last year. I worked in a café, which was a lot of fun.	☐	32.1, 32.5
PHRASAL VERBS DE TRES PALABRAS	It's important to get along with clients.	☐	34.1
PHRASAL VERBS CON PRONOMBRES	Here's a form. Please can you fill it in?	☐	34.6, 34.7
HABLAR SOBRE POSIBILIDADES	We might have to recruit more staff. You will definitely be promoted.	☐	35.1, 35.6

36 Vocabulario

36.1 EQUIPO DE OFICINA Y PRESENTACIONES

computer

screen

keyboard

mouse

laptop

tablet

touch screen

cursor

power button

charger

power cable

low battery

USB drive / flash drive

hard drive

router

laminator

scanner

webcam

video camera

voice recorder

printer

slides

handout

projector

projector screen

lectern

clicker

pointer

cue cards

microphone

speakers

chairs

flipchart

whiteboard

erasable markers

graph

pie chart

flow chart

table

report

Cuando hables ante un público, es importante estructurar el discurso para que sea claro y fácil de entender. Existen diversas expresiones que te ayudarán a conseguirlo.

⚙ **Lenguaje** Lenguaje orientador
Aa Vocabulario Material para presentaciones
🧩 **Habilidad** Estructurar una presentación

37.1 PUNTO CLAVE LENGUAJE ORIENTADOR

Puedes ayudar al público a seguir tu discurso con expresiones que lo organicen. Así el público sabe qué pasará a continuación.

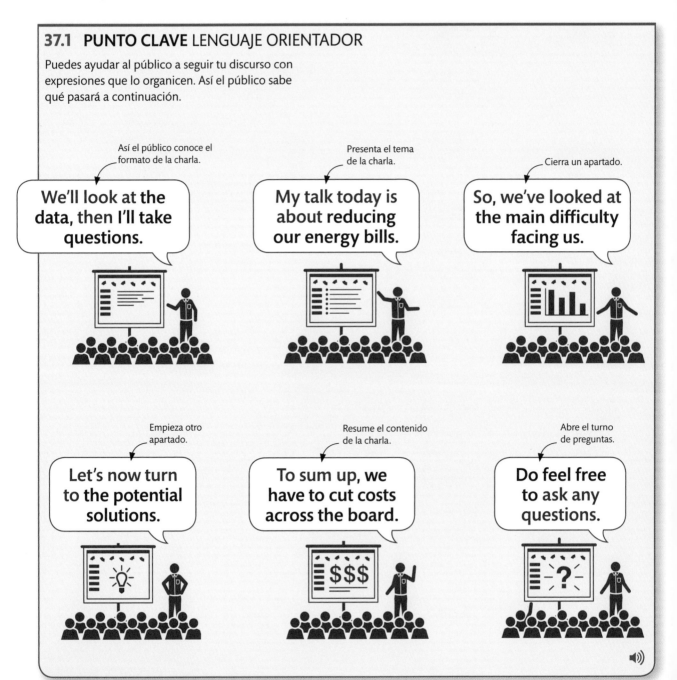

Así el público conoce el formato de la charla.

We'll look at the data, then I'll take questions.

Presenta el tema de la charla.

My talk today is about reducing our energy bills.

Cierra un apartado.

So, we've looked at the main difficulty facing us.

Empieza otro apartado.

Let's now turn to the potential solutions.

Resume el contenido de la charla.

To sum up, we have to cut costs across the board.

Abre el turno de preguntas.

Do feel free to ask any questions.

37.2 ESCUCHA EL AUDIO Y RESPONDE A LAS PREGUNTAS

El propietario de un café presenta propuestas de futuro a los inversores.

> The speaker invites questions during the talk.　　**True** ☐　**False** ☐　**Not given** ☑

❶ The café is not very successful.　　**True** ☐　**False** ☐　**Not given** ☐

❷ One option is adding 20 more tables.　　**True** ☐　**False** ☐　**Not given** ☐

❸ Any expansion would require more restrooms.　　**True** ☐　**False** ☐　**Not given** ☐

❹ The choice is to expand or close the café.　　**True** ☐　**False** ☐　**Not given** ☐

❺ The speaker wants to expand the café.　　**True** ☐　**False** ☐　**Not given** ☐

37.3 VUELVE A ESCRIBIR LAS FRASES PONIENDO LAS PALABRAS EN SU ORDEN CORRECTO

| talk. | end | my | That | me | brings | the | to | of |

That brings me to the end of my talk.

❶ | up, | bright | To | a | future. | sum | have | we | very |

_____

❷ | ask | questions. | feel | me | Do | to | any | free |

_____

❸ | the | figures. | turn | predicted | Let's | sales | to |

_____

❹ | we've | alternatives. | looked | all | So, | at | main | the |

_____

331

37.4 CONECTA LAS DEFINICIONES CON EL MATERIAL

a device that loads a battery with electricity → charger

1. part of a computer that stores information
2. a device used to highlight parts of a slide
3. the switch which turns a device on or off
4. projected documents with images and information
5. a wire that connects to an electrical device
6. a tall stand that a presenter stands behind
7. a gadget you click to change presentation slides

remote
cable
charger
pointer
lectern
slides
hard drive
power button

37.5 COMPLETA LOS ESPACIOS CON LAS PALABRAS DEL RECUADRO Y DI LAS FRASES EN VOZ ALTA

You can ask for copies of the _____slides_____ after the talk.

1. Be careful of the _____ in front of the stage.

2. I will return to the _____ to answer questions.

3. If you follow my _____, you can see the graph.

4. I'll use my _____ to forward to the final slide.

5. This projector's noisy. I'll turn the _____ off.

cable   ~~slides~~   lectern   pointer   remote   power button

37.6 LEE EL ARTÍCULO Y RESPONDE A LAS PREGUNTAS

> We often see similar pictures in presentations.
> **True** ☑ **False** ☐ **Not given** ☐

❶ Images always make presentations exciting.
True ☐ **False** ☐ **Not given** ☐

❷ The writer often gives presentations himself.
True ☐ **False** ☐ **Not given** ☐

❸ Slides can add extra meaning to the presentation.
True ☐ **False** ☐ **Not given** ☐

❹ It can be better to use your own images.
True ☐ **False** ☐ **Not given** ☐

❺ It is better to have a lot of text on slides.
True ☐ **False** ☐ **Not given** ☐

❻ You must have slides to give a good presentation.
True ☐ **False** ☐ **Not given** ☐

PRESENTATIONS AND TALKS

Visual Aids: tips and tricks

Make the most of the images you use in your presentations

The internet contains millions of images and yet, when we sit through presentations, we often see the same old pictures of cogs and handshakes. These images add little value to any presentation. Here are some simple tips for using visual aids in presentations. First, use clear slides with simple images that add to the meaning of the presentation. Also, don't forget that you can use your own photographs, rather than the impersonal images taken from the internet. Next, ensure that slides are not covered in lots of tiny text that is either difficult to read, or that you intend to read out anyway. Finally, consider if you need slides at all. If they don't add anything, you may be better off without them.

37.7 ESCUCHA EL AUDIO Y LUEGO NUMERA LAS FRASES EN EL ORDEN EN QUE APARECEN

Ⓐ My talk today is about the advertising budget for the next year. ☐

Ⓑ Let's now turn to the advertising plans for next year. ☐

Ⓒ Do feel free to ask any questions or for more information. ☐

Ⓓ Good morning. Thank you for coming to my presentation this morning. ☐ 1

Ⓔ So, we've looked at last year's advertising successes and failures. ☐

Ⓕ To sum up, we will have even more publicity for less money. ☐

Ⓖ If you follow my pointer, you'll see last year's figures on the left. ☐

Ⓗ I'll quickly go through the figures and then I'll take any questions. ☐

37 ✓ CHECKLIST

⚙ Lenguaje orientador ☐   **Aa** Material para presentaciones ☐   Estructurar una presentación ☐

38 Desarrollar un argumento

Durante una presentación dispones de expresiones concretas para desarrollar tu argumento y hacer que el público sepa qué va a pasar.

⚙ **Lenguaje** Lenguaje útil para presentaciones
Aa Vocabulario Presentaciones
🧩 **Habilidad** Desarrollar un argumento

38.1 PUNTO CLAVE GENERALIZAR, HACER EXCEPCIONES Y CENTRARSE

Si dispones de datos concretos, es útil proporcionarlos. No obstante, quizá te convenga utilizar términos más generales si no tienes este tipo de datos o si quieres evitar repetirte.

> **Generally speaking, consumers are buying the latest models...**

Sirve para aclarar que estás generalizando.

> **...except for this older model, which is still popular.**

Expresiones como esta sirven para destacar excepciones a la regla general.

> **If we focus on last year's sales, we can see things have shifted.**

Tras cualquier afirmación general, utiliza esto para centrarte en un área concreta.

🔊

⚙ 38.2 ESCRIBE LAS EXPRESIONES DEL RECUADRO EN LAS CATEGORÍAS CORRESPONDIENTES

GENERALIZAR	EXCEPCIONES	CENTRARSE
on the whole		
____	____	____
____	____	____
____	____	____

except for   with the exception of

generally   if we focus on

aside from   ~~on the whole~~

if we home in on   excepting

concentrating on   focusing on

in general   by and large

🔊

334

38.3 VUELVE A ESCRIBIR LAS FRASES PONIENDO LAS PALABRAS EN SU ORDEN CORRECTO

| rule, | our | love | As | promotions. | a | customers |

As a rule, our customers love promotions.

① | launch | the | interview. | successful, | The | from | was | aside |

_____

② | let's | in | positive | Now, | on | home | the | news. |

_____

③ | and | poster | a | By | disaster. | large, | campaign | the | was |

_____

④ | our | Most | except | clients | one. | of | liked | the | design |

_____

⑤ | Today | social | we're | focus | going | on | to | media. |

_____

38.4 ESCUCHA EL AUDIO Y RESPONDE A LAS PREGUNTAS

Un responsable de marca presenta una gama nueva de productos.

ValenTova's is going to take over Tina's.
True ☐ **False** ☐ **Not given** ☑

① Both brands have a good reputation.
True ☐ **False** ☐ **Not given** ☐

② The new partnership will have a website.
True ☐ **False** ☐ **Not given** ☐

③ You can only buy Tina's in London.
True ☐ **False** ☐ **Not given** ☐

④ They will sell mail order chocolate.
True ☐ **False** ☐ **Not given** ☐

⑤ The ice cream will be called Valentina's.
True ☐ **False** ☐ **Not given** ☐

38.5 PUNTO CLAVE DAR EJEMPLOS

Tras explicar detalladamente tu argumento, incluye ejemplos para reforzar el discurso.

"For instance" puede ir al principio, en medio o (en pocas ocasiones) al final de la oración.

For instance, our new distribution method has been a huge success.

También puedes decir "As an illustration..." al principio de la oración.

As an example, our products have been very popular in Asia.

We've made progress in new sectors such as the travel market.

"Such as" aparece en el medio de la oración, antes del sustantivo que ilustra.

38.6 PUNTO CLAVE REBATIR LA OPINIÓN GENERAL

Existen diversas expresiones concretas para rebatir algo que se considera o se entiende como la opinión general.

Estas expresiones suelen ir al principio de la oración.

In fact...

Actually...

As a matter of fact...

In actual fact...

In reality...

However...

38.7 LEE EL ARTÍCULO Y RESPONDE A LAS PREGUNTAS

The article is about creating slides.	**True** ☐	**False** ☑

1. Start with a joke. **True** ☐ **False** ☐
2. Research each audience. **True** ☐ **False** ☐
3. You should not stay still. **True** ☐ **False** ☐
4. You should look serious. **True** ☐ **False** ☐

15 LIFE HACKS

PRESENTING

We put a lot of effort into writing presentations, so it's important to keep the audience's attention. Start with a good, relevant story and include facts and images that are aimed directly at your audience. This shows you have researched them and their needs. Use the space that you have and move around the stage. Lastly, make sure that you look up regularly and smile.

38.8 COMPLETA LOS ESPACIOS CON LAS PALABRAS DEL RECUADRO Y CONTESTA AL AUDIO EN VOZ ALTA

How do our customers spend their free time?

Our research shows that, ___*as a rule*___ , they are very active.

1 So, were all the media campaigns failures?

No. _____ the posters, we can see they were very successful.

2 Did all the stores improve sales last year?

Yes, _____ our Madrid store.

3 So, it was yet another poor year for the company.

_____ it was very successful.

4 Where do you think we should open the next store?

Cities _____ Seoul and Busan could have successful stores.

5 Have sales increased after the launch of our new TV advert?

They haven't yet. _____ , it's too soon to see what the impact will be.

| If we focus on | As a matter of fact | However | ~~as a rule~~ | such as | with the exception of |

---

39 Promocionar un producto

Al describir un producto a un cliente potencial, es útil compararlo con los de la competencia mediante adjetivos comparativos y superlativos.

⚙ **Lenguaje** Comparativos y superlativos
Aa Vocabulario Marketing de productos
Habilidad Comparar productos

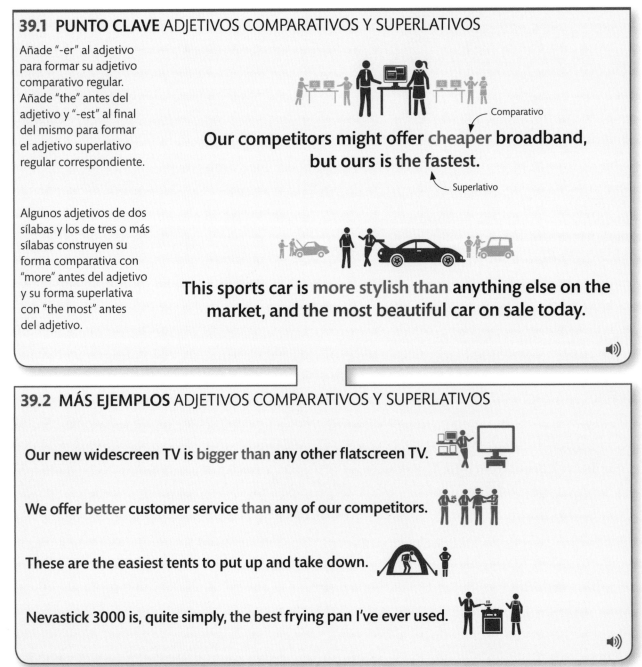

39.1 PUNTO CLAVE ADJETIVOS COMPARATIVOS Y SUPERLATIVOS

Añade "-er" al adjetivo para formar su adjetivo comparativo regular. Añade "the" antes del adjetivo y "-est" al final del mismo para formar el adjetivo superlativo regular correspondiente.

Comparativo

Our competitors might offer cheaper broadband, but ours is the fastest.

Superlativo

Algunos adjetivos de dos sílabas y los de tres o más sílabas construyen su forma comparativa con "more" antes del adjetivo y su forma superlativa con "the most" antes del adjetivo.

This sports car is more stylish than anything else on the market, and the most beautiful car on sale today.

39.2 MÁS EJEMPLOS ADJETIVOS COMPARATIVOS Y SUPERLATIVOS

Our new widescreen TV is bigger than any other flatscreen TV.

We offer better customer service than any of our competitors.

These are the easiest tents to put up and take down.

Nevastick 3000 is, quite simply, the best frying pan I've ever used.

39.3 VUELVE A ESCRIBIR LAS FRASES CORRIGIENDO LOS ERRORES

Our phones are much more reliabler than our competitors' phones.
Our phones are much more reliable than our competitors' phones.

❶ Our new smartwatch is easyer to operate than the old one.

❷ Our new designer jeans are stylish than last year's products.

❸ Our tablet is cheapest on the market.

❹ This is the more beautiful dress in our range.

❺ This is the goodest laptop I have ever owned.

39.4 ESCUCHA EL AUDIO Y CONECTA LOS PRODUCTOS CON LAS EXPRESIONES QUE LOS DESCRIBEN

| the most reliable | the thinnest | more affordable | lighter | more comfortable |

39.5 PUNTO CLAVE COMPARACIONES CON "AS... AS"

Las comparaciones con "as... as" se utilizan con un adjetivo para comparar cosas similares.

Our laptops are as fast as our competitors' laptops, but are much cheaper.

39.6 MÁS EJEMPLOS COMPARACIONES CON "AS... AS"

Utiliza "just as... as" para destacar la similitud entre dos cosas.

Our new watch is just as light as any other design on the market.

Utiliza "not as... as" para contrastar cosas que son diferentes.

This drill is not as noisy as many existing brands.

This sports drink is as healthy as the leading brand, but much cheaper.

Our washing machine is as quick as more expensive models.

39.7 MARCA LAS FRASES QUE SEAN CORRECTAS

These energy-efficient light bulbs are just as effective as the old ones. ☑

These energy-efficient light bulbs are as just effective as the old ones. ☐

1. Our new phone is cheap as existing models, but has a much wider range of features. ☐

   Our new phone is as cheap as existing models, but has a much wider range of features. ☐

2. Our latest DVD is as more exciting as anything I've ever seen. ☐

   Our latest DVD is as exciting as anything I've ever seen. ☐

3. Our chairs are excellent value, and just as comfortable as more expensive models. ☐

   Our chairs are excellent value, and as just as comfortable as more expensive models. ☐

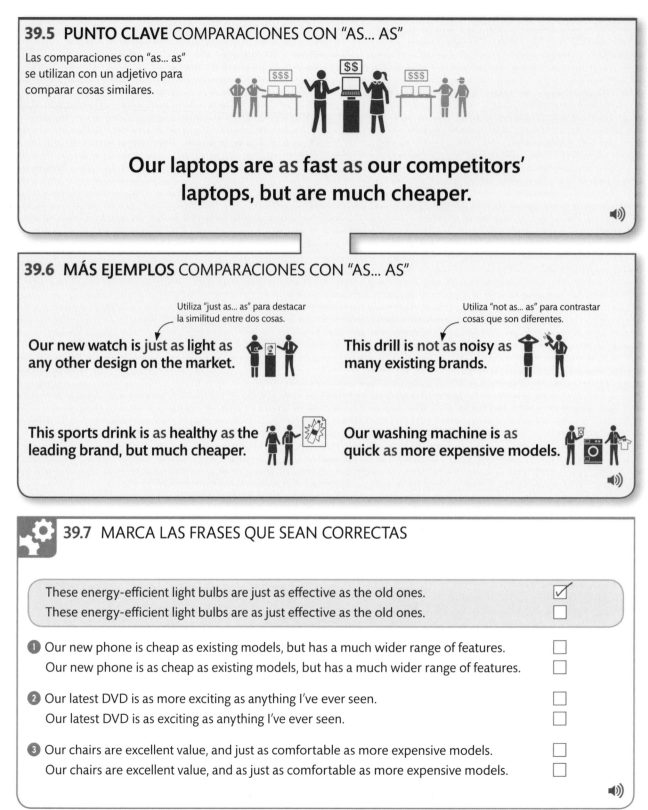

39.8 LEE EL ANUNCIO Y RESPONDE A LAS PREGUNTAS

GARDENER'S WEEKLY

ORGANIC VEG BOX

Perfect organic goodness, delivered to your door

In our veg box, you'll find the freshest lettuce, picked the day before delivery, and delicious, ripe, seasonal fruit. You and your family will love it!

Our vegetables are just as cheap as supermarket produce. And we deliver them free to your door every week!

Vegetables in the box are grown in the UK.
True ☐ **False** ☐ **Not given** ☑

❶ The ad claims that the fruit tastes delicious.
True ☐ **False** ☐ **Not given** ☐

❷ The veg box contains apples.
True ☐ **False** ☐ **Not given** ☐

❸ Vegetables in the supermarket are cheaper.
True ☐ **False** ☐ **Not given** ☐

❹ There is no extra charge for home delivery.
True ☐ **False** ☐ **Not given** ☐

❺ The box is available in different sizes.
True ☐ **False** ☐ **Not given** ☐

39.9 TACHA LAS PALABRAS INCORRECTAS DE CADA FRASE Y DI LAS FRASES EN VOZ ALTA

This car is ~~reliabler~~ / **more reliable** than other models, and good value for money.

❶ Our new laptop is much **lighter** / **more light** than its competitors.

❷ This fitness tracker is **just effective as** / **just as effective as** more expensive models.

❸ Organic fruit is not **as cheap** / **as cheap as** supermarket fruit, but it tastes better.

❹ A consumer survey voted our pizzas the **tastiest** / **most tastyest** on the market.

---

39 ✓ CHECKLIST

⚙ Comparativos y superlativos ☐   **Aa** Marketing de productos ☐   🧩 Comparar productos ☐

Proporcionar datos y cifras

Al hacer una presentación o redactar un informe, es importante describir los cambios y las tendencias con un lenguaje preciso y que suene natural.

⚙️ **Lenguaje** Colocaciones
Aa Vocabulario Tendencias del negocio
🧩 **Habilidad** Describir datos y cifras

40.1 PUNTO CLAVE DESCRIBIR TENDENCIAS CON COLOCACIONES

Utiliza un verbo modificado con un adverbio para describir la velocidad o el grado de un cambio. Estas parejas de palabras son colocaciones que suenan "naturales" en inglés.

NOTA
Las colocaciones suelen ser de dos o más palabras; lo más normal es que tengan dos. Si las utilizas bien, tu discurso será más fluido.

VERBO   **ADVERBIO**

Sales have **declined considerably**.

House prices are **fluctuating wildly**.

Public interest has **fallen steadily**.

The markets have **rallied slightly**.

Algunas colocaciones para describir tendencias son adjetivos seguidos de un sustantivo.

ADJETIVO   **SUSTANTIVO**

There was a **steady increase** last quarter.

We expect a **considerable drop** in the new year.

After the news, there was a **dramatic spike** in sales.

There was a **sharp rise** in profits over the winter.

40.2 ESCUCHA EL AUDIO Y LUEGO NUMERA LAS TENDENCIAS EN EL ORDEN EN QUE SE DESCRIBEN

40.3 CONECTA LAS FRASES QUE SIGNIFICAN LO MISMO

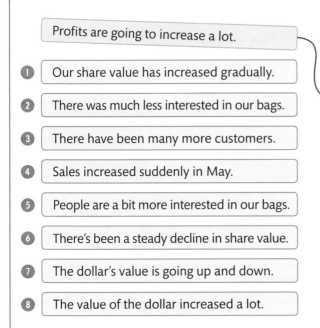

Profits are going to increase a lot.

1. Our share value has increased gradually.
2. There was much less interested in our bags.
3. There have been many more customers.
4. Sales increased suddenly in May.
5. People are a bit more interested in our bags.
6. There's been a steady decline in share value.
7. The dollar's value is going up and down.
8. The value of the dollar increased a lot.

We've had a sharp rise in customer numbers.

Sales of our bags have rallied slightly.

We expect a sharp rise in profits.

The value of the dollar saw a dramatic spike.

Interest in our bags declined considerably.

The value of the dollar is fluctuating wildly.

There was a dramatic spike in sales in May.

The value of our shares has fallen steadily.

There was a steady increase in our share value.

343

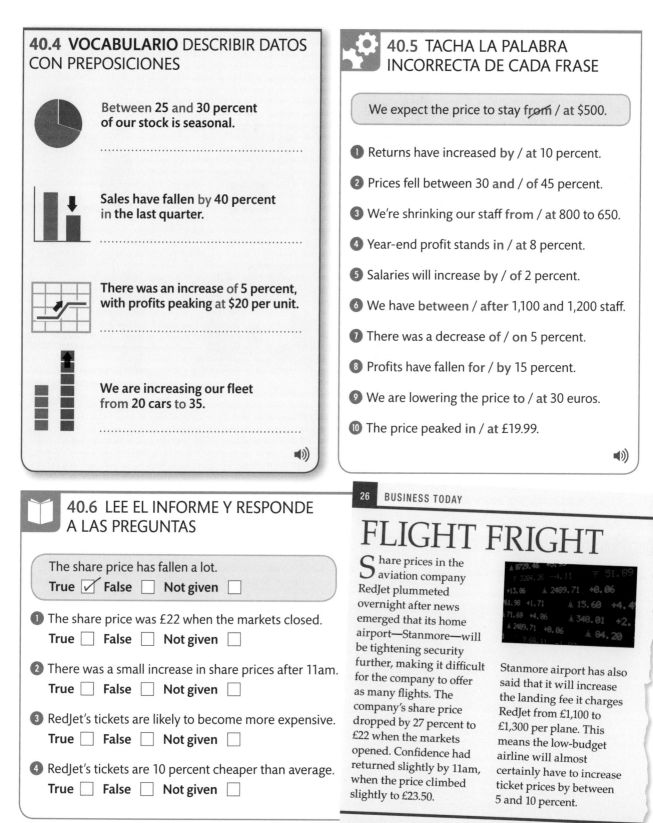

40.4 VOCABULARIO DESCRIBIR DATOS CON PREPOSICIONES

Between 25 and 30 percent of our stock is seasonal.

....

Sales have fallen by 40 percent in the last quarter.

....

There was an increase of 5 percent, with profits peaking at $20 per unit.

....

We are increasing our fleet from 20 cars to 35.

....

40.5 TACHA LA PALABRA INCORRECTA DE CADA FRASE

We expect the price to stay ~~from~~ / at $500.

1. Returns have increased **by** / **at** 10 percent.

2. Prices fell between 30 **and** / **of** 45 percent.

3. We're shrinking our staff **from** / **at** 800 to 650.

4. Year-end profit stands **in** / **at** 8 percent.

5. Salaries will increase **by** / **of** 2 percent.

6. We have **between** / **after** 1,100 and 1,200 staff.

7. There was a decrease **of** / **on** 5 percent.

8. Profits have fallen **for** / **by** 15 percent.

9. We are lowering the price **to** / **at** 30 euros.

10. The price peaked **in** / **at** £19.99.

40.6 LEE EL INFORME Y RESPONDE A LAS PREGUNTAS

The share price has fallen a lot.
True ☑ **False** ☐ **Not given** ☐

1. The share price was £22 when the markets closed.
True ☐ **False** ☐ **Not given** ☐

2. There was a small increase in share prices after 11am.
True ☐ **False** ☐ **Not given** ☐

3. RedJet's tickets are likely to become more expensive.
True ☐ **False** ☐ **Not given** ☐

4. RedJet's tickets are 10 percent cheaper than average.
True ☐ **False** ☐ **Not given** ☐

26   BUSINESS TODAY

FLIGHT FRIGHT

Share prices in the aviation company RedJet plummeted overnight after news emerged that its home airport—Stanmore—will be tightening security further, making it difficult for the company to offer as many flights. The company's share price dropped by 27 percent to £22 when the markets opened. Confidence had returned slightly by 11am, when the price climbed slightly to £23.50.

Stanmore airport has also said that it will increase the landing fee it charges RedJet from £1,100 to £1,300 per plane. This means the low-budget airline will almost certainly have to increase ticket prices by between 5 and 10 percent.

40.7 COMPLETA LOS ESPACIOS CON LAS PALABRAS DEL RECUADRO Y DI LAS FRASES EN VOZ ALTA

Last year, our sales _declined steadily_.

2 It's been _____ since the announcement.

1 There was a _____ at the start of the year.

3 We're expecting them to _____ next quarter.

fluctuating wildly   rally considerably   ~~declined steadily~~   sharp increase

---

40 ✓ CHECKLIST

⚙ Colocaciones ☐   **Aa** Tendencias del negocio ☐   🧩 Describir datos y cifras ☐

♻ REPASA LO QUE HAS APRENDIDO EN LAS UNIDADES 36–40

NUEVO LENGUAJE	FRASE DE EJEMPLO	☑	UNIDAD
ESTRUCTURAR UNA PRESENTACIÓN	So, we've looked at **the main difficulty facing us**. Let's now turn to **some solutions**.	☐	37.1
GENERALIZAR, HACER EXCEPCIONES Y CENTRARSE	Generally speaking, **customers are buying the latest models**, except for **this older model**.	☐	38.1
INCLUIR EJEMPLOS Y REBATIR	For instance, **our new distribution model has been a huge success**.	☐	38.5, 38.6
PROMOCIONAR UN PRODUCTO CON COMPARATIVOS Y SUPERLATIVOS	**Our competitors might offer** cheaper **broadband, but ours is** the fastest.	☐	39.1, 39.5
DESCRIBIR TENDENCIAS	**Sales have** declined considerably. **There was a** steady increase.	☐	40.1
DESCRIBIR DATOS CON PREPOSICIONES	Between **25** and **30 percent** of our stock is seasonal.	☐	40.4

41 Planes y sugerencias

Utilizamos los verbos modales para hacer sugerencias y las preguntas indirectas o la voz pasiva para solicitar información o avisar de un error de manera educada.

✿ **Lenguaje** Preguntas indirectas
Aa Vocabulario Negociación empresarial
🧩 **Habilidad** Negociar educadamente

41.1 PUNTO CLAVE NEGOCIACIÓN Y SUGERENCIAS

Durante una negociación, se utilizan verbos modales o el past continuous para que suene más educado e indirecto.

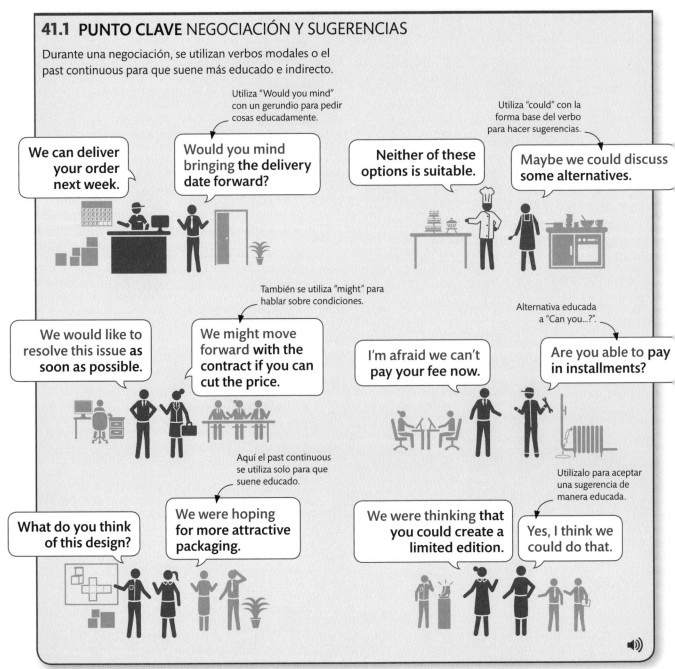

Utiliza "Would you mind" con un gerundio para pedir cosas educadamente.

We can deliver your order next week.

Would you mind bringing **the delivery date forward?**

Utiliza "could" con la forma base del verbo para hacer sugerencias.

Neither of these options is suitable.

Maybe we could discuss **some alternatives.**

También se utiliza "might" para hablar sobre condiciones.

We would like to resolve this issue **as soon as possible.**

We might move forward **with the contract if you can cut the price.**

Alternativa educada a "Can you...?".

I'm afraid we can't pay your fee now.

Are you able to **pay in installments?**

Aquí el past continuous se utiliza solo para que suene educado.

What do you think of this design?

We were hoping for more attractive packaging.

Utilízalo para aceptar una sugerencia de manera educada.

We were thinking **that you could create a limited edition.**

Yes, I think we could do that.

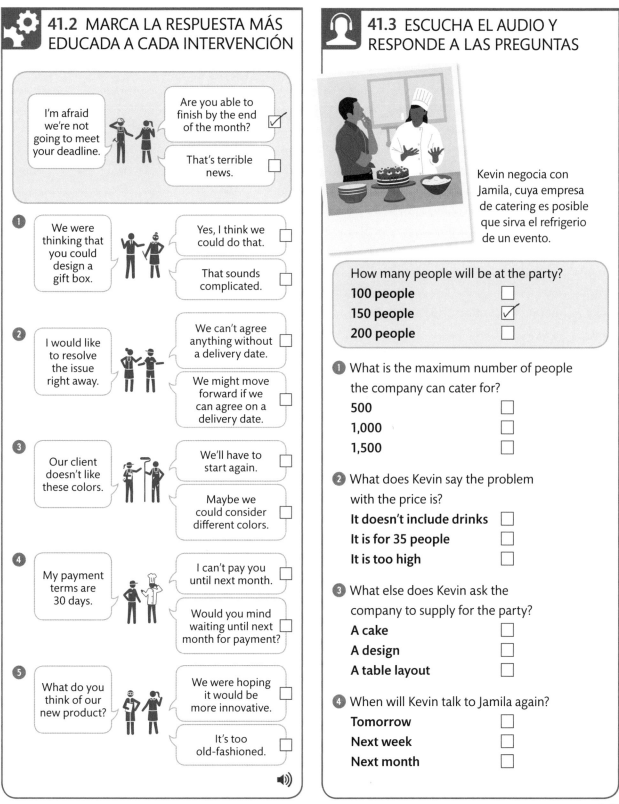

41.2 MARCA LA RESPUESTA MÁS EDUCADA A CADA INTERVENCIÓN

I'm afraid we're not going to meet your deadline.

Are you able to finish by the end of the month? ☑

That's terrible news. ☐

1 We were thinking that you could design a gift box.

Yes, I think we could do that. ☐

That sounds complicated. ☐

2 I would like to resolve the issue right away.

We can't agree anything without a delivery date. ☐

We might move forward if we can agree on a delivery date. ☐

3 Our client doesn't like these colors.

We'll have to start again. ☐

Maybe we could consider different colors. ☐

4 My payment terms are 30 days.

I can't pay you until next month. ☐

Would you mind waiting until next month for payment? ☐

5 What do you think of our new product?

We were hoping it would be more innovative. ☐

It's too old-fashioned. ☐

41.3 ESCUCHA EL AUDIO Y RESPONDE A LAS PREGUNTAS

Kevin negocia con Jamila, cuya empresa de catering es posible que sirva el refrigerio de un evento.

How many people will be at the party?
100 people ☐
150 people ☑
200 people ☐

1 What is the maximum number of people the company can cater for?
500 ☐
1,000 ☐
1,500 ☐

2 What does Kevin say the problem with the price is?
It doesn't include drinks ☐
It is for 35 people ☐
It is too high ☐

3 What else does Kevin ask the company to supply for the party?
A cake ☐
A design ☐
A table layout ☐

4 When will Kevin talk to Jamila again?
Tomorrow ☐
Next week ☐
Next month ☐

41.4 PUNTO CLAVE PREGUNTAS INDIRECTAS

Las preguntas indirectas comienzan a menudo con una frase de cortesía. Al contrario que en las preguntas directas, en las indirectas el verbo se sitúa después del sujeto.

Las preguntas indirectas comienzan a menudo con una frase de cortesía.

Could you tell me when my order will be ready?

[When **will** my order be ready?]

Las preguntas directas y las indirectas ordenan las palabras de maneras diferentes.

41.5 MÁS EJEMPLOS PREGUNTAS INDIRECTAS

Si la expresión de inicio es "Could you tell me", la pregunta indirecta acaba con signo de interrogación.

Could you tell me how much your product costs?

Las preguntas indirectas prescinden del verbo auxiliar "do".

Could you tell me when we can expect payment?

Si la expresión de inicio es "I was wondering", la pregunta indirecta acaba con punto.

I was wondering what time your store closes.

I was wondering if you are free for a meeting.

41.6 CÓMO FUNCIONA PREGUNTAS INDIRECTAS

EXPRESIÓN DE INICIO	PRON. INTERROGATIVO	SUJETO	VERBO
Could you tell me	when	the store	closes?

También puedes utilizar "I was wondering".

En preguntas indirectas, el verbo va después del sujeto.

41.7 VUELVE A ESCRIBIR LAS FRASES PONIENDO LAS PALABRAS EN SU ORDEN CORRECTO

| tell | Could | the | me | you | been | start | has | delayed? | why | date |

Could you tell me why the start date has been delayed?

① | wondering | have | I | another | these | whether | size. | you | in | was |

_____

② | you | ready? | when | tell | list | be | Could | me | the | will | price |

_____

③ | expect | me | I | you | delivery? | tell | Could | when | can |

_____

◀))

41.8 CORRIGE LOS ERRORES Y DI LAS FRASES EN VOZ ALTA

I was wondering if would you be able to give me a discount.

I was wondering if you would be able to give me a discount.

① Could you tell me when can I start buying the new products?

② I was wondering what is the warranty period.

③ Could you tell me how is the new product different from the old one?

④ I was wondering if would you be free to discuss a new job opening.

◀))

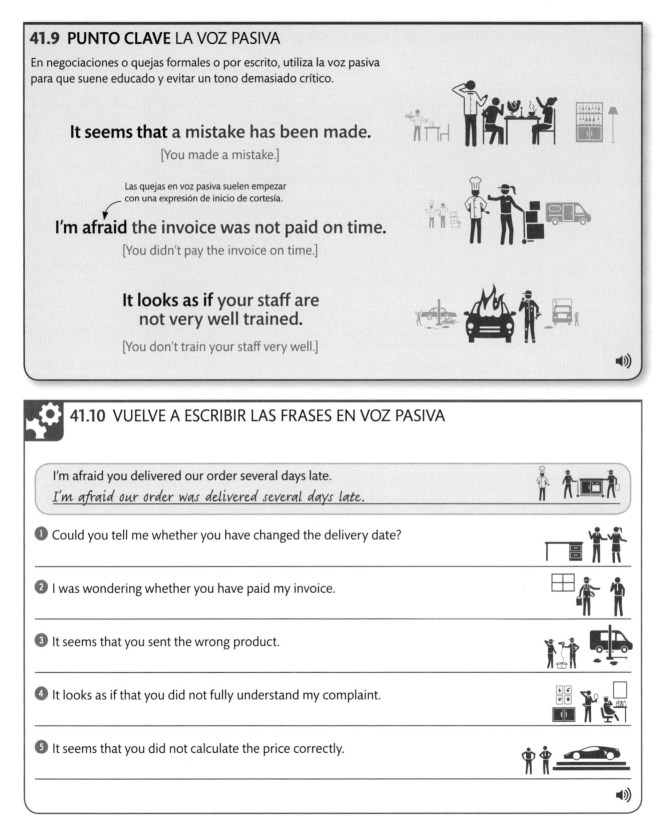

41.9 PUNTO CLAVE LA VOZ PASIVA

En negociaciones o quejas formales o por escrito, utiliza la voz pasiva para que suene educado y evitar un tono demasiado crítico.

It seems that a mistake has been made.

[You made a mistake.]

Las quejas en voz pasiva suelen empezar con una expresión de inicio de cortesía.

I'm afraid the invoice was not paid on time.

[You didn't pay the invoice on time.]

It looks as if your staff are not very well trained.

[You don't train your staff very well.]

41.10 VUELVE A ESCRIBIR LAS FRASES EN VOZ PASIVA

I'm afraid you delivered our order several days late.
I'm afraid our order was delivered several days late.

❶ Could you tell me whether you have changed the delivery date?

❷ I was wondering whether you have paid my invoice.

❸ It seems that you sent the wrong product.

❹ It looks as if that you did not fully understand my complaint.

❺ It seems that you did not calculate the price correctly.

Aa 41.11 CONECTA EL INICIO Y EL FINAL DE CADA FRASE

We would like to resolve	the sales start?
1 I'm afraid I can't access	the discount has not been applied.
2 It looks as if	this issue as soon as possible.
3 I was wondering why the	the computer system right now.
4 Could you tell me when	has been contacted.
5 It seems that the wrong customer	deadline has been missed.

We would like to resolve → this issue as soon as possible.

41.12 LEE EL CORREO ELECTRÓNICO Y RESPONDE A LAS PREGUNTAS

Bettina's order arrived on May 5.
True ☐ **False** ☐ **Not given** ☑

1 The shipments from Ms. Liang are often late.
True ☐ **False** ☐ **Not given** ☐

2 Ms. Liang said the order was sent before April 26.
True ☐ **False** ☐ **Not given** ☐

3 Bettina has the shipping information.
True ☐ **False** ☐ **Not given** ☐

4 Ms. Liang won't be charged for the late delivery.
True ☐ **False** ☐ **Not given** ☐

5 Bettina will cancel her next order.
True ☐ **False** ☐ **Not given** ☐

✉ ∨ ✕

To: Jennifer Liang

Subject: Shipment of jeans overdue

Dear Ms. Liang,

I'm afraid we have still not received the shipment of jeans that was due to arrive on May 5. I contacted you on April 26, when you confirmed that the order had been sent and would arrive on time. Could you please send me the shipping information and tell me when the order will arrive?

I'm afraid we will have to make a deduction from your final invoice to compensate us for the late delivery.

I look forward to hearing from you,
Bettina Koehl

---

41 ✓ CHECKLIST

⚙ Preguntas indirectas ☐ **Aa** Negociación empresarial ☐ 🧩 Negociar educadamente ☐

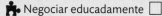

42 Destacar tu opinión

Existen muchas expresiones en inglés para destacar educadamente tu punto de vista. Son útiles cuando hay desacuerdos en el lugar de trabajo.

⚙ **Lenguaje** Marcadores de énfasis
Aa Vocabulario Desacuerdos en el trabajo
🧩 **Habilidad** Destacar tu opinión

42.1 PUNTO CLAVE MARCADORES DEL DISCURSO PARA ENFATIZAR

Existen diversas palabras y expresiones para destacar más tu posición sin ser maleducado.

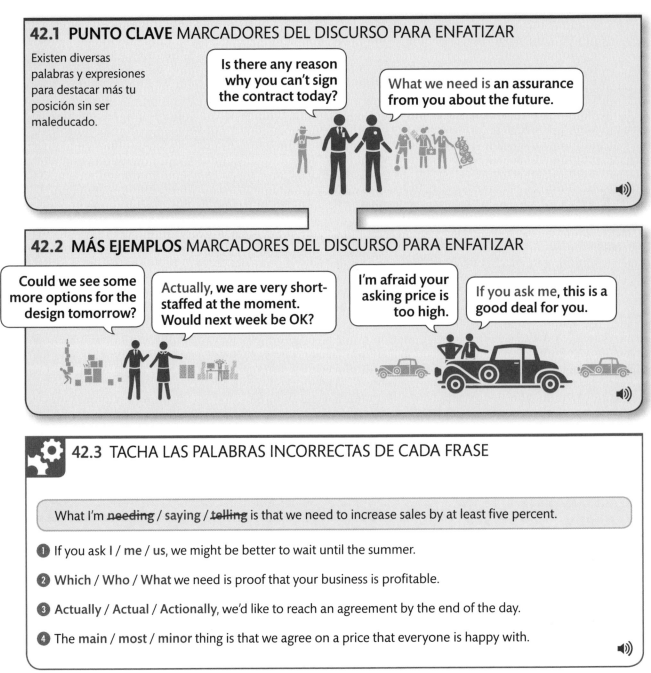

Is there any reason why you can't sign the contract today?

What we need is **an assurance from you about the future.**

42.2 MÁS EJEMPLOS MARCADORES DEL DISCURSO PARA ENFATIZAR

Could we see some more options for the design tomorrow?

Actually, we are very short-staffed at the moment. Would next week be OK?

I'm afraid your asking price is too high.

If you ask me, this is a good deal for you.

42.3 TACHA LAS PALABRAS INCORRECTAS DE CADA FRASE

What I'm ~~needing~~ / saying / ~~telling~~ is that we need to increase sales by at least five percent.

❶ If you ask I / **me** / us, we might be better to wait until the summer.

❷ Which / Who / **What** we need is proof that your business is profitable.

❸ **Actually** / Actual / Actionally, we'd like to reach an agreement by the end of the day.

❹ The **main** / most / minor thing is that we agree on a price that everyone is happy with.

42.4 ESCUCHA LA NEGOCIACIÓN Y LUEGO NUMERA LAS FRASES EN EL ORDEN EN QUE APARECEN

A If you ask me, these colors are quite bright already. ☐

B We need assurance that you can supply 1,000 umbrellas a month. ☐

C Actually, we're worried about the colors. 1

D The main thing is that our company logo should really stand out. ☐

E What I'm saying is I can send you samples in brighter colors next week. ☐

42.5 COMPLETA LOS ESPACIOS CON LAS PALABRAS DEL RECUADRO Y RESPONDE AL AUDIO EN VOZ ALTA

Is there any chance you could reduce your asking price?

I'm afraid not. If _____*you ask me*_____ , you won't find a lower price.

1 Are you ready to sign the contract?

Not quite. _____ some references from your customers.

2 I'm afraid I can't start on this job until December.

That's OK. The _____ we find the right person to do the work.

3 Is it possible for you to offer free delivery?

_____ , our quote already includes free delivery.

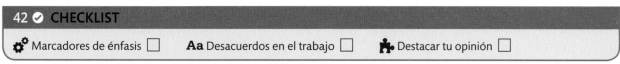

| What we need are | ~~you ask me~~ | Actually | main thing is that |

43 Debatir condiciones

Se suele utilizar el first conditional y el second conditional para negociar con clientes y colegas, mientras que el zero conditional sirve para hablar de verdades generales.

⚙ **Lenguaje** Condicionales
Aa Vocabulario Negociar y regatear
🧩 **Habilidad** Debatir posibilidades

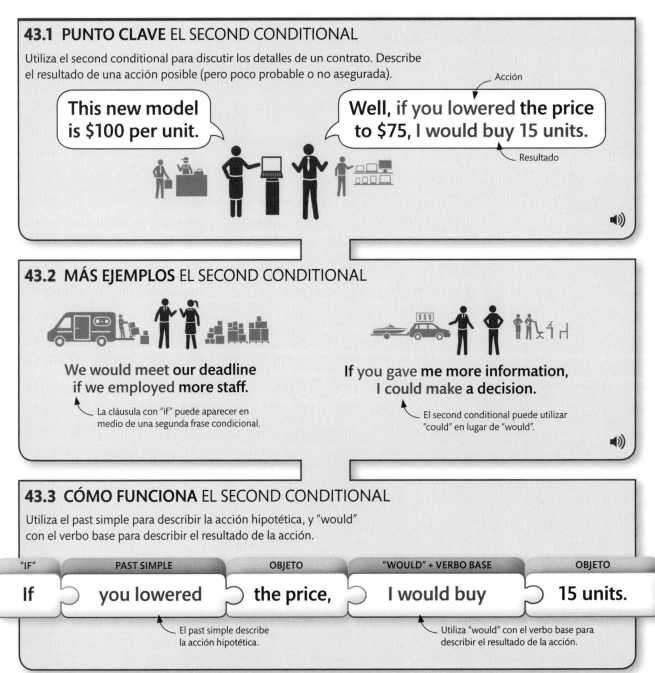

43.1 PUNTO CLAVE EL SECOND CONDITIONAL

Utiliza el second conditional para discutir los detalles de un contrato. Describe el resultado de una acción posible (pero poco probable o no asegurada).

Acción

This new model is $100 per unit.

Well, if you lowered the price to $75, I would buy 15 units.

Resultado

43.2 MÁS EJEMPLOS EL SECOND CONDITIONAL

We would meet our deadline if we employed more staff.

La cláusula con "if" puede aparecer en medio de una segunda frase condicional.

If you gave me more information, I could make a decision.

El second conditional puede utilizar "could" en lugar de "would".

43.3 CÓMO FUNCIONA EL SECOND CONDITIONAL

Utiliza el past simple para describir la acción hipotética, y "would" con el verbo base para describir el resultado de la acción.

"IF"	PAST SIMPLE	OBJETO	"WOULD" + VERBO BASE	OBJETO
If	you lowered	the price,	I would buy	15 units.

El past simple describe la acción hipotética.

Utiliza "would" con el verbo base para describir el resultado de la acción.

43.4 VUELVE A ESCRIBIR LAS FRASES EN SECOND CONDITIONAL CORRIGIENDO LOS ERRORES

If you give me a discount, I would book.
If you gave me a discount, I would book.

❶ I would placed an order if they delivered sooner.

_____

❷ If your product is cheaper, we would buy it.

_____

❸ If you moved the deadline, we could to meet it.

_____

❹ I work with them if they answered my questions.

_____

❺ If they would check their work, I would use them.

_____

◀))

43.5 ESCUCHA EL AUDIO Y RESPONDE A LAS PREGUNTAS

Diane negocia un precio mejor para el material de oficina con Josef, el agente comercial de una empresa de material de oficina.

Diane has talked to another company.
True ☑ **False** ☐ **Not given** ☐

❶ Diane is impressed with Office Hub's offers.
True ☐ **False** ☐ **Not given** ☐

❷ Diane has always bought stationery from Josef.
True ☐ **False** ☐ **Not given** ☐

❸ Josef can't offer free next-day delivery.
True ☐ **False** ☐ **Not given** ☐

❹ Josef offers free delivery after four days.
True ☐ **False** ☐ **Not given** ☐

❺ The two-for-one deal is a new offer.
True ☐ **False** ☐ **Not given** ☐

43.6 COMPLETA ESTAS FRASES EN SECOND CONDITIONAL Y DILAS EN VOZ ALTA

If you _offered_ (offer) a discount,
I _would order_ (order) now.

❶ We _____ (sign) the contract
if it _____ (be) clearer.

❷ I _____ (accept) the job offer
if the pay_____ (be) better.

❸ If they _____ (improve) the quality,
we_____ (place) an order.

❹ If I _____ (have) more time today,
I_____ (check) the contract.

◀))

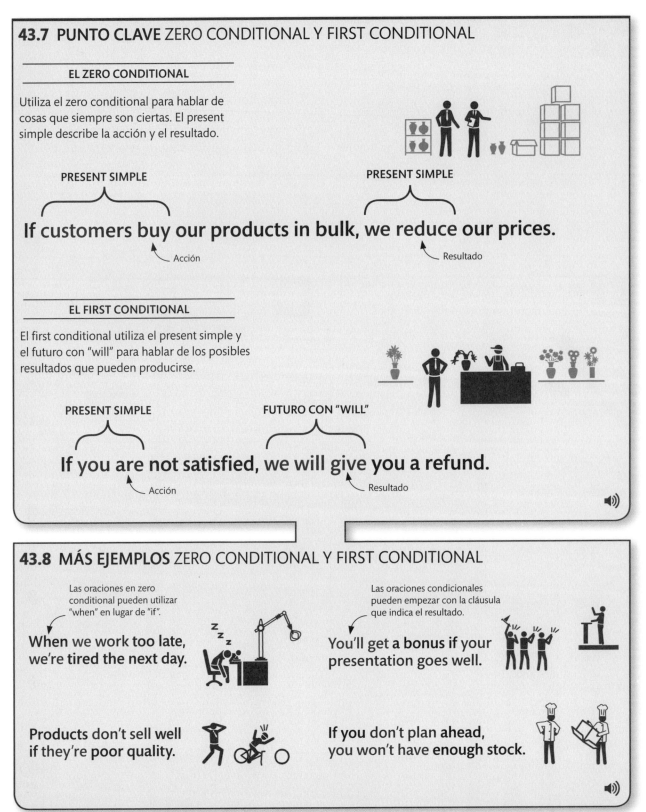

43.7 PUNTO CLAVE ZERO CONDITIONAL Y FIRST CONDITIONAL

EL ZERO CONDITIONAL

Utiliza el zero conditional para hablar de cosas que siempre son ciertas. El present simple describe la acción y el resultado.

PRESENT SIMPLE   PRESENT SIMPLE

If customers buy our products in bulk, we reduce our prices.

Acción   Resultado

EL FIRST CONDITIONAL

El first conditional utiliza el present simple y el futuro con "will" para hablar de los posibles resultados que pueden producirse.

PRESENT SIMPLE   FUTURO CON "WILL"

If you are not satisfied, we will give you a refund.

Acción   Resultado

43.8 MÁS EJEMPLOS ZERO CONDITIONAL Y FIRST CONDITIONAL

Las oraciones en zero conditional pueden utilizar "when" en lugar de "if".

When we work too late, we're tired the next day.

Las oraciones condicionales pueden empezar con la cláusula que indica el resultado.

You'll get a bonus if your presentation goes well.

Products don't sell well if they're poor quality.

If you don't plan ahead, you won't have enough stock.

43.9 VUELVE A ESCRIBIR LAS FRASES DE ZERO CONDITIONAL PONIENDO LAS PALABRAS EN SU ORDEN CORRECTO

| receive | day. | after | we | 3pm, | it | If | we | the | next | an | ship | order |

If we receive an order after 3pm, we ship it the next day.

① | you | by | a | credit | fee. | card, | we | If | charge | 2 | pay | percent |

_____

② | helpline | 24 | hours | Our | a | assistance. | if | day | is | you | open | need |

_____

③ | it. | we | are | When | our | quality, | we | high | mean | say | products |

_____

④ | get | overtime. | money | extra | I | every | month | if | I | work |

_____

◀))

43.10 COMPLETA LOS ESPACIOS CON LOS VERBOS EN LOS TIEMPOS CORRECTOS PARA FORMAR ORACIONES EN FIRST CONDITIONAL

If you ___*order*___ (order) today, we ___*will guarantee*___ (guarantee) delivery tomorrow.

① If you _____ (sign) the contract now, we _____ (begin) production next week.

② We _____ (charge) a 10 percent fee if you _____ (not pay) on time.

③ If you _____ (buy) more than 50 units, we _____ (give) you a 5 percent discount.

④ We _____ (send) you a contract if you _____ (want) to proceed.

◀))

43.11 PUNTO CLAVE RESUMEN DE ZERO, FIRST Y SECOND CONDITIONALS

ZERO CONDITIONAL

Utiliza el zero conditional para hablar de verdades generales y cosas que pasan siempre.

If employees are friendly to clients, they get better tips.

FIRST CONDITIONAL

Utiliza el first conditional para hablar de cosas que es probable que pasen.

If Lisa's meeting goes well, she will get a raise.

SECOND CONDITIONAL

Utiliza el second conditional para hablar de cosas que es poco probable que pasen, pero que continúan siendo posibles.

If Ethan was more polite to clients, he would be promoted.

🔊

43.12 CONECTA EL INICIO Y EL FINAL DE CADA FRASE

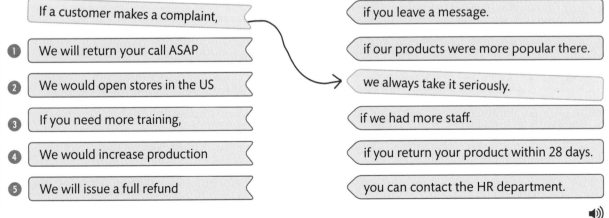

If a customer makes a complaint,   we always take it seriously.

1. We will return your call ASAP   if you leave a message.

2. We would open stores in the US   if our products were more popular there.

3. If you need more training,   you can contact the HR department.

4. We would increase production   if we had more staff.

5. We will issue a full refund   if you return your product within 28 days.

🔊

Business Tips

HOME | ENTRIES | ABOUT | CONTACT

EFFECTIVE NEGOTIATION

Many businesspeople are required to handle negotiations, but few receive any training in how to do it. Here are my top negotiating tips.

Before negotiating

- Do your research. Find out about your business partner. If you understand the other party, you'll understand his or her strengths and weaknesses.
- Before the meeting, decide what you can compromise on. For example, if your business partner offered you Deal A, would you accept it? If not, what would you accept?

During the negotiation

- If you haven't met your business partner before, hold the meeting face to face. Research has shown that meetings in person help to build rapport, so the other party will be more likely to meet you halfway.
- Don't talk more than is necessary. If you talk too much, you run the risk of revealing information that could be useful to the other party.
- Remember, if you keep the meeting professional and listen to each other, you'll reach the goal of any negotiation: finding common ground so that you can reach an agreement and close the deal.

Why might you need negotiation advice?

Few businesspeople are trained to negotiate.

❶ Why should you understand the other party?

_____

❷ What should you decide before negotiating?

_____

❸ Why are face-to-face meetings important?

_____

❹ Why shouldn't you talk too much?

_____

❺ What is the goal of any negotiation?

_____

---

43 ✓ CHECKLIST

⚙ Condicionales ☐　　**Aa** Negociar y regatear ☐　　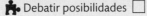 Debatir posibilidades ☐

Se utiliza el third conditional para hablar de un pasado irreal o de acontecimientos que no pasaron. Es útil para hablar sobre errores en el lugar de trabajo.

⚙ Lenguaje Third conditional
Aa Vocabulario Errores en el trabajo
✦ Habilidad Hablar sobre errores anteriores

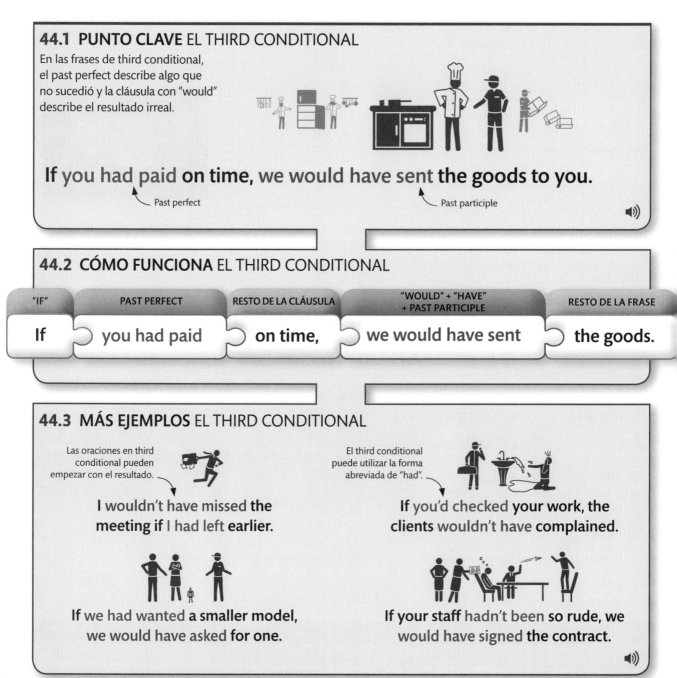

44.1 PUNTO CLAVE EL THIRD CONDITIONAL

En las frases de third conditional, el past perfect describe algo que no sucedió y la cláusula con "would" describe el resultado irreal.

If you had paid **on time, we would have sent the goods to you.**

Past perfect — Past participle

44.2 CÓMO FUNCIONA EL THIRD CONDITIONAL

"IF"	PAST PERFECT	RESTO DE LA CLÁUSULA	"WOULD" + "HAVE" + PAST PARTICIPLE	RESTO DE LA FRASE
If	you had paid	on time,	we would have sent	the goods.

44.3 MÁS EJEMPLOS EL THIRD CONDITIONAL

Las oraciones en third conditional pueden empezar con el resultado.

I wouldn't have missed the meeting if I had left earlier.

El third conditional puede utilizar la forma abreviada de "had".

If you'd checked your work, the clients wouldn't have complained.

If we had wanted a smaller model, we would have asked for one.

If your staff hadn't been so rude, we would have signed the contract.

If you ___had spoken___ (speak) more calmly, people ___would have listened___ (listen) to you.

❶ If he _____ (use) the correct figures, his report _____ (not be) so out of date.

❷ The boss _____ (not shout) if you _____ (admit) your mistake earlier.

❸ If you _____ (run) a spell check, the report _____ (not contain) so many errors.

❹ We _____ (not embarrass) ourselves if we _____ (research) local customs before our trip.

❺ I _____ (work) late last night if I _____ (know) our deadline was so soon.

🔊

44.5 ESCUCHA EL AUDIO Y MARCA LAS COSAS QUE REALMENTE PASARON

44.6 PUNTO CLAVE FIRST CONDITIONAL CON "UNLESS"

Utiliza "unless" en lugar de "if... not" en frases de first conditional. En oraciones con "unless", el resultado solo se produce si la acción no tiene lugar.

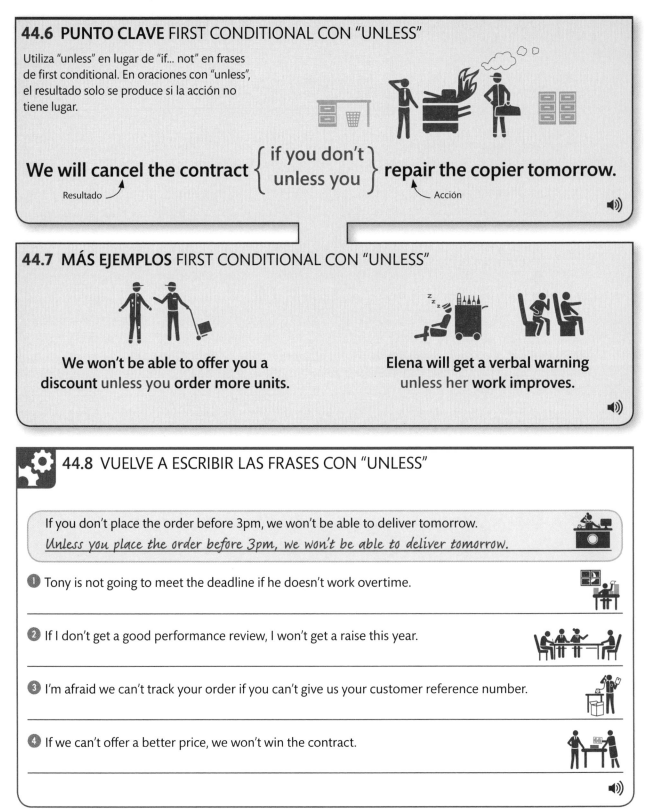

We will cancel the contract { if you don't / unless you } **repair the copier tomorrow.**

Resultado →   Acción

44.7 MÁS EJEMPLOS FIRST CONDITIONAL CON "UNLESS"

We won't be able to offer you a discount unless you **order more units.**

Elena will get a verbal warning unless her **work improves.**

44.8 VUELVE A ESCRIBIR LAS FRASES CON "UNLESS"

If you don't place the order before 3pm, we won't be able to deliver tomorrow.
Unless you place the order before 3pm, we won't be able to deliver tomorrow.

❶ Tony is not going to meet the deadline if he doesn't work overtime.
_____

❷ If I don't get a good performance review, I won't get a raise this year.
_____

❸ I'm afraid we can't track your order if you can't give us your customer reference number.
_____

❹ If we can't offer a better price, we won't win the contract.
_____

44.9 LEE EL INFORME Y RESPONDE A LAS PREGUNTAS

> Customer response to the product was as expected.
> **True** ☐ **False** ☑ **Not given** ☐

1 Avatar has been a competitor for a long time.
True ☐ **False** ☐ **Not given** ☐

2 It was known when Avatar would launch its product.
True ☐ **False** ☐ **Not given** ☐

3 Vivo knew how much Avatar's watch cost.
True ☐ **False** ☐ **Not given** ☐

4 The Avatar watch is cheaper than the Vivo watch.
True ☐ **False** ☐ **Not given** ☐

5 The new watch will be ready in six months.
True ☐ **False** ☐ **Not given** ☐

VIVO PRODUCT LAUNCH REPORT

Six months ago we launched our new smartwatch, the Vivo. Sales have been very disappointing and interest in the product is low.

WHY?

Our main competitor, Avatar, launched its new smartwatch one week after us. If we had known this, we would have launched our product later. Furthermore, they priced their smartwatch $50 lower than our product. We would have priced our watch lower if we had known about their competitive price.

WHAT NOW?

Unless we reduce the price of our product to match Avatar's watch, we won't make many sales. I suggest we reduce the price to $125. Furthermore, we need to develop a new, better product. We won't beat Avatar unless we can offer a more functional, better-looking watch.

---

44 ✅ CHECKLIST

⚙️ Third conditional ☐   **Aa** Errores en el trabajo ☐   🧩 Hablar sobre errores anteriores ☐

♻ REPASA LO QUE HAS APRENDIDO EN LAS UNIDADES 41–44

NUEVO LENGUAJE	FRASE DE EJEMPLO	☑	UNIDAD
PREGUNTAS INDIRECTAS	Could you tell me **when my order will be ready?**	☐	41.4
LA VOZ PASIVA Y LA EDUCACIÓN	It seems that a mistake **has been made.**	☐	41.9
DESTACAR TU OPINIÓN	What we need is **an assurance from you about the future.**	☐	42.1
SECOND CONDITIONAL	If you lowered **the price, I would order more units.**	☐	43.1
THIRD CONDITIONAL	If you had paid **on time, we would have delivered the goods.**	☐	44.1
FIRST CONDITIONAL CON "UNLESS"	We will cancel the contract unless **you repair the copier tomorrow.**	☐	44.6

Respuestas

1.2 🔊
1. Hi, Katherine. I think I **met you at the Market Max conference**.
2. I'm not sure whether you **have met each other before**.
3. Yes, we met in Barcelona. **It's great to see you again.**
4. You must be Gloria from the design team. **Guvan told me about your great work.**
5. This is Brian from customer services. **Brian, meet Tonya. She's joining our team.**

1.3 🔊
1. Did we **meet** at a conference?
2. Really good to **see** you again.
3. Roula, meet Maria, **our** new assistant.
4. I'd like to **introduce** you to Karl.
5. Have you two **met** each other before?

1.4
1. False
2. True
3. Not given
4. Not given
5. True

1.6
1. Shy
2. Good ones
3. Ex-colleagues
4. Say sorry
5. Unprofessional
6. Their eyes
7. Your business card

1.7 🔊
1. Hi James. I'm Vanisha. I don't think **we've met** before.
2. Ashley, I'd like **to** introduce you to my colleague Neil.
3. I **am** enjoying the presentations. Are you?
4. Nice to meet you Bethany. How do you **do**?

1.8 🔊
1. Hello Frank. **Are you enjoying** the conference?
2. Wilfred, I'd like you to **meet** Roger, our new press officer.
3. Serena, it's really great to **see** you again after so long.
4. I usually enjoy workshops, but I am not **finding** this one interesting.

2.3 🔊
1. They **were beginning** to sell more when the shop suddenly closed last year.
2. I **lost** my job when the factory closed last December.
3. I was delighted when I **got** promoted to senior manager in 2015.
4. We moved here when my wife **found** a new job two years ago.
5. I **was training** to be a chef when I was given this award.
6. When I worked 90 hours a week, I **felt** exhausted all the time.
7. When I was a photographer, I **met** a lot of famous people through my work.

2.5 🔊
1. I was looking for another job.
2. I was wondering if you could help.
3. Were you working as a waiter?
4. They weren't employing young people.
5. I didn't enjoy my last job.
6. Did you work in a hotel?

2.8 🔊
1. He **has taken** 15 days off sick this year and it is only May!
2. Julia has a lot of experience. She **has managed** this department for years.
3. They **have employed** more than 300 people over the years.
4. John **has trained** lots of young employees across a few different teams.
5. I'm so happy! I **have finished** my apprenticeship at last.
6. My manager **has approved** my vacation days. I'm going to Italy in July.

2.9
1. True
2. False
3. Not given
4. True
5. Not given

2.10 🔊
1. I **was driving** taxis when I saw this job advertised.
2. I **have managed** accounts for this company for seven years.
3. I **bought** my first business in 2009.
4. I was studying in college when I **saw** this job.
5. They **have invested** in this company since 2010.
6. In 2014, I **sold** the company to an investor.

4.3
1. I used to travel to work by car.
2. She's used to giving big presentations.
3. I'll get used to my new job eventually.
4. We didn't use to get paid a bonus.
5. Did he use to work in marketing?

4.4
- (A) 2
- (B) 1
- (C) 4
- (D) 3

4.5 🔊
1. We used to finish at noon on Fridays.
2. She didn't use to be so serious.
3. I am used to working for a strict boss.
4. Did you use to work in London?

4.6 🔊
1. I got used to long hours in my first job.
2. He didn't use to have a law degree.
3. I am used to working long hours.
4. You didn't use to work such long hours.
5. Did he use to work in a bank?

4.7
1. True
2. Not given
3. False
4. False
5. True

4.8 🔊
1. I'm not used to starting at 6am!
2. Yes, what a disappointment!
3. Yes, please. It looks delicious.
4. That's a very short commute!
5. Yes, I think it's going to rain.

4.9 🔊
1. When I was young, I **didn't use to** like mushrooms.
2. My grandfather **used to** walk four miles to school every morning.
3. Are you **used to** your new job yet?
4. I grew up in Florida, so I **am used to** the heat.
5. We **used to** go to the south of France every year.

05

5.3 🔊
1. We have got to ask **for some support on this project**.
2. You must put the finished **proposal on my desk tomorrow**.
3. We must not forget **to look after this project while he's away**.
4. I have to help Sami produce **a report about recycling**.
5. You don't have **to complete it today**.

5.4 🔊
1. We need to increase sales to Europe.
2. We can't reveal our new product yet.
3. You don't have to work late.
4. I will need the accounts by tomorrow.
5. We have got to find a new IT manager.
6. You need to produce a spreadsheet.
7. We must reach our sales target.

5.5
1. True
2. False
3. False
4. False
5. Not given

5.7 🔊
1. Could you answer my phone?
2. Would you call the supplier?
3. We have to finish today.
4. Would you book a meeting?
5. Could you send this today?

5.8 🔊
1. **Could** you deliver this letter for me, please?
2. **Would** you show the new employee around the office?
3. Jess, I **need to** leave early today. Could you let Philippe know?

5.9
1. Not given
2. True
3. True
4. Not given
5. True

07

7.4 🔊
1. We **changed** our logo because a lot of people **had complained** about it.
2. Some of our goods **had arrived** broken, so we **asked** for a refund.
3. There **were** problems in the warehouse because our manager **had resigned**.
4. Sales of umbrellas **were** poor because we **had had** a dry summer.
5. Our clients **were not** happy because we **had missed** our deadline.
6. Yasmin's presentation **had gone** very well, so I **gave** her a promotion.
7. Our sales **increased** because we **had launched** a new product range.

7.5
2

7.7 🔊
1. The purpose of this report is **to** review our sales figures for the last quarter.
2. Our **principal** recommendation is to complete the sale of the downtown store.
3. The **following** report presents the results of extensive customer satisfaction research.
4. Our main client **stated** that the recent changes were beneficial for his business.

7.8 🔊

① As can be seen in the table, **the figures for this period were excellent.**
② It is clear from the research **that there were a number of problems.**
③ A number of focus groups **were consulted for this report.**
④ The purpose of this report is **to present the findings of our survey.**

7.9 🔊

① The focus group clients had all **used** both the original and new products.
② The following chart **compares** the sales figures for the two periods.
③ We **asked** the customers who had complained why they didn't like the change.
④ The **purpose** of this report is to present the results of our online trial.
⑤ We started this online trial after our store costs had **risen** by 10 percent.

08

8.2 🔊

① Yes, we'll give you a full refund.
② Yes, it's AMLGW14.
③ OK. No problem.
④ Our courier has been having difficulties.
⑤ I'm very sorry to hear that, Mrs. Singh.
⑥ Yes, we'll send you a new one tomorrow.

8.3
Ⓐ 3
Ⓑ 1
Ⓒ 6
Ⓓ 5
Ⓔ 2
Ⓕ 4

8.4 🔊

① We'll **look** into the problem for you.
② We'll **give** you a discount voucher.
③ Could you hold the **line** a moment?
④ Let's see **what** we can do.

8.8 🔊

① The customers **have been waiting** for us to contact them.
② Our engineers **have been working** on the line for two days.
③ What **have** you **been doing** to solve the problem?
④ I **have been watching** your program and I want to complain.
⑤ We **have been repairing** the broken cables this morning.
⑥ They **have been updating** my software and now it doesn't work.

8.9
① True ② Not given ③ True
④ False ⑤ Not given

10

10.2
③

10.3 🔊

① I just wanted to **check** that you will be able to make it to the meeting.
② Don't worry if you have any questions. Just let me **know**.
③ I'm **copying** Maxine in on this as she may have some more information.
④ How **about** coming to the restaurant with us this evening?
⑤ I was **wondering** if you and Ana could come to the meeting tomorrow.
⑥ Give me a call if you can't **make** the presentation at 10 o'clock

---

11

11.2
① Presente ② Futuro
③ Futuro ④ Presente

11.3
Respuestas modelo
① The delivery van was involved in an accident yesterday.
② The company is receiving new stock tomorrow.
③ She is hoping to confirm a new delivery date next week.
④ She can cancel her order online.
⑤ Yasmin should contact Janice if she has any questions.

11.4 🔊
① to hesitate ② to prefer ③ to obtain
④ to confirm ⑤ to inform
⑥ to contact ⑦ to request

11.6
① I am hoping
② We are currently waiting
③ we are expecting
④ I was wondering
⑤ I assure you
⑥ We will be doing
⑦ please do not hesitate to contact me

11.7 🔊
① I was **wondering** if you would meet the clients at their factory.
② We **are** having difficulties with deliveries due to the weather.
③ Will you be **paying** for the order by bank transfer or credit card?
④ We are aiming **to** finish the redecorating by next Wednesday.

11.8 🔊

① We are still waiting to hear from our supplier.
② I was wondering if you could call me back.
③ Will you be attending the progress meeting next week?

12

12.3 🔊

① I'll look **into** the problem now.
② The printer has run **out** of ink.
③ I need to **catch** up with you.
④ Sorry, I have to hang **up** now.
⑤ Could you deal **with** this order?
⑥ I'll **look** into Mr. Li's query.
⑦ My client just **hung** up on me!

12.4

Ⓐ 6
Ⓑ 3
Ⓒ 5
Ⓓ 1
Ⓔ 2
Ⓕ 4

12.5 🔊

① bring up ② turn up ③ chill out
④ fill out ⑤ figure out

12.8 🔊

① James, can you **pass on** the message to Zane?
② Welcome to Jo's. Please **fill** the visitor's form **out**.
③ Can you stand at the exit and **hand** the leaflets **out**?
④ **Put** a helmet **on** before entering the site.
⑤ Before I update the software, **back** your files **up**.

12.9 🔊

① Could you please **pass** the message **on** to Gary?
② I have an important meeting, so I **put** a suit **on** this morning.
③ Howard, we should really **fix** a meeting **up** for this week.
④ After a busy day in the office, I usually **chill out** at home.

14

14.2

① True
② False
③ False
④ Not given
⑤ False

14.3 🔊

① Over the last year, an exciting new line has been **developed**.
② This design **was** patented in 1938. Nobody has ever managed to make a better product!
③ Their new line **is being** launched next Saturday. Everyone is talking about it.
④ Our factory floor **was** cleaned before the CEO visited. He was happy things looked good!
⑤ You don't need to worry about dinner. The food **is** cooked to order so that it is fresh.
⑥ The first cars made in this factory **were** sold in the UK in 1972, and worldwide the next year.
⑦ Our original designers **were** influenced by Japanese artists.
⑧ To prepare for the launch, advertising posters **are being** put up around town as we speak.

14.6 🔊

① Their new products **are being promoted** on TV now.
② 80,000 packets **are produced** in the factory each week.
③ A thousand new cars **will be sold** next week.
④ Our latest gadget **was invented** by Ronnie Angel.
⑤ The production line **is stopped** during the summer.
⑥ Great advances in design **have been made** recently.

14.7 🔊

① All the cars are checked by someone before they leave the factory.
② The new photo app for professional artists was invented by Maxine.
③ All Carl Osric's books were bought by customers on the publication date.
④ All our vegetarian ingredients are bought from the market by Ron.
⑤ All of the invoices are checked by Samantha before they are sent out.

14.8

Ⓐ 3
Ⓑ 1
Ⓒ 6
Ⓓ 2
Ⓔ 7
Ⓕ 8
Ⓖ 4
Ⓗ 5

14.10 🔊

① These flowers must have been bought today.
② They can't be marked down yet! They're new.
③ This picture couldn't have been drawn by Sanjit.
④ The price shouldn't have been accepted.
⑤ These glasses must be packaged carefully.
⑥ Faults in the product shouldn't be ignored.
⑦ The oven has been turned up.

14.11

1. The chassis parts are placed on the **assembly line**.
2. The engine and radiator **are lifted** by a robot as they are very heavy.
3. The engine and radiator **are secured** to the chassis by an assembly worker.
4. The bodywork is fully **assembled and welded** on a separate line.
5. The assembled bodywork is inspected before **being painted** by a robot.
6. The chassis and bodywork are joined together before the vehicle **is checked**.

15

15.3

OPINIÓN:
awesome, **awful**
TAMAÑO:
enormous, **tiny**
EDAD:
modern, **out-dated**
COLOR:
green, **red**
NACIONALIDAD:
Swiss, **Indian**
MATERIAL:
wooden, **fabric**

15.4

1. Have you seen the ugly, plastic desks?
2. We're launching the new, metallic range tomorrow.
3. Would you prefer these tiny, diamond ones?

15.5

1. B 2. A 3. A
4. A 5. B

15.7

1. I'm interested in that **incredible** modern device we saw at the sales fair.
2. Our competitors are still selling those really **ugly**, large cotton shirts.
3. The office has a **friendly**, old black cat that visits regularly.
4. Frances, have you seen these Peruvian **silver** earrings that I brought back?
5. Did you get one of those new **plastic** business cards?
6. A lot of customers have been asking for the **new** red version.
7. My boss has asked me to design a small, **paper** package for the product.
8. I have bought some new **leather** chairs for the boardroom.

15.8

1. True
2. Not given
3. False
4. False
5. False

15.9

1. We offer great, **delicious** food that people can afford.
2. Look at that **enormous** new billboard across the street.
3. I love buying **antique** wooden furniture for the office.
4. My boss drives a tiny **green** car to work. It's definitely easy to spot!
5. We aim to offer awesome, **friendly** customer service at all times.

17

17.3

EXTREMOS:
awful, **fantastic**, **tiny**, **disgusting**, **enormous**
ABSOLUTOS:
unique, **impossible**, **right**, **perfect**, **wrong**
CLASIFICADORES:
organic, **digital**, **industrial**, **electronic**, **chemical**

17.4

1. True
2. True
3. Not given
4. False
5. False
6. Not given

17.7

1. The new gadget is completely digital.
2. This draft design is practically perfect.
3. The client said it was totally fantastic.
4. His decision to invest was entirely right.
5. This area of town is largely industrial.

17.9

1. mainly European
2. pretty confident
3. absolutely delicious

18

18.2

1. Is the office big enough for us?
2. The delivery times are too slow.
3. Are these shelves strong enough?

18.3
1. B
2. A
3. A
4. A
5. B

18.4
1. False
2. True
3. Not given
4. True
5. False

18.6 🔊
1. It's such a great product.
2. The meeting was so boring.
3. His news was such a surprise.
4. My boss is so ambitious.
5. Their phones are so cheap.
6. Her company is so big!
7. Our launch was such a surprise!

18.7 🔊
1. The slogan is far **too** complicated. We need to simplify it.
2. They have created **such** a brilliant poster campaign.
3. We haven't done **enough** market research. We need to understand our consumers.
4. Our supervisor is **such** a creative person. She designed our new logo.
5. Marion is **so** persuasive when she delivers a sales pitch.

19

19.3 🔊
1. You must tell your boss it will be late.
2. You shouldn't start work so early.
3. You shouldn't work such long shifts.
4. You should take a walk outside right now.

19.4 🔊
1. My wife said I **could try** yoga and relaxation techniques.
2. You **should stop** working right away if you feel sick.
3. You **ought to take** a break if you're really tired.
4. You **shouldn't feel** exhausted at the beginning of the week.
5. You **must delegate** some of your work to your assistant.

19.5 🔊
1. You **ought to** relax more.
2. You **must stop** taking work home every day.
3. He **could try** to delegate more tasks.
4. You **shouldn't worry** so much about work.
5. She **should talk** to her colleagues.
6. He **ought to quit** his job if he hates it.

19.6
1. No
2. Sí
3. Sí
4. Sí

19.10 🔊
1. What about taking a break?
2. What about buying better equipment?
3. What about training new employees?
4. Why don't we take a break?
5. Why don't we buy better equipment?
6. Why don't we train new employees?

19.11 🔊
1. Why don't we **buy** new chairs?
2. Why don't we **go** for a walk outside?
3. What about **drinking** less coffee?
4. Why don't we **provide** free fruit?
5. What about **making** a list of your tasks?
6. What about **delegating** this to Jo?
7. Why don't we **ask** Paul to help us?

19.12
1. True
2. False
3. True
4. False
5. True
6. False

21

21.3 🔊
1. She doesn't like meeting new people. She **can't** work in the HR department.
2. Shaun **can** work really well with new employees, so he should help run our training course.
3. Have you seen her brilliant photographs? She **can** create our posters and flyers.
4. Lydia failed her driving test, so, unfortunately, she **can't** drive the delivery van.

21.5 🔊
1. Peter **couldn't** use the new coffee machine. He didn't know how it worked.
2. Varinder **couldn't** write reports very well at first, but she can now that she's had more practice.
3. No one in the office **could** read his handwriting. It was awful.
4. Bill was the only person who **couldn't** figure out how to use the photocopier.

21.7 🔊
1. Futura
2. Pasada
3. Futura
4. Pasada
5. Futura

21.8

1. True
2. Not given
3. True
4. False
5. False

21.9

1. James's team was weak, but he's trained them well and now they **can** do anything.
2. We think that you are really creative and **would** make a great addition to the PR team.
3. I don't know what is wrong with me today. I **can't** get anything finished.
4. My confidence is much better now. Before, I **couldn't** talk in public.

22.3

1. **Although** I attended the training session, I'm not sure I learned very much.
2. You got a high score for the IT test, and you've done **equally** well on the team-building course.
3. Team A built a small boat out of plastic bottles, **whereas** Team B used wood to make theirs.
4. The training day is a great way to learn new skills. It's **also** a good way to get to know people.

22.4

1. Walked across bridges high in the air
2. Overcome fear and help each other
3. The tallest and the most scared
4. Disagreed with each other
5. Work more slowly and listen to their teammates

22.6

1. The course taught us how to lead a team. As a consequence, I feel more confident.
2. I'd never ridden a horse before. For this reason, I was quite scared during the training.
3. Team Lion completed the challenge first. Consequently, they all received medals.

22.7

1. Team A had to build a cardboard tower, **while Team B had to bake a cake.**
2. Although I liked going to the beach, **I didn't enjoy swimming in the ocean.**
3. I love learning new things. **As a result, I really enjoyed the training day.**
4. Team building is a good way to learn new skills **and it's also a chance to relax.**

22.8

1. Not given
2. True
3. False
4. Not given
5. True

22.9

Respuestas modelo
1. This course will teach you new skills. It will help you to get to know each other, **too.**
2. **Although** Team B completed the task first, they had some major communication problems.
3. By doing this task, we'll not only identify the team's weaknesses, but **also** its strengths.
4. Team A worked together very well. Team B were **equally** cooperative.

23.4

1. Mara has offered **to organize** the accommodation for our guests.
2. I keep **suggesting** that our company should organize a golf day, but my boss disagrees.
3. We like **to offer** our clients a wide range of food at our conferences.
4. I enjoy **helping** out at company open days because I get to meet lots of people.
5. Before I start planning, I usually make a list of all the customers I want **to invite.**
6. I expect **to stay** late tonight to help Martina decorate the conference hall.

23.5

Respuestas modelo
1. The SmartTech Fair opened in 1987.
2. It is helping us to live healthier lives.
3. They could shape the future of the car industry.
4. You can register your interest online.
5. You can buy tickets from the SmartTech website.

23.8

1. We stopped holding breakfast meetings **because few people attended them.**
2. We regret to announce **that there will be some job losses.**
3. I'm sure Shona will remember **to book the conference room.**
4. Sahib went on working **until midnight in order to finish the report.**

23.9

1. False
2. Not given
3. False
4. Not given
5. True
6. True

23.10 🔊

1. I remember meeting him in Tokyo.
2. I was supposed to book a nice hotel room.
3. I wanted to book a nice hotel room.
4. She was supposed to book a nice hotel room.
5. She wanted to book a nice hotel room.
6. We remember meeting him in Tokyo.
7. We wanted to book a nice hotel room.
8. They remember meeting him in Tokyo.
9. They wanted to book a nice hotel room.

23.14 🔊

1 My boss asked me **to arrange** a meeting with our clients.
2 Our clients **asked us** to visit them in Paris.
3 We expect all our staff **to arrive** on time.
4 We **invited all our clients** to attend our end-of-year party.
5 I expect my manager **to give** me a promotion soon.

23.15 🔊

1 Our clients expect to receive excellent service.
2 My boss invited me to attend a conference.
3 My business degree allowed me to get this job.

25.4 🔊

1 She said she paid the invoice.
2 He said he would pay the invoice.
3 He said he would arrange a meeting.
4 He said he was arranging a meeting.
5 She said she had finished writing the report.
6 She said she would finish writing the report.

25.5 🔊

1 She **said (that) she would interview the candidates**.
2 He **said (that) he met the CEO on Monday**. / He **said (that) he'd met the CEO on Monday**.
3 He **said (that) he could book the meeting room**.
4 She **said (that) she was writing a press release**.
5 He **said (that) he could use design software**.

25.8

Ⓐ 2
Ⓑ 4
Ⓒ 5
Ⓓ 1
Ⓔ 3

25.10 🔊

1 She said that she didn't understand the email.
2 He said there was a problem with his computer.
3 She said we need to reply to those customers.

25.14 🔊

1 Sharon **confirmed** that the sales figures would be ready by 5pm.
2 Lilia **promised** that she would stay late to help me finish the report.
3 Mr. Lee **announced** that we had beaten our sales target for the year.
4 Ben **complained** that the coffee from the machine tasted awful.
5 She **suggested** that I could ask my boss about a raise.

26

26.4 🔊

1 He asked me why I was late again.
2 Lara asked me where the meeting was.
3 She asked me why I had missed the interview.
4 He asked me who had taken the minutes.

26.5

1 True
2 False
3 True
4 Not given
5 True
6 False
7 Not given

26.6

1 Not given
2 False
3 True
4 Not given
5 False
6 Not given

26.7 🔊

1 The boss is angry with Max. He told him to **do his work** before he leaves.
2 Mr. Tan promised that I would **get promoted** to manager if I worked hard.
3 Could you **do me a favor**? Could you make 20 copies of this, please?
4 Can I **make a suggestion**? Finish the proposal first, then work on the spreadsheet.
5 Paola said that she usually **gets home** from work at 6:30pm.
6 Paul said that he **had an appointment** with his boss, but he was really late.

26.9 🔊

1 She asked (me) what the consumer feedback was.

2 He asked (me) whether I had a strategy. / He asked (me) if I had a strategy.

3 She asked (me) who was getting promoted.

4 He asked (me) what the main points were.

5 She asked (me) if he was the new marketing manager. / She asked (me) whether he was the new marketing manager.

27

27.2 🔊

1 We'll have to reduce the price. Very few customers have bought our new jeans.

2 So few people pay by check these days that we no longer accept this form of payment.

3 Unfortunately, we've had few inquiries about our new spa treatments.

27.4 🔊

1 Unfortunately, there is **little** chance of us winning this contract.

2 I have **a few** ideas that I really think could improve our brand image.

3 There is still **a little** time left before we need to submit the report.

4 Kelvin has **little** understanding of accountancy.

5 So **few** people have bought this TV that we're going to stop production.

27.6 🔊

1 All you can do is apologize for your mistake.

2 All I expect is for staff to complete their tasks.

3 I'm sure all will be well in the interview.

4 All I want is a raise.

5 We have all the information we need.

27.7 🔊

1 The only thing we need is a photo.

2 We have some money.

3 We have some time.

4 Not many people like Mr. Jenkins.

5 Bertha is an expert in IT.

6 Some people like Mr. Jenkins.

7 We don't have much time.

27.8

1 Not given

2 False

3 True

4 True

5 False

6 False

28

28.4 🔊

1 Who is the manager?

2 What's in the report?

3 Who answers the telephone?

4 Who approves annual vacation?

5 What is the deadline?

6 Who wrote the ad?

7 Who will take questions?

8 What are the objectives?

9 What's the complaint about?

28.5 🔊

1 What are our most popular products?

2 Do you need to book the meeting?

3 Who answers customer emails?

4 Did Savannah write this report?

5 What is our lowest price?

6 Is James on vacation next week?

28.8 🔊

1 You haven't read my proposal, **have you**?

2 Sean could give the presentation, **couldn't he**?

3 Zoe got promoted, **didn't she**?

4 We're not ready for the conference, **are we**?

5 You work in marketing, **don't you**?

28.9 🔊

1 Alice would know the answer, **wouldn't she**?

2 I'm not dressed formally enough, **am I**?

3 You've worked in Berlin, **haven't you**?

4 They could tell us before 6pm, **couldn't they**?

5 Kate's going to Bangkok, **isn't she**?

6 I should double check the figures, **shouldn't I**?

7 Richard didn't get a raise, **did he**?

28.11

1 Not given

2 False

3 False

4 True

5 True

28.12 🔊

1 What was the name of the company? I didn't **hear**.

2 **Who** is working on the project for the new office?

3 You identified the mistake, **didn't you**?

4 Could you repeat that, please? I didn't **catch** it.

5 **What** is the theme of this year's conference?

30.2 🔊
1 **The** deadline for applications is Friday.
2 This job is based in **the** Berlin office.
3 We are recruiting **a** new designer.
4 I've got **an** interview for a new job.
5 **The** application form for this job is long.
6 Please complete **the** form on our website.
7 **The** ideal candidate enjoys teamwork.
8 There's an ad for **an** English teacher.

30.3
Ⓐ 2
Ⓑ 1
Ⓒ 4
Ⓓ 3
Ⓔ 5

30.6 🔊
1 The jobs I'm really interested in are based in Los Angeles. They're in IT.
2 The people who interviewed me for the job were really nice. They were the managers.
3 Clients can be very demanding. The clients I met today had lots of complaints.

30.9 🔊
1 I often travel to **Hong Kong** on business.
2 **Zenith Accounting** has three job openings.
3 I have a meeting with **the company director**.
4 He works for **the World Health Organization**.
5 I'm a strong candidate because I speak **Russian**.

30.10
1 Europe
2 an opening
3 Flight attendants
4 The hours
5 build a career

30.11 🔊
1 Your meeting is with **the HR manager**.
2 We're recruiting more staff in **France**.
3 I'm looking for a job as **an education consultant**.
4 We need someone who can speak **Italian**.
5 **Omnitech** is advertising several vacancies in its marketing department.
6 I work in **the sales department** of a large company.

31.3 🔊
1 In our department, we focus **on** sales and marketing.
2 Katrina graduated **from** college with a degree in Biological Sciences.
3 Our technicians are fully trained **in** all aspects of health and safety.
4 I've applied **for** a job in the IT department of a big company in Los Angeles.

31.4
1 Not given
2 Not given
3 True
4 False
5 True
6 True

31.5 🔊
1 to be responsible for something
2 to look forward to something
3 to amount to
4 to apply for a job
5 to be passionate about
6 experience in something

31.8 🔊
1 When can I expect to hear **from** you about the job?
2 Unfortunately, there has been a rise **in** complaints from customers.
3 I work **for** the CEO of a big IT company. I'm her assistant.
4 I heard **about** the job through a friend who works at the company.
5 Our profits went up last year. There was a rise **of** about five percent.

31.9
1 résumé
2 reliable
3 team
4 skills
5 salary
6 referee

31.10

Dear Mr. Khan,

I am writing to **apply for** the **position** of head web designer with your company.

I have **experience in** managing large commercial websites. Last year, sales from the website that I designed for a major online store **amounted to** more than $6 million.

I am eager to develop my **skills** and broaden my knowledge of other **industries**. I believe this job would be a fantastic **opportunity** for me, and I'd add a great deal to your company. I am enthusiastic and **passionate about** being at the cutting edge of web development. I'm also very **reliable** and I enjoy working in a team.

I have attached my **résumé** and details of my referees. I look forward to **hearing from** you.

Yours sincerely,
Amy Quah

32.2 ◀))

❶ The office that I work in **is modern and open-plan**.
❷ The customers who gave us **feedback were all very positive**.
❸ One thing that I don't like **about my job is the long hours**.
❹ The people who are on my team **say they enjoy working with me**.
❺ The product that we've just launched **is already selling very well**.

32.3 ◀))

❶ The main thing **that** I hope to gain by working here is more experience.
❷ The area **that** I live in is very close to the bus routes into the business district.
❸ The tasks **that** I perform best usually involve customer relations.
❹ The exams **that** I passed last year mean that I am now fully qualified.
❺ The person **who** I have learned the most from is my college professor.
❻ The countries **that** order most of our umbrellas are in Europe.
❼ The achievement **that** I am most proud of is winning "employee of the year."

32.5 ◀))

❶ I have completed all the training, **which** means you wouldn't need to train me.
❷ My boss, **who** is very talented, always encourages me not to work too late.
❸ IT development, **which** is my favorite part of the job, is very fast-paced.
❹ My co-workers, **who** are all older than me, have taught me a lot.
❺ I worked at the reception desk, **which** taught me how to deal with customers.
❻ I take my job very seriously, **which** means I always follow the company dress code.
❼ In my last job, **which** was in Paris, I learned to speak French fluently.

32.6

Ⓐ 3
Ⓑ 6
Ⓒ 5
Ⓓ 2
Ⓔ 1
Ⓕ 4

32.8 ◀))

❶ The place **where** I can concentrate the best is at home.
❷ The person **whose** career inspires me the most is Muhammad Ali.
❸ Last year, **when** I was an intern, I learned how to give presentations.
❹ My parents, **who** are both doctors, inspired me to study medicine.

32.9 ◀))

❶ My current salary, **which is** $20,000 a year, is not very high.
❷ The thing **that gets** me excited about my job is seeing our products on sale.
❸ Yes. I always know **who has** the responsibility for getting a task done on my team.
❹ I can identify things **that need** to change, to make your business more efficient.
❺ My boss, **who is** quite flexible, would allow me to leave after six weeks' notice.

34.3 ◀))

❶ to live up to something
❷ to look forward to something
❸ to come across as something
❹ to get away with something
❺ to run out of something
❻ to keep up with someone

34.4

❶ True
❷ Not given
❸ False
❹ Not given
❺ True
❻ False

34.5
1 Please could you **come** up with a proposal on how to improve punctuality?
2 I can't **keep** up with Thom when he goes through the accounts. He's too quick.
3 Liza comes **across** as very serious, but outside of work she's a lot of fun.
4 The two interns don't get **along** with each other very well. They don't see eye to eye.
5 I'm really looking **forward** to welcoming our new clients to London.

34.8 🔊
1 Can you **take it on**?
2 We're **giving them away**.
3 Let's **look it up** on social media.
4 I think we should **call it off**.
5 Can we **talk it over**?

34.9
1 Needs a modern image
2 Advertise the event
3 Increase awareness of the company
4 Tariq volunteers to do it

34.10 🔊
1 I need the report today. Please don't let **me down**.
2 Josef complains a lot. I can't put **up** with it.
3 I'm looking forward **to** finishing my training.
4 If you have a problem, we can talk **it** over.
5 Don't look down **on** Rachel. She's still new.
6 Our company is giving **away** three cars.

35

35.3 🔊
1 Tanya has used up all her leave.
She won't go on vacation this year.
2 Toby is great at managing people.
He will be promoted to lead his team.
3 Josef doesn't get along with his boss.
He might not stay here much longer.
4 We have some meetings in Japan.
You may have to go to Tokyo.

35.4 🔊
1 We can't hire any staff at the moment, so you might not get an assistant until May.
2 You're great with new staff, so we may ask you to become a mentor.
3 It's been a bad year for the company, so you won't get a raise.
4 This report needs to be finished by Friday. You might need to work overtime.
5 If Lucinda's work doesn't improve, we may have to fire her.

35.5
1 True
2 False
3 True
4 False
5 True
6 False
7 True
8 False

35.7 🔊
1 He **definitely won't** get the job.
2 You probably **won't need** any training.
3 We **will probably hire** some more staff soon.
4 She **will definitely** get a raise.
5 I **definitely won't** move to the head office.
6 I **probably won't** go on vacation this year.

35.8 🔊
1 We will **probably** get a thank-you gift.
2 I **definitely** won't change jobs this year.
3 You will **definitely** get a bonus.
4 We **probably** won't invite him to the meeting.

35.9
1 may happen
2 might not happen
3 probably won't happen
4 definitely won't happen

37

37.2
1 False
2 True
3 True
4 False
5 Not given

37.3 🔊
1 To sum up, we have a very bright future.
2 Do feel free to ask me any questions.
3 Let's turn to the predicted sales figures.
4 So, we've looked at all the main alternatives.

37.4 🔊
1 hard drive
2 pointer
3 power button
4 slides
5 cable
6 lectern
7 remote

37.5 🔊
① Be careful of the **cable** in front of the stage.
② I will return to the **lectern** to answer questions.
③ If you follow my **pointer**, you can see the graph.
④ I'll use my **remote** to forward to the final slide.
⑤ This projector's noisy. I'll turn the **power button** off.

37.6
① False
② Not given
③ True
④ True
⑤ False
⑥ False

37.7
Ⓐ 2
Ⓑ 6
Ⓒ 8
Ⓓ 1
Ⓔ 5
Ⓕ 7
Ⓖ 4
Ⓗ 3

38.2 🔊
GENERALIZAR:
on the whole, generally, in general, by and large
EXCEPCIONES:
except for, with the exception of, aside from, excepting
CENTRARSE: **if we focus on, if we home in on, concentrating on, focusing on**

38.3 🔊
① The launch was successful, aside from the interview.
② Now, let's home in on the positive news.
③ By and large, the poster campaign was a disaster.
④ Most of our clients liked the design except one.
⑤ Today we're going to focus on social media.

38.4
① True
② Not given
③ False
④ Not given
⑤ True

38.7
① False
② True
③ True
④ False

38.8 🔊
① No. **If we focus on** the posters, we can see they were very successful.
② Yes, **with the exception of** our Madrid store.
③ **As a matter of fact** it was very successful.
④ Cities **such as** Seoul and Busan could have successful stores.
⑤ They haven't yet. **However**, it's too soon to see what the impact will be.

39.3 🔊
① Our new smartwatch is **easier** to operate than the old one.
② Our new designer jeans are **more** stylish than last year's products.
③ Our tablet is **the** cheapest on the market.
④ This is the **most** beautiful dress in our range.
⑤ This is the **best** laptop I have ever owned.

39.4
① more comfortable
② the most reliable
③ lighter
④ more affordable

39.7 🔊
① Our new phone is as cheap as existing models, but has a much wider range of features.
② Our latest DVD is as exciting as anything I've ever seen.
③ Our chairs are excellent value, and just as comfortable as more expensive models.

39.8
① True ② Not given ③ False
④ True ⑤ Not given

39.9 🔊
① Our new laptop is much **lighter** than its competitors.
② This fitness tracker is **just as effective as** more expensive models.
③ Organic fruit is not **as cheap as** supermarket fruit, but it tastes better.
④ A consumer survey voted our pizzas the **tastiest** on the market.

40

40.2
(A) 6
(B) 1
(C) 2
(D) 7
(E) 5
(F) 8
(G) 3
(H) 4

40.3 ◀))
1 There was a steady increase in our share value.
2 Interest in our bags declined considerably.
3 We've had a sharp rise in customer numbers.
4 There was a dramatic spike in sales in May.
5 Sales of our bags have rallied slightly.
6 The value of our shares has fallen steadily.
7 The value of the dollar is fluctuating wildly.
8 The value of the dollar saw a dramatic spike.

40.5 ◀))
1 Returns have increased **by** 10 percent.
2 Prices fell between 30 **and** 45 percent.
3 We're shrinking our staff **from** 800 to 650.
4 Year-end profit stands **at** 8 percent.
5 Salaries will increase **by** 2 percent.
6 We have **between** 1,100 and 1,200 staff.
7 There was a decrease **of** 5 percent.
8 Profits have fallen **by** 15 percent.
9 We are lowering the price **to** 30 euros.
10 The price peaked **at** £19.99.

40.6
1 False
2 True
3 True
4 Not given

40.7 ◀))
1 There was a **sharp increase** at the start of the year.
2 It's been **fluctuating wildly** since the announcement.
3 We're expecting them to **rally considerably** next quarter.

41

41.2 ◀))
1 Yes, I think we could do that.
2 We might move forward if we can agree on a delivery date.
3 Maybe we could consider different colors.
4 Would you mind waiting until next month for payment?
5 We were hoping it would be more innovative.

41.3
1 1,000
2 It is too high
3 A cake
4 Next week

41.7 ◀))
1 I was wondering whether you have these in another size.
2 Could you tell me when the price list will be ready?
3 Could you tell me when I can expect delivery?

41.8 ◀))
1 Could you tell me when **I can** start buying the new products?
2 I was wondering **what the warranty period is**.
3 Could you tell me how **the new product is** different from the old one?
4 I was wondering if **you would** be free to discuss a new job opening.

41.10 ◀))
1 Could you tell me whether **the delivery date has been changed**?
2 I was wondering whether **my invoice has been paid**.
3 It seems that **the wrong product was sent**.
4 It looks as if **my complaint was not fully understood**.
5 It seems that **the price was not calculated correctly**.

41.11 ◀))
1 I'm afraid I can't access **the computer system right now**.
2 It looks as if **the discount has not been applied**.
3 I was wondering why the **deadline has been missed**.
4 Could you tell me when **the sales start**?
5 It seems that the wrong customer **has been contacted**.

41.12
1 Not given
2 True
3 False
4 False
5 Not given

42

42.3 🔊
1 If you ask **me**, we might be better to wait until the summer.
2 **What** we need is proof that your business is profitable.
3 **Actually**, we'd like to reach an agreement by the end of the day.
4 The **main** thing is that we agree on a price that everyone is happy with.

42.4
Ⓐ 2
Ⓑ 4
Ⓒ 1
Ⓓ 3
Ⓔ 5

42.5 🔊
1 Not quite. **What we need are** some references from your customers.
2 That's OK. The **main thing is that** we find the right person to do the work.
3 **Actually**, our quote already includes free delivery.

43

43.4 🔊
1 I would **place** an order if they delivered sooner.
2 If your product **was** cheaper, we would buy it.
3 If you moved the deadline, we **could meet** it.
4 I **would** work with them if they answered my questions.
5 If they **checked** their work, I would use them.

43.5
1 True
2 Not given
3 True
4 False
5 Not given

43.6 🔊
1 We **would sign** the contract if it **was** clearer.
2 I **would accept** the job offer if the pay **was** better.
3 If they **improved** the quality, we **would place** an order.
4 If I **had** more time today, I **would check** the contract.

43.9 🔊
1 If you pay by credit card, we charge a 2 percent fee.
2 Our helpline is open 24 hours a day if you need assistance.
3 When we say our products are high quality, we mean it.
4 I get extra money every month if I work overtime.

43.10 🔊
Nota: todas las respuestas también pueden ir en la forma abreviada del futuro con "will".
1 If you **sign** the contract now, we **will begin** production next week.
2 We **will charge** a 10 percent fee if you **don't pay / do not pay** on time.
3 If you **buy** more than 50 units, we **will give** you a 5 percent discount.
4 We **will send** you a contract if you **want** to proceed.

43.12 🔊
1 We will return your call ASAP **if you leave a message**.
2 We would open stores in the US **if our products were more popular there**.
3 If you need more training, **you can contact the HR department**.
4 We would increase production **if we had more staff**.
5 We will issue a full refund **if you return your product within 28 days**.

43.13
Respuestas modelo
1 You will understand his or her strengths and weaknesses.
2 You should decide what you can compromise on.
3 They help to build rapport if you don't know your business partner.
4 If you talk too much, you run the risk of revealing useful information.
5 To find a common ground so that you can reach an agreement.

44

44.4 🔊
Nota: todas las respuestas también pueden redactarse en su forma abreviada.
1 If he **had used** the correct figures, his report **would not have been** so out of date.
2 The boss **would not have shouted** if you **had admitted** your mistake earlier.
3 If you **had run** a spell check, the report **would not have contained** so many errors.
4 We **would not have embarrassed** ourselves if we **had researched** local customs before our trip.
5 I **would have worked** late last night if I **had known** our deadline was so soon.

44.5
1 B
2 A
3 A
4 B
5 A

44.8 🔊
1 Tony is not going to meet the deadline **unless he works overtime**.
2 **Unless I get** a good performance review, I won't get a raise this year.

3 I'm afraid we can't track your order **unless you can** give us your customer reference number.
4 **Unless we can** offer a better price, we won't win the contract.

44.9
1 Not given
2 False
3 False
4 True
5 Not given

Índice

Los temas se indexan por el número de la unidad. Las entradas que comienzan con **L1** se refieren a unidades del nivel **1**. Las entradas que comienzan con **L2** se refieren a unidades del nivel **2**. (Por ejemplo, **L1-8** se refiere a la unidad 8 del nivel **1**.) Las entradas en **negrita** indican la unidad que incluye más información.

382

Agradecimientos

Los editores expresan su agradecimiento a:
Amy Child, Dominic Clifford, Devika Khosla y Priyansha Tuli por su asistencia de diseño; Dominic Clifford y Hansa Babra por sus ilustraciones adicionales; Sam Atkinson, Vineetha Mokkil, Antara Moitra, Margaret Parrish, Nisha Shaw y Rohan Sinha por su asistencia editorial; Elizabeth Wise por el índice; Jo Kent por la redacción de textos adicionales; Scarlett O'Hara, Georgina Palffy y Helen Ridge por la corrección de pruebas; Christine Stroyan por la gestión del proyecto; ID Audio por las grabaciones y la producción de audio; David Almond, Gillian Reid y Jacqueline Street-Elkayam por su asistencia de producción.

DK agradece su permiso para la reproducción de sus fotografías a:
25 **Fotolia**: semisatch (centro).
37 **Fotolia**: Leonid Smirnov (abajo, centro).
55 **Dorling Kindersley**: NASA (arriba a la derecha)
257 **Fotolia**: Maksym Dykha (abajo, derecha).
336 **Alamy**: MBI (abajo, derecha).

Los derechos del resto de las imágenes son propiedad de DK.

Para más información se puede visitar: **www.dkimages.com**.